STRESS AND ANXIETY

THE SERIES IN CLINICAL PSYCHOLOGY

CHARLES D. SPIELBERGER
and IRWIN G. SARASON · Consulting Editors

STRESS AND ANXIETY

Volume 2

EDITED BY

IRWIN G. SARASON
University of Washington

CHARLES D. SPIELBERGER
University of South Florida

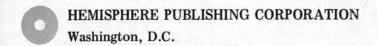

HEMISPHERE PUBLISHING CORPORATION
Washington, D.C.

A HALSTED PRESS BOOK

JOHN WILEY & SONS
New York   London   Sydney   Toronto

Copyright © 1975 by Hemisphere Publishing Corporation. All rights
reserved. No part of this book may be reproduced in any form, by
photostat, microform, retrieval system, or any other means, without
the prior written permission of the publisher.

Hemisphere Publishing Corporation
1025 Vermont Ave., N.W., Washington, D.C. 20005

Distributed solely by Halsted Press, a Division of John Wiley & Sons,
Inc., New York.

Library of Congress Cataloging in Publication Data

Main entry under title:

Stress and anxiety.

(The Series in clinical psychology)
Includes indexes.
1. Stress (Psychology)—Addresses, essays, lectures.
2. Anxiety—Addresses, essays, lectures. I. Sarason,
Irwin G. II. Spielberger, Charles Donald, 1927–
[DNLM: 1. Anxiety. 2. Stress, Psychological.
WM172 S755s]

BF575.S75S76   155.9   75-12807
ISBN 0-470-75412-5

Printed in the United States of America

CONTENTS

II EMPIRICAL APPROACHES TO STRESS

III LIFE STRESS AND ANXIETY

IV COPING WITH STRESS AND ANXIETY

CONTRIBUTORS

A. T. Beck, Philadelphia General Hospital, Philadelphia, Pennsylvania, United States

Sam Burstein, University of Waterloo, Waterloo, Ontario, Canada

H. J. Eysenck, Institute of Psychiatry, University of London, London, England

Walter D. Fenz, University of Waterloo, Waterloo, Ontario, Canada

Charles V. Ford, University of California, Los Angeles, California, United States

Vernon Hamilton, Reading University, Reading, England

Robert D. Hare, Department of Psychology, University of British Columbia, Vancouver, Canada

Heinz Heckhausen, Ruhr University, Bochum, German Federal Republic

Jean E. Johnson, Center for Health Research, College of Nursing, Wayne State University, Detroit, Michigan, United States

Keijo Kata, Research Group for Comparative Sociology, University of Helsinki, Helsinki, Finland

Edward S. Katkin, State University of New York at Buffalo, Buffalo, New York, United States

D. Paul Lumsden, Anthropology Department, York University, Downsview, Ontario, Canada

Richard Lynn, University of Ulster, County Londonderry, Coleraine, Northern Ireland

Paul McReynolds, University of Nevada, Reno, Nevada, United States

Donald Meichenbaum, University of Waterloo, Waterloo, Ontario, Canada

A. J. Rush, Philadelphia General Hospital, Philadelphia, Pennsylvania, United States

Irwin G. Sarason, University of Washington, Seattle, Washington, United States

Yona Teichman, Tel-Aviv University, Tel-Aviv, Israel

Richard Trumbull, American Institute of Biological Sciences, Arlington, Virginia, United States

Dennis Turk, University of Waterloo, Waterloo, Ontario, Canada

PREFACE

The papers in this second volume deal with issues and problems that are currently attracting growing inquiry among researchers. The topics include the physiological, personality, and social dimensions of human distress and the need to adapt to persistent, and often unforeseen, unwanted conditions of life. Among the questions to which the authors address themselves are these:

How might the cognitive dimensions of anxiety most effectively be conceptualized?

In what ways do psychophysiological reactions to stress pattern themselves?

What are the predominant patterns of psychological reactions to life stress and unusual environmental settings?

Can coping skills needed for successful adaptation be taught to persons susceptible to the unwanted effects of stress?

The specific questions posed in this volume vary widely, ranging from Katkin's programmatic psychophysiological investigations to

Beck and Rush's analysis of clinical problems to Eysenck's ideas about the genetics of anxiety to Fenz's and Meichenbaum, Turk, and Burstein's studies of the acquisition of coping skills. Yet they share a common commitment to objective evidence and its thoughtful application to human welfare.

This volume is one effort to adapt to novelty and trauma. Its papers had been scheduled for presentation at an international conference that, at the last moment, could not be held due to political and military exigencies. Amid much stress and anxiety the conference was rescheduled and the decision made to publish the papers before the conference was held. This has two major advantages. One is that workers in the field can become aware as quickly as possible of the findings and analyses contained in the papers. The other is the opportunity for the conference participants to read and think about the papers before attending the conference and thus derive greater benefit from their attendance.

The volume reflects the importance the editors attach to furthering international communication among scholars. Six countries are represented among the seventeen papers. In some instances—for example, the papers by Teichman and Kata—the research reported deals with problems unique to a given society or situation, while in others, the problems represent essentially universal laboratory inquiries. The way in which all the contributors show their awareness of scholars throughout the world is impressive and encouraging.

We are deeply grateful to the Scientific Affairs Division of the North Atlantic Treaty Organization for its support. The encouragement and assistance of B. A. Bayraktar has helped us at a number of points. We appreciate also the support of Roche Laboratories and the encouragement given us by Bruce Medd. Many individuals helped at important points in the preparation and production of this volume. The contributions of the following were especially important: Evelyn Pettit, Isabelle Reynolds, and Jane E. Sarason. Needless to say, out greatest debt is to the scholars whose work is presented in this volume.

Irwin G. Sarason
Charles D. Spielberger

ANXIETY: THEORETICAL AND EMPIRICAL ISSUES

CHANGING CONCEPTIONS OF ANXIETY: A HISTORICAL REVIEW AND A PROPOSED INTEGRATION

Paul McReynolds

University of Nevada
Reno, Nevada, United States

The feeling of anxiety is an intrinsic part of the condition of being human. It is a natural response, built into the human design, to certain environmental and psychological factors. It may, therefore, seem somewhat odd, not to say misguided, to approach the study of anxiety from a historical point of view. What, one may ask, can one possibly learn about anxiety from such an approach? The answer, I think, is twofold: first, a historical perspective of anxiety can furnish us with a better appreciation for, and a deeper understanding of the current theoretical scene in the psychology of anxiety; and, second, it is a worthwhile endeavor in its own right, in the sense that a fuller insight into a significant area of the human past needs no further excuse for being.

EARLY CONCEPTIONS OF ANXIETY

Presumably, man has always experienced anxiety, as long as he has existed as a species, though the contents of his anxieties, and the ways in which these affects are felt and categorized phenomenally, as well as the kinds of circumstances that give rise to them, are no doubt to a considerable degree a function of the mores and assumptions of the cultures in which he has lived. Development of the *concept* of anxiety, on the other hand, apparently did not come about until well into the historical era, in the classical Greek period, and particularly in the Hellenistic era.

The theme of anxiety—not a delineation of the concept, but an awareness of the affect—appears in the first literary narrative (Mason, 1972), the *Epic of Gilgamesh*, which is believed to have reached its present form in Babylonia at the beginning of the second millenium, and parts of which go back to Sumerian myths of the third millenium. The story concerns Gilgamesh's anxiety about the fact that he is mortal and must die, and his attempt to gain some degree of immortality by achieving fame. The Homeric epics include vivid descriptions of grief and sorrow, as when Telemachus, upon being received by Menelaus, first hears mention of his father (Homer, 1946, p. 65). A concern with inner anguish is expressed in the works of the eighth century prophets of Israel, as in Isaiah 41:10: "Fear thou not; for I am with thee: be not dismayed, for I am thy God. . . ."

The Concept of Ataraxia

Throughout much of early Greek thought there is a concern with the seeking of tranquility, or *ataraxia*. This is, in a sense, the opposite and more positive end of the dimension of anxiety, and it says something, I think, for the optimism of the ancient Greek world that their emphasis was on unanxiousness rather than on anxiousness. Democritus of Abdera, the fifth century father of atomic theory, was apparently the first to state this orientation. He is described by Diogenes Laertius (1925) as believing, "The end of action is tranquillity, which is not identical with pleasure, as some by a false interpretation have understood, but a state in which the soul continues calm and strong, undisturbed by any fear or superstition or any other emotion [p. 455]." Democritus used the term *cheerfulness* to refer to the kind of tranquility that he recommended. Cheerfulness, he felt, comes from an attitude of moderation and from not attempting things that lie beyond one's power (Nahm, 1964).

The feeling of anxiety, in the sense of an inner experience of intense anguish, is intimately associated with self-awareness and the appreciation of one's own individuality and reponsibility. These psychological conditions for the most part did not exist until about the seventh or sixth centuries (Barbu, 1960; Snell, 1960). Prior to that time, in what had been called the preindividualistic period of civilization, man tended to categorize himself primarily as a member of his group, and only secondarily to view himself as a person having within himself the sources of actions and decisions. Characteristically, man in this period conceived of himself in a passive way, and attributed his major decisions to the gods. Under such a philosophical orientation, feelings of anxiety must have had a vastly different phenomenonolgy than is true in today's inner-directed world. This attitude is suggested clearly in Homer's works, as indicated by Snell (1960):

In Homer, a man is unaware of the fact that he may think or act spontaneously.... Whatever "strikes" him, whatever "thought comes" to him, is given from without, and if no visible stimulus has affected him, he thinks that a god has stood by his side and given him counsel.... It follows that Homer's men act with perfect assurance, and that they do not know what it means to be burdened with scruples or doubts [p. 123].

Classical Greek Individuality

It was in the classical Greek drama—particularly in the plays of Aeschylus and Euripides—that the developing concept of individuality and self-awareness first became clearly manifest. Not surprisingly, these dramas contain a great deal of affect which, while not termed anxiety, is easily recognized as such. In the plays of Aeschylus, the *Oresteia* trilogy and others, man is presented for the first time as being responsible for his own actions,[1] indeed, as being unable to avoid responsibility for himself. The general paradigm employed by Aeschylus, as Snell has observed, was to contrive a dramatic situation in which the hero is faced with the necessity of making a choice between two alternatives, each of which has powerful positive and negative aspects. In the *Oresteia*,

---

[1] This interpretation can also be found to some extent in Homer, as Smith (1974) has pointed out; however, its representation there is much more limited and tentative.

for example, Orestes feels obligated to avenge his father, yet this means that he must slay his mother. In Sophocles, and particularly in Euripides, e.g., in *Medea*, the same lesson is even stronger: here the conflict is sharpened and placed squarely in the minds of individual men and women. These dramatic analyses of human motivation are the ancestors of today's conflict theories of anxiety.

In philosophy Socrates changed the emphasis of study from the external to the internal frame of reference and furthered the shift toward a personal, self-oriented world view. His contributions, as reported by Plato, do not seem to have added directly to the developing concept of anxiety, but they helped to prepare the way for later introspective analyses of the affect. Plato's own emphasis on the separation between reason and the passions laid the basis for the later detailed development of theories of the passions, which encompassed the concept of fear, and which I will return to shortly. Aristotle, for his part, discussed the emotion of fear at some length. In his delineation of fear, as in that of many other writers, the concept is fairly close, though not identical, to that of anxiety. In *The Rhetoric*, Aristotle writes as follows:

> Fear may be defined as a pain or disturbance arising from a mental image of impending evil of a destructive or painful sort. [The evil must be of a destructive or painful sort]; for men do not fear all evils—as, for example, the prospect of becoming wicked or slothful—but only such as mean great pain or ruin, and these only when they appear to be, not remote, but close at hand, imminent. Of evils that are very remote men are not afraid; thus everyone knows that he must die, but since people think they will not die soon, they do not care. From our definition, then, it must follow that fear is caused by whatever seems to have a great power of destroying us or of working injuries that are likely to bring us great pain. Accordingly, the very indication [signs] of such things cause fear, since they suggest that the thing is at hand; "danger" means just this—the proximity of anything we dread [Cooper, 1932, pp. 107-108].

In the last sentence of this quotation Aristotle approaches rather closely to the notion of conditioned fear, though he does not develop this idea. In the material following the quotation, he gives a number of examples of the causes of fear; interestingly, almost all of these are interpersonal in nature.

Hellenistic Stresses

The era that began with the conquests of Alexander the Great is called the Hellenistic period. Though it was a highly creative age, it was also in many respects—especially in its earlier phases—an anxious and disturbed period.[2] It was a time of great political and social flux, when the cultural verities and the ideological assumptions of the contemporary world were undergoing rapid change, and new ways of conceiving reality and man's place in it had not yet been worked out. May (1974) suggests that the reason for the general rise of anxiety that seems to have been characteristic of this age was that "man had lost his world," that he no longer had the power to communicate "with this world, with others, and with himself [p. 291]." I suspect that careful research would show that all times of rapid and unpredictable cultural change—e.g., the periods of the Italian Renaissance, the French revolution, and the industrial revolution in England, as well as many aspects of the present scene—always lead to heightened anxiety. The converse is also probably true, in that periods of especially high anxiety are probably particularly liable to undergo change until some kind of cultural stability is achieved. However, we would not want to conclude that a situation of rapid, uncertain change in a society is the *only* broad cultural condition that can lead to increased anxiety; another condition that appears to have a similar effect (though the anxiety in this case would have a different, somewhat more depressive tone) would be a historical condition in which there is a general fearfulness associated with the lack of satisfaction of basic human needs, as in parts of late medieval Europe, when cultural anxiety focused so much on the concept of death.[3]

---

[2] It seems possible that the same factors which lead to increased anxiety in a culture may, at least on some occasions, lead also to enhanced creativity. Thus, anxiousness and creativeness appear to have been correlated not only in the Alexandrian period, but also in the Italian Renaissance (May, 1950, p. 161), and possibly in contemporary Western culture as well.

[3] An analysis of the relations between anxiety and cultural values and changes would be an excellent assignment for the newly emerging discipline of psychohistory. Such an analysis would have a much better hope of success than do the currently popular attempts to analyze contemporary political figures.

With respect to the cultural factors leading to anxiety in the Alexandrian world, there is a particular type of cultural change that needs to be emphasized. This is the rising level of self-awareness and individuality that I spoke about earlier. This developing current, the course of which we shall be following throughout this chapter, can be seen in its first great surge in antiquity as something of a quantum change in the way man characteristically experienced anxiety. In the period we are discussing, the last three centuries B.C., this tide of individuation (Barbu, 1960) had, under the stimulus of Hellenic and Judaic thought and literature, reached the point of influencing the general, popular culture. The situation has been well described by Parkes (1965), who uses the term "Axial Period" to refer to the period from 800 to 200 B.C. Parkes states: "When man began to distinguish between objective reality and his own subjective mental processes, he began to lose his sense of unity with nature. . . . The problem of human loneliness and alienation had its roots in the thinking of the Axial Period. . . . This, in fact, was the true expulsion from Eden. . . [p. 81]."

As a result, at least in part, of the heightened anxiety of this historical period, three philosophical movements, each of which offered some degree of relief from personal stress, arose and gained wide acceptance. The two earliest of these were Epicureanism and Stoicism, and the third was Christianity. I will consider these three orientations, which include theoretical conceptions of anxiety as well as ways of coping with anxiety, in order. It is noteworthy that all three placed their main emphasis on man's inner life.

Epicureanism

As a quasi-religious movement, Epicureanism, which was prominent from the 3rd century B.C. to the 4th century A.D., was recognized in its own time as a message of salvation from anxiety. Epicurus, like Democritus, after whom his views were to some extent modeled, did not talk about the presence of anxiety, but rather about its lack, i.e., tranquillity, or peace of mind. It is quite clear, however, that the topic of his concern was what we refer to as anxiety. In this sense, Epicurus proposed a sweeping theory of motivation, based on the thesis that all behavior is determined by the tendency to reduce pain and fear. This view is, in principle, not unlike the notion of anxiety reduction as a generalized motivator in certain contemporary theories. Epicurus is popularly remembered as an advocate of unbridled pleasure, but this is, of course, inaccurate. Though Epicurus was a hedonist, he conceived of happiness as tranquillity of mind, as indicated in this statement: "When we say that pleasure is the end, we do not mean the pleasure of the profligate or that which depends on physical enjoyment...but by pleasure we mean the state wherein the body is free from pain and the mind from anxiety [Epicurus, 1964, p. 57]." The factors that cause anxiety, according to Epicurus, are any conditions that cause mental disturbances. Of these he emphasized two in particular, the fear of death and the fear of the gods. Much of Epicurus' direct teaching, as well as the import of the rather communal societies that grew up around him, was directed toward combatting these two sources of anxiety.

Stoicism

Stoicism, like Epicureanism, with which it was contemporary, was attuned to coping with the anxieties of man in a troubled world. Though its views changed somewhat during its long history, basically it consisted of a world view which, if one could accept it completely, would make the real problems of life less troublesome. Thus, the Stoics conceived that there is a grand design in the universe; that man is a part of this design; and that all things, including vices and misfortunes, serve some purpose in the overall scheme of things and should be accepted with as much equanimity as possible. Anxiety was attributed to a person's becoming too emotionally involved in, and too committed to personal performances and goals. This view is evident in the following comments by the first century (A.D.) Roman philosopher Epictetus (1944). These comments are taken from a discourse that the translator has appropriately titled "On Anxiety," and that must be considered the earliest systematic discussion of this topic. Epicetus states:

When I see anyone anxious, I say, what does this man want? Unless he wanted something or other not in his own power, how could he still be anxious? A musician, for instance, feels no anxiety while he is singing by himself; but when he appears upon the stage he does, even if his voice be ever so good, or he plays ever so well. For what he wishes is not only to sing well but likewise to gain applause. But this is not in his own power. In short, where his skill lies, there is his . courage.... Therefore Zeno, when he was to meet Antigonus, felt no anxiety. For over that which he prized, Antigonus had no power; and those things over which he had power, Zeno did not regard. But Antigonus felt anxiety when he was to meet Zeno, and with reason, for he was desirous to please him; and this was external ambition. ... When, therefore you see anyone pale with anxiety, just as the physician pronounces from the complexion that such a patient is disordered in the spleen, and another in the liver, so do you likewise say, this man is disordered in his desires and aversions; he cannot walk steadily; he is in a fever. For nothing else changes the complexion, or causes trembling, or sets the teeth chattering [pp. 117-119].[4]

The modern psychologist will observe a similarity between these examples of Epictetus and contemporary views on the roles of self-esteem and high achievement strivings in the genesis of anxiety. It is interesting to note that in the latter Roman period the writings of Epicetus, as well as of certain other philosophers, were addressed, according to Edman (1944), "to an educated public seeking personal security and equilibrium." The words were thus intended to serve a popular therapeutic role, much as books such as Leibman's (1946) *Peace of Mind* do in our time.

Christianity

The third, and last, of the early philosophical orientations that arose in this period and that offered solace to anxious men was Christianity, as presented by Paul of Tarsus on his missions throughout the Greco-Roman world. Over the period of the first three centuries A.D., Christianity proved more successful in handling anxiety than did either Epicureanism or Stoicism; this success

[4] At this point Epictetus gives a brief, abridged quotation, referring to overt signs of anxiety, from Homer. The full description in *The Iliad* (Homer, 1950) is as follows: "A coward changes colour all the time; he cannot sit still for nervousness, but squats down, first on one heel, then on the other; his heart thumps in his breast as he thinks of death in all its forms, and one can hear the chattering of his teeth. But the brave man never changes colour at all and is not unduly perturbed, from the moment when he takes his seat in ambush with the rest [p. 241]."

was, no doubt, a major factor in the rapid rise of this new faith. There were, of course, major differences between the Christian philosophy, on the one hand, and Epicureanism and Stoicism, on the other hand. These differences can best be seen in the context of the growing trend toward individualization. In this sense Christianity was the wave of the future, whereas Epicureanism and Stoicism were desperate attempts to cling to a past that man was growing beyond. Thus, Epicureanism and Stoicism assumed that man's troubles were due to discrepancies between his desires and his capacities to attain them, and they advised that he inhibit his desires: this amounted, in effect, to an attempt to attenuate the rising growth of individuality. Christianity, on the other hand, emphasized the personal individuality of each man and woman. This contrast has been put as follows by Parkes (1965):

Pagan philosophy had no true concept of human personality; man's body after death would return to the elements, while his soul would be absorbed into divinity. For Christianity, however, each man was endowed with a separate individual existence both in this life and in the next [p. 376].

Christianity, then, can properly be conceived as another step in the progression toward greater emphasis on individuality in Western culture; it also came to represent a world view which could bring some degree of stability to the uncertainties of troubled minds in a transitional era. The wide appeal of early Christianity, then, was in giving man the solace, as well as the dignity, that he sought. It must, then, have included a theory of anxiety. This theory was the Paulian notion of sin. Anxiety is due to guilt. It is important to note that this postulate is essential; i.e., as soon as one adopts the thesis that man is responsible for himself, he necessarily becomes subject to the possibility—one could say the inevitability—of guilt from his failure to meet his responsibilities. This guilt hypothesis of anxiety is quite different from the conceptions of Epicurus and Epictetus, and it called for different ways to relieve the anxiety. In the long run it prevailed over these other hypotheses of late antiquity, not because they were totally wrong—certainly they were not—but because, at least at that stage in history, and probably today as well, there was greater psychological truth in the Paulian position. As Parkes (1965) has written,

In preaching that all men were sinners Paul was not trying to envelop all human life in a pall of gloom or expressing a vindictive and neurotic hatred of the world and the flesh; he was stating a psychological fact. Man was a divided creature, driven by egotistical passions that conflicted with his own moral principles, capable of envisaging ideals, but unable to realize them [p. 408].

The legacy for anxiety theory of the early Christian revolution in thought has been great. It amounted, in Freudian terms, to a shift from the id-ego discrepancies of the Epicurean and Stoic philosophies, to an emphasis on id-superego discrepancies. The idea that guilt is crucially involved in much anxiety is, of course, central in many contemporary conceptions of anxiety, e.g., those of Freud and Mowrer. In later antiquity the Christian position on guilt, anxiety, and the obtaining of relief through acceptance of the world view of the Christian eschatology was brilliantly reflected in *The Confessions* of St. Augustine (1907). In this work, which represents a further major advance in the emphasis on individuality and self-examination (Misch, 1950), St. Augustine trenchantly probes his inner life. His anxiety, and the comforting balm of his beliefs, is poignantly revealed in the line, "our heart is restless, until it repose in Thee [p. 1]."

I want next to quote from a brief treatment titled "Of Fear," written by Nemesius of Emesa about 390 A.D., in order to illustrate the thinking about fear and anxiety in that period. Though Nemesius was a Christian bishop, this selection is in no sense theological, but rather represents the secular learning of that time. The selection is also instructive in that it includes a quotation from Galen. After noting that fear may appear in six different manifestations—diffidence, shyness, shame, consternation, terror, and anguish—Nemesius writes as follows:

Fear starts with a chilling of the extremities, all the hot blood running to the heart, as to the centre of control, just as the mob, when frightened, rushes to the rulers of the city. The organ of such grief is the pit of the stomach, for this it is that, at onsets of fear, feels a gnawing sensation. So Galen, in his work, *On Demonstration*, Book III, says something to this effect: "People attacked by fear experience no slight inflow of yellow bile into the stomach, which makes them feel a gnawing sensation, and they do not cease feeling both distress of mind and the gnawing until they have vomited up the bile [Telfer, 1955, pp. 360-361].

THEORY OF THE PASSIONS

We must now turn to a brief examination of the history of the theory of the passions. This is one of the most intriguing narratives in the whole of the history of psychology, but we will go into it in only a very limited way here. The relevance of the topic to our present inquiry, as I implied earlier, is that the concept of fear, with overtones of what we today mean by anxiety, was systematically embedded in an overall conception of human passions throughout the Middle Ages.

Origins

The theory of the passions, which began with Plato and lasted, in its various versions, until well into the eighteenth century, was by far the most durable personality theory that man has ever developed. Plato divided the soul into three parts: the rational functions, located in the head; courage and anger, located in the area of the heart; and desires, assigned to the lower part of the body. The latter two of these divisions formed the basis for the conception of the passions, with those mental functions in the heart area coming to be categorized as the irascible passions, and those of the abdominal area as the concupiscible passions. This distinction, along with related taxonomies, was used for some two millenia. The Stoic Chrysippus, in the third century B.C., proposed a four-fold classification of passions—pleasure (*hedonè*) and mental pain (*lupè*) from present good or evil, and desire (*epithumia*) and fear (*phobos*) from future good or evil—which had considerable influence throughout history. One of the more prominent taxonomies was that of Thomas Acquinas (1911-1922; Gardiner, Metcalf, and Beebe-Center, 1937) in which fear was categorized as an evil, irascible passion.[5]

[5] Other relevant works on the passions include those by Vives (1959), Coeffeteau (1630), de La Chambre (1658, 1662, 1663), Reynolds (1971), and Descartes (1967). For general discussions of this interesting topic, consult Gardiner et al. 1937) and Levi (1964).

The importance of the various treatments of the passions for the history of anxiety is in, first, their attempts to relate fear systematically to other emotions, which implies at the very least the realization that fear can best be understood as part of a broader psychology; and second, various insightful descriptions of the nature of fear. I will now give several instances of this latter category. It is to Vives, the highly original 16th century Spanish psychologist, that we are indebted for an observation that is suggestive of the notion of conditioning, and which can therefore perhaps be interpreted as an early adumbration of the concept of conditioned anxiety. Vives relates it in this way: "When I was a boy at Valencia I was ill of a fever: while my taste was deranged, I ate cheeries: for many years afterwards, whenever I tasted fruit, I not only recalled the fever but seemed to experience it again [Peters, 1962, p. 324]." Vives conceived (Gardiner et al., 1937, p. 136) that pallor, coldness, trembling of the limbs, stammering, and other indications of fear are caused by the fact that the heart is weakened by the fear, with the result that the blood rushes from the periphery to the aid of the heart. He further suggested—and this is a most interesting anticipation of Freud's notion of anxiety as a signal—that emotion may be felt as a warning to a person to take appropriate defensive action (Gardiner et al., 1937, p. 136).

Claramontius, in a book published in 1625, suggested (Gardiner et al., 1937, p. 136) that pulse and respiration provide the most reliable indications of emotion. This report is most interesting in that many contemporary investigators employ measures of these variables as assays of anxiety; the reasoning behind Claramontius' conclusion, however, is less impressive, though it was typical of the period: it was that emotion is a function of the heat of the heart, and such heat is reflected in the pulse and respiration. Another systematic writer on the passion of fear was de La Chambre, a physician to Louis XIV. In his *Les Caractéres Des Passions*, de La Chambre (1658, 1662, 1663) suggested that each passion has its own peculiar pattern of physiological manifestations. He failed, however, to work this out in any detail.

The Renaissance

In bringing the narrative this far I have bypassed several important components of the cultural background which must now be examined briefly. Earlier I devoted considerable attention to the growth of self-awareness and individuality in the human personality. Historically, there was an interregnum—indeed, perhaps something of a retrogression—in this developing process from about the time of Augustine to the 12th century. In the 12th century, however, there occurred a striking cultural renaissance, centered in Paris. This period, which has recently been examined from the psychohistorical point of view in a brilliant work[6] by Colin Morris (1972), emphasized again the development of individuality. In the 15th century, of course, there was the larger, more famous Renaissance, centered in Italy, which also enormously fostered the fulfillment of individuality, as Burckhardt (1958, p. 143) pointed out over a century ago. I bring these matters up here because of the close relationship between experienced anxiety and the concept of selfness, and because of the necessary dependence of theories of anxiety on the nature of the cultures from which they derive, in which anxieties inevitably play a significant role.

Because anxiety, in its various adjectival forms, is so intimately a characteristic of human societies, one would expect that its presence would necessarily be a part of the literature that most

---

[6] Despite the excellence of this work, its title (*The Discovery of the Individual, 1050-1200*) should not be taken too literally. First, the individual was not so much discovered as rediscovered in this period. Second, the concept of the individual was not so much a discovery, in any event, as an invention. The same criticism can be made of Snell's (1960) *The Discovery of the Mind*, as Sarbin (1964) observed. From a psychological perspective, concepts like the self, the person, and the individual are not real (i.e., concrete, tangible) entities, but rather are mental categories, a part of the cognitive representations by which one structures his world. This interpretation, of course, does not reduce by a whit the brilliance of the extraordinary achievement by which man, over the last three millenia, has been able to create his self-image. This self-image is, however, not entirely by invention: thus, there are real limitations, in the nature of the world and of man's psychological apparatus, that set the boundaries within which concepts of selfness can be developed. These limits are undoubtedly sufficiently broad, however, as to permit great variations among persons and cultures with respect to the degree and nature of their concepts of selfness. Most people, except perhaps those who have endured great personal suffering, or have examined themselves in intense psychotherapy, probably take their intimations of selfness and individuality rather directly from their cultures. It is a rather amazing thought that the notion of psychological individuality, which to us has a certain obvious quality about it, had to be developed, over a long period of time, just like all other difficult abstractions.

clearly reflects the nature of a period. I have already given a number of examples of this generality, and I will now give several additional instances. One of the most readable essays on fear was (as one would expect) that by Michel Montaigne. It is particularly interesting for its point that fear itself is a highly unpleasant emotion. The phrase Montaigne used was, "The thing I fear most is fear [Frame, 1965, p. 53]," a line that calls to mind Franklin Roosevelt's more recent, and more famous lines at the height of the 1933 depression, "the only thing we have to fear is fear itself—nameless, unreasoning, unjustified terror. . . ."[7] The tragedies of Shakespeare are, of course, replete with instances of strong anxiety, as in these lines from Macbeth: "Now o'er the one half-world/Nature seems dead, and wicked dreams abuse/The curtained sleep. . ." (II,1). Shakespeare, even more than Euripides, placed the origins of man's anguish within himself: "The fault, dear Brutus, is not in our stars/But in ourselves, that we are underlings."

THE ENLIGHTENMENT

Turning back now to the contributions of systematic philosophers, we may examine next the ideas of Benedict de Spinoza. Spinoza, writing in 1675, defined fear as "an inconstant pain arising from the idea of something past or future, whereof we to a certain extent doubt the issue [Spinoza, 1955, p. 176]." He notes further that "there is no hope unmingled with fear, and no fear unmingled with hope [p. 176]." Spinoza's most interesting suggestion is, "Anything whatever can be, accidentally, a cause of hope or fear [p. 162]." He is referring here to superstitions and omens, and he appears to approach—though, as was true of previous authors, without quite reaching it—the notion that specific

---

[7] Roosevelt's thoughts on the paralyzing effects of fear were expressed earlier (1621) by Robert Burton in these words: "Many men are so amazed and astonished with fear, they know not where they are, what they say, what they do; and (that which is worse) it tortures them, many dayes before, with continual affrights and suspicion [Burton, 1838, p. 173]." An earlier observation along the same line is found in Lucretius (1926), as follows: "For even as children tremble and fear everything in blinding darkness, so we sometimes dread in the light things that are no whit more to be feared than what children shudder at in the dark, and imagine will come to pass [pp. 66-67]."

fears can be learned by the association of neutral cues with existent fears.

Fifteen years after Spinoza completed his *Ethics*, John Locke's (1959) *An Essay Concerning Human Understanding* appeared in England. This classic work was, of course, primarily concerned with the relation of experience to knowledge, but it also included an excellent examination of what Locke refers to as "uneasiness." In my judgment this is one of the more significant early discussions relevant to anxiety, though it has not previously been considered in this light. The term "uneasiness" is another of the many words that connote—and particularly connoted in Locke's day, before the word "anxiety" had come into general use—a state of mental unrest, worry, and distress. Locke used the term "uneasiness" in a way almost synonymous with the present motivational meaning of "anxiety." Specifically, Locke states that "All pain of the body, of what sort soever, and disquiet of the mind, is uneasiness [p. 333]." Uneasiness leads to desire, and desire to action; thus, all action is asserted to be determined by the reduction of uneasiness. Among the factors that may cause uneasiness, Locke lists such bodily states as hunger, thirst, weariness, and sleepiness; such unsatisfied strivings as the needs for "honour, power, or riches"; and passions such as aversion, fear, and anger. The historical significance of Locke's theory of uneasiness is that it represents the first systematic attempt, after that of Epicurus, to develop an anxiety-reduction model of motivation.

With Francis Hutcheson, who was Professor of Moral Philosophy at the University of Glasgow in the early 1700's, we arrive at an accurate statement, after many earlier false starts, of the concept of conditioned anxiety (McReynolds, 1969, p. xiii), though Hutcheson of course does not use this term. He discusses how one can go about "rooting out the Prejudices of Education" which arise "from Associations of Ideas without any natural Connection [McReynolds, 1969, p. 93]." By "Prejudice" Hutcheson means (as determined both in terms of the context and of the way the term was then used) a perceptual or affective bias, and by "Education" he means one's previous experience. An example given by Hutcheson of the Association of a Prejudice with a particular situation, such that we would call it an instance of conditioned fear, is "the case of our Fear of *Spirits* in the *dark*, and in *Church-yards* [p. 93]." Not only does Hutcheson identify, in principle, the existence of conditioned fear, but he presents a sophisticated analysis of how the fear can be removed. Thus he suggests, in an anticipation of what today we term "extinction," that the disagreeable association may be disjoined by the frequent repetition of representations of objects (conditioned stimuli) separated from the "disagreeable Idea." Hutcheson's discussion also includes the notions of counter-conditioning and the greater resistance to extinction brought about by intermittent than by periodic reinforcement.

In 1747 a book titled *An Enquiry into the Origin of the Human Appetites and Affections* appeared. The author of this interesting volume has still not been definitely determined, but it may have been a James Long (McReynolds, 1969). The particularly interesting point that we find given in this book for first time is the idea that a state of uncertainty can lead to anxiety. Long uses the term "uneasiness," after Locke, to whom his generally associationist approach is much indebted; but he also uses the word "anxiety" in a technical sense, and he is the first author we have considered who does so. After noting that uneasiness arises in part because of the absence of an object or condition that one desires, he suggests that there is in addition another reason for uneasiness, namely, "The Uncertainty of possessing what is desired. Because a State of Uncertainty is always accompan'd with Anxiety. But when Certainty is once substituted in the Room of it, Anxiety, and its inseparable Attendant (Uneasiness) then cease [McReynolds, 1969, p. 353]." The suggestion that anxiety may reflect a state of uncertainty is, of course, in accord with modern anxiety theory.

The next work that we are to consider is William Battie's (1969) *A Treatise on Madness*, published in 1758. A truly epochal work, it was the first serious treatment of anxiety, by this name, from a psychiatric perspective, and one of the most original analyses, from any point of view, up to this time. Battie, an important, though largely unknown figure in the early history of psychiatry, was the superintendent of St. Luke's Hospital, and is said to have been the first teacher of psychiatry in England, perhaps in the world (Brussel, 1969). As might be expected from an English theorist of this period, in which the influence of Locke's emphasis upon the psychology of sensations was still very great, Battie framed his theory in terms of the different effects of sensations. "Sensation," he assumed, "is always accompanied with some degree of pleasure or uneasiness (Battie, 1969, p. 27)." He then posited three different classes of sensory effects (cutting across the different sensory modalities): first, an exceedingly high state of sensation, brought about by "too great and too lively a perception of objects that really exist [p. 4]"; second, a very low state of sensation, caused by "too little and too languid a perception of things that really exist [p. 5]"; and third, the perception of objects that do not really exist. The first situation leads to a feeling of uneasiness, or, if it is intense enough, *anxiety*, and the second to a condition of *insensibility*; the third is referred to as *deluded imagination*, and is considered to be the essential characteristic of madness.

The striking point about this theory of anxiety is its modernity. The idea that anxiety is somehow a function of the intensity, or overload, of stimulus input is central in such contemporary approaches to anxiety as that of Freud, Neil Miller, J. G. Miller, and others. Battie conceived that anxiety may arise either from "the too great or too long continued force of external objects [p. 34]," or by an "illconditioned" state of the nerves, such that they are more sensitive. A distinction was made by Battie between *Original* and *Consequential* anxiety (p. 90), with the former referring to inherent, and the latter to experiential factors. Another up-to-date idea of Battie's, and one with certain evolutionary overtones well prior to Darwin, is that the presence of anxiety is held to be adaptive; it is, he suggests, "absolutely necessary to our preservation, in such a manner, that without its severe but useful admonitions the several species of animals would speedily be destroyed [p. 28]." Another important advance made by Battie in this book is the designation of anxiety as a separate mental disorder. He made a number of suggestions for treatment of this disorder; these now sound rather quaint,[8] but on the whole, Battie felt fairly optimistic about the medical treatment of anxiety.

ANXIETY AND THE MODERN ERA

Throughout this chapter I have emphasized the continuing historical development of man as a self-knowing, self-probing

[8] Battie's recommendations for the treatment of anxiety primarily involve chemotherapy. Wines, he suggests, may sometimes procure tranquillity. Often, he states, he has prescribed *Extractum Thebaicum* (opium). Other drugs that may be helpful include Camphire, Sagapenum, Peruvian Bark, iron, vitriol, and mineral waters. Cold bathing is also suggested.

organism with a gradually deepening sense of individuality, and I have related this trend to the nature of his experiencing of anxiety. It is particularly in periods of the general breakdowns of widely accepted world views that increments in individuation are most likely to occur. At such points in history men are likely to feel that their particular gods, whoever and whatever they may be, are dead; and they are likely to seek new ways of assimilating their worlds. The modern era, I think it would be agreed, is such a time. This has been suggested by a number of recent commentators, including May (1950, 1974), Baumer (1960), and others, and is reflected in the inward-probing writings of such authors as James, Proust, Joyce, Camus, Auden, and Koestler.

It is not clear when this present period began, but perhaps it would be accurate to consider Søren Kierkegaard as its chief progenitor. Kierkegaard is particularly relevant here because of his classic work on anxiety, *Begrebet angest*, written in 1844 and translated into English in 1944 under the title *The Concept of Dread*.[9] Kierkegaard brings to an explicit statement many of the culturally implicit trends that I have already identified, in particular the relations among personal responsibility, guilt, and anxiety, as represented in early Christianity; it is thus not surprising that Kierkegaard was a theologian as well as a psychologist. Kierkegaard distinguished between two different kinds of anxiety. The first, which is especially evident in children, is the apprehension associated with "a seeking after adventure, a thirst for the prodigious, the mysterious [p. 38]." The second is the anxiety concerned with the choices that one faces as a function of his responsibilities as a person. It is the second of these that is most significant in Kierkegaard's philosophy and in the existential approach to anxiety that he inaugurated. The basis of Kierkegaard's interpretation of anxiety is that strong individuation and self-awareness necessarily make man free in—and at the same time responsible for—his choices from a multitude of possibilities. In the awareness of his necessity to make choices, together with the

[9] In terms of contemporary English usage a better translation would be "The concept of anxiety," and I have so interpreted Kierkegaard's meaning here. This question of the translation of the word *angst* has been elaborated by May (1950, p. 32). It is signficiant that Freud's *Hemmung, symptom und angst* was translated as *The Problem of Anxiety*.

possibilities of failure and guilt, lie the sources of one's anxiety. Anxiety is thus a necessary accompaniment of increased individuation. Though these views of Kierkegaard's seem to me correct, I think that he was wrong in assuming, as he apparently did, that in stating them he was describing the inherent nature of man; rather, the human characteristics that he identified were the results of a long history of culturally based individuation in Western man.

Let us return now to the medical tradition. In 1826 the pioneer Belgian psychiatrist, Joseph Guislain, proposed that anxiety is influential in the development of psychopathology. In 1859 in Germany, Heinrich Neumann, in his influential textbook of psychiatry, developed an interpretation of anxiety (*Angst*) as a danger signal. Anxiety, according to Neumann, arises when the person becomes aware of threats to vital concerns (Ellenberger, 1970, p. 214). By the period of, say, 100 years ago, the term "anxiety" was appearing as a standard term in the medico-psychiatric literature.[10] For example, there was a report of a case of "Jaundice after anxiety" in the *British Medical Journal* in 1870 (Tuke, 1884, p. 302). In this context Sigmund Freud, in 1895, in a paper of great historical importance, proposed the delineation of a new diagnostic entity, the "anxiety-neurosis." Freud[11] identified two immediately preceding authors who, in 1893, had also given prominent attention to morbid anxiety, though not to the extent of conceiving of it as a separate disease entity. Freud's conception of the cause of anxiety, as distinct from anxiety-neurosis, in this early paper was this: "The psyche develops the affect of anxiety," Freud

[10] For an examination of the linguistic history of the word "anxiety" see Sarbin (1964). The meaning of the term, as reflected in its usages, has undergone, and is continuing to undergo, constant change. The same is also true of linguistic analogues in other languages. It would be a gross error, however, to assume, as Sarbin seems to, that because the word "anxiety" is relatively new, that the general area of human experience to which it points is also new. As this paper has made clear, the general concept that we today designate in English as anxiety has a very long history ineed, though of course with constantly accruing and changing meanings.

[11] Though some writers seem to be under the impression that Freud discovered anxiety, the fact—as indicated in this paper—is that the significance of anxiety in personology and psychopathology had been recognized well before Freud, and indeed, was "in the air" at the time he began his work. This factual statement, of course, does not detract from the importance of Freud's contribution.

proposed, "when it feels itself incapable of dealing (by an adequate reaction) with a task (danger) approaching it externally [Freud, 1959, pp. 101-102]." This appraisal-and-threat notion, though in some respects at variance with Freud's later conceptions of anxiety, has a distinctly modern ring. Anxiety-neurosis, Freud suggested in this early paper, arises when the psyche feels unable to master endogenous sexual excitation.

With Freud we have reached the contemporary period, and I need not outline the later development of his theory of anxiety, nor the theories of other recent authorities, in detail. Instead, let me simply note a few later highlights.[12] In 1920 Watson and Raynor reported their now well-known study on the conditioning of fear. Then in 1926 Freud published his *Hemmung, Symptom und Angst*; this was translated into English, under the title *Inhibition, Symptom and Anxiety*, in 1927, and under the title *The Problem of Anxiety*, in 1936. Mowrer, in 1939, published his influential paper on a stimulus-response analysis of anxiety, and in 1950 May's important book, *The Meaning of Anxiety*, appeared. Since that time the amount published in this area, of course, has been enormous.

Overall Trends

I want now to examine the present situation in anxiety theory from the perspective of the historical background we have surveyed. If we examine the whole course of the history of conceptions of anxiety, there are, I believe, two main currents that can be identified. I am speaking now from the scientific point of view, with respect to the question of just what it is about the way that man is biologically put together that causes him, under certain conditions, to become anxious. The two theoretical approaches that I am referring to are what, in today's terminology, are termed the "cognitive orientation" and the "conditioning orientation." The essence of the cognitive approach to anxiety theory is that a person's anxiety is the natural resultant of a state of discrepancies, imbalances, or conflicts (there are many ways of phrasing the fundamental idea) among his mental thoughts, feelings, and memories. The general assumption of the conditioning approach to

[12] The recent history of certain aspects of anxiety theory is discussed in McReynolds (1975).

anxiety theory is that anxiety is the result of some kind of fortuitous temporal association between neutral, or accidental cues, and certain mentally traumatic events, such that thereafter the previously neutral cues elicit a negative affect, anxiety. Though these two distinct theoretical approaches each have a number of somewhat different versions, together they encompass all, or practically all of the variety of theoretical approaches to anxiety (McReynolds, 1973, 1975). A possible third approach is the intensity, or overstimulation hypothesis, though I believe (McReynolds, 1975) that this can be subsumed under the cognitive orientation. In contemporary theory, the broadly cognitive approach is represented by the existential and psychoanalytic conceptualizations, by the dissonance, incongruence, and disparity interpretations, and by my own cognitive backlog model (McReynolds, 1975); the conditioning model is represented in stimulus-response (S-R) formulations and in behavior-modification theory.

Now, it is particularly noteworthy, I think, that if one surveys the past history of anxiety theory he will find these same two orientations represented. Let us consider the cognitive approach first. This has certainly been the most widely used orientation throughout history, in attempting to understand anxiety: thus, finds it reflected, in diverse ways, of course, in the conceptio human anguish developed by Aeschylus, Euripides, Aristotle, curus, Epictetus, Paul, Locke, Long, Kierkegaard, and Freud. The conditioning orientation is represented, at least in part, in the writings of Aristotle, Vives, Spinoza, Hutcheson, and Watson. The overstimulation hypothesis, if one wishes to consider it as a distinct approach, is represented by Battie and Freud.

It is striking that these two or three theoretical approaches have had such a long past, and that they have kept recurring throughout the history of thought. This fact certainly says something about their heuristic value. Further, a great deal of evidence is now available in support of each of the approaches. Yet they are obviously quite different theoretically. The question arises: Is it possible to integrate them into a single, overall conceptualization of the etiology of anxiety?

I believe that it is. I have elsewhere (McReynolds, 1973, 1975) proposed, as a resolution of the apparent contradiction between the cognitive and the conditioning formulations of anxiety, that in actuality both are correct, that despite appearances there is no real contradiction between them, and that in fact they deal with different aspects of the anxiety-arousing process. The matters discussed by the cognitive theories, I suggest, concern the *initial causes* of a person's anxiety, i.e., what we may call *primary anxiety*; the matters discussed by the conditioning theories, on the other hand, concern the *spread* of anxiety, *once it has occurred*, i.e., what we may call *secondary anxiety*. Both types are real, and perhaps indistinguishable phenomenally, and both are inherent in the sense of being functions of the way man is put together.

Throughout this paper I have alternated between discussions of particular formulations of anxiety, on the one hand, and comments on the relations between cultural conditions and anxiety, on the other hand. These two approaches, though quite different, are by no means unrelated, and this is why I have considered them both in the same paper. Science, though it should not be at the whim of cultural currents, is never separate from its cultural medium; this is particularly true with something as intimate and pervasive as anxiety.

REFERENCES

Acquinas, T. *Summus theologica*. (English trans.). London: Washbourne, 1911–22. 18 vols.

Barbu, Z. *Problems of historical psychology*. New York: Grove, 1960.

Battie, W. *A treatise on madness*. New York: Brunner/Mazel, 1969. (Originally published, 1758)

Baumer, F. L. *Religion and the rise of skepticism*. New York: Harcourt Brace, 1960.

Brussel, J. A. *Introduction to W. Battie*, A treatise on madness. New York: Brunner/Mazel, 1969.

Burckhardt, J. *The civilization of the Renaissance in Italy*. (Trans. by S. G. C. Middlemore) New York: Harper & Row, 1958. (Originally published 1860)

Burton, R. *The anatomy of melancholy*. London: B. Blake, 1838.

Coeffeteau, N. *Tableau des passions humaines, de leurs causes et de leurs effets*. Paris, 1630.

Cooper, L. *The Rhetoric of Aristotle*. New York: D. Appleton & Co., 1932.

Descartes, R. The passions of the soul. In *The philosophical works of Descartes*. Vol. 1. (Trans. by E. S. Haldane & G. R. T. Ross) Cambridge: University Press, 1967.

Diogenes Laertius. *Lives of eminent philosophers*. Vol. 2. (Translated by R. D. Hicks) Cambridge, Mass.: Harvard University Press, 1925.

Edman, N. Introduction. In Epictetus, *Discourses*. New York: Walter J. Black, 1944.

Ellenberger, H. E. *The discovery of the unconscious*. New York: Basic Books, 1970.

Epictetus. *Discourses*. (Trans. by T. W. Higginson) Roslyn, N.Y.: Walter J. Black, 1944.

Epicurus. *Letters and principal doctrines and Vatican sayings*. (Trans. by R. M. Geer) New York: Bobbs-Merrill, 1964.

Frame, D. M. (Ed. and Trans.) *The complete essays of Montaigne*. Stanford, Calif.: Stanford University Press, 1965.

Freud, S. *Hemmung, symptom und angst*. Leipzig, Vienna, & Zurick: Internationaler Psychoanalytischer Verlag, 1926.

Freud, S. *Inhibition, symptom and anxiety*. Stanford, Conn.: Psychoanalytic Institute, 1927.

Freud, S. *The problem of anxiety*. New York: The Psychoanalytic Quarterly Press, 1936.

Freud, S. The justification for detaching from neurasthenia a particular syndrome: The anxiety-neurosis. In *Sigmund Freud: Collected papers*. Vol. 1. New York: Basic Books, 1959.

Gardiner, H. M., Metcalf, R. C., & Beebe-Center, J. G. *Feeling and emotion: A history of theories*. New York: American Book Company, 1937.

Guislain, J. *Traité sur l'aliénation mentale*. Amsterdam, 1826.

Homer, *The Odyssey*. (Trans. by E. V. Rieu) Hammondsworth, Middlesex: Penguin, 1946.

Homer. *The Iliad*. (Trans. by E. V. Rieu) Hammondsworth, Middlesex: Penguin, 1950.

Hutcheson, F. *An essay on the nature and conduct of the passions and affections*. Gainsville, Fla.: Scholars' Facsimiles and Reprints, 1969. (Originally published 1742)

Kierkegaard, S. A. *Begrebet angest. En simpel psychologisk-paapegende overveielse i retning af det dogmatiske problem om arvesynden af Vigilius Haufniensis* [*pseud.*] Kjøbenhavn: C. A. Reitzel, 1844

Kierkegaard, S. A. *The concept of dread*. (Trans. by W. Lowrie) Princeton: Princeton University Press, 1944.

La Chambre, M. C. de. *Les caractéres des passions*. Amsterdam: Vols. 1-2, 1658; Vols. 3-4, 1662; Vol. 5, 1663.

Leibman, J. L. *Peace of mind*. New York: Simon & Schuster, 1946.

Levi, A. *French moralists: The theory of the passions 1585-1649*. Oxford: Clarendon Press, 1964.

Locke, J. *An essay concerning human understanding*. Vol. 1. New York: Dover, 1959.

Lucretius. *On the nature of things*. (Trans. by C. Bailey) Oxford: Clarendon Press, 1926.

Mason, H. *Gilgamesh*. New York: Mentor, 1972.

May, R. *The meaning of anxiety*. New York: Ronald Press, 1950.

May, R. *Love and will*. New York: Dell, 1974.

McReynolds, P. (Ed.) *Four early works on motivation*. Gainsville, Fla.: Scholars' Facsimiles & Reprints, 1969.

McReynolds, P. A theoretical integration of conditioning and cognitive conceptions of anxiety. Paper presented at a symposium on "New concepts and methods in anxiety and emotions: Effects of anxiety on learning and retention." American Psychological Association Meeting, Montreal, August 28, 1973.

McReynolds, P. Anxiety and assimilation. In M. Zuckerman & C. D. Spielberger (Eds.), *Emotions and anxiety: New concepts, methods and applications*, 1975, in press.

Misch, G. *Autobiography in antiquity*. London: Routledge & Kegan Paul, 1950, 2 vols.

Morris, C. *The discovery of the individual. 1050-1200*. New York: Harper & Row, 1972.

Mowrer, O. H. A stimulus-response analysis of anxiety and its role as a reinforcing agent. *Psychological Review*, 1939, 46, 553-565.

Nahm, M. C. *Selections from early Greek philosophy*. New York: Appleton-Century-Crofts, 1964.

Neumann, H. *Lehrbuch der Psychiatrie*. Erlanger: F. Enke, 1859.

Parkes, H. B. *Gods and men: The origins of Western culture*. New York: Random House, 1965.

Peters, R. S. *Brett's history of psychology*. (Abridged) Cambridge, Mass.: Massachusetts Institute of Technology Press, 1962.

Reynolds, E. *A treatise of the passions and faculties of the soule of man*. Gainsville, Fla.: Scholars' Facsimilies and Reprints, 1971. (Originally published 1640)

Saint Augustine. *The confessions*. (Trans. by E. B. Pusey) London: J. M. Dent & Sons, 1907.

Sarbin, R. R. Anxiety: The reification of a metaphor. *Archives of General Psychiatry*, 1964, 10, 630-638.

Smith, N. W. The ancient background to Greek psychology and some implications for today. *Psychological Record*, 1974, 24, 309-324.

Snell, B. *The discovery of the mind*. (Trans. by T. G. Rosenmeyer) New York: Harper, 1960.

Spinoza, B. *The chief works of Benedict de Spinoza*. (Trans. by R. H. M. Elwes) Vol. 2. New York: Dover, 1955.

Telfer, W. *Cyril of Jerusalem and Nemesius of Emesa*. London: S. C. M. Press, 1955.

Tuke, D. H. *Influence of the mind upon the body*. Philadelphia: Henry C. Lea's Son & Company, 1884.

Vives, J. L. *De anima et vita*. Turin, 1959 (Photographic reproduction of Basle, 1538, ed.).

Watson, J. B., & Raynor, R. Conditioned emotional reactions. *Journal of Experimental Psychology*, 1920, 3, 1-14.

2
ANXIETY AND SELF-PREOCCUPATION

Irwin G. Sarason

University of Washington
Seattle, Washington
United States

This chapter presents a cognitive social learning interpretation of anxiety. It deals particularly with the effects of self-preoccupation on attention to environmental cues, information processing, and overt behavior. Anxiety is viewed as a type of self-preoccupation characterized by self-awareness, self-doubt, and self-depreciation. These cognitive activities exert impacts on both overt behavior and physiological reactivity. A proposition considered here is that contrary to classical psychoanalytic theory, self-preoccupation and not an anxiety drive is of pivotal importance in the development of maladaptive behavior.

There seems to be increasing recognition of the need to establish a middle ground between the limited and more precise domain of behaviorism and the broad but murkier domain of the inner life of the individual. Cognitive social learning theory is directed

I am indebted to the following colleagues who reviewed earlier drafts of the manuscript: Elizabeth F. Loftus, G. Alan Marlatt, Ronald E. Smith, and Keith Sonnanburg.

particularily toward an explication of the thought processes and covert problem-solving activities that occur before, during, and following overt behavior. These covert behaviors and activities are assumed to be products of the individual's history and to function as mediators between experience and behavior. They are not completely at the mercy of changes in stimulus conditions because, once cognitive competencies, structures, and styles have been established, they serve to influence stimulus reception and interpretation, on the one hand, and overt behavior, on the other.

Personality can be viewed from an information-processing perspective. The term "cognitive events" refers to ways in which a person searches the environment for cues, selects cues that are relevant to thought and action, integrates new information with old, and makes decisions that eventuate in observable behavior. A cognitive event can be thought of as being as much behavior as a muscle twitch or a signature on a piece of paper. However, cognitive events are not directly observable. Inferential support for their existence must come from other behaviors that can be observed.

Research on test anxiety illustrates this inferential process with regard to attention and information processing. Let us briefly review some of the empirical evidence that supports a cognitive view of anxiety.

TEST ANXIETY, ATTENTION, AND INFORMATION PROCESSING

A number of researchers have viewed test anxiety as a proneness to emit self-centered interfering responses when confronted with evaluative conditions (Liebert & Morris, 1967; Mandler & Sarason, 1952; Phillips, Martin, & Meyers, 1972; Sieber, 1969). This interpretation typically emphasized two response components. One is autonomic reactivity—sweating, accelerated heart rate, etc. The other component is cognitive events, for example, saying to oneself while taking a test, "I am stupid" or "Maybe I won't pass." It seems reasonable that saying such things to oneself during a test might interfere considerably with attention to the task at hand, be it one that requires learning or figuring out the answers to certain questions. Worry is unmistakably an attentionally demanding and emotionally arousing cognitive activity.

Wine (1971) reviewed the literature from the standpoint of selective attention and pointed out that a large portion of research using test anxiety scales focused on cues to which high scorers respond with personalized, task-irrelevant responses (e.g., worry). Studies of the perceptual, attentional, and cognitive factors that influence how information is used and interpreted are relevant to this research (Easterbrook, 1959; Egeth, 1967; Mandler, 1959). Wine (1970) also reported a study of attentional training as a means of reducing the negative effects of test anxiety. Her approach included instructions to the subject to attend to task-relevant behavior, and her findings indicated that highly test anxious persons were helped by the training they received.

The writer's recent research has used evidence of differences in direction of attention among groups differing in test anxiety as a basis for developing methods to facilitate the performance of high scorers. One line of investigation has been concerned with the effects of preperformance communications (Sarason, 1960; Sarason, Kestenbaum, & Smith, 1972). Reassuring and neutral instructions at the outset of an experimental session facilitate the performance of high test anxious groups. Unfortunately, the same conditions may be detrimental for low test anxious groups. For example, reassurance about the nonevaluative nature of a performance situation seems to lessen the effort of subjects low in test anxiety.

A promising line of research has dealt with modeling and its relationship to performance. Modeling is an important component of social learning theory because significant social models provide the observer not only with demonstrations of overt responses, but covert ones (by "thinking through" problems and tactics aloud) as well. Models can shape and reshape one's views and expectancies concerning oneself and others. Whereas exposure to models who have failure experiences has a negative effect on the performance of high test anxious subjects (Sarason, 1972a), exposure to models displaying adaptive behavior plays a discernible positive role in facilitating learning and performance (Sarason, 1972b). Exposure to prosocial models also seems to strengthen adaptive social behavior in juvenile delinquents, especially those whose level of anxiety is high (Sarason, 1968; Sarason & Ganzer, 1973). Research on cognitive modeling has shown that persons high in anxiety are particularly responsive to demonstrations of how problems can be analyzed and approached (Sarason, 1973).

An example of the broadening role of modeling techniques in research on anxiety is provided by a recent experiment (Sarason, in press). It dealt with the role of the model, but not as a demonstrator of responses targeted to improve subjects' performance on a specific task. Rather, the model disclosed information about her typical reactions to testing and evaluation situations. Because evaluative threat has been shown to be a significant factor in comparisons between groups differing in test anxiety, arousal of an achievement orientation was included as an independent variable in the investigation. The modeling condition preceded the achievement orientation condition, and the experiment asked two basic questions: Are high and low test anxious groups differentially sensitive to the experimenter's modeled self-disclosures? Do preperformance instructions temper or exacerbate the effects of modeled self-disclosure? The measure used in the study was the Test Anxiety Scale (TAS) (Sarason, 1972a).

There were five modeling conditions:

1. *Coping anxious model.* Model describes herself as high in test anxiety but describes how she copes with it (e.g., by concentrating on the task at hand).
2. *Noncoping anxious model.* Model describes herself as high in test anxiety but does not refer to coping tactics.
3. *Low anxious model.* Model describes herself as typically being unworried about taking tests.
4. *Neutral model.* Model talks about campus life (subjects were college students).
5. *Control.* The experimenter proceeds directly to administer the task.

After listening to the experimenter's self-disclosures, the subjects performed on the experimental task, which involved learning difficult verbal learning material. The Test Anxiety X Instructions interaction, consistent with earlier work, showed that while the superiority of low TAS subjects was evident under achievement-orienting conditions, in the absence of these threats the performance levels of groups differing in test anxiety were comparable. Table 2-1 presents the results of the experiment from the standpoint of modeling. While low anxious were correct more often than high anxious subjects, and while modeling increased the

Table 2-1

Mean Number of Correct Responses for Groups Differing in Test Anxiety (TAS) Scores and Modeling Conditions

Group	Coping model	Noncoping model	Low anxious model	Campus model	No model
High TAS ($N = 20$)	137.25	83.45	94.35	107.65	104.45
Low TAS ($N = 20$)	121.30	117.55	113.65	112.35	114.40
All subjects ($N = 40$)	129.28	100.50	104.00	110.00	109.40

Source: Sarason, I. G. Test anxiety and the self-disclosing, coping model. *Journal of Consulting and Clinical Psychology*, in press. With permission.

number of correct responses, the interaction effects are of the greatest relevance to the present discussion. The high TAS-Coping Model mean was not only significantly higher than the means for the other high TAS groups, but was also higher than the low TAS group means as well. The superiority of this group suggests the receptiveness of high test anxious persons to modeled information and their ability to apply it.

Attentional processes may provide clues to the behavior of high anxious persons in situations in which they are being evaluated. The highly test anxious individual seems prone to emit self-centered interfering responses when confronted with an evaluative threat. These responses include such cognitions as "What will happen if I fail?" It seems reasonable that saying such things to oneself during a test might interfere considerably with the task at hand, be the task one that requires the acquisition of a new skill (e.g., learning to drive a car) or figuring out the answers to certain questions (e.g., items on an income tax form). In one study college students were asked the reason why they failed a test (Doris & Sarason, 1955). Low test anxious college students tended to put the blame on external factors ("It was a bad exam"), whereas high test anxious students tended to blame themselves ("I got confused"), suggesting that they are having such interfering cognitions about themselves. Since external attributions (e.g., anger directed toward a teacher), as well as internal ones (e.g., self-blame), can interfere with attention to a task, research on the interfering effects of the former as well as the latter is needed.

Although worry and self-blame are clearly attentionally demanding activities, their roles as cognitive mediators of overt behavior remain to be delineated. Studies relating test anxiety and modeling suggest that while high scorers have a tendency to become self-centered under evaluative stress, the direction of their attention is not completely one sided. Except, perhaps, for the most extreme form of pathological withdrawal, anxious persons—even those described here as being self-centered—attend to both internal and external stimuli. Whereas test anxiety would appear to be a type of trait anxiety, the balance in any given case between an inner-directed preoccupation with oneself and sensitivity to external cues, such as the behavior of a model, can be expected to vary with the level of evaluative stress, task characteristics, and the interpersonal dimensions of the setting in which the performance takes place.

Why is it that under appropriate conditions (for example, a difficult task and achievement-orienting instructions) the performance of highly test anxious subjects deteriorates? One interpretation is that the highly test anxious individual becomes self-preoccupied, attending to internal events rather than the task at hand. This self-focusing in the face of external challenges is maladaptive, but has been shown to be modifiable (Sarason, 1972a; Wine, 1971). Because self-preoccupation is not peculiar to the highly test anxious individual, it seems useful to explore this general concept, its relationship to the problem of anxiety, and its possible heuristic value in accounting for both adaptive and maladaptive behavior.

PREOCCUPATION AND SELF-PREOCCUPATION

The preoccupied individual is engrossed in thought. Preoccupations include worry over the future of mankind, concern about food shortages throughout the world, fearful thoughts about snakes or failing in school, and anger over perceived slights and insults. The range of self-preoccupations is narrower because it is limited to being lost in thought about oneself. When Einstein was pondering the theory of relativity he probably was preoccupied, but not self-preoccupied. The person who habitually responds to perceived slights and frustrations with feelings of anger is self-preoccupied, as is the person who responds by a retreat into Walter

Mitty fantasy. Self-preoccupation may intrude on information-processing at three points: attention to environmental cues, encoding and transformation of these data, and selection of an overt response.

The cognitive preoccupations of the angry person may interfere with the veridical preception of environmental cues, their interpretation, and decisions about responses to them. Similarly, but probably for different reasons, the person engulfed in private fantasies may also experience maladaptive functioning at these stages of information processing.

The variegated nature of self-preoccupation is illustrated in Read's (1974) account of the harrowing experiences of the Uruguayan rugby players whose flight to compete against a Chilean group was interrupted by a crash in the Andes mountains. Although several died in the initial crash, as well as afterwards as a result of crash injuries, there were survivors who lived to tell the tale.

The aspect of the adventure that received the most attention is that survival was possible because the survivors ate meat cut from the bodies of the dead. Of more interest from a psychological standpoint is the wide variability in the survivors' behavior. There appeared to be three groups. One group, the copers, after surveying their plight in the cold, snow-covered mountains with only the plane wreckage for their home and a larder consisting of a few candy bars and bottles of liquor, proceeded to the task at hand, survival. They organized the survivors, arranged the best sanitary conditions that they could set up, made plans for food distribution, cared for the sick and injured, made efforts to attract the attention of planes that might pass by, and conducted scouting expeditions. If these task-oriented men were self-preoccupied they either kept it to themselves or engaged in self-preoccupation during periods when they were not confronted with tasks to carry out. A second group was clearly self-preoccupied and bore characteristics in common with the sketch of the test anxious individual drawn previously. They seemed in varying degrees to focus on themselves, to worry about their assorted discomfortures, to be constantly worrying and anticipating the next disasterous event, and, in the face of no indication that their plight would end, to experience despair at performing the routine hour-by-hour task required for survival. A third group also focused their attention on themselves, but the content of their self-preoccupations took the form of annoyance and anger at their plight, suspicion of the motives and behavior of other members of the group, and dependence on the copers for the wherewithal to survive.

Many clinical examples could be given of the diversity of cognitions with which persons become self-preoccupied; the degree to which self-preoccupation influences attentiveness to external cues; and the way in which information from the environment is stored, retrieved, and acted upon. It seems clear that self-preoccupation is not restricted to the domain of worry or anxiety. In the following case it might at first seem that the patient was preoccupied with the number 13 rather than being preoccupied with himself. However, unlike Einstein's preoccupation with the abstractions of relativity theory, this man was really quite self-preoccupied with the *personal* significance he invested in the number 13.

The patient was a 49-year-old man whose main symptom was an obsession with the number 13. If he heard the word he felt "shock" and experienced a subsequent period of acute anxiety. His everyday life was a continuous effort to avoid any reference to 13, so much that his activities were seriously handicapped. In some way or another, it seems as if everyone was always saying 13 to him. If they met him in the morning they would say "Oh, good morning," or later in the day it would be "Good afternoon." (13 letters in each). He stayed in bed on the 13th day of each month, skipped the 13th tred in a stairway, and found it necessary to count letters and phrases, his steps, and streets, to avoid the number 13. As long as he was occupied with the avoidance of the number 13, preoccupation with unpleasant, immoral thoughts was impossible [Ross, 1937, pp. 219–221].

The delusions of a schizophrenic individual also illustrate the powerful role that self-preoccupations can play. The account that follows was given by a medical student with a Ph.D. degree in psychology who had a psychotic episode. It illustrates not only this role, but also the fact that cognitive self-focusing can be wavering and is mutable:

Conversations had hidden meaning. When someone told me later that I was delusional, though, I seemed to know it. But I was really groping to understand what was going on. There was a sequence with my delusions: first panic, then groping, then elation at having found out. Involvement with the delusions would fade in and out. One moment I would feel I certainly didn't believe these things; then, without realizing it, I would be caught up in them again. When reality started coming back, when I realized where I was and what had happened, I became depressed. There were times when I was aware, in a sense, that I was acting on a delusion. One part of me seemed to say, "Keep your mouth shut, you know this is a delusion and it will pass." But the other side of me wanted the delusion, preferred to have things this way. The experience was a passive one; that is, I just sat back as these things happened to me. Getting better was passive too; it just happened, so to speak, as I watched [Bowers, 1968, p. 353].

ANXIOUS SELF-PREOCCUPATION

Anxious self-preoccupation consists of heightened concern over one's inadequacies and shortcomings. The anxious person is concerned about any dangers, threats, and the inability to cope with them. This does not mean that danger and threat necessarily cause anxious self-preoccupation. Self-preoccupation of any type is a function not only of objective life events but also of the interpretation of those events by the individual. Whether self-preoccupation occurs depends on the skills a person has learned in coping with dangers and threats. The anxious person seems deficient in these skills.

From a traditonal psychodynamic point of view, maladaptive behavior is caused by unconsciously felt anxiety. Anxiety has usually been regarded as a basic process upon which other processes and behavior depend. *Perhaps anxiety, while important, is not quite so pivotal. Perhaps the more basic process is not anxiety, but self-preoccupation or self-focusing.* If this is true, a need to understand the process by which particular self-preoccupations are acquired, strengthened, and weakened.

Patterns of self-preoccupying thought function as schemas that direct explorations of objects in the environment and interpersonal relationships. However, the person may have articulated neither these schemas nor their functional relationship to behavior. Self-preoccupations not only interfere with or otherwise influence performance, but also they serve, correctly or incorrectly, to identify problems that require solution. There may be considerable value in approaching a number of psychological problems from the standpoint of cognitive events and processes that develop in a social environment.

Whereas we have focused mainly on self-preoccupations that are excessive, undesirable, or maladaptive, the examples of many writers and artists make clear that personal introspections can yield valuable insights for mankind as well as for the individual. What appears critical is the orientation the individual takes toward himself as a stimulus. Constructive self-examination requires the capacity to look at oneself in a detached, objective way. Perhaps Freud's self-analysis falls into this category of self-preoccupation. The orientation taken toward oneself might be viewed as a cognitive style, as acquired approach to stimulation, or a competency (if it is, in fact, adaptive).

Self-preoccupation or self-focusing may be a basic process involved in attention to objects of the environment and the way in which information is used and acted upon. Those who are described as being high in anxiety tend to worry about and anticipate threats and dangers. Others, for example certain psychotics, may be equally self-preoccupied but have different cognitive contents. Still others may not be strongly self-preoccupied with anxiety, anger, or other cognitive contents, but preoccupied with events and problems external to their personal lives. Identifying such persons and the factors that contribute to their preoccupations is of considerable interest. The ability to concentrate on and involve oneself in a task or project is as deserving a focus of psychological study as are the personal maladaptations. Perhaps if we could achieve a better understanding of the ability to immerse oneself in external events, our understanding of internal (self) preoccupations might be elucidated in the process.

A task confronting the researcher preoccupied with anxiety is identification of the operations and transformations the individual performs on information that result in high levels of worry and anticipations of unpleasant outcomes. Accomplishing this task will require empirical inquiry into the assumptions, strategies, and expectancies of people falling at different points along the continuum of anxious self-preoccupation, as well as into the rules by which the person labels and makes judgments about whether an environmental event represents a personal threat. Experimental studies of performance on tasks that are sensitive to the interfering effects of self-preoccupation are needed. These include short term memory, incidental learning, and tasks similar to those that have been fruitfully employed in testing hypotheses about the role of interference effects in schizophrenia. Research is also needed on individual differences in information processing as a function of personality characteristics.

SELF-PREOCCUPATION AND BEHAVIOR

Figure 2-1 contains a diagram of steps that may be part of the process by which self-preoccupation influences behavior. Step 1 refers to the stimulus configuration that confronts a person at a given point. Step 2 refers to the aspects of the configuration to which the individual is sensitive. The amount and type of self-preoccupation (A) influences the degree to which the person is receptive to the available stimulus information and the amount of physiological arousal. The task-oriented person who is deeply immersed in his job will be especially attentive to cues that might contribute to job completion. The student who is worried about failure will be especially attentive to stimuli suggestive of possible evaluations of his work. The paranoid will be especially attentive to cues that relate to his distinctive system of ideation. To the extent that environmental cues are attended to, they are then dealt with by the distinctive information-processing system developed by the individual (Step 3). The self-preoccupations of the individual (B) influence the data processing of Step 3. When the doctor gives

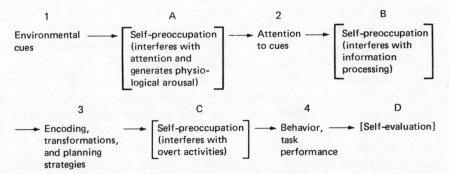

Fig. 2-1. Steps in an information-processing analysis of the role of self-preoccupation in behavior.

pills to his patients, some will worry about side effects, some will accept the medicine matter of factly, and still others will become angry about the high cost of drugs. A major task in the field of personality assessment is identification and measurement of individual differences involved in information processing. The fourth step in the sequence is the behavior of the person, whether it be in the social, educational, or work spheres. Selection of a behavioral response, also, is influenced by the personal focus of the individual (C). After the person has responded, self-evaluation (D) of his behavior and its outcomes may significantly influence responses to environmental cues.

This sequence of steps provides a framework within which a number of research domains might be integrated. Earlier in this chapter, research on test anxiety was discussed particularly with regard to Step 2, which is concerned with attentional processes. There is a considerable body of related research on stress and behavior. Individual differences in attention (Step 2) encompass the appraisal process that Lazarus and Averill (1972) and others have used to account for individual differences in reactions to various types of stresses. There is a burgeoning literature on the encoding and transformation of information (Step 3). Unfortunately, research in this area has been conducted almost independent of efforts at integration with work on the psychology of personality.

There are some important implications of the emphasis placed here on the role of self-preoccupation in behavior. As mentioned previously, one of these concerns personality assessment. With a few exceptions, most assessment work has dealt with categorizing people in various diagnostic ways, e.g., as psychopaths, schizophrenics, and obsessive-compulsives. Little or no theory is involved in the use of several prominent instruments, the Minnesota Multiphase Personality Inventory being the most notable example. The belief expressed here is that personality researchers should be more preoccupied with the assessment of cognitive processes that may underlie overt patterns of behavior such as those seen in anxiety, schizophrenia, and criminality. These processes include attentional patterns, assumptions people make about the nature of interpersonal relationships, ways in which the person deals with information from the environment and the bases of personal decisions.

The study of self-preoccupation probably requires innovations not only in *what* is assessed, but also *how* assessment is conducted. Fortunately, recent emphasis on behavioral approaches has significantly broadened the base of personality assessment. It seems reasonable to assume that much of an individual's behavioral repertory is created through experience and learning. Factors that may significantly influence self-preoccupation and its contents include the amount of time someone spends alone, the type of models to which he is exposed, the reinforcements available for various types of activity, debilitating physical illnesses, instigations to aggression, and informational overloads. In some cases the prsence of these factors can be assessed in specially created situations in the clinic or laboratory; in others, retrospective accounts may be the only feasible alternative.

The proposals of this chapter are to (*a*) analyze anxiety as one type of self-preoccupying response, (*b*) view self-preoccupation as cognitive contents shaped by social learning, and (*c*) explore objectively the cognitive and learning mechanisms by which a person makes use of information. The latter is a task with beginnings identifiable in the literature on cognitive styles (e.g., reflectivity-impulsivity, field dependence-independence, curiosity, and creativity).

The formulation presented here omits a number of popular chapter-heading words including emotion, drive, stress, and motivation. The writer agrees with Cofer's (1972) caution concerning the explanatory role played by motivational concepts:

Little is accomplished by invocation of the work *motivation.* . . . What is needed is a close examination of the conditions under which a behavior pattern of interest was developed and is sustained, and it is not very helpful to emphasize motivational concepts in the process of making the analysis [p. 153].

Perhaps a similar statement might be made about anxiety. Perhaps study of the elements of anxious self-preoccupation will prove more useful than pursuit of the drives and emotions in terms of which anxiety has often been described.

CLINICAL IMPLICATIONS

Identification of the cognitive elements of self-preoccupation may be of considerable practical value since adaptive and maladaptive behavior may be thought of as outcomes of a coping process. The components of this process are summarized in Fig. 2-1. By coping process is meant the ways in which the individual attends to, assimilates, and responds to information provided by the environment and by information stored in memory. As already implied, self-preoccupation, including anxious self-preoccupation, can result from a variety of factors (available models of coping styles and behavior, reinforcement regimens, unexpected events such as illnesses). As these factors are delineated and understood, new approaches to eliminating maladaptive and strengthening adaptive behavior may become available. With an analysis of behavior in terms of its cognitive substrate, training programs can be developed to teach not only new overt responses but new ways of construing and thinking about the world and of processing information. Research on cognitive modification has shown that focalized instruction and practice in attending to relevant external cues and ignoring internal responses that interfere with task performance have a significant facilitating effect on anxious people (Meichenbaum, 1972; Sarason, 1972a; Wine, 1971).

Outside the anxiety literature, a study by Smith (1973) provides further encouragement to the development of training programs for strengthening specific coping skills, both of the overt and cognitive variety. One goal of Smith's study was the improvement of police officers' skills in attention to relevant events, critical thinking, and maintaining objectivity under stress. He prepared a training program to aid police officers in handling family disputes. The program involved live and videotaped modeling, information about the effects of stress on behavior, techniques for dealing with personal feelings of inadequacy, and periods of practice and feedback. A significant portion of the program dealt with monitoring one's own behavior and controlling idiosyncratic preoccupations, particularly when under stress. Using as dependent measures behavior in simulated and actual domestic intervention situations, self-confidence, and supervisor's ratings, Smith demonstrated that a training program emphasizing cognitive skills can increase the effectivenss of police officers.

Work with police officers, the research described earlier on anxiety and attention, and efforts to change thought patterns in deviant groups such as delinquents and schizophrenics share a number of characteristics. Most pertinent to the present discussion is the need for self-preoccupied persons to gain better control over their self-oriented thinking and thus become more adept at coping with the task at hand. Training in attentional skills and in critical and objective thinking seems especially relevant to situations that require decision-making under unpredictable, dangerous conditions.

The story of the old-time airplane pilot suggests the need to establish such cognitive programs (Glass & Singer, 1972). The pilot often flew long distances over water, looking for a small island in the sea. The pilot, before his departure, would carefully plot his course. After several hours in the air, he would sometimes find himself past the point in time when he should have sighted his destination. While he carefully calculated his speed, drift, and direction throughout the flight, the thought that he had indeed passed his island and would end up running out of fuel over the sea was compelling. It was important for him to have confidence in his navigational skills despite the second thoughts of the moment. The pilot who decided to abort his navigational plan and fly in wide circles to look for the island would probably end up in the sea. The pilot who systematically followed his plan, despite the lack of cues from the environment, generally made his landfall.

Can training programs be developed to meet the needs of such diverse groups as test anxious students and airplane pilots? There is every reason to argue for an affirmative answer to this question, as long as it is understood that one master program will not be applicable in every case. The following are components of cognitive training programs suggested by the available literature:

1. *Information.* People often are woefully ignorant of basic information about themselves, others, their jobs, and their responsibilities. At present, it is difficult to estimate how much human maladaptation, inefficiency, and unhappiness is due largely to poor information. At a minimum, test anxious persons need applicable information about study and test-taking skills.
2. *Modeling.* The opportunity to observe someone cope with a task or think through a problem can provide a shortcut to

weeks, months, and years of frustration and failure. Adaptive models provide valuable information in usable form.

3. *Self-monitoring and self-control.* People can learn to monitor and control both their behavior and their thoughts.
4. *Attentional training.* Skill at attending to the task at hand can be learned and represents an important aspect of self-control.
5. *Relaxation.* Knowing how to relax under specifiable conditions can be especially valuable for people who must work under tension, personal threat, and danger. The literature on systematic desensitization has much to contribute to lowering anxiety in people so that they can learn needed coping skills.
6. *Practice and reinforcement.* Whether the person is performing a task or thinking about a problem to be solved, practice, together with reward, is needed in shaping adaptive psychological functioning.

These principles may be as relevant to groups characterized by serious behavioral disorder as to those who simply desire to function more effectively on the job, in school, or with their friends. An early step in determining if this is true will be clarification of the nature and consequences of self-preoccupying thought and activity. For example, the content of self-preoccupation may be noxious for some people (for example, anxiety neurotics) but a pleasant fantasy retreat for others (for example, some schizophrenics). Among certain people who are ridden with anxiety (self-preoccupying worry), there may be intense physiological reactions, while others are relatively free of these symptoms. If the approach to personality assessment suggested here bears fruit, it might contribute to a classification system of maladaptive behavior that is more internally consistent than the present one.

The purpose of this chapter was to consider an approach to anxiety that treats it, not as a principle underlying all forms of behavior, but as a particular type of self-preoccupation. As such it is a distinctive form of self-oriented cognitive activity characterized by worry, self-doubt, and anticipations of danger. This activity, like arithmetic skills and letter writing, is a product of experience and can be influenced by learning either unsystematically in everyday life or through carefully programed activities in the laboratory, school, or clinic.

SUMMARY

This chapter analyzed anxiety from the standpoint of cognitive social learning. Anxiety is a subset of the self-preoccupations experienced by people (anger and fantasy are others). The self-preoccupying thoughts of the highly anxious individual may interfere with adaptation at several points in the course of information processing. They may narrow or otherwise influence the attentional focus on environmental cues; distort encoding, transformation, and planning strategies; and influence responses that are selected to cope with situations. Cognitive skills can be assessed and learned, and this fact has important implications for clinical practice and programs aimed at strengthening of coping skills.

REFERENCES

Bowers, M. B., Jr. Pathogenesis of acute schizophrenia psychosis. *Archives of General Psychiatry*, 1968, 19, 348–355.

Cofer, C. N. *Motivation and emotion*. Glenview, Ill.: Scott, Foresman, 1972.

Doris, J., & Sarason, S. B. Test anxiety and blame assignment in a failure situation. *Jorunal of Abnormal and Social Psychology*, 1955, 50, 335–338.

Easterbrook, J. A. The effect of emotion on cue utilization and the organization of behavior. *Psychological Review*, 1959, 66, 183–201.

Egeth, H. Selective attention. *Psychological Bulletin*, 1967, 14, 41–57.

Glass, D. C., & Singer, J. E. *Urban stress: Experiments on noise and social stressors*. New York: Academic Press, 1972.

Lazarus, R. S., & Averill, J. R. Emotion and cognition: With special reference to anxiety. In C. D. Spielberger (Ed.), *Anxiety: Current trends in theory and research*. Vol. 2. New York: Academic Press, 1972.

Liebert, R. M., & Morris, L. W. Cognitive and emotional components of test anxiety: A distinction and some initial data. *Psychological Reports*, 1967, 20, 975–978.

Mandler, G. Stimulus variables and subject variables: A caution. *Psychological Review*, 1959, 66, 145–149.

Mandler, G., & Sarason, S. B. A study of anxiety and learning. *Journal of Abnormal and Social Psychology*, 1952, 47, 166–173.

Meichenbaum, D. H. Cognitive modification of test anxious college students. *Journal of Consulting and Clinical Psychology*, 1972, 39, 370–380.

Phillips, B. N., Martin, R. P., & Meyers, J. School-related interventions with anxious children. In C. D. Spielberger (Ed.), *Anxiety: Current trends in theory and research.* Vol. 2. New York: Academic Press, 1972.

Ross, T. A. *The common neuroses.* Baltimore: Wood, 1937.

Read, P. P. *Alive.* Philadelphia: Lippincott, 1974.

Sarason, I. G. Empirical findings and theoretical problems in the use of anxiety scales. *Psychological Bulletin*, 1960, 57, 403–415.

Sarason, I. G. Verbal learning, modeling, and juvenile delinquency. *American Psychologist*, 1968, 23, 254–266.

Sarason, I. G. Experimental approaches to test anxiety: Attention and the uses of information. In C. D. Spielberger (Ed.), *Anxiety: Current trends in theory and research.* Vol. 2. New York: Academic Press, 1972. (a)

Sarason, I. G. *Abnormal psychology.* New York: Appleton-Century-Crofts, 1972. (b)

Sarason, I. G. Test anxiety and cognitive modeling. *Journal of Personality and Social Psychology.* 1973, 28, 58–61.

Sarason, I. G. Test anxiety and the self-disclosing, coping model. *Journal of Consulting and Clinical Psychology*, in press.

Sarason, I. G., & Ganzer, V. J. Modeling and group discussion in the rehabilitation of juvenile delinquents. *Journal of Counseling Psychology*, 1973, 20, 442–449.

Sarason, I. G., Kestenbaum, J. M., & Smith, D. H. Test anxiety and the effects of being observed. *Journal of Personality*, 1972, 40, 242–250.

Sieber, J. E. A paradigm for experimental modification of the effects of test anxiety on cognitive processes. *American Educational Research Journal*, 1969, 6, 46–61.

Smith, D. Domestic crisis intervention: A comparison of observational learning models with police officers. Unpublished doctoral dissertation, University of Washington, 1973.

Wine, J. Investigations of an attentional interpretation of test anxiety. Unpublished doctoral dissertation, University of Waterloo, 1970.

Wine, J. Test anxiety and direction of attention. *Psychological Bulletin*, 1971, 76, 92–104.

3

SOCIALIZATION ANXIETY AND INFORMATION PROCESSING: A CAPACITY MODEL OF ANXIETY-INDUCED PERFORMANCE DEFICITS

Vernon Hamilton

Reading University
Reading, England

INTRODUCTION

This chapter offers a contribution to theories of the effects of anxiety on cognitive performance and briefly describes a conceptually related investigation of the relationship between anxiety-inducing maternal attitudes and strategies and the suboptimal development in the child of the important cognitive skill of conservation. The reanalysis of anxiety attempted here belongs to the group of "interference" theories, but an answer will be proposed to the question of *why* anxiety interferes with performance. To this end, existing models of anxiety/performance interaction require elaborations in which the emphasis in a definition of anxiety is placed on cognitive structures containing individually aversive information. The two major elaborations are as follows:

Anxiety at its most fundamental level of *behavioral* analysis consists of connotative signals presenting information to an organism's cognitive processing system.

45

The many demonstrated effects of anxiety on perceptual, learning, and thinking processes are due to the limited capacity of the human information-processing apparatus.

This limitation restricts the processing of externally presented task-relevant information in the presence of other information in the processing system interpreted as threatening and potentially harmful. If it is further proposed that the presence, the proliferation, and the intensity of such connotative signals are primarily the result of learning experiences during critical periods of socialization, predictions concerning the information-processing capacity of children reared in anxiety-inducing settings may be validly made.

Our research program originated in three previously established facts obtained from work with long-term, nonparanoid, male, process schizophrenics. First, institutionalized schizophrenics are capable of responding to *industrial rehabilitation* techniques presented under conditions of low social anxiety and graded information-processing requirements, after periods of physical and chemical treatment extending to up to 30 years (Hamilton, 1963, 1964; Hamilton & Salmon, 1962). Second, the *size constancy* abnormalities in this type of schizophrenic appears to be related to a lowered capacity to use the information presented in an experimental display (Hamilton, 1963, 1966, 1972a). Third, this type of subject may demonstrate deficits in *conservation*, even when of average intelligence, and differences in the conserving ability supply some explanation for divergent findings of, respectively, overconstancy and underconstancy in this type of population (Hamilton, 1966, 1972a). Abnormalities in conservation, like those of size constancy, can be redefined as abnormalities in the utilization and integration of objective cues and, thus, as deficits in the capacity to process relevant, available information.

It is a moot point whether these deficits have a basis in internally generated information on themes of social anxiety, though we do have Venables' evidence (1964) that this type of patient shows electrophysiological arousal. Heilbrun (1973) gave an indirect account of the cognitive strategies of students with a background of aversive maternal attitudes defined by low nurturance and high control; but he provided consistent evidence that schizotypic cognitive processes may be relatable to the presence of task-irrelevant anxieties. Whatever data may be produced by progress in experimental sophistication, however, it is still necessary to find a plausible set of mechanisms and processes that account for the indubitable fact that high anxiety impairs performance.

AN INFORMATION-PROCESSING CAPACITY MODEL OF ANXIETY-INDUCED PERFORMANCE DEFICITS

Present Status of Anxiety/Performance Interference Models

There are two major approaches to the study of anxiety/ performance interaction. The first of these derives from the Yerkes-Dodson "Law" and conceives anxiety as a generalized state of arousal or emotionality. It leaves the reasons for performance decrements unspecified except that it postulates some type of interference from autonomic drive or from high arousal through the ascending reticular formation. It may be assumed, though without much support from the existing literature, that the proponents of an inverted U-shaped relationship between performance and emotionality or arousal think of the mediating mechanisms in terms of signals from a highly active neurochemical system. These signals become intrusive and unavoidable "noise" in a central-processing and response-integrating system, thus reducing its powers of freedom and its capacity to deal with external cues in a manner consistent with their stimulus and task requirements. Apart from a number of useful suggestions by Easterbrook (1959) and Wachtel (1967), however, the nature of the interference still remains to be elucidated.

The second major model has a Hullian basis. It considers anxiety as a drive and postulates mechanisms of response competition to account for performance decrements. Response competition theory appears to have attracted the greatest amount of support. Anxiety is seen as a drive that like other drives, obeys systematic relationships between performance, drive, and habit strength (e.g., Spence, K. W., 1956; Spence, K. W., & Farber, 1954; Spence, J. T., & Spence, K. W., 1966; Taylor & Spence, K. W., 1952). An important feature of the theory is the necessary assumption that the energising characteristic of high anxiety drive would increase the number of competing response tendencies drawn from a wider range of a response repertoire when new responses had to be learnt. Its fertility has been seen in the work by the Sarasons and their associates (e.g., Mandler & Sarason, S. B., 1952; Sarason, I. G., 1957, 1961; Sarason, S. B., Mandler, & Craghill, 1952; Sarason, S. B., Davidson, Lighthall, Waite, & Ruebush, 1960; Sarason, S. B., Hill, & Zimbardo, 1964), Spielberger (1966, 1972), Denny (1966), Dunn (1968), Gaudry and Spielberger (1971), and many others. The response competition theory was refined by Broen and Storms (1961) by drawing attention to possible ceiling effects for dominant habits so that further increases in drive would strengthen only competing responses. This elaboration, supported by Wilder's "Law of Initial Value," enabled them, additionally, to offer explanations for a number of behavior abnormalities observed in schizophrenics (Broen, 1966, 1968; Broen & Storms, 1966). Although this sustained approach provided a first systematic attack on the nature of interference processes, its conception of an anxiety *drive*, rather than anxiety *processes*, shows it to be closely related to a Yerkes-Dodson position of a nonspecific emotionality or arousal concept. This limitation prevents an analysis of the antecedents of anxiety interpreted as threat and the coping processes that intervene between threat and reaction (Lazarus, 1966), which may account for the amount and type of response competition.

There are other imperfections in the drive analysis of anxiety:

1. It has not been possible to consider results from what would undoubtedly be unethical experiments, in which performance was monitored under conditions of anxiety increasing in regular steps to intolerable levels for the same sample of human subjects.
2. No distinction has been made between competing responses that might be considered plausibly related to the task requirements, and the other type of competition arising from responses that are irrelevant to the performance of the task because they belong to different cognitive structures, subserving the perception of social stimulation.
3. Apart from the recent introduction of intelligence as a moderator variable in the drive/performance relationship, and the distinction between state or situational anxiety and trait

anxiety, no other individual differences appear to have been systematically investigated.

4. An anxious subject, or one in whom anxiety is induced, may actually demonstrate a reduction in relevant and irrelevant competing responses by responding rapidly but incorrectly, by offering a stereotyped response that provides an anchor of subjective certainty, or by restricting the amount of information processing that could be potentially induced by input from an externally presented task in order to avoid discomfort from multiple-choice decision-making.

Some success has been achieved more recently with elaborations and specifications of the arousal concept of anxiety implied by drive theory. These reanalyses have started to emphasise cognitive components that distinguish between anxiety and other emotions such as anticipation and uncertainty (Lazarus & Averill, 1972); expectancy, incongruity, and response unavailability (Epstein, 1972); the presence of self-depreciation and rumination (Sarason, I. G., 1972), or of task-irrelevant self-instruction (Mandler, 1972) in the performances of test anxious subjects. Lazarus and Averill's and Epstein's concepts can be seen as instigators and representations of anxiety with specific implications for relatable behavior. They do not define the concept, however, and do not appear to contribute to an understanding of deficits in cognitive power under conditions of anxiety except, again, in terms of arousal. Sarason and Mandler appear to come close to a new conceptualization of the role of anxiety in performance decrements by considering it as interference from task-irrelevant information, as does Wine (1971) by pointing to the division between self-relevant and task-relevant variables in test anxious subjects.

Anxiety as Internally Generated Information

The brilliantly conceived experiments of Schachter and Singer (1962) made it clear that the essential elements of a differentiated emotional response are cognitive, so that arousal is a necessary but not sufficient condition for a specific type of emotional behavior and experience (Lykken, 1968). Many research efforts, however, have continued primarily along physiological and neurochemical lines. The energising as well as interfering qualities of physiologically mediated emotionality are not questioned. They ought to be distinguished, however, from what has been called a "worry" component (Liebert & Morris, 1967; Morris & Liebert, 1969) and basically need to be conceived as signals conveying information, even if this information is confined to the distracting and unpleasant awareness of the somatic aspects of emotionality. It seems, however, that even when cognitive terms are used in the analysis of anxiety, the implications are not fully recognized (Spielberger, 1972). It is possible that the obvious does not require mention: that stimuli cannot be coded or interpreted as belonging to cognitive systems subserving anxiety-awareness, control, avoidance, or other coping strategies, until a considerable number of retrieval, scanning, and matching operations have been carried out by a cognitive-processing system.

Again, perhaps, it does not require restating that the identification of stimuli as anxiety signals rather than pleasure or satisfaction signals, depends on a continuous succession of experience. The individual differences in identification of the signals must then depend on differential response disposition hierarchies, with different degrees of elaboration; differences in lengths of associative chains; and differences in evocation, retrieval, or threshold values. In this context, *anxiety can be defined as internally generated cycles of connotative signals elicited by external stimuli, which a central interpreting or appraisal process codes as requiring avoidance, and as indicating physical danger, injury to self-esteem, rejection, and loss of affection in valued social settings*, and any other consequences that a person has learnt to be potentially harmful.

Each cycle of signals, whether single or organized in "chunks" or schemata, presents information to a central, cognitive processing system. The more anxious the individual, the greater and more extended the amount of information and the number of cognitive operations on unpleasant associations and conceptualized unwanted consequences. The greater the number of unpleasant associations and conceptualized unwanted consequences, the greater will be the information load on the system. If, in the course of individual development under adverse or suboptimal circumstances, stimuli interpreted as potentially harmful and unpleasant have not become habituated or extinguished, then a wide range of stimuli may continue to elicit overdifferentiated and overelaborated systems of unpleasant, aversive, and threatening signals. In the context of a neutral and unstressful experimental or occupational setting, this type of self-generated information is irrelevant. Under conditions of experimental manipulation with problem-solving tasks, which contain instructions of potential loss of self-esteem, reward, status, or personal acceptability, the person with the more differentiated and elaborated aversive long-term memory structures will generate and process greater amounts of task-irrelevant information. To the extent that all conceptual operations are based on codes carrying information, an overactive retrieval process will present large amounts of information to a code-analysing and response-organising system. To the extent that these processes may be excessive during the performance of an objective and emotionally neutral task, excessive amounts of interfering information will press for central processing.

Anxiety in a Limited Capacity Processing System

Elaborations of Broadbent's theory of a limited capacity information processing system (1958, 1971) can provide a novel approach to the explanation of information-processing deficits associated with anxiety interference. At a simplified level, Broadbent's theory consists of two major, related statements: (a) a single, central information processing channel restricts the amount of possible cognitive processes, especially in connection with simultaneous tasks; and (b) increases in arousal, postulated to occur with loud noise, lead to performance decrements as predicted by the Yerkes-Dodson "Law."

It is fair to comment that detailed aspects of this model are presently under attack because of inadequacies in conceptualizing input filter and short term or temporary memory operations, as well as problems concerning possible simultaneous, parallel processes. For the present purpose and level of analysis, however, this model is adequate with three plausible extensions: (a) defining anxiety as internally presented stimuli or signals containing information; (b) postulating pathways from a long-term memory store to parts of the processing system dealing with current sensory inputs and central, integrating processes conveying anxiety signals; and (c) reserves of processing capacity for raised levels of information input and of motivation. Arguments supporting the first modification of the theory have been presented previously.

The second modification may be crucial for the present model. If a person reports that he is unable to concentrate on a set task because of distractions from fears of failure, or frustration as a result of his slowness, or imagined or actual incompetence, two conclusions may be reached from this evidence. First, the self-reported distractions belong to cognitive anxiety structures and associations retrieved from a long-term memory store. These are channelled as information towards parts of the processing system dealing with current stimulus input and its integration and are additional to the information presented by the external stimulus field. Second, this information will compete with relevant task-induced information for space and time in a processing system with limited capacity for sensory transmission, temporary or short term memory storage, and simultaneous tasks.[1] There is no evidence of the extent to which "chunking" skills arising from long experience will extend the postulated limits of simultaneous, complex information processing (Miller, 1956). On the other hand, it may be presumed that a processing system already given the task of solving an externally presented problem is given a second task by the intrusion of cognitive material seeking an end state of anxiety avoidance. In this event a second, central control program may be stimulated into activity (Broadbent, 1971), to achieve an individually acceptable solution for what may be loosely termed an "anxiety problem." But this problem, by definition, is irrelevant to the primary task.

At this point, the third proposed modification of Broadbent's model becomes relevant since high levels of information-processing demands on a system would stimulate efforts to cope. Kahneman's (1973) concept of "spare capacity" appears to supply a useful conceptual tool. He defines it as the difference between total available capacity and the capacity demanded by the primary task. The greater the spare capacity (of obvious relevance to test intelligence and intellectual development), the greater its capacity

---

[1] It may be reasonable to suppose that a similar type of processing competition occurs when a person is not fully aware of the nature of the distractions. The point of interference need not be in the short term memory component of the processing system.

to deal with complex tasks. Moreover, if the system in its analysis of demand priorities gives precedence to the demands of "enduring dispositions" (such as anxiety avoidance), then it is likely to activate in the first instance a program for allocating effort and spare capacity to the solution of the "anxiety problem." In this event, and with primary tasks requiring high levels of information-processing capacities, less spare capacity is available, and complex tasks will become impaired before more simple tasks show the effect of limited processing capacity. Increasing the likelihood of anxiety associations by introducing instructions containing elements of threat to already anxious subjects would increase the probability of secondary, rather than primary task problem solving.

Questionnaire measures of anxiety—whether *manifest, state, test,* or *trait*—are unlikely to yield accurate data on the presence or availability of associations with cognitive anxiety content. It is easier to control the external stimuli by varying, in a systematic way, the processing demands of experimentally presented problems, as was done in the series of experiments reported here. If in addition some independent measures of processing capacity are obtained from subjects under two conditions of motivation, some predictions could be formalized concerning information-processing capacity in relation to anxiety.

This could read:

Successful Performance occurs when $APC + SPC > I_{ept} + I_{ist}$

where APC is average processing capacity, SPC is spare processing capacity, I_{ept} is externally presented primary task information, and I_{ist} is internally generated secondary information.

An elaboration of the term "internally generated secondary information" is necessary as well as possible. In the context of the present reanalysis of anxiety it refers to task-irrelevant cognitive structures containing threatening or individually dangerous information. This may be written $I_{ist(A)}$. While more emphasis has been placed here on its interfering, nonproductive effects, drive theory has demonstrated the energising effects of anxiety. This must mean three things: (*a*) facilitation *or* interference of performance depends on the ease with which $I_{ist(A)}$ is generated; (*b*) in a raised drive state, plausibly task-related competing responses are available which produce a dominance hierarchy; and (*c*) competing responses plausibly related to the task can achieve dominance over $I_{ist(A)}$. Task-related competing responses are also internally generated and must be drawn from a memory store of stimulus differentiation and conceptualization. The greater this store, the greater the number of available plausible competing response tendencies. The greater the amount of response competition, the greater the number of choice or decision operations for the subject. Let us term this "*task-relevant*, internally generated information," $I_{ist(C)}$, and let us remember that its size is affected by $I_{ist(A)}$. (as required by drive theory), and, broadly speaking, by intelligence.

We may now try to relate this attempt at formalization to some existing findings. Denny (1966) showed that high anxiety impairs concept formation in subjects of low intelligence, but facilitates it in those of high intelligence. Where performance is low, $I_{ist(A)} > I_{ist(C)}$, and $I_{ist(A)} + I_{ist(C)} + I_{ept} > APC + SPC$. Where performance is good, $I_{ist(A)} < I_{ist(C)}$ and $I_{ist(A)} + I_{ist(C)} + I_{ept} \lessgtr APC + SPC$. Spielberger and Smith (1966) demonstrated the facilitating effect of high anxiety on serial learning for university students. By definition, anxiety is subpathological and intelligence is high in this population, so that $I_{ist(C)} > I_{ist(A)}$, and $I_{ist(A)} + I_{ist(C)} + I_{ept} < APC + SPC$. The poorer performance of high anxiety subjects in the early stages of learning is then due to high values of $I_{ist(C)}$ as well as $I_{ist(A)}$, which at that point, in conjunction with I_{ept}, must exceed $APC + SPC$. Only I_{ept} and $I_{ist(A)}$ in these statements are under possible experimental control: the first by varying the complexity of the task, the second by threatening instructions, and both have been shown to lead to performance deficits (Dunn, 1968; Hodges & Spielberger, 1969). Since Dunn varied complexity as well as stressfulness of the tasks and found a significant interaction between degrees of complexity and high anxiety, it is possible to say that the energising aspects of anxiety operate in a favourable direction only when all the I terms together are smaller than $APC + SPC$.

The retrieval of internal task-relevant or irrelevant information is substantially outside voluntary control. If the total information-processing demands exceed an available value for $APC + SPC$, the simplest control that may be exercised by a person is to reduce the input from I_{ept}. This may be achieved at the level of sensory operations by narrowing the area focused for selective attention or by restricting attention to a small number of foci (Wachtel, 1967). According to Easterbrook (1959), this would lead to a narrowing of the range of cue utilization, with peripheral signals the first victims. Since the definition of what is peripheral depends on present task instructions and their interpretation, the terms "narrowing" and "peripheral" must be seen as more complex than suggested by Easterbrook (Cornsweet, 1969). Other methods for controlling the value of I_{ept} are more central, as suggested by the cognitive style theorists. By this method, the value of I_{ept} may be indirectly reduced by restricting the level of $I_{ist(C)}$ operations.

One additional point should be made before the implications of this approach for some other theories can be considered. On the basis of early and later learning it is possible to predict for some people an increase in $I_{ist(A)}$ as a result of raising the level of $I_{ist(C)}$. Competing responses are alternatives for consideration in a decision-making process. Alternatives of apparent equal strength are experienced as being in conflict. Where past experience has linked conflict with anxiety, $I_{ist(A)}$ will rise, and subsidiary processing program may be activated to avoid excess levels of $I_{ist(C)}$. If this occurs, response strategies may become oversimplified and even irrational, so as not to exceed the total processing capacity of the system.

Some Implications of an Informational Approach to Anxiety

The application of a capacity model of information processing need not be confined to theories involving the concept of anxiety. Processing capacity may be low because *APC* and/or *SPC* are endogenously low, with the consequence that $I_{ist(C)}$ may be low. It is likely that this applies in some cases of low intelligence and in cases of brain damage. A more productive approach, however, is available by considering situations and people where there is evidence of restrictions on the input of externally generated primary task information, I_{ept}, or where behavior suggests that a consistent type of restriction, or unidirectional elaborations are imposed on the processing of secondary competing response tendencies, $I_{ist(C)}$. It is possible to describe a number of social psychological processes in these terms. For example, *rigidity*, *stereotypy*, *dogmatically held beliefs*, and attitude shifts towards *consonance*, *congruity* or *balance* require a limitation of information, whether externally or internally generated; and they require an inability or reluctance to use all potentially available information and to respond to new information by excluding it either at peripheral or at central stages of a processing system. It is no longer fashionable, as it was in the 1950's, to define these strategies and outcomes by reference to personality dimensions. For behavior theory it is indeed sufficient to hold that rapid, or even premature closure, is a function of societal norms, which, by strengthening social conformity and expectancies, provide for an economy of effort and subjective certainty in social interaction. It is easier to conform to expectation than to be idiosyncratic, especially in epochs when the information-processing demands of the wider environments are increasing in complexity and, more especially, when a full knowledge of all present and potential events may generate threatening internal information. As Mowrer (1944) suggested long ago, it is possible that the least effortful skills are learnt best.

The processing capacity model appears to permit a tougher analysis of the concept of *intolerance of ambiguity*, which has provided a useful explanatory tool for some basic processes in ethnic prejudice (Frenkel-Brunswik, 1948, 1949, 1951) and the neuroses (Hamilton, 1957, 1960). Both authors defined intolerance of ambiguity in terms of perceptual conflict, with the prediction that for people in whom emotional conflict was associated with anxiety, even perceptual conflict can induce avoidance responses. According to the proposed model it can be postulated that $I_{ist(A)}$ is basically high in prejudiced subjects and very high in neurotic subjects. The competing response tendencies built into perceptually unstable stimuli will induce attempts at classifying inputs capable of activating mutually exclusive, but equally possible decision processes. Where $I_{ist(A)}$ is sufficiently high and SPC has not been exhausted, the drive potential of the former will generate cognitive elaborations to aid the decision processes, and thus produce increments in $I_{ist(C)}$. In deliberately ambiguous situations, a categorical solution is precluded, leading to increments in $I_{ist(A)}$. Thus, a positive feedback loop between $I_{ist(A)}$ and $I_{ist(C)}$ is set up that can be interrupted only when $I_{ist(A)} + I_{ist(C)} (+ I_{ept}) \rightarrow APC + SPC$. A decision, at this point, that something ambiguous is in fact classifiable indicates that information-processing limits have been reached. In clinically identified patients, this limit is likely to be reached sooner and in a wider variety of settings than for adapted subjects scoring high on an anxiety questionnaire, because small increments of either information (A) or (C) are likely to raise dominant responses close to a response ceiling, and the generalization gradient for less plausible responses is thus lengthened. Since further increases in anxiety are likely to be experienced as extremely unpleasant, nonveridical decisions may gain dominance at the level of final response selection.

In the context of *neurosis*, this degree of control of information appears to possess defensive characteristics, and it seems possible that some reanalysis of previously vaguely conceptualized psychodynamic processes in information-processing terms may be productive, as already suggested by Peterfreund (1971). This may be unpopular in some quarters and may be considered to have low priority in furthering behavioral science. No serious attempt to do so will be made here, apart from drawing attention to three relatively uncontentious psychoanalytic concepts interpretable by reference to cognitive process theories.

1. *Unconscious processes* may be defined as operations of a central processing system that fail to reach awareness for four reasons: because they contain too much concurrent information (A); because an excess of concurrent information is subject to cognitive masking and other inhibiting processes, which in turn affect the range of selective attention through restrictions on coding; because excessive information simultaneously reaching a short term or temporary memory store facilitates its own rapid decay; and because some information contains nonprocessing instructions. All these may be facilitated by what recently has been termed "cortical recurrent lateral inhibition," which appears to increase under conditions of high arousal (Walley & Weiden, 1973).

2. The *mechanisms of defence* of psychoanalytic theory, by definition, are not available to consciousness, and so share the basic features of some other mechanisms such as may be found during experimental instructions not to respond to one of two dichotically presented messages. The nonattended message is processed, however, since it could not be otherwise excluded, but this process is not the subject of awareness. If a stimulus generates information that a central

scanning and interpreting process has coded as strongly aversive, it may fail to reach awareness for the reasons given previously. If a strong neurochemical reaction is set up by these cognitive processes, however, subsidiary adaptive programs may be activated. These are likely to contain primarily information type (C) processing a low probability of eliciting further information type (A), or further bodily disturbances. Response substitution or displacement phenomena appear to be amenable to an alternative explanation along these lines. Other mechanisms of defence may yield to similar reinterpretation. In each case, the given anxiety levels and the given information processing capacity and limits of the individual may be crucial to the development of defensive operations.

3. The *developmental basis of* normal and abnormal adult *personality characteristics* is explicable not only in terms of drive reduction reinforcement theories or modeling, but in terms of hierarchies of adaptive programs for the processing of information. Here, the "instructions" may be conceived as chains of associations or information elicited from a long-term memory store by key stimuli occurring in the external environment. In as far as they do not contain individually threatening information, and assuming that the memory banks do not contain priority subroutines for $I_{ist(A)}$, adaptation occurs as the result of operations on $I_{ist(C)}$. With low thresholds and large amounts of $I_{ist(A)}$, however, processing limits or overload conditions will be reached sooner for given levels of I_{ept}; and maladaptation and suboptimal cognitive development may result. In the context of the experiments reported here, what is coded and programed as $I_{ist(A)}$ may plausibly contain those socialization experiences that at the time induced the greatest number of neurochemical as well as cognitive anxiety responses, and that did not subsequently benefit from other experiences that may have modified the earlier, aversively coded information.

The application of information-processing concepts to the study of *the schizophrenias* has made some progress, but even modified classifications of clinical subtypes have left a number of issues confused. It is unclear, for example, to what extent different types of schizophrenics are able to deploy selective attention appropriately and efficiently, because deficiencies in input filter operations suggested by Payne (e.g., Payne & Hewlett, 1960; Payne, 1966) and McGhie (1966; McGhie, Chapman, & Lawson, 1965), to account for thought disorder and distractibility, now appear insufficient to explain the wealth of available data (Payne, 1973). This is not surprising, perhaps, since in the context of the present model only externally generated information I_{ept} is being considered. Elaborations of the response competition theory, postulating ceiling effects, would explain longer and flatter generalization gradients in some schizophrenics and appear to account for overinclusive thought disorder and paranoid delusions (Broen, 1968, 1973). This may be restated by reference to high levels of $I_{ist(C)}$ operations, which are energized by $I_{ist(A)}$. As in neurosis, the positive feedback loop may be broken by a response that is experienced as a drop in $I_{ist(A)}$ and its concomitant autonomic disturbance; but because of the wider range of semi-appropriate or inappropriate associations elicited, the response is likely to be more unusual or inappropriate. The findings of Venables (1963, 1964) and Silverman (1964, 1967) suggest that at some point in the history of some schizophrenics, the nature of adaptive strategies changes. Whereas in acute and in paranoid schizophrenics excessive scanning seems to occur that would irrelevantly increase the information load from I_{ept}, chronic and process nonparanoid schizophrenics appear to engage in minimal scanning only, so that I_{ept} input is reduced. The level of reduction may be considerable and appears to involve the basic skills of perceptual constancy and conservation. If Venables is correct in his conclusions that arousal levels in this kind of patient are high despite evidence of behavioral withdrawal, then it is appropriate to suggest that limitations on external stimulus input have defensive functions (Broen, 1966; Broen & Storms, 1966). With activity of the $I_{ist(A)}$ and $I_{ist(C)}$ type outside voluntary control, only I_{ept} can be reduced by a person in an attempt to control for processing overload conditions. If this strategy is adopted, however, response competition as well as selection would have a primarily subjective or internal basis with obvious consequences for stimulus-appropriate behavior.

In all the instances cited where task-irrelevant information is thought to interfere with the selection of objective, logical, and appropriate responses, information type (A) appears to be involved.

This conclusion seems unavoidable in the light of the evidence from the clinical and counseling literature, from child guidance, and from the results of pretherapy and posttherapy experiments. Since the physiological and neurochemical responses are solidly linked to the aversive cognitive information, chemotherapy has palliative effects as long as medication is continued and as long as the external information *remains* at the level where internal information of types (A) and (C) can be controlled by a drug of specified dosage. These therapies, however, cannot, and are not expected to change the stored information that appears in excessive amounts of $I_{ist(A)}$ and $I_{ist(C)}$.

SUBOPTIMAL MATERNAL ATTITUDES AND INFORMATION-PROCESSING DEFICITS IN CHILDREN

The quasi-quantitative model, of anxiety interpreted as information, appears to supply a parsimonious basis for predictions concerning the differential processing capacity of children brought up under divergent conditions of maternal attitudes and strategies. It is a testable assumption, if not a fact, that certain types of mother-child interactions generate anxiety in the child. This will contribute particular types of data to the informational structure, contents, and elaborations available or retrievable in children's cognitive, social, and affective long-term memory stores. If the assumption is correct, *and* the child interprets the mother's responses as emotional rejection and coldness, strictness and control, rigidity, criticism, and lack of empathy, the memory store will accumulate information coded as anxiety. This will consist of chains of associations and of an appropriate number of cognitive structures encoding the child's reactions to the agent's behavior. The child's coded evaluation will be in terms of whether he is deserving of love and nurturance, whether he is obedient and competent in order to deserve rewarding rather than punishing, whether it is safe to play and explore freely with enjoyment, and whether he may anticipate unpleasant and unwanted events as the result of his actions. If these conceptualizations were only partially correct, they would have at least two effects: (*a*) a possible restriction on interaction with the environment, leading to limitations on the input of externally available information, with unfavourable consequences for the development of basic cognitive skills and an acquired reduction in potential information-processing capacity; and (b) the development of information coded as anxiety—$I_{ist(A)}$. In the event of the nonhabituation or nonextinction of this type of information with the growth of competence and cognitive self-evaluation, task-irrelevent anxiety responses will continue to occupy, on a priori grounds, a high position in a response competition hierarchy. The greater the impairment of potential processing capacity and the greater the intrusion of task-irrelevant information, the smaller will be the capacity of the information-processing system to cope with increases in externally presented information. As an initial test of this proposition, it was predicted that a comparison of the children of criterion groups of "accepting" and "rejecting" mothers would produce evidence of lowered competence in conservation for the children of rejecting mothers. An experiment testing this prediction was carried out employing only partially validated techniques for the assessment of maternal attitude and an ad hoc instrument for the measurement of fine-grain differences in conservation of quantity. The results supported the predictions to a substantial degree (Hamilton, 1972 b, c).[2]

This study required replication for a number of reasons. Maternal acceptance-rejection seemed an unnecessarily limited dimension for the assessment of socialization anxiety, and it required external validation. The instrument for the demonstration of difference in conservation was psychometrically impure, a systematic rationale for the construction of problems differing in information content was not available, and the application of information-processing concepts to conservation had not been validated. Three studies dealing with these problems have now been completed.[3] Conservation was chosen as the primary task because it had been found impaired in some types of schizophrenia, but particularly because the fundamental skill of conceiving identity and equivalence between objects and quantities, as required in the conserving response, develops at the time when socialization pressures in a child's home are stepped up. If anxiety has an impairing effect on congitive learning, then anxiety-inducing socialization attitudes

[2] Supported by Canada Council grant 67–0285.
[3] Supported by Social Science Research Council grant HR 1556.

and strategies could be accompanied by retardation and/or impairment of skills and operations that normally would develop at
that time. Validation of the techniques for the assessment of
maternal attitude was obtained from a comparison of two groups
of 40 mothers, one, whose children were attending child guidance,
the other, whose children were receiving medical or dental attention. By the method of paired-comparison, rank order data were
obtained on the socialization dimensions of acceptance-rejection,
permissiveness-strictness, autonomy-control, warmth-coldness, and
intellectual stimulation-nonstimulation. In addition, protocols from
three TAT plates were scored as well as mothers' free description
of their children, all on the basis of presence or absence of
operational definitions of optimal and suboptimal maternal attitudes. Regression and discriminant function analyses yielded
highly reliable separations of the criterion groups with a mis-
classification error of under 9%.

Details of a new technique for assessing the information content
of conservation problems are available elsewhere (Hamilton &
Moss, 1974). It was possible to demonstrate that an essential step
in the solution of a conservation problem is the processing of an
equation. By increasing the number of originally equal quantities,
the number of distributions and redistributions, the number of
parts formed thereby, and the number of so-called reversibility
steps necessitated by a particular test question, equations could be
generated to define systematically the contents of problems. The
greater the value of these parameters, the larger the number of
equations presented by it. The larger the number of equations
involved in a problem, the greater its informational content.[4] The
correlation between subjects' pass rate and information load was
-0.943 ($N = 150$).

---

[4] Information content of problems is formalized by the statement

$$n(\text{steps}) = n_{C_2} + \Sigma_i \, (m_i + p_i + 2q_i + d_i) + 1$$

where n_{C_2} is the number of originally equal standard quantities, m is the
number of parts resulting from distributions, p is the number of times given
quantities were distributed or divided, $2q$ is the number of distributions of
quantity necessary to deduce a conserving response, d is the number of
quantities that were only deformed but not divided, and 1 is the equation
representing the solution statement.

The assumption that conservation conceived as a scalable dimension requires the capacity to process increasing amounts of information was validated in two more traditional settings for the assessment of this capacity: speed of binary choice decision-making in sorting playing cards and errors in a coding task of increasing complexity defined by the number of coding steps (Hamilton, V., & Launay, G. The role of information processing capacity in the conserving operation. Unpublished manuscript, 1974). The differences for both tasks between criterion groups of nonconservers, poor conservers, and good conservers were highly reliable.

The refined and validated techniques were applied in a larger study to test the prediction that the children of suboptimal mothers ($N = 40$) had a lower information-processing capacity than did the children of optimal mothers ($N = 40$). With substantial control for the effects of age, sex, socioeconomic group, and intellectual and educational status, highly significant differences consistent with the hypothesis were obtained (Fig. 3-1). Each child was given two versions of the conservation test instrument, the first without, the second with maternal participation, by means of tape-recorded messages. A second prediction that the difference between groups of optimally and suboptimally reared children would increase with maternal participation was generally confirmed, particularly for females (Fig. 3-2).

Since anxiety levels in the children were not directly assessed, it is necessary to go beyond the data to infer that the deficits in the suboptimally reared children are due to socialization anxiety. This anxiety, it is assumed, was generated by a test situation which for

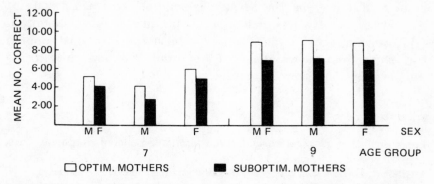

Fig. 3-1. Conservation scores of optimally and suboptimally reared children (session 1).

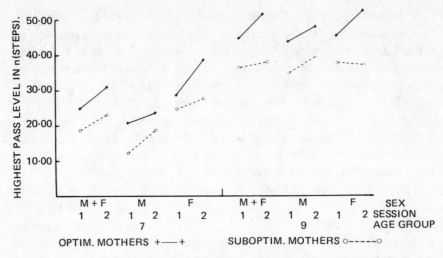

Fig. 3-2. Effect of maternal participation on conservation.

them, in the light of their earlier experiences, aroused aversive and threatening associations. In these conditions, suboptimally reared children may be required to process more information elicited by a given task than children of optimal mothers. Because the capacity to process information is limited at any given stage of development, internally generated task-irrelevant information will interfere with performance on a primary task. The interference effect will become most evident with systematic increases in task difficulty, defined by its information-processing requirements, and as the system approaches overload conditions. The greater the demands made on a system operating at or near overload conditions, the more radical may be the acceptable solutions to reach a state of adaptation or of stress reduction. Depending on the amount of $I_{ist(A)}$ generated by a socialization history, the solutions adopted may range from the avoidance of incongruity and ambiguity to the total avoidance of sensory input.

REFERENCES

Broadbent, D. E. *Perception and communication*. London: Pergamon Press, 1958.

Broadbent, D. E. *Decision and stress*. London: Academic Press, 1971.

Broen, W. E., Jr. Response disorganization and breadth of observation in schizophrenia. *Psychological Review*, 1966, **73**, 579–585.

Broen, W. E., Jr. *Schizophrenia: Research and theory*. New York: Academic Press, 1968.

Broen, W. E., Jr. Limiting the flood of stimulation: A protective deficit in chronic schizophrenia. In R. L. Solso (Ed.), *Contemporary issues in cognitive psychology: The Loyola Symposium*. New York: Wiley, 1973.

Broen, W. E., Jr., & Storms, L. H. A reaction potential ceiling and response decrements in complex situations. *Psychological Review*, 1961, 68, 405-415.

Broen, W. E., Jr., & Storms, L. H. Lawful disorganization: The process underlying a schizophrenic syndrome. *Psychological Review*, 1966, 73, 265-279.

Cornsweet, D. M. Use of cues in the visual periphery under conditions of arousal. *Journal of Experimental Psychology*, 1969, 80, 14-18.

Denny, J. P. Effects of anxiety and intelligence on concept formation. *Journal of Experimental Psychology*, 1966, 72, 596-602.

Dunn, R. F. Anxiety and verbal concept learning. *Journal of Experimental Psychology*, 1968, 76, 286-290.

Easterbrook, J. A. The effect of emotion on cue-utilization and the organization of behavior. *Psychological Review*, 1959, 66, 183-201.

Epstein, S. The nature of anxiety with emphasis upon its relationship to expectancy. In C. D. Spielberger (Ed.), *Anxiety—current trends in theory and research*. New York: Academic Press, 1972.

Frenkel-Brunswik, E. Dynamic and cognitive categorization of qualitative material: II. Interviews of the ethnically prejudiced. *Journal of Psychology*, 1948, 25, 261-277.

Frenkel-Brunswik, E. Intolerance of ambiguity as an emotional and perceptual personality variable. *Journal of Personality*, 1949, 18, 108-143.

Frenkel-Brunswik, E. Personality theory and perception. In R. R. Blake & G. V. Ramsay (Eds.), *Perception—An approach to personality*. New York: Ronald Press, 1951.

Gaudry, E., & Spielberger, C. D. *Anxiety and educational achievement*. Sydney: Wiley, 1971.

Hamilton, V. Perceptual and personality dynamics in reactions to ambiguity. *British Journal of Psychology*, 1957, 48, 200-215.

Hamilton, V. Inperception of Phi: Some further determinants. *British Journal of Psychology*, 1960, 51(3), 257-266.

Hamilton, V. Size constancy and cue responsiveness in psychosis. *British Journal of Psychology*, 1963, 54, 25-39.

Hamilton, V. Psychological changes in chronic schizophrenics following differential activity programmes: A repeat study. *British Journal of Psychiatry*, 1964, 110, 282-286.

Hamilton, V. Deficits in primitive perceptual and thinking skills in schizophrenia. *Nature*, 1966, 211(5047), 389-392.

Hamilton, V. The size constancy problem in schizophrenia: A cognitive skill analysis. *British Journal of Psychology*, 1972, 63, 73-84. (a)

Hamilton, V. Continuities and individual differences in conservation. *British Journal of Psychology*, 1972, 63, 429-440. (b)

Hamilton, V. Conservation and maternal attitude: An analysis of suboptimal cognition. *Journal of Child Psychology and Psychiatry*, 1972, 13, 147-166. (c)

Hamilton, V., & Moss, M. A method of scaling conservation of quantity problems by information content. *Child Development*, 1974, 45, 737-745.

Hamilton, V., & Salmon, P. Psychological changes in chronic schizophrenics following differential activity programmes. *Journal of Mental Science*, 1962, 108, 505-519.

Heilbrun, A. B., Jr. *Aversive maternal control: A theory of schizophrenic development.* New York: Wiley, 1973.

Hodges, W. F., & Spielberger, C. D. Digit span: An indicant of trait or state anxiety? *Journal of Consulting and Clinical Psychology*, 1969, 33, 430-434.

Kahneman, D. *Attention and effort.* New Jersey: Prentice-Hall, 1973.

Lazarus, R. S. *Psychological stress and the coping process.* New York: McGraw-Hill, 1966.

Lazarus, R. C., & Averill, J. R. Emotion and cognition: With special reference to anxiety. In C. D. Spielberger (Ed.), *Anxiety—current trends in theory and research.* New York: Academic Press, 1972.

Liebert, R. M., & Morris, L. W. Cognitive and emotional components of test anxiety: A distinction and some initial data. *Psychological Reports*, 1967, 20, 975-978.

Lykken, D. T. Neuropsychology and psychophysiology in personality research. In E. F. Borgatta & W. W. Lambert (Eds.), *Handbook of personality theory and research.* Chicago: Rand McNally, 1968.

Mandler, G. Comments on Dr. Sarason's paper. In C. D. Spielberger (Ed.), *Anxiety—current trends in theory and research.* Vol. 2. New York: Academic Press, 1972.

Mandler, G., & Sarason, S. B. A study of anxiety and learning. *Journal of Abnormal and Social Psychology*, 1952, 47, 166-173.

McGhie, A. Psychological studies of schizophrenia. *British Journal of Psychology*, 1966, 39, 281-288.

McGhie, A., Chapman, J., & Lawson, J. S. The effect of distraction on schizophrenic performance: 2. Perception and immediate memory. *British Journal of Psychiatry*, 1965, 111, 383-390.

Miller, G. A. The magical number seven, plus or minus two: Some limits on our capacity for processing information. *Psychological Review*, 1956, 63, 81-97.

Morris, L. W., & Liebert, R. M. The effects of anxiety on timed and untimed intelligence tests: Another look. *Journal of Consulting and Clinical Psychology*, 1969, 33, 240-244.

Mowrer, O. H. Dynamic theory of personality. In J. McV. Hunt (Ed.), *Personality and the behavior disorders.* New York: Ronald Press, 1944.

Payne, R. W. The measurement and significance of overinclusive thinking and retardation in schizophrenic patients. In P. H. Hoch & J. Zubin (Eds.), *Psychopathology of schizophrenia.* New York: Grune & Stratton, 1966.

Payne, R. W. Cognitive abnormalities. In H. J. Eysenck (Ed.), *Handbook of psychology*. (2nd ed.) London: Pitman, 1973.

Payne, R. W., & Hewlett, J. H. G. Thought disorder in psychotic patients. In H. J. Eysenck (Ed.), *Experiments in personality*: Vol. 2. *Psychodiagnostics and psychodynamics*. London: Routledge & Kegan Paul, 1960.

Peterfreund, E. Information, systems and psychoanalysis: An evolutionary biological approach to psychoanalytic theory. *Psychological Issues*, 1971, 7, Monographs No. 25-26.

Sarason, I. G. Test anxiety, general anxiety and intellectual performance. *Journal of Consulting Psychology*, 1957, 21, 485-490.

Sarason, I. G. The effects of anxiety and threat on solution of a difficult task. *Journal of Abnormal and Social Psychology*, 1961, 62, 165-168.

Sarason, I. G. Experimental approaches to test anxiety: Attention and the uses of information. In C. D. Spielberger (Ed.), *Anxiety—current trends in theory and research*. New York: Wiley, 1972.

Sarason, S. B., Mandler, G., & Craghill, P. C. The effect of differential instructions on anxiety and learning. *Journal of Abnormal and Social Psychology*, 1952, 47, 561-565.

Sarason, S. B., Davidson, K. S., Lighthall, F. F., Waite, R. R., & Ruebush, B. K. *Anxiety in elementary schoolchildren: A report of research*. New York: Wiley, 1960.

Sarason, S. B., Hill, K. T., & Zimbardo, P. G. A longitudinal study of the relation of test anxiety to performance on intelligence and achievement tests. *Monographs of the Society for Research in Child Development*, 1964, 29(98).

Schachter, S., & Singer, J. E. Cognitive, social and physiological determinants of emotional state. *Psychological Review*, 1962, 69, 379-399.

Silverman, J. The problem of attention in research and theory of schizophrenia. *Psychological Review*, 1964, 71, 352-379.

Silverman, J. Variations in cognitive control and psychophysiological defense in the schizophrenias. *Psychosomatic Medicine*, 1967, 29, 225-245.

Spence, J. T., & Spence, K. W. The motivational components of manifest anxiety: Drive and drive stimuli. In C. D. Spielberger (Ed.), *Anxiety and behavior*. London: Academic Press, 1966.

Spence, K. W. *Behavior theory and conditioning*. New Haven: Yale University Press, 1956.

Spence, K. W., & Farber, I. E. The relation of anxiety to differential eyelid conditioning. *Journal of Experimental Psychology*, 1954, 47, 127-134.

Spielberger, C. D. (Ed.) *Anxiety and behavior*. New York: Academic Press, 1966.

Spielberger, C. D. (Ed.) *Anxiety—current trends in theory and research*. New York: Academic Press, 1972. 2 vols.

Spielberger, C. D., & Smith, L. H. Anxiety (drive) stress and serial position effects in serial-verbal learning. *Journal of Experimental Psychology*, 1966, 72, 589-595.

Taylor, J., & Spence, K. W. The relationship of anxiety level to performance in serial learning. *Journal of Experimental Psychology*, 1952, 44, 61-64.

Venables, P. H. Selectivity of attention, withdrawal, and cortical activation. *Archives of General Psychiatry*, 1963, 9, 92–96.

Venables, P. H. Input dysfunction in schizophrenia. In B. A. Maher (Ed.), *Progress in experimental personality research*. Vol. 1. New York: Academic Press, 1964.

Wachtel, P. L. Conceptions of broad and narrow attention. *Psychological Bulletin*, 1967, 68, 417–429.

Walley, R. E., & Weiden, T. D. Lateral inhibition and cognitive masking: A neuropsychological theory of attention. *Psychological Review*, 1973, 80, 284–302.

Wine, J. Test anxiety and direction of attention. *Psychological Bulletin*, 1971, 76(2), 92–104.

4

A COGNITIVE MODEL OF ANXIETY FORMATION AND ANXIETY RESOLUTION

A. T. Beck and A. J. Rush

Philadelphia General Hospital
Philadelphia, Pennsylvania
United States

Anxiety neurosis has commonly been equated with free-floating anxiety: that is, the neurosis is related to a fear, the source of which is not recognized (Marks & Lader, 1973). This conceptualization has resulted in a relative inertia in explorations of the patient's phenomenal field. The patient's spontaneous explanations have been discounted as rationalizations (Marks, 1969).

In an earlier study of 30 patients with "free-floating" anxiety treated in long-term psychodynamic psychotherapy, a meaningful correlation between the patient's cognitions and fluctuations in his level of anxiety was noted (Beck, 1963, 1971). A detailed examination of these cognitions was accomplished in 10 cases of phobia and 50 cases of anxiety neurosis in three separate studies (Beck, Laude, & Bohnert, 1974; Laude, R., & LaVigne, G. The role of cognition in anxiety neurosis and phobic neurosis. Unpublished manuscript, 1974). A summary of these cases, including 18 new cases of anxiety neurosis and 10 phobias, is presented. Implications for the conceptualization of anxiety neurosis and its therapy are discussed.

METHOD

Patient Sample

Initially, an assessment was made of the fantasies and cognitions in 12 private patients with anxiety neurosis. Subsequently, a more specific examination of the nature of the cognitions associated with anxiety in 20 outpatients was undertaken. Each case was evaluated at the Hospital of the University of Pennsylvania outpatient clinic and was diagnosed as anxiety neurosis (Diagnostic Statistical Manual II). Each received a 1-1/2-hour structured interview consisting of general questions of symptomatology followed by open-ended questions regarding the ideation related to each patient's subjective anxiety. In many cases, patients spontaneously volunteered information regarding specific cognitions without interviewer prompting. Direct questions were used to elicit specific content of cognitions and visual imagery. Finally, each patient was asked to reproduce a fantasy or daydream he had experienced just before or during his anxiety spells (Beck et al., 1974).

A second group of clinic patients, not previously reported on, included 18 new cases of anxiety neurosis and 10 with phobic neurosis (Laude & LaVigne, previously cited unpublished manuscript). A structured interview was similarly used to assess their cognitions and fantasies.

The findings of all three studies were remarkably similar and are presented in summary here.

RESULTS

Anxiety Neurosis

Of the 50 cases of anxiety neurosis, 32 were female and 18 were male. Mean age for the males was 29.2 years, for the females 28.2. Nine of the 10 cases of phobic neurosis were female, with a mean age of 23.4 years. The young-adult range for nearly all patients seeking treatment for these two disorders has been consistently observed in the literature (Marks & Gelder, 1966; Wheeler, White, Reed, & Cohen, 1970). In all, 18 cases were acute, 14 subacute, and 18 chronic in onset. Males predominantly suffered from chronic onset (10 out of 18), whereas females suffered from more acute (13 out of 32) and subacute (11 out of 32) symptoms.

Acute onset means that the anxiety state developed over a period of days. Several cases of acute onset had intermittent anxiety episodes with interspersed symptom-free periods. Most though, had fluctuating levels of anxiety, but were never entirely anxiety free. In the *subacute* cases, the onset of symptoms was more gradual, usually occurring over weeks to a few months. *Chronic* onset refers to a slow, insidious development of the condition or to cases of such prolonged duration that the patient was unable to recall any completely anxiety-free times. In both subacute and chronic conditions, a relatively loose temporal association between specific life events (precipitating events) and the onset of anxiety symptoms was noted. These patients generally were less certain of the etiologic significance of specific events and their illness, as compared with the acute onset cases.

With one exception, all cases, whether acute or chronic onset, reported acute anxiety attacks superimposed on a base level of anxiety. The "attacks" lasted from minutes to hours and were of a highly variable frequency.

In anxiety neurosis, the levels of anxiety were related to environmental events in two specific ways. Fourteen of 20 in one study and 14 of 18 in the second reported at least one "precipitating event," i.e., an event subsequent to which their basal anxiety level increased and their anxiety "attacks" began. For those who reported more than one such event characteristically, the initial event resulted in a period of mild to moderate anxiety, whereas the second event resulted in a higher level. Moreover, their anxiety levels increased to maximal when the patient was about to enter or was in specific stimulus situations.

The meaning of these stimulus situations to each patient was assessed by collecting the thoughts or fantasies (cognitions) that occurred just before or during the onset of attacks. These cognitions were analogous to those surrounding the precipitating event.

The theme of *all* these cognitions consisted of an anticipation or visualization of *danger*, either physical or psychological harm. A trend was detectable in the content as compared to the "acuteness" of onset. The chronic-onset patients anticipated criticism, rejection, or interpersonal failure. The cognitions in the acute-onset cases related to more imminent danger involving physical well-being or loss of bodily or mental control.

Cognitions before the onset or exacerbation of anxiety similarly reflected ideas of imminent danger, but were experienced as *discrete* thoughts (e.g., "I am having a heart attack," "I will look foolish.") A high degree of probability was attached to the feared event's happening. In fact, even with a history of repeated disconfirmations, the expectancies of danger recurred when the patient was exposed to the typical stimulus events.

The anxiety-associated cognitions included not only verbal information, but visual fantasies (images) in 35 of 38 cases. When asked to repeat these fantasies in the interview, the patients felt anxious as the visualized scenario developed.

The unique personal content of these cognitions is notable. The personal variations clearly related to the unique aspects of the patient's past experience and conceptual configurations. Thus, these personal variations reflected on the relationship between the patient's mode of integrating his experience and the arousal of anxiety.

For instance, 11 of 38 patients had recurrent anxiety-associated ideations of dying. The nature of the feared event, the situations associated with such anticipations, and the presumed consequences of dying were idiosyncratic to each person's past experience. Two patients feared acute suffocation, two feared acute heart attacks, two feared being frightened to death by an intruder, two feared a slowly deteriorating illness, two feared an acute sudden death by an unspecified illness, and one feared punishment after death.

Similarly, a variety of personal meanings were attached to a theme of fear of "rejection." These included fears of ridicule for sexual inadequacy, peer group rejection, total social ostracism, disgrace and humiliation in performance before a group of strangers, intellectual attack and defeat, and humiliation from stuttering.

These studies did not specifically examine another aspect of the relation between cognitions and affect suggested by an earlier work (Beck, 1963): i.e., the relationship of the content of the stream of consciousness to anxiety without respect to environmental events. The studies did suggest that such a relationship exists—that cognitive events unrelated to external stimuli do occur, signal "danger" to the patient, and are associated with feelings of anxiety. Perhaps this accounts for the elevated basal anxiety levels in these patients.

Comparison of Cognitions in Anxiety
Neurosis and Phobic Neurosis

Significantly cognitive processes involving recurrent danger-related ideation was found in *all* cases of anxiety neuroses and phobias (Table 4-1). The arousal and intensification of anxiety was regularly associated with the occurrence of discrete thoughts or ideas centering on the theme of danger. In both syndromes, this was expressed as the *fear* of consequences resulting from specific events or situations. Both involved an *unrealistic* appraisal of the situation with a consistent overestimation of the dangerous aspects. This overestimation included an exaggeration of (*a*) the *degree* of harm and (*b*) the *likelihood* of harm. Further, in both groups a relationship between specific environmental stimuli and the occurrence of these cognitions was noted.

However, the phobic cognitions were distinguishable from those reported by anxiety neuroses in several ways. For anxiety neuroses, stimulus situations were more frequent and categorically broader. Secondly, the stimuli for anxiety neurotics were less specific than for phobics (e.g., "any gastrointestinal symptoms" as compared with fear of a rat).

In addition, the stimuli in anxiety neuroses were more frequently "internal," whereas phobic stimuli were more frequently "external."

Table 4-1
A Comparison of Cognitions in Anxiety and Phobic Neuroses

Anxiety neuroses	Phobias
1. Anxiety associated with discrete thoughts/fantasies	Same
2. Theme of danger	Same
3. Unrealistic situation appraisal	Same
4. Precipitating event present	Same
5. More frequent stimuli	Less frequent stimuli
6. Broader classes of stimuli	More specific class of stimuli
7. Less easily avoided stimuli	More easily avoided stimuli
8. Stimuli more frequently internal	Stimuli more frequently external
9. Cognitive content *less* directly related to content of stimulus situations	Cognitive content *more* directly related to content of stimulus situations
10. ? More frequent danger-related ideation in the "stream of consciousness"	? Less frequent danger-related ideations in the "stream of consciousness"

For instance, bodily sensations and thought processes themselves were more frequently included in the cognitions of those with anxiety neurosis. For example, the cognition of "I am dying" was associated with an interpretation of feelings of chest pain or difficulty breathing. For the phobics the cause of danger was experienced as outside the patient (e.g., a rat). The more frequent use of avoidance in phobics as compared with anxiety neurotics is explicable by these cognitive differences. When the sources of danger are external, one can successfully avoid them; this is impossible if danger is construed as coming from within.

Finally, the connection between the anxiety neurosis stimulus situations and the concomitant cognition was less discrete and direct than that for phobias. Thus, the fearful thoughts were associated with broader range of environmental triggers than for phobias. This fact would also reduce the effectiveness of avoidance behaviors.

The question as to the content of the "stream of consciousness" in both types of neurosis remains open for further study. The data suggested, however, that anxiety neurotics more frequently experienced anxiety-associated cognitions even without direct relation to environmental stimuli more frequently than did phobics.

DISCUSSION

Fear Versus Anxiety

A conceptual clarification of the definitions of "fear" and "anxiety" is postulated on the basis of this data. *Fear* is a particular kind of *ideation*, whereas *anxiety* is an *emotion*. Fear is an anticipation of "the possibility that something dreaded or unwanted may occur." Anxiety is "an unpleasant emotional state." Fear may be regarded as a predisposition to perceive a specific set of conditions as a threat and to react with anxiety when exposed to these conditions.

From the data with phobias, it is clear that the object or situation is not feared, per se, but rather the *possible consequences* of exposure to such an object. For example, fear of a rat is really fear of being bitten by the rat. Similarly, in anxiety states the *possible consequences* of situations or sensations are feared. For example, the sensations of chest pains are associated with anxiety and the fearful cognition "I am having a heart attack and might die."

Thus, a person's fear is a *concept* oriented toward the future referring to possibility of personal harm. When a fear is activated, a general state of anxiety ensues unless the person can alter the situation to change the feeling of imminent danger (e.g., escape, fantasize, etc.)

These definitions obviate common semantic contradictions such as "realistic anxiety" or "irrational or rational anxiety." These adjectives are properly applied to ideas or concepts, not feeling states. Is a bellyache "irrational"? A fear is labeled "objective" or "realistic" if there is a realistic danger; i.e., a disinterested observer would label the situation as realistically dangerous. The fear is rational or irrational depending on whether it is based on sensible assumptions, logic, or reasoning.

Phobic-Anxiety Neurosis Continuum

Anxiety neurosis appears to consist of "attacks" of anxiety occurring against a "background" of anxiety. This is in contrast to phobias in which there is no "background" of anxiety between exposure to feared situations or objects. In both neuroses, however, cognitions play a central role. These cognitions reflect the theme of "danger," represent an unrealistic appraisal of the stiuation, and are associated with anxiety. In this respect, phobic and anxiety neurosis may be viewed on a continuum of a chronic construing of situations to mean "danger."

However, these syndromes are distinguishable in certain respects. The more frequent occurrence of avoidance behavior in phobias is well documented (Laude & LaVigne, previously cited unpublished manuscript). Further, greater functional impairment has been demonstrated in anxiety neurosis. It is hypothesized that these features can be accounted for by cognitive differences in the two syndromes. In both cases, attacks of anxiety are associated with environmental stimuli. The stimuli in anxiety neurosis are broader, less specific, more frequently "internal," less easily avoided, and less directly related to the content of cognitions as compared with phobias.

The concept of free-floating anxiety has been applied to situations in which there is no apparent danger (to the objective observer). From the patient's frame of reference, though, he construes such situations as imminently dangerous. His interpretation may involve overgeneralization, arbitrary inferences, etc. Thus, anxiety is not free floating but is directly associated with cognitions signaling danger.

The interpretation of an unavoidable event as fearful activates the "danger" schema and results in anxiety. The feeling of anxiety itself may reinforce this underlying attitude, resulting in a vicious circle of fear-anxiety reinforcement.

What about the background of "basal anxiety" found in anxiety neurosis? The level of "basal anxiety" has been correlated with the severity of functional impairment (interference with daily activities) (Laude & LaVigne, previously cited unpublished manuscript). It is hypothesized that the background anxiety found in anxiety neurosis as compared with phobias may result from (a) more multiple and diffuse types of situations acting as anxiety-provoking stimuli; (b) the higher frequency of internal events acting as stimuli; (c) less easily avoided situations construed as "dangerous"; and, possibly, (d) more fear-producing cognitions in the "stream of consciousness" without respect to environmental events. The net result of such repeated cognitions is a more marked functional impairment in anxiety neurosis compared with phobias. The unavoidability of such situations may further add to the anxiety level in that the patient is aware that he cannot cope, even by escaping, with such situations.

A Model for Anxiety: Neurosis

It is hypothesized that a precipitating event (or series of events) elicits or magnifies an underlying attitude of fear. These events may impinge on the patient's specific vulnerabilities to elicit such danger-related ideation. Subsequently, the patient is overly vigilant of danger. He scans internal and external stimuli for "dangerous" properties. When new situations with possibilities of unpleasant outcomes are encountered, they are construed as dangerous. That is, the patient magnifies the possibility and intensity of unpleasant outcomes in his cognition of the situation. The resulting tendency to "catastrophize" develops (Ellis, 1962).

Danger-related ideation is subsequently more easily activated by less specific, less avoidable, more internal classes of stimuli. Even more subtle aspects of relatively nonthreatening situations begin to be associated with such cognitions. Such ideation is accompanied by experiences and bodily sensations of anxiety, which reinforce the underlying attitude. As the situations become less avoidable, more frequent, and unpredictable, the patient becomes more apprehensive about losing control of his anxiety. Perhaps his "stream of consciousness" regularly contains more danger-related ideation with only slight or no relevance to environmental events. Prolonged activation of such ideation results in anxiety neurosis.

Although stimulus situations may initially be rather analogous to the precipitating events, after repeated hypervigilance they become less clearly related to the precipitating events. This contention is supported by comparison of the content of acute- and chronic-onset cases. An increasingly fixed cognitive organization ensues so that once a situation is labeled as "dangerous" by the patient, the association is left unquestioned: his thinking is dominated by the concept of danger. The patients fix on specific possibilities of situations and anticipate "danger" with which they believe they cannot cope. Other less dangerous possibilities are apparently discounted or not experienced at all. The likelihood of danger is felt as high. This conceptualization is consistent with the work of Lader and Marks (1971) in which anxious patients were unable to habituate to moderately frightening stimuli with repeated exposures.

The specific cognitive distortions in anxiety neurosis include the following: (a) repetitive thoughts of danger, (b) "stimulus generalization" such that a wide and wider range of environmental stimuli evoke the "fear" concept, and (c) reduced ability to "reason" with fearful thoughts (i.e., even though they are questionable, their validity is predominantly believed.)

It is suggested that a *dual belief* system is operative in patients with anxiety. A rational, mature system is available to reflect realistically on the probability and intensity of danger inherent in specific situations associated with anxiety. A second "irrational" system becomes activated as the patient is exposed to or approaches being exposed to these situations. For the phobics, the situations triggering the irrational system are more concrete, external, and therefore avoidable. In anxiety neurosis, the perimeter of this belief system is less distinct; it is therefore operative in more situations. Clinical data about the danger-laden cognitions in the "streams of consciousness" of anxiety neurotics without specific relation to environmental events are consistent with this hypothesis.

Implications for Therapy

The previously cited data and the model suggest that alteration of danger-laden cognitions associated with anxiety will relieve the anxiety itself. Such cognitive changes can be accomplished by a broad range of techniques. The *intellectual* approach consists of identifying the misconceptions, testing their validity, and substituting more appropriate concepts. Often the need for broad attitudinal changes emerges as the individual recognizes that the rules he has relied on to guide his thinking and behavior have served to deceive and defeat him.

The *experiential* approach exposes the patient to experiences that are in themselves powerful enough to change misconceptions. Interaction with others in organized situations (e.g., encounter groups and individual psychotherapy) may help a person perceive them more realistically, thereby altering his cognitive distortions.

Cognitive therapy helps patients with anxiety neurosis identify their automatic thoughts or the "things they tell themselves." These thoughts are maladaptive or unrealistic. Training in the collection of automatic thoughts can be accomplished by directing the patient to record the thoughts he has between the stimulus situation and his emotional response. For example, a patient experienced anxiety when exposed to dogs even though he had no reason for fearing them (e.g., the dog was too small or was chained). By this technique, when exposed subsequently to dogs, he reported the thought, "It's going to bite me." Thus, he automatically regarded every dog as dangerous. An alternative method to help the patient become aware of such thoughts involves asking him to fantasize the precipitating event(s) (Beck, 1970).

Once the automatic thoughts are identified, the patient is increasingly able to view them objectively (with his more rational belief system). This process of regarding thoughts objectively is called *distancing*. Thus, a person who can examine his automatic thoughts as psychological phenomena rather than as identical to reality is exercising the capacity for *distancing*, i.e., for distinguishing between "I believe" (an opinion subject to validation) and "I know" (a nonnegotiable fact) (Beck, 1970).

Even after a patient is able to make a clear distinction between his internal mental processes and the outside world that stimulates them, it may still be necessary to educate him regarding procedures for acquiring accurate knowledge. The therapist works with the patient to apply the rules of evidence to his conclusions.

Finally, a theme is frequently detectable in a series of such cognitions that can be identified with the patient. Once identified this theme can be assessed, tested, and corrected if maladaptive. For example, a theme of fear of failure in front of strangers was identified; after examination, the patient concluded that such failure was indeed a setback but not the catastrophe he initially felt it was.

The sequence of cognitive therapy involves (a) self-observations that led directly to the ideation preceeding the anxiety (identifying the automatic thoughts or fantasies), (b) establishing the relationship between such thoughts and anxiety attacks, (c) learning to regard thoughts as hypotheses rather than facts (distancing), (d) piecing together the assumptions that underlie and generate these hypotheses, and (e) demonstrating that these rules comprising the belief system are incorrect (Beck, 1974).

Since 34 of 38 patients with anxiety neurosis had visual fantasies associated with the onset of anxiety episodes, these patients may be particularly susceptible to treatment by *fantasy modification* (Allport, 1955). Anxious neurotics can be trained to control autonomous fantasies. Fantasies can be modified at the therapist's direction allowing the patient to experience alternative consequences. Fantasy repetition in the office frequently leads to a more realistic fantasy content. In addition, a reduction in the unpleasantness of affect has resulted from a fantasy rehearsal. This treatment probably involves a lessening of generalizations of the "danger" attitudes, and thereby allows a more realistic, reasonable assessment of the situation (Beck, 1970).

Behavioral techniques have been designed to alter such cognitive distortions as well. Wolpe and Lazarus' (1966) systematic desensitization used cognitive rehearsal of induced fantasies as an integral part of treatment. Other behavioral tasks have been used to facilitate any of the preceding five general steps in cognitive reorientation. For example, the patient may be asked to write down his automatic thoughts and "answer them" logically on the basis of the environmental data. He may be assigned a specific task to test one of his underlying assumptions.

In summary, the patient is armed with a variety of intellectual and behavioral methods he can use to evaluate and respond realistically to subsequent situations without the therapist.

REFERENCES

Allport, F. H. *Theories of perception and the concept of structure.* New York: Wiley, 1955.

Beck, A. T. Thinking and depression: 1. Idiosyncratic content and cognitive distortions. *Archives of General Psychiatry*, 1963, 9, 324–333.

Beck, A. T. Role of fantasies in psychotherapy and psychopathology. *Journal of Nervous and Mental Diseases*, 1970, 150, 3–17.

Beck, A. T. Cognition, affect and psychopathology. *Archives of General Psychiatry*, 1971, 24, 495–500.

Beck, A. T. *Cognitive modification in depressed suicidal patients*. Paper presented to the Society for Psychotherapy Research, Denver, Colo., June 1974.

Beck, A. T., Laude, R., & Bohnert, M. Ideational components of anxiety neurosis, *Archives of General Psychiatry*, 1974, 31, 319–325.

Ellis, A. *Reason and emotion in psychotherapy*. New York: Lyle Stuart, 1962.

Lader, M., & Marks, I. M. *Clinical anxiety*. New York: Grune & Stratton, 1971.

Marks, I. M. *Fears and phobias*. New York: Academic Press, 1969.

Marks, I. M., & Gelder, M. Different onset ages in varieties of phobia. *American Journal of Psychiatry*, 1966, 123, 218.

Marks, I. M., & Lader, M. Anxiety states (anxiety neurosis): A review. *Journal of Nervous and Mental Diseases*, 1973, 156, 3–18.

Wheeler, E. O., White, P. D., Reed, E. W., & Cohen, M. E. Neurocirculatory asthenia (anxiety Neurosis, effort syndrome neurasthenia). *Journal of the American Medical Association*, 1970, 142, 878.

Wolpe, J., & Lazarus, A. A. *Behavior therapy technique: A guide to the treatment of neuroses*. New York: Pergamon Press, 1966.

5

A GENETIC MODEL
OF ANXIETY

H. J. Eysenck

Institute of Psychiatry
University of London
London, England

STRESS, STRAIN, AND PERSONALITY

In looking at stress and anxiety, it may be useful to take seriously the physical model of stress and strain that has been so widely adapted to serve our psychological purposes. This physical model finds its expression in Hooke's classical law of elasticity: Stress $= k \times$ Strain, where k is a constant (the modulus of elasticity) that depends upon the nature of the material and the type of stress used to produce the strain. This constant k, i.e., the ratio stress/strain, is called Young's modulus and is illustrated, with certain simplifications, in Fig. 5-1 (top). A and B are two metals differing in elasticity; they are stressed by increasing loads, and the elongation corresponding to each load is plotted on the abscissa. Identical loads θ give rise to quite divergent elongations, α and β, depending on k. Figure 5-1 (bottom) illustrates a similar analysis of human or rat behaviour in an experimental situation productive of emotion. Again the stress (independent variable) is plotted on the ordinate, and the strain (dependent variable) on the abscissa. A

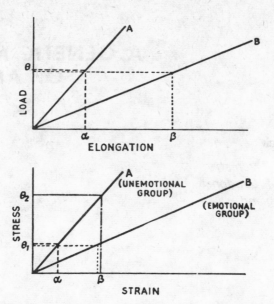

Fig. 5-1. Hooke's Law as applied to physical stress-strain relations (top) and to psychological stress-strain relations (bottom.) A and B refer to different materials, or to different genetic predispositions with respect to anxiety. θ represents two identical loads; α and β represent different elongations (top) and stress or strain (bottom).

and B represent stable and neurotic groups of human subjects, or perhaps the specially bred unemotional and emotional Maudsley strains of rats. Identical stress θ_1 gives rise to quite different strains α and β. It would require stress θ_2 to make the strain in A animals equal to that produced by θ_1 in B animals. Differences between θ_1 and θ_2 are the kind of differences traditionally studied by experimental psychologists; differences between A and B are the kinds of differences traditionally studied by personality psychologists and behavioural geneticists. Physicists have never attempted to make a choice between these two sets of variables, or to study them in isolation; it seems equally futile for psychologists to do so. Provided the modulus employed is even moderately correct, and more than a mere analogy, the experimental possibilities suggested by this method of approach seem promising (Savage & Eysenck, 1964).

In animal work this constant k (emotionality, fearfulness, anxiety) has been studied genetically in considerable detail, using the defecation score in the open field test as the selection measure. Figure 5-2 shows a selection experiment that has been going on for some three dozen generations in our laboratories; the figure shows the trend over the first 15 generations. The mean defecation scores of the animals in the emotionally reactive strain have risen to 4+, whereas those of the animals in the emotionally nonactive strain have fallen to 0; there is practically no overlap between descendants of parents in the two strains. There is ample evidence that this genetic selection has not simply been along the lines of high and low defecation; the two strains behave quite differently from each other in experimental situations where the evidence entitles us to expect different behaviour on the basis of high and low emotionality, respectively. Thus, reactives show greater conditional emotional responses (CER's), learn less efficiently in escape-avoidance conditioning, show greater response to shock, are more susceptible to frustration, develop conditioned inhibition more quickly, and so on. There are also physiological differences: emotionally reactive animals have more body fat, heavier thyroids, more cholesterol in the blood, heavier adrenals, more 17-Ketosteroid output, more thyrotrophic hormone content, and heavier pituitaries (Eysenck, H. J., & Broadhurst, 1964).

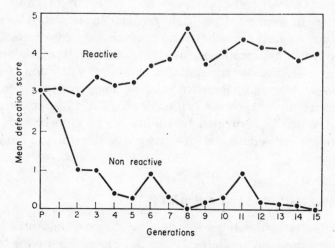

Fig. 5-2. Mean defecation scores (measures of emotional reactivity) in rats bred for high or low defecation over 15 generations.

We might say that we can trade organismic variables against experimental variables; a very elastic metal does not require much stress to produce a given strain, whereas a nonelastic metal might require a considerable stress. Thus we can obtain the same result by trading the modulus of elasticity of the metal against the stress required. In the same way, to produce the same degree of fear/anxiety, we can take an emotionally unreactive rat (or human) and subject the organism to a very frightening experience, or we can take an emotionally reactive rat (or human) and subject the organism to a much less frightening experience, using an appropriate scale of "frighteningness."

To illustrate this argument, consider the work of Rosenbaum (1953, 1956). He found that threat of a strong shock led to greater generalization of a voluntary response than did threat of a weak shock. He also discovered that anxious subjects showed greater generalization to identical stimuli than did nonanxious subjects. In other words, to attain any given degree of generalization, we can either manipulate the stress (strength of shock) or the organismic property of fearfulness or anxiety which is a characteristic of the person. This principle of *trading off* may be useful because we can use the one to measure the other; we could, in the Rosenbaum experiment, express differences in anxiety along a scale the units of which were marked out in terms of strength of shock. Or we could compare both strength of shock, in its psychological meaning, and trait anxiety in terms of degree of generalization. Last, threat (stress) produces certain effects that are identical to those produced by trait anxiety; thus, the measure used for trait anxiety is validated. A similar validation is seen in the case of our rats. Reactive rats, as compared with nonactive rats, behave in a typically different fashion in an experimental situation which is known to be productive of anxiety stress; thus, the measure of emotional reactivity used with the animals is validated.

THE DIMENSIONALITY OF ANXIETY

Anxiety, unfortunately, is not a unidimensional variable; it is implicit in the construction of such devices as the Taylor Manifest Anxiety Scale (MAS) that what is being measured is in some sense univocal, but this is not so. Anxiety is conceived as conditioned fear reactions (Eysenck, H. J., & Rachman, 1965); and the strength of such conditioned fear reactions depends on two independent variables, not one: (a) degree of emotionality or fearfulness, which determines the strength of the unconditioned stimulus (UCS) and (b) strength of conditioning, which determines the degree to which the conditioned stimulus (CS) and the UCS will be associated. In terms of personality theory, emotionality or fearfulness is measured as the personality dimension of neuroticism (N), and conditionability is closely associated with the personality dimension of extraversion-introversion (E–I) (Eysenck, H. J., 1967). Thus, people whose personality puts them in the dysthymic quadrant (high N, low E) are most predisposed to neurotic disorders and anxiety generally, both because of their strong fear reactions, and their ability to form strong conditioned responses. Scores on the MAS, as one would expect from this analysis, correlate both with N (positively) and with E (negatively); the former correlations are higher than the latter ones (Eysenck, H. J., & Eysenck, S. B. G., 1969). The experimental evidence is strongly in favour of a positive correlation between introversion and strength of conditioning, provided that certain parametric requirements of the theory are fulfilled. Figure 5-3

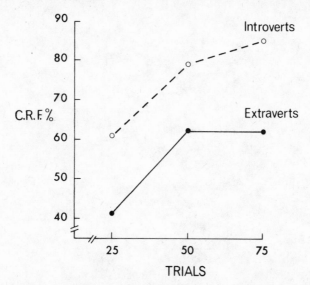

Fig. 5-3. Proportions of conditioned eyeblink responses given by extraverted and introverted subjects during three sessions of 25 trials each. CRF represents conditioned response frequency.

shows some recent results of work with the eyeblink conditioning task; data are shown for the frequency of conditioned responses (CR's) during three sets of 25 conditioning trials. Differences are highly significant for all three sets of data; it is noteworthy that extraverts reach an asymptote during the second set of trials, whereas introverts are still improving during the third set. Figure 5-4 shows, for the same subjects, differences in a work-rate measure; this is defined as the ratio of CR amplitude at unconditioned response (UCR) onset over peak UCR amplitude and is considered to be an estimate of the amount of "physiological work" taken over by the CR from the UCR (Martin & Levey, 1969). Clearly, conditioned responses are not only more frequent in introverts, but also more effective. This "conditionability" is not confined to one test; there is good evidence of a more general factor of "conditionability," which extends from aversive to appetitive conditioning (Barr & McConaghy, 1972).

This general view of anxiety as a conditioned response, determined in part by personality factors N and E, agrees well with the useful distinction between trait and state anxiety, a distinction first drawn by Cicero almost 2,000 years ago. He distinguished

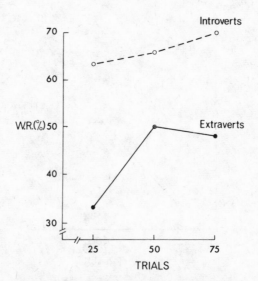

Fig. 5-4. Work rate (WR) (percent) of introverted and extraverted subjects on eyeblink conditioning task during three sessions of 25 trials each.

carefully between *angor* and *anxietas*; *angor* is a transitory attack, provoked by a specified stimulus, *anxietas* is an abiding predisposition. *"Anxium proprie dici qui pronus est ad aegritudinem animi, neque enim omnes anxii, qui anguntur aliquando; nec qui anxii, semper anguntur."* (He is anxious who is prone to the sorrows of the soul, but they are not necessarily anxious who sometimes feel fear; nor do those who are anxious always feel fear.) *Anxietas*, on this account, would be similar in conception to N, i.e., general fearfulness or emotionality; *angor* would correspond with state anxiety, i.e., the evocation of specific conditioned fear responses.

Factor analytic work with such fear schedules as that of Geer (1965) has shown that, as expected on these grounds, fears for a variety of objects and concepts have both general and specific properties. The work of Rubin, Katkin, Weiss, and Efram (1968) and Landy and Gaupp (1971) has unearthed a number of factors that group such fear-producing stimuli into meaningful groups, such as interpersonal events, discrete objects, death and illness, animate nonhuman organisms, and fears of the unknown. In addition, each item, of course, possesses some unique variance; items differ markedly in this respect. The communality for "deep water" is .80, that for "untimely death" is .78, and that for "heights" is .94; this may be contrasted with "sharp objects," which has a communality of .46, "strange dogs" (.41), and "arguing with parents" (.42). These values, of course, are dependent to some extent on the particular sample of items and subjects chosen; but they are characteristic of the range of generality of fears in our civilisation.

Practically all factor analytic studies in the personality field agree on the overwhelming importance of two major factors resembling N and E, although the names used are often different (Eysenck, H. J., & Eysenck, S. B. G., 1969.) Some writers, in particular Cattell, prefer to work at the primary factor level, using a much larger number of factors; the evidence now seems conclusive that these alleged "primary" factors can no longer be posited. It has been shown that Cattell's 16 Primary Factor (PF) scales have unacceptably low reliability; that they are not replicable in independent researches; that when corrected for attenuation the correlations between them are so high as to approach unity, making them simply rather unreliable measures of E and N (and possibly one or two additional higher order factors.) Reference may be made here to the work of Becker (1961); Borgatta (1962); H. J. Eysenck (1971, 1972); H. J. Eysenck and S. B. G. Eysenck (1969); Greif (1970); Howarth and Browne (1971); Levonian (1961 a, b); Peterson (1960); Sells, Demaree, and Will (1968); and Timm (1968). These works leave no doubt that work on "primary" factors in personality research is not yet advanced enough to make the use of such factor scores feasible.

It seems reasonable to assume that powerful human reactions, such as fear and conditioning, are mediated by well-demarcated physiological and neurological systems, anatomically identifiable; and there is good evidence to suggest that neuroticism is mediated by an especially labile autonomic system, coordinated in its activity through the visceral brain, while extraversion-introversion is mediated through the cortical arousal system, interacting with the ascending reticular activation system. Those systems are essentially independent most of the time, except when the sympathetic system is strongly aroused; this, like all types of external and internal stimulation, produces strong cortical arousal and washes out any differences that might exist in the resting state between introverts and extraverts (Eysenck, H. J., 1967).

ANXIETY AND HERITABILITY

Having thus, briefly, introduced our psychological and underlying physiological conception of anxiety, we must next turn to the question of heritability. At first sight it might seem unlikely that conditioned fear reactions could be determined to any large extent by hereditary causes, because by definition these reactions are learned, i.e., determined by environmental factors. But this is not the proper way to look at things. It is proposed that people differ systematically from each other in the degree to which they experience fear in the presence of pain and other stimuli which are perceived as threatening life or organic integrity; both the strength of fear experienced, and the length of time over which such fears persist, are determined by the autonomic system, coordinated in its activity by the visceral brain, and are strongly based on polygenic hereditary aspects of the individual's constitution. Similarly, such fears become attached to formerly neutral aspects of the situation in which these fears are experienced (conditioned stimuli), and the speed with which, and the degree to which such conditioning proceeds are also determined genetically. Thus given random exposure to fear-producing stimuli, some people (high N, low E) are genetically predisposed to develop conditioned fear responses because of strong UCR's and strong CS-CR associations. Even if exposure is not random, these genetic predispositions will still powerfully influence a person's behaviour; it is the task of empirical study to determine the degree to which these various components of the anxiety response are heritable. Current orthodoxy in psychiatry and psychology attributes minimal (or even no) importance to hereditary predispositions, and stresses exclusively the role of environmental variables; we shall see that this stress is one sided and that heredity plays a very powerful part indeed in the causation of neurotic and other anxiety responses.

An example will illustrate the present "orthodox" position of total environmentalism; this is what Redlich and Freedman (1966) (in a widely read textbook of psychiatry) have to say about the influence of heredity on neurotic and sociopathic disorders characterized by anxiety: "The importance of inherited characteristics in neuroses and sociopathies is no longer asserted except by Hans J. Eysenck and D. B. Prell"—referring to a paper in which Eysenck and Prell (1951) demonstrated a high degree of heritability for a factor of neuroticism derived from a battery of psychological tests, administered to monozygotic (MZ) and dizygotic (DZ) twins. Note that there was no discussion of the experiment in question, or criticism of it; neither was there any mention of the large number of authors who have reported empirical results demonstrating the importance of heredity in these types of disorder, or of those experts in the field of behavioural genetics who share this belief and might be quoted as "asserting" it. An equally widely read psychological text by Ullman and Krasner (1969) completely fails to mention genetics or heredity in the Index, and refers to twins only in connection with schizophrenia. Textbooks on personality almost universally refuse to discuss genetic factors; occasionally they mention the completely out-of-date Newman, Freeman, and Holzinger (1937) study as demonstrating the lack of heritability of personality variables.

THE DEFINITIONS OF HERITABILITY

Before looking at the evidence, we must define with some precision the notion of heritability, because psychologists have used this term in many divergent and often meaningless ways; even the statistical definition given it by Newman et al. in the classic study mentioned previously and widely used by investigators ever since, has no assignable genetic meaning. Briefly, heritability (usually written h^2) is a population statistic which expresses the proportion of population variance in a given phenotypic characteristic attributable to genetic factors. It is usually estimated from a sample of the population and is therefore subject to sampling errors, the magnitude of which is inversely related to the square root of the sample size; representativeness of the sample is of course vitally important in drawing conclusions from the sample to the population. Being a population statistic, h^2 is clearly not a constant in the physical sense, nor does it apply to individuals. It may be defined by reference to the components of variance that enter into it:

$$h^2 = \frac{V_G}{V_P}$$

where V_G is the genetic variance and V_P is the phenotypic or total observed variance. The genetic variance can be divided into four main components:

$$V_G = V_A + V_D + V_{Ep} + V_{AM}$$

where V_A refers to the additive genetic variance; V_D to that portion of the nonadditive genetic variance due to dominance at the same gene loci; V_{Ep} to that portion of the nonadditive genetic variance due to interaction between different gene loci, called *epistasis*; and V_{AM} to genetic variance due to assortative mating, i.e., the increment in total variance attributable to degree of genetic resemblance between mates on the characteristic in question.

The phenotypic variance is made up of the following:

$$V_P = V_G + V_E + V_{GE} + \text{Cov. } GE + V_e$$

where V_G is the genetic variance already defined, V_E is the additive environmental variance that is independent of the genotype, V_{GE} is variance due to interaction of genotypes and environments, Cov. *GE* is covariance of genotypes and environments, and V_e is error variance due to unreliability of measurements.

There are three different ways in which environment and heredity can interact. First, if a particular change in the environment has a uniform effect in raising or lowering the score of every member of the sample on the test used, this effect would be indexed under V_E. Second, if the environmental change interacts with genotypes to produce different phenotypic effects in different genotypes, this source of variance would be indexed under Cov. *GE*; this covariance increases the total population variance in the trait. Roberts (1967) and other geneticists include Cov. *GE* as part of the total genetic variance rather than as part of the environmental variance, and define V_E accordingly as those environmental effects that are independent of the genotype. Finally, V_{GE} denotes interaction of genotype and environment.

It will be clear that we have, not one definition of heritability, but several. Heritability in the narrow sense ($h_N{}^2$) is the proportion of additive genetic variance:

$$h_N{}^2 = \frac{V_A}{V_P}$$

while heritability in the broad sense (h^2) is V_G/V_P. If we follow Roberts and include Cov. *GE* in the numerator, we obtain:

$$h^2 = \frac{V_G + \text{Cov. } GE}{V_P}$$

Generally this latter formula is in fact used, either on the assumption that the covariance is due to the genotype, or because the particular method of estimating h^2 used does not permit separation of V_G and Cov. *GE*. Doubts also arise about the inclusion of V_e in the phenotypic variance; it is not clear why errors in measurement due to unreliability of the measuring instruments should be attributed to phenotypic variance. It seems best to correct empirical results for unreliability before carrying out calculations that would attribute the remaining variance to *G* and *E*.

One further distinction is important in understanding the work that has been done on the heritability of personality variables. V_G

and V_E may both be partitioned into two components, one due to differences *between* families and the other due to differences *within* families. The terms used express the fact that, on the genetic side, there are differences between the average value of the trait measurements of different families in the population, and also genetic differences among the offsprings within each family: $V_G = V_{GB} + V_{GW}$. Similarly, there are systematic environmental differences *between* families that do not make for differences among offsprings reared together in the same family, and there are environmental influences *within* families which make for differences among offsprings reared together in the same family: $V_E = V_{EB} + V_{EW}$. The portions of G and E contributed by these different factors are sometimes referred to as G_1 and G_2, on the genetic side, and E_1 and E_2, on the environmental side.

MODELS OF GENE ACTION

Empirical work requires us to construct first of all a model to which we can then proceed to fit the data; we also require statistical tests of significance to tell us whether our model is adequate in fitting the data or not. Obviously the various components of V_P cannot be measured directly; they must be estimated indirectly, using estimates made from correlations (or preferably covariances) among persons of differing degrees of kinship (twins, siblings, cousins, etc.) and relationship (reared together or reared apart.) It would not be useful or possible here to go into the detailed formulae which make this possible. The reader is referred to Mather and Jinks (1971) or to Jinks and Fulker (1970); the latter reference gives detailed examples of the application of the formulae to data from studies of intelligence and personality.

Jinks and Fulker (1970) stated:

There are currently three alternative approaches to the genetical analysis of human twin and familial data. There is what might be termed the classical approach through correlations between relatives, culminating in the estimation of various ratios describing the relative importance of genetic and environmental influences on trait variation. This approach leads to ratios such as the H of Holzinger (1929), the E of

Neel and Schull (1954), and the HR of Nicholls (1965), each of which measures an aspect of the relative importance of heredity and environment. There is the more systematic and comprehensive approach of the Multiple Abstract Variance Analysis (MAVA) developed by Cattell (1960, 1965) leading to both the estimation of nature : nurture ratios, and an assessment of the importance of the correlation between genetic and environmental influences within the family as well as within the culture.... Finally, there is the biometrical genetical approach initiated by Fisher (1918), and extended and applied by Mather (1949), which includes the first two approaches as special cases, and attempts to go beyond them to an assessment of the kinds of gene action and mating systems operating in the population [p. 311].

Of these approaches, it is in practice largely the classical Holzinger-type of analysis which has been used in the genetic study of personality; unfortunately, this has such serious drawbacks that we can do no more than answer the question of whether the intraclass correlation for MZ twins is significantly larger than that for DZ twins. If it is, and provided that certain objections to the twin method can be satisfactorily discounted, we may conclude that heredity has played some part in causing variation in the trait under investigation; however, we can say nothing about its heritability in any quantitative fashion, nor can we answer any questions about the contribution of nonadditive sources of variance. We are further restricted to a consideration of within-family variance; in interpreting the results in terms of heritability we have to assume that between-family variance is nonexistent. Nor can we answer questions about interaction between E and G in any manner.

These (and other) defects of the classical method are responsible for the frequently heard remark that we cannot apportion genetic and environmental variance quantitatively, or that it is impossible to assign any meaningful value to the heritability of a given trait or ability. This is true provided we are restricted to the classical method of analysis and are unwilling to make certain simplifying assumptions that would enable us to make at least an estimate of the heritability of the traits or abilities involved. It is not true, however, of the new biometrical genetical methods; these enable us to construct a proper genetic model, to estimate the various parameters of that model, and to make quantitative judgments regarding the closeness of fit of the data to the model. These are important advances, and they enable us to make certain quantitative estimates in the genetic field which take us a great deal nearer to the proper understanding of the dynamics of heredity.

RESEARCHES USING THE CLASSICAL METHOD: THE BEGINNING

Before turning to studies which have used these modern methods, we must briefly look at the large number of investigations using the classical methods of analysis. A detailed survey has been published by H. J. Eysenck (1975), and there would be little point in undertaking another review here. We shall selectively mention some of the more important studies and summarize the remainder. We shall then turn to concordance studies, which share some of the defects of investigations using the classical twin method, and finally close with a discussion of the studies that have used the methods of biometrical general analysis. The first study is the now classical book by Newman et al. (1937), the results of which are still widely quoted as representative of the literature.

These writers compared 50 paris of MZ and 50 pairs of DZ twins with respect to a number of physical measurements and mental and educational tests; they concluded:

the physical characteristics are least affected by the environment; that intelligence is affected more; educational achievement still more; and personality or temperament, if our tests can be relied upon, the most. This finding is significant, regardless of the absolute amount of the environmental influence.

The lack of hereditary influence on personality here suggested is still assumed to be a true statement of the fact in the accounts given by most textbooks of psychology and psychiatry; but there are reasons for regarding it with suspicion, not only in the light of more recent work, but also in view of the many criticisms to be made of this early work. These have been summarized by H. J. Eysenck (1967) as follows:

There are two main criticisms. In the first place, the measures used would not now be regarded as either reliable or valid. They included the Woodworth-Mathews Personality Inventory, the Kent-Rosanoff Scale, the Pressey Cross-Out Test, and the Downey Will-Temperament Test. It is doubtful whether any psychologist would nowadays wish to make very strong claims for these measures; even if they could be regarded as reliable and valid, the question would still have to be asked; valid for what? The Woodworth-Mathews Inventory is the only one for which detailed statistics are presented, and we discover that for identical twins the intraclass correlation is .562, for fraternal twins it is .371, and for identical twins brought up in separation it is .583. If we regard, as the original authors certainly did, this questionnaire as an inventory of neurotic tendency, then we would here seem to have some mild indication of the importance of heredity, seeing that identical twins are distinctly superior in point of intraclass correlation to fraternals. Moreover, and this is a particularly interesting feature of this table, identical twins brought up in separation are more alike than are identical twins brought up together; this is the only test used, including physical measurements, where this is true. The authors comment that "the Woodworth-Mathews Test appears to show no very definite trend in correlations, possibly because of the nature of the trait and also because of the unreliability of the measure." It is not quite clear to the present writer why there is this denial of a definite trend; it seems fairly clear that identical twins, whether brought up in separation or together, are more alike than are fraternal twins, and we shall see, later modern work has amply justified such a conclusion.

We must now turn to our second criticism, which has curiously enough not to our knowledge been made before. The personality tests used by Newman, Freeman, and Holzinger were essentially tests for adults; the Woodworth-Mathews Inventory for instance was constructed specifically for selection purposes in the army and in hospitals. It is quite inadmissible to use tests of this kind on children, and as is made clear on page 106 of the twin study, the average age of the whole group of identical and fraternal twins is only about thirteen years. No details are given, but it is clear that there must have been children as young as eight or even younger in this group, and it is doubtful whether a large proportion of the children were in a position to understand the terms used in the tests or to give meaningful replies to them. Our own work in questionnaire construction (S. B. G. Eysenck, 1965) has clearly shown the difficulties attending the construction of personality inventories for children, and the difficulties which children may encounter in answering questions even when these are specifically constructed for them. Taking together these two criticisms of the Newman, Freeman, and Holzinger study, it is perhaps justifiable to say that the data do not support their conclusions. Identical twins whether brought up together or in separation are clearly more alike than are fraternal twins, thus suggesting the importance of heredity in contributing to the temperamental differences studied; the poor reliability and inappropriate nature of the test used suggest that the differences found would have been larger and possibly much larger had more suitable tests been employed. We shall indeed find in our examination of the evidence that later studies using more appropriate methods of examination have resulted in a much better discrimination between identical and fraternal twins. It must of course be remembered that the Newman, Freeman and Holzinger study was a pioneering venture and that at the time few if any personality tests existed, particularly as far as children were concerned. More to blame perhaps are later writers who have cited their work as support for the proposition that heredity is a relatively unimportant factor in the causation of individual differences in temperament and personality, without a closer look at the details of the evidence offered.

The Newman et al. study thus emerges with a heritability of about 30%, which is not negligible when we consider the inappropriateness of the tests; more impressive perhaps is the fact that MZ twins brought up separately are, if anything, more alike than MZ twins brought up together. It is possible that this odd result caused the authors to be hypercautious in their conclusions; we will see that later studies have found similar results, so that we may consider the finding as probably nonartefactual. (It should be added here that our strictures apply only to that portion of the

Newman et al. work concerned with personality; for the rest, their book fully deserves its high standing in the literature. They themselves obviously did not feel happy with the section on personality, as their caveat, already quoted, makes clear.)

RESEARCHES USING THE CLASSICAL METHOD: LATER WORK

Since the work of Newman et al., quite a number of studies have appeared using MZ and DZ twins as subjects and questionnaires as personality measures; Table 5-1 lists the more important ones, as well as the inventories employed. The outcome of all this work can be stated quite simply; for practically all measures used, MZ twins show higher intraclass correlations than do DZ twins, and the differences are mostly statistically significant, although for some subscales significance may not be reached, particularly when number used are small. Lindzey, Loehlin, Manosevitz, and Thiessen (1971) surveyed some of the more recent of these studies,

Table 5-1

Twin Studies Using Personality Inventories To Discover Genetic
Determination of Individual Differences in Personality

Author and date	Scale used
Carter, 1935	Bernreuter
Cattell, Blewett, & Beloff, 1955	Cattell High School Personality Questionnaire
Vandenberg, 1962	Cattell High School Personality Questionnaire
	Thurstone Temperament Schedule
Gottesman, 1963	Minnesota Multiphasic Personality Inventory (MMPI)
	Cattell High School Personality Questionnaire
Wilde, 1964	Maudsley Personality Inventory (Adaptation)
Gottesman, 1965	MMPI
Partanen, Bruun, & Markkanen, 1966	Sociability Inventory
Nicholls, 1966	California Personality Inventory
Gottesman, 1966	California Personality Inventory
Vandenberg, 1966	Myers-Briggs Type Indicator
Reznikoff & Honeyman, 1967	MMPI
Vandenberg, Comrey, & Stafford, 1967	Comrey Personality and Attitude Factor Scales
Schoenfeldt, 1968	California Personality Inventory
Young, Fenton, & Lader, 1971	Middlesex Hospital Questionnaire

and have derived certain "fairly clear conclusions" that also apply to the earlier reports.

Lindzey et al. concluded the following:

1. There is ample evidence that MZ twins are more alike with respect to personality than are DZ like-sexed twins.
2. Correlations are lower, in both groups, for personality traits than they are for IQ test scores; even when corrected for reliability (personality tests are usually less reliable) correlations only come up to .61 and .37, respectively, assuming reliabilities of .75.
3. Heritability is considerably lower than in the case of IQ tests; even when corrected for attenuation, coefficients would be below 50%.
4. The fourth point is perhaps the most interesting. It appears from some calculations made by Thompson and Wilde (1971) that when different studies are compared for the order of heritability coefficients for component scales, no similarity whatever appears; in other words, scale A may have a higher heritability than scale B in one study, but a lower one in another. Lindzey et al. (1971) concluded that "for the present, the most economical interpretation of the data would seem to be that while the genotype may have an appreciable effect on personality, the network of causal pathways between genotype and phenotype is so complex in this realm that the effect of the genotype is spread almost evenly across the broad phenotypic measures that personality and interest questionnaires provide."

An alternative explanation, and one which I would prefer, is that the "spreading" is due to the failure to use univocal trait measures, by failing to employ factor analysis in the purification of the scales in question. Where scales are based on relatively arbitrary collocation of items, nothing else really can be expected.

In addition to studies using personality questionnaires, investigations have also been carried out using psychophysiological measures (Block, 1967; Eysenck, H. J., 1956; Goodman, Luke, Rosen, & Hackel, 1959; Jost & Sontag, 1944; Kryshova, Beliaeva, Dmitrieva, & Zhilinskaia, 1963; Lader & Wing, 1966; Vandenberg, Clark, & Samuels, 1965.) These are so diversified that it is difficult to give any sort of interpretation without going into tedious detail. The results reported leave no doubt that autonomic functioning under a variety of different types of stimulation is to a large extent under genetic control, but beyond that it would not be wise to go at the present moment. It is unfortunate that investigators have seldom if ever linked their psychophysiological studies with personality investigations; hence our gain in knowledge has not been commensurate with the amount of work done.

STUDIES USING CHILDREN

The studies reviewed so far were carried out on adults and adolescents; do young children give results dissimilar to those reported on older groups? Scarr (1966 a, b, 1969) studied 24 MZ and 28 DZ pairs of girl twins of elementary school age, using ratings and observations in standardized situations; mothers' ratings on the Adjective Check List (ACL) were also used. Median intraclass correlations for the former type of observation were .39 and .23, and for the mothers' ACL ratings they were .40 and .11; again there is overall evidence for greater personality similarity of MZ twins, as compared with DZ twins. The work of Koch (1966) lends some mild support to this conclusion. For even younger twins, Brown, Stafford, and Vandenberg (1967) assessed eight variables, ratings being based on interviews with the mother. MZ twins were more alike on seven of these variables, impressively so on feeding and sleeping problems. Freedman (1965) had films of a small group of twins rated for behaviour in standard situations; smiling and fear of strangers showed the most marked MZ similarities. Lindzey et al. (1971) pointed out:

> These data on younger twins, taken together, tend to support the common observation that the greater resemblance of identical twins has early roots, but the data are insufficient to cast much light on the differential influence of heredity and environment on different traits, and thus to assist much in the interpretation of findings at later ages. A really large study of twins followed through the early years of life would be most welcome.

This conclusion is supported by the work of Juel-Nielsen (1965), who presented detailed case-history-type information of 12 Danish pairs of MZ twins reared apart from early infancy, or early childhood in some cases. Unfortunately, he relied on projective tests, notoriously unreliable and lacking in validity (Zubin, Eron, & Schumer, 1965) and subjective interviews that are difficult to quantify; a proper study of this kind would be extremely interesting and important.

Using factor analysis of parental ratings, Buss, Plomin, and Willerman (1973) found that "four inherited tendencies are suggested for humans: emotionality, activity, sociability, and impulsivity." Activity, sociability, and impulsivity are three of the main components of extraversion; emotionality corresponds closely to neuroticism. The actual H values calculated for twins under and over 55 months of age are given in Table 5-2; the numbers in the cells are not very large, and it would not be wise to read too much into the results other than that heredity plays a powerful part in producing individual differences in these four components of personality.

The work of H. J. Eysenck & Prell (1951) differs in two important directions from most of the studies so far reviewed. In the first place, they argued that objective tests of behaviour are superior to personality questionnaires, particularly when used on children, and are in any case less liable to faking. In the second place, they argued that conceptions such as neuroticism are essentially based on the notion of intercorrelated traits and measurements, and that twin studies carried out on single measures

Table 5-2

Holzinger H Values for 4 Components of Personality

Component	Boys		Girls	
	Under 55 months	Over 55 months	Under 55 months	Over 55 months
Emotionality	.55	.76*	.71*	.69*
Activity	.83*	.73*	.24	.70*
Sociability	.72*	.42	.36	.22
Impulsivity	.87	.86*	—	.66*

*$p < .01$.

Source: Buss, A. H., Plomin, R., & Willerman, L. The inheritance of temperaments. *Journal of Personality*, 1973, 41, 513–524.

confound the issue by mixing up variance due to the trait under investigation and specific variance relative to the test in question. They suggested, therefore, that a whole battery of tests should be given and factor analysed and that a score based on a combination of tests having the highest saturations with the factor in question should be used. In addition, they suggested that these factor scores should be validated against some form of external control; in their own work they did so by comparing experimental groups of children under treatment at a child guidance clinic with normal children in school, demonstrating significant differences on "neuroticism" between the two groups of children (Eysenck, H. J., & Prell, 1952).

Using this approach, H. J. Eysenck and Prell found that the factor score derived from all the tests gave an intraclass correlation of .851 for identical twins and of .217 for fraternal twins; this factor score showed a greater difference between identical and fraternal twins than any single constituent test, thus suggesting that it was indeed a general factor of neuroticism which was inherited rather than specific variance for any single test. The Holzinger h^2 coefficient showed a hereditary determination of .810 if we are willing to assume that this coefficient can indeed be used to measure hereditary determination in this manner.

In another, similar study, H. J. Eysenck (1956) reported results on a battery of tests of intelligence, extraversion, and autonomic activity. Again, intraclass correlations for identical and fraternal twins were calculated for three factors corresponding to these concepts rather than individual tests. For extraversion, the correlation for identical twins was .50; for fraternal ones, −.33: for the autonomic factor, the two correlations were, respectively, .93 and .72. For intelligence, the values were .82 and .38. Holzinger's h^2 statistic was calculated for all three factors, giving very similar results in the neighbourhood of .7 for all three. The appearance of a negative intraclass correlation for the fraternal twins is unusual, and H. J. Eysenck (1956) concluded:

[It seems] likely that this value represents a chance deviation from a true correlation of zero, or of some slight positive value, an assumption strengthened by the fact that a correlation of the observed size is not statistically significant. Under the circumstances, however, we cannot regard the h^2

statistic derived for the factor of extraversion as having very much meaning. . . . Much more reliance fortunately can be placed on the significance of the differences between identical and fraternal twins for this factor which. . . is fully significant.

The results of the Eysenck studies give values indicating a greater influence of hereditary causes than would be true of the other studies quoted so far. Apart from the possibility of chance deviations, it may be suggested that the following causes have possibly been operative: (a) behavioural tests are more likely than questionnaires to reveal deep-seated constitutional features of the personality; (b) factor scores are more reliable and valid than single tests; and (c) the measures selected have been chosen on the basis of a theory of personality that perhaps has more experimental and theoretical backing than the theory that gave rise to the measures used by the earlier workers. It is possible that any or all of these causes may have been operative, and it must be left to future investigation to discover to what extent these hypotheses can be upheld.

CLINICAL AND CONCORDANCE STUDIES

Heritability estimates, using questionnaires or objective laboratory tests, give an unequivocal indication of the importance of genetic factors in determining a person's neuroticism and extraversion; similar results are produced when we turn to concordance studies of criminals and neurotics. These are relevant when we consider that theoretically (and in actual fact) neurotics tend to fall into the N+E− quadrant, while criminals fall into the N+E+ quadrant (Eysenck, H. J., 1970; Eysenck, H. J., & Eysenck, S. B. G., 1969). If these relationships are truly causal, then we would expect greater concordance for MZ twins than for DZ twins; this is of course what has been the general finding. Table 5-3 shows concordance figures for criminality, Table 5-4 for neurosis. It will be seen that of almost 800 pairs of twins, concordance is shown for criminality by MZ twins in 55% of all cases, by DZ twins in only 13% of all cases, i.e., in a ratio of over 4 to 1. For neurosis, the ratio is only 2 to 1, out of over 300 pairs of twins.

Other data, e.g., from foster children, support the conclusion that crime and neurosis are in part produced by a genetic

Table 5-3

Concordance Rates for Criminality: Identical and Fraternal Twins

Author and date	Identical		Fraternal	
	Proportion	Percent	Proportion	Percent
Lange, 1929	10/3	77	2/15	12
Legras, 1932	4/0	100	0/5	0
Rosanoff, Handy, & Plesset, 1934	25/12	68	6/54	10
Krantz, 1936	20/11	65	23/20	53
Stumpfl, 1936	11/7	61	7/12	37
Borgström, 1939	3/1	75	2/3	40
Yoshimasu, 1961	17/11	61	2/16	11
Hayashi, 1967	11/4	73	3/2	60
Christiansen, 1968, 1970	27/54	33	23/340	6
Total	128/103	55	68/467	13

Source: Eysenck, H. J. *The inequality of man.* London: Temple Smith, 1973.

predisposition (Eysenck, H. J., 1973.) A review of clinical work on the genetic aspects of anxiety, specifically, is given by Slater and Shields (1969). They concluded that "genetic factors play a part in determining the predisposition to anxiety [p. 70]."

All the studies cited so far depend on three hypotheses that may be of doubtful standing. First, it is assumed that MZ twins are in fact 100% identical with respect to heredity; this is almost certainly untrue (Eysenck, H. J., 1967), and calculations based on

Table 5-4

Concordance Rates for Neurosis: Identical and Fraternal Twins

Author and date	Identical		Fraternal	
	Proportion	Percent	Proportion	Percent
Slater, 1953	2/6	25	8/35	19
Ihda, 1960	10/10	50	2/3	40
Braconi, 1961	18/2	90	13/17	43
Tienari, 1963	12/9	57	[not included]	
Parker, 1964, 1965	7/3	70	4/7	30
Shields & Slater, 1966	25/37	40	13/71	15
Total	76/67	59	40/133	30

Source: Eysenck, H. J. *The inequality of man.* London: Temple Smith, 1973.

this hypothesis seriously *underestimate* the contribution of heredity to an unknown extent. Second, it is assumed that the fact that twins are MZ or DZ does not by itself cause parents and others to treat them more or less alike. The evidence suggests that this is not so, and that MZ twins are treated more alike; however, Scarr (1966c) presented evidence to show that this factor is of no great importance in this connection. She examined the child-rearing practices of mothers who were wrong about the zygosity of their twins, and found that actual zygosity had more effect on child-rearing practices than did the (incorrect) zygosity assumed by the mother. Insofar as this difference is important, it would lead us to *overestimate* the contribution of heredity to an unknown extent. Third, it is assumed that conditions in the womb are alike for MZ and DZ twins; this is not so. MZ twins show much more evidence of serious interference of one twin with the other; the effects of this would show up as environmental effects, although it would be stretching the usual meaning of that word to include intrauterine conditions of this kind. On the whole, these three departures from the model are likely to lead to an underestimation of hereditary contributions; and conclusions are therefore likely to be on the conservative side (Eysenck, H. J., 1975).

APPLICATIONS OF THE GENETIC MODEL

We must now turn to a consideration of the most recent work, using more adequate models and methods of analysis. A suitable start is a study by Shields (1962), in which he used a self-rating questionnaire devised by the writer which is very similar to the MPI, sharing a number of items in common with it; this questionnaire provides scores for extraversion and neuroticism. Shields applied it and two tests of intelligence to a collection of pairs of twins who had been separated from one another in childhood; he also had a control group of twins who had been brought up together. There were 44 MZ, 44 nonseparated MZ control pairs, and 32 pairs of DZ twins, 11 of which had been brought up apart. His findings with the questionnaire are given in Table 5-5. It will be seen that identical twins are much more alike than fraternal twins, regardless of whether they are brought up together or in separation; in each case the twins brought up separately are more

Table 5-5

Intraclass Correlation Coefficients for Monozygotic (MZ)
Twins Brought Up Together (C), MZ Twins
Brought Up Apart (S), and Dizygotic
(DZ) Twins Brought Up Together

Item	MZ		DZ
	C	S	
Height	+0.94	+0.82	+0.44
Weight	+0.81	+0.37	+0.56
Dominoes	+0.71	+0.76	−0.05
Mill Hill	+0.74	+0.74	+0.38
Combined Intelligence	+0.76	+0.77	+0.51
Extraversion	+0.42	+0.61	−0.17
Neuroticism	+0.38	+0.53	+0.11

Source: Shields, J. *Monozygotic twins.* London: Oxford University Press, 1962.

alike than twins brought up together. These results are therefore in good accord with those originally reported by Newman, Freeman, and Holzinger as well as with those of later writers. They are rather more clear-cut perhaps, due to two possible causes: (a) the subjects of the experiment were adults rather than children, and consequently the questionnaires applied to them much more readily than they would apply to children; and (b) the questionnaires used had been elaborated for many years on the basis of factor analytic studies of personality and were consequently perhaps more reliable and valid than those used earlier.

Table 5-5 shows that the fraternal twins have a negative intraclass correlation for extraversion, very much as in the study of H. J. Eysenck (1956). Again this intercorrelation is not significantly different from zero, but the coincidence is certainly striking, although I cannot present any reasonable hypothesis which would account for such a negative correlation.

Results similar to those of Shields were reported by J. S. Price (personal communication, 1969), who tested 102 pairs of MZ twins, of whom 57 pairs had been living apart, and 45 pairs living together. Using the EPI, he found that for N the former pairs showed an intra-pair correlation of .69, as compared with one of .57 for the latter pairs; for all pairs $r = .65$. For E, correlations were .45 and .29, averaging .38 over all pairs. Thus, here, too, twins living apart were more alike than twins living together.

So far we are still in the field of classic "heritability"; we now turn to the reanalysis of Shields' data by Jinks and Fulker (1970). They were concerned with the construction of genotype-environment models, including interaction variables, and in doing so they went far beyond the simplistic classical models. As they pointed out, even in the absence of genotype-environment interaction, partitioning the total variation between two components, the genetic G and the environmental E, must lead on to a partitioning of these two components into within-family and between-family (G_1 and G_2, E_1 and E_2.) Classical formulae ignore explicity important sources of variation (Holzinger's H ignores G_2 and E_2, for example.) Nor do classical formulae enable us to test for interaction, or for dominance, or for assortative mating. Jinks and Fulker developed a model that does enable us to do these things, and then apply this model to the data collected by Shields and briefly described previously. What is the outcome of their analysis?

The model requires first of all that the four groups used (male and female MZ and DZ twins) should be homogeneous with respect to N (the first variable to be discussed); the data pass this test. The second assumption to test is the possible importance of genotype-environment interaction. There is no evidence of GE_1 or GE_2, nor are correlated environments found to be a complication in these data. "Thus on the basis of these tests we are justified in fitting the simple G and E model to the data."

When the calculations are done (they are given in detail in the original paper), G and E_1 are clearly significantly greater than 0, while E_2 is not. There is some slight indication of assortative mating, but the figures are not significant.

At the same time, the absence of dominant gene action is clearly indicated by the fact that $G_1 > G_2$. The absence of dominant gene action strongly suggests that an intermediate level of neuroticism has been favoured by natural selection, and constitutes the population optimum for this personality trait [Jinks & Fulker, 1970].

Further tests confirm the adequacy of the simple model, and "this simplified model, which fits the data extremely well, . . . may now be used to calculate heritabilities with some degree of confidence." The broad heritability = narrow heritability = .54, which is fully significant. Cattell's nurture : nature ratios were also calculated and indicated that although environment is more important than genotype in producing differences among siblings, the differences in neuroticism observed between families is entirely genotypic in origin. "Evidently cultural and class differences have no effect on this major personality dimension."

We now turn to the analysis of extraversion scores. Here too "we conclude that the types of family represent reasonably adequate samples from the same population." Testing for interaction, it is found:

> there is evidence of a certain amount of GE_1, but not GE_2 . . . Introvert genotypes are more susceptible to environmental influences than extravert genotypes, the latter being relatively impervious. This finding is, of course, fully consistent with Eysenck's (1967) theory that the introvert is more conditionable than the extravert [Jinks & Fulker, 1970].

Broad heritability was calculated as accounting for 67% of variation, but it should be added that this figure depends on certain assumptions that must be made because the simple model does not fit the data as well as it does in the case of neuroticism. Jinks and Fulker raise the possibility that failure may be due to "competition" (intrauterine or later), particularly between DZ twins; Eysenck's (1956) data, giving a negative intraclass correlation on E for DZ twins, support this view. Jinks and Fulker discuss the reasons for the failure of the simple model in some detail; it would take us too far to follow them in this.

An interesting further analysis of some of these data was undertaken by Fulker and Eaves (Unpublished manuscript). Using only MZ twins pairs, they plotted mean scores for each pair against differences, arguing that mean scores were the best available estimate of the degree of extraversion (or neuroticism) of the pair while the difference would indicate the action of environment (and errors of measurement.) These plots are shown in Figs. 5-5 and 5-6; they are clearly bowed, rather than linear, and indicate very

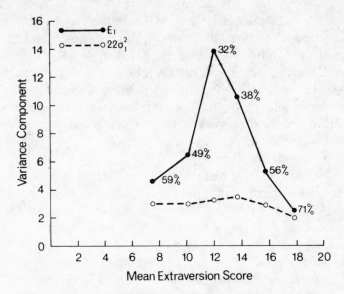

Fig. 5-5. Plot of means and differences between monozygotic twins on extraversion questionnaire. Percentage
figures indicate heritability at different points of the
extraversion continuum.

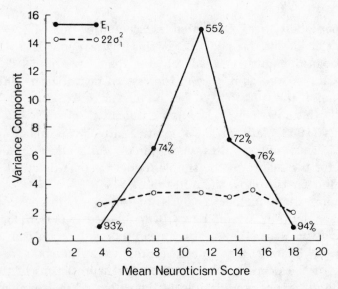

Fig. 5-6. Plot of means and differences between monozygotic twins on neuroticism questionnaire. Percentage figures indicate heritability at different points of the neuroticism continuum.

clearly that environmental factors are more important in the middle range of scores than at the extremes. In part this must be a statistical artefact; very high or low mean scores are incompatible with large within-pair differences. However, this is clearly not the whole story; when the same analysis was done on IQ data, the plotted data were almost entirely linear, with a very weak quadratic component. The data suggest, then, that hereditary influences are stronger for E and N when these personality traits are either very strong or very weak; ambiverts are more determined in their conduct by environmental determinants. This finding may be worthy of being followed up in future work.

FURTHER STUDIES OF THE MODEL

So far, we have assumed that factors like neuroticism and extraversion are unitary; this has been disputed, and Eaves (1973) published a genetic analysis of the PEN scale in which, while N appeared as a unitary factor, E items were found "not to form a single genotypic factor, possible because the observed phenotypic unity of E depends on the correlated environmental modification of more than one underlying genotypic factor [p. 281]." An exhaustive genetical analysis of this problem was undertaken by Eaves and Eysenck (in press); using a much larger number of twins than any previous study, they subjected separately measured traits of "sociability" and "impulsivity" (the two major components of E) to a test of model fitting. They found that between 60% and 70% of the "reliable" variation was genetically determined, and that both genetic and environmental factors contributed to the covariation of sociability and impulsiveness. "Combining Soc and Imp scores by addition to provide a measure of extraversion provides the most powerful single means of discriminating between individuals with respect to the genetical and environmental determinants of their responses to the Soc and Imp items of the questionnaire." The data were consistent with the view that the genetical variation was mainly additive, and there was no evidence for a large effect of the family environment on any of the traits studied. Mating was effectively random for the traits in question, and the genetical and environmental determinants of variation were homogeneous over sexes, suggesting that the effects of sex linkage and sex limitation are negligible. More detailed analyses of this kind, using variation and covariation of primary traits in the genetical analysis of the higher order factors like extraversion and neuroticism, will undoubtedly provide us with much clearer evidence for the precise action of genetic factors in the causation of individual differences in personality.

It will be obvious that certain aspects of the genetic model can be investigated directly, as well as in terms of the biometrical genetical formulae. One example is assortative mating (V_{AM}), which can to some extent be studied by correlating the relevant personality inventory scores for married couples. (This is only partly relevant, because it is possible that married couples change after marriage; ideally one ought to have the personality test scores of men and women before marriage, but this is rather difficult.) A review of the literature reveals that the degree of assortative mating for N and E is slight or nonexistent; this is in good agreement with the results of the biometrical work reviewed (Eysenck, H. J., 1975.) In a recent study, which did not form part of that review, H. J. Eysenck (1974) tested 241 couples with a personality questionnaire; correlations between spouses were .06 for E and .22 for N. The figure for N is significant, but not high enough to affect the issue; this is in accord with the Jinks and Fulker analysis which suggested some slight degree of assortative mating, for N, but not for E. We thus have external support for the accuracy of the biometrical genetical analysis.

Several recent large-scale reviews, in several different languages, have surveyed the field of genetic influences on personality and anxiety (Bracken, 1969; Roubertoux & Carlier, 1973; Shields, 1973); all are agreed on the important role heredity has to play in this field. In particular, the major personality dimensions of N and E, and their constituent factors, emerge again and again in the various studies surveyed as being determined to an important degree (usually in excess of 50%) by heredity. This leaves little doubt that it is not feasible to study anxiety without taking these genetic components into account; research designs that attempt to assess only environmental variables inevitably lead to ambiguous conclusions that leave the door open to alternative, genetic interpretations. There are good reasons for regarding the estimates of heritability for both E and N reviewed in these pages as underestimates; few authors have corrected their figures for V_e, for instance. Failure of the tests employed to have perfect validity also detracts from the "true" heritability of the traits in question. H. J.

Eysenck and Prell, using a whole battery of tests for the measurement of N, obtained higher heritability estimates than other authors; their results indicated that the use of single tests is less likely to optimize findings. But even when we take up the minimum estimates found in the literature, we must conclude that something like one-half of the total variance in the personality variables associated with anxiety is accounted for by heredity. This is an important finding, and it is to be hoped that future work will allow us a more detailed breakdown of this figure and permit us to construct a more detailed model than is currently available. The methods of analysis are now available for carrying out this task, and we know enough about the demands of the experimental design to be able to carry out these improvements (Eaves, 1969, 1970, 1972 a, b); it will not be long before our knowledge in this field will be adequate to the demands we would like to make on it.

REFERENCES

Barr, R. F., & McConaghy, N. A general factor of conditionability: A study of galvanic skin responses and penile responses. *Behaviour Research and Therapy*, 1972, **10**, 215-228.

Becker, V. C. A comparison of the factor structure and other properties of the 16PF and the Guilford Martin personality inventories. *Educational and Psychological Measurement*, 1961, **21**, 393-404.

Block, J. P. Monozygotic twin similarity in multiple psychophysiologic parameters and measures. In J. Wortis (Ed.), *Recent advances in biological psychiatry*. Vol. 9. New York: J. Wiley, 1967.

Borgatta, E. F. The coincidence of subtests in four personality inventories. *Journal of Social Psychology*, 1962, **56**, 227-244.

Borgstrom, C. P. Eine Serie von Kriminellen Zwillingen. *Archiv für Rassenwissenschaft und Gesellschaftsbiologie*, 1939, **33**, 334-343.

Bracken, H. V. Humangenetische Psychologie. In P. E. Becker (Ed.), *Humangenetik*. Vol. 1/2. Stuttgart: G. Thieme, 1969.

Braconi, L. Le psiconeurosi & le psiocosi nei jemelli. *Acta geneticae medicae Gemellologiae*, 1961, **10**, 100-136.

Brown, A. M., Stafford, R. E., & Vandenberg, S. G. Twins: Behavioral differences. *Child Development*, 1967, **38**, 1035-1064.

Buss, A. H., Plomin, R., & Willerman, L. The inheritance of temperaments. *Journal of Personality*, 1973, **41**, 513-524.

Carter, H. D. Twin similarities in personality traits. *Character and Personality*, 1935, **4**, 61-78.

Cattell, R. B. The multiple abstract variance analysis equations and solutions for nature-nurture research on continuous variables. *Psychological Review*, 1960, **67**, 353-372.

Cattell, R. B. Methodological and conceptual advances in evaluating hereditary and environmental influences and their interactions. In S. G. Vandenberg (Ed.), *Methods and goals in human behavior genetics*. New York: Academic Press, 1965.

Cattell, R. B., Blewett, D. B., & Beloff, J. R. The inheritance of personality. *American Journal of Human Genetics*, 1955, 7, 122-146.

Christiansen, K. O. Threshold of tolerance in various population groups illustrated by results from Danish Criminological Twin Study. In A. V. S. de Renck & R. Porter (Eds.), *The mentally abnormal offender. A Ciba Foundation symposium*. London: Churchill, 1968.

Christiansen, K. O. Crime in a Danish twin population. *Acta geneticae medicae Gemellologiae*, 1970, 19, 323-326.

Eaves, L. J. The genetic analysis of continuous variation: A comparison of experimental designs applicable to human data: II Estimation of heritability and comparison of environmental components. *British Journal of Mathematical and Statistical Psychology*, 1969, 22, 131-137.

Eaves, L. J. *British Journal of Mathematical and Statistical Psychology*, 1970, 23, 189-198.

Eaves, L. J. Computer simulation of sample size and experimental design in human psychogenetics. *Psychological Bulletin*, 1972, 77, 144-152. (a)

Eaves, L. J. The multivariate analysis of certain genotype-environment interactions. *Behavioural Genetics*, 1972, 2, 241-247. (b)

Eaves, L. J. The structure of genotypic and environmental covariation for personality measurements: Analysis of the PEN. *British Journal of Social and Clinical Psychology*. 1973, 12, 275-282.

Eaves, L. J. & Eysenck, H. J. The nature of extraversion: A genetical analysis. *Journal of Personality and Social Psychology*, 1976, (in press).

Eysenck, H. J. The inheritance of extraversion-introversion. *Acta psychologica*, 1956, 12, 95-110.

Eysenck, H. J. *The biological basis of personality*. Springfield, Ill.: Charles C Thomas, 1967.

Eysenck, H. J. *Crime and personality*. London: Paladin, 1970.

Eysenck, H. J. On the choice of personality tests for research and prediction. *Journal of Behavioural Science*, 1971, 1, 85-89.

Eysenck, H. J. Primaries or second-order factors: A critical consideration of Cattell's 16 PF battery. *British Journal of Social and Clinical Psychology*, 1972, 11, 205-269.

Eysenck, H. J. *The inequality of man*. London: Temple Smith, 1973.

Eysenck, H. J. Personality, premarital sexual permissiveness and assortative mating. *Journal of Sexual Research*, 1974, 10(1), 47-51.

Eysenck, H. J. Genetic factors in personality development. In A. R. Kaplan (Ed.), *Human behavior genetics*. Springfield, Ill.: Charles C Thomas, 1975.

Eysenck, H. J., & Broadhurst, P. L. Experiments with animals: Introduction. In H. J. Eysenck (Ed.), *Experiments in motivation*. London: Pergamon Press, 1964.

Eysenck, H. J., & Eysenck, S. B. G. *Personality structure and measurement*. London: Routledge & Kegan Paul, 1969.

Eysenck, H. J., & Prell, D. B. The inheritance of neuroticism: An experimental study. *Journal of Mental Science*, 1951, 97, 441-465.

Eysenck, H. J., & Prell, D. A note on the differentiation of normal and neurotic children by means of objective tests. *Journal of Clinical Psychology*, 1952, 8, 202-204.

Eysenck, H. J., & Rachman, S. *The causes and cures of neurosis.* London: Routledge & Kegan Paul, 1965.

Eysenck, S. B. G. *The Junior E.P.I. Manual.* London: University of London Press, 1965.

Fisher, R. A. The correlation between relatives on the supposition of Mendelian inheritance. *Transactions of the Royal Society (Edinburgh)*, 1918, 52, 399-433.

Freedman, D. An ethological approach to the genetical study of human behavior. In S. G. Vandenberg (Ed.), *Methods and goals in human behavior genetics.* New York: Academic Press, 1965.

Geer, J. H. The development of a scale to measure fear. *Behaviour Research and Therapy*, 1965, 3, 45-53.

Goodman, H. O., Luke, J. E., Rosen, S., & Hackel, E. Heritability in dental caries, certain oral microflora and salivary components. *American Journal of Human Genetics*, 1959, 11, 263-273.

Gottesman, I. I. Heritability of personality: A demonstration. *Psychological Monographs*, 1963, 77, No. 9.

Gottesman, I. I. Personality of natural selection. In S. G. Vandenberg (Ed.), *Methods and goals in human behavior genetics.* New York: Academic Press, 1965.

Gottesman, I. I. Genetic variance in adaptive personality traits. *Journal of Child Psychology and Psychiatry*, 1966, 7, 199-208.

Greif, S. Untersuchungen zur deutschen Ubersetzung des 16PF Fragebogens. *Psychologische Beiträge*, 1970, 12, 186-213.

Hayashi, S. A study of juvenile delinquency in twins. In: H. Mitsuda, (Ed.), *Problems in nosological classification.* Tokyo: Igaku Shoin, 1967.

Holzinger, K. J. The relative effect of nature and nurture influences on twin differences. *Journal of Educational Psychology*, 1929, 20, 245-248.

Howarth, E., & Browne, A. An item factor analysis of the 16PF. *Personality*, 1971, 2, 117-139.

Ihda, S. A study of neurosis by twin method. *Psychiatria et Neurologica Japonica*, 1960, 63, 861-892.

Jinks, J., & Fulker, D. V. A comparison of the biometrical genetical MAVA and classical approaches to the analysis of human behavior. *Psychological Bulletin*, 1970, 73, 311-349.

Jost, H., & Sontag, L. W. The genetic factor in autonomic nervous system functions. *Psychological Medicine*, 1944, 6, 308-310.

Juel-Nielsen, N. *Individual and environment.* Copenhagen: Munksgaard, 1965.

Koch, N. L. *Twins and twin relatives.* Chicago: University of Chicago Press, 1966.

Krantz, H. *Lebensschicksale Krimineller Zwillinge.* Berlin: Springer, 1936.

Kryshova, N. A., Beliaeva, Z., Dmitrieva, A. E., Zhilinskaia, U. S., & Pervor, L. G. Investigation of the higher nervous activity and of certain vegetative features in twins. *Soviet Psychology and Psychiatry*, 1963, 1, 36-41.

Lader, M. H., & Wing, L. Physiological measures, sedative drugs, and morbid anxiety. London: Oxford University Press, 1966.

Landy, F. J., & Gaupp, L. S. A factor analysis of the fear survey schedule—III. *Behaviour Research and Therapy*, 1971, 9, 89-93.

Lange, J. *Verbrechen als Schicksal*. Leipzig: Thieme, 1929.

LeGras, A. M. *Psychose en Criminaliteit bij Tweelingen*. Utrecht: University of Utrecht, 1932.

Levonian, E. A statistical analysis of the 16 Personality Factor Questionnaire. *Educational and Psychological Measurement*. 1961, 21, 589-596. (a)

Levonian, E. Personality measurement with items selected from the 16 PF Questionnaire. *Educational and Psychological Measurement*, 1961, 21, 937-946. (b)

Lindzey, G., Loehlin, J., Manosevitz, M., & Thiessen, D. Behavioral genetics. *Annual Review of Psychology*, 1971, 22, 39-94.

Martin, I., & Levey, S. B. The genesis of the classical conditioned response. London: Pergamon Press, 1969.

Mather, K. Biometrical genetics: The study of continuous variation. London: Methuen, 1949.

Mather, K., & Jinks, J. L. *Biometrical genetics*. (2nd ed.) London: Chapman & Hall, 1971.

Neel, J. V., & Schull, W. J. *Human heredity*. Chicago: University of Chicago Press, 1954.

Newman, H. N., Freeman, F. S., & Holzinger, K. J. *Twins: A study of heredity and environment*. Chicago: University of Chicago Press, 1937.

Nicholls, R. C. The national merit twin study. In S. G. Vandenberg (Ed.), *Methods and goals in human behavior genetics*. New York: Academic Press, 1965.

Nicholls, R. C. The resemblance of twins in personality and interests. *National Merit Scholarship Corporation Research Report*, 1966, 8, 1-23.

Parker, N. Close identification in twins discordant for obsessional neurosis. *British Journal of Psychiatry*, 1964, 110, 496-504.

Parker, N. Twins: A psychiatric study. Unpublished M.D. thesis, University of Queensland, Australia, 1965.

Partanen, J., Bruun, K., & Markkanen, T. Inheritance of drinking behavior. Vol. 14. Helsinki: Finnish Foundations for Alcohol Study, 1966.

Peterson, D. R. The age generality of personality factors derived from ratings. *Educational Psychological Measurement*, 1960, 20, 461-474.

Redlich, F. C., & Freedman, D. T. *The theory and practice of psychiatry*. London: Basic Books, 1966.

Reznikoff, M., & Honeyman, G. M.M.P.I. profiles of monozygotic and dizygotic twin pairs. *Journal of Consulting Psychology*, 1967, 31, 100.

Roberts, R. G. Some concepts and methods in quantitative genetics. In J. Hirsch (Ed.), *Behavior—Genetic Analysis*. New York: McGraw-Hill, 1967.

Rosanoff, A. J., Handy, L. H., & Plesset, I. R. Criminality and delinquency in twins. *Journal of Criminal Law and Criminology*, 1934, 24, 929-934.

Rosenbaum, R. Stimulus generalization as a function of level of experimentally induced anxiety. *Journal of Experimental Psychology*, 1953, 45, 35-43.

Rosenbaum, R. Stimulus generalization as a function of clinical anxiety. *Journal of Abnormal and Social Psychology*, 1956, 53, 281-285.

Roubertoux, P., & Carlier, M. Analyse génétique des comportements: II. Les résultats. *Annee Psychologique*, 1973, 73, 151-223.

Rubin, B. M., Katkin, E. S., Weiss, B. W., & Efram, J. S. Factor analysis of a fear survey schedule. *Behaviour Research and Therapy*, 1968, 6, 65-75.

Savage, R. D., & Eysenck, H. J. The definition and measurement of emotionality. In H. J. Eysenck (Ed.), *Experiments in motivation*. London: Pergamon Press, 1964.

Scarr, S. Genetic factors in activity motivation. *Child Development*, 1966, 37, 663-673. (a)

Scarr, S. The origin of individual differences—adjective check list scores. *Journal of Consulting Psychology*. 1966, 30, 354-357. (b)

Scarr, S. Environmental bias in twin studies. Paper presented at the Second Invitational Conference on Human Behavior Genetics, University of Louisville, May 2, 1966. (c)

Scarr, S. Social introversion-extraversion as a heritable response. *Child Development*, 1969, 40, 823-852.

Schoenfeldt, L. F. The hereditary components of the project TALENT two-day test battery. *Measurement and Evaluation Guide*, 1968, 1, 130-140.

Sells, S. B., Demaree, R. G., & Will, D. P. *A taxonomic investigation of personality*. Tex.: Christian Institute of Behavior Research, 1968.

Shields, J. *Monozygotic twins*. London: Oxford University Press, 1962.

Shields, J. Heredity and psychological abnormality. In H. J. Eysenck (Ed.), *Handbook of abnormal psychology*. London: Pitman, 1973.

Shields, J., & Slater, E. La similarité du diagnostic chez les jumeaux et le problème de la specificité biologique dans les neuroses et les troubles de la personalité. *Evolution Psychiatrique*, 1966, 31, 441-451.

Slater, E. Psychotic and neurotic illnesses in twins. *Medical Research Council; Special Report Series*, No. 278. London: H.M.S.O., 1953.

Slater, E., & Shields, J. Genetical aspects of anxiety. *British Journal of Psychiatry* (*Studies of anxiety*, Special Publication No. 3.), 1969.

Stumpfl, F. *Die Ursprünge des Verbrechens dargestellt am Lebenslauf von Zwillingen*. Leipzig: Thieme, 1936.

Thompson, V. R., & Wilde, G. J. S. Behavior genetics. In S. Valman (Ed.), *Handbook of psychology*. New York: McGraw-Hill, 1971.

Ticnari, P. Psychiatric illnesses in identical twins. *Acta psychiatrica Scandinavica. Supplement*, 171, 1963.

Timm, U. Reliabilität und Faktorenstruktur von Cattells 16PF test bei einer deutschen Stichprobe. *Zeitschrift für experimentelle und angewandte Psychologie*, 1968, 15, 354-373.

Ullman, L. P., & Krasner, L. *A psychological approach to abnormal behavior*. London: Prentice-Hall, 1969.

Vandenberg, S. G. The hereditary abilities study: Hereditary components in a psychological test battery. *American Journal of Human Genetics*, 1962, 14, 220-237.

Vandenberg, S. G. Contribution of twin research to psychology. *Psychological Bulletin*, 1966, 66, 327-352.

Vandenberg, S. G., Clark, P. J., & Samuels, I. Psychophysiological reactions of twins: Heritability factors in galvanic skin resistance, heartbeat, and breathing rates. *Eugenics Quarterly*, 1965, 12, 3-10.

Vandenberg, S. G., Comrey, S. L., & Stafford, L. E. Hereditary factors in personality and attitude scales in twin studies. Research Report No. 16, Louisville twin study, University of Louisville, 1967.

Wilde, G. J. S. Inheritance of personality traits. *Acta Psychologica*, 1964, 22, 37-51.

Young, J. P. D., Fenton, G. S., & Lader, M. H. The inheritance of neurotic traits in a twin study of the Middlesex Hospital Questionnaire. *British Journal of Psychiatry*, 1971, 119, 393-398.

Zubin, J., Eron, L. D., & Schumer, F. An experimental approach to projective techniques. London: Wiley & Son, 1965.

6

FEAR OF FAILURE AS
A SELF-REINFORCING
MOTIVE SYSTEM

Heinz Heckhausen

Ruhr University
Bochum, German Federal Republic

The exploding research on achievement motivation in the early 1950's saw, rather soon, the necessity to conceptualize an avoidance motive. However, the emerging fear-of-failure (FF) motive remained, so to speak, a step-twin of the need for achievement, the straightforward hope-of-success (HS) motive. Like a problem child, the FF motive had not been loved in his own right. It was taken care of because it was just there and soon proved useful to set its buoyant brother motive into a still more radiant light.

MEASURES OF FEAR OF FAILURE

American researchers, particularly the Atkinson group, are content with using a self-report measure for the FF motive, primarily the Test Anxiety Questionnaire (TAQ) by George Mandler and Seymour Sarason (1952). For the achievement (HS) motive, researchers continue to rely on a projective TAT measure, The TAQ measures self-perceived symptoms of psychophysiological arousal in test situations. There are, however, thematic apperceptive measures

117

of the FF motive. Birney, Burdick and Teevan (1969) developed the hostile press (HP) code, which taps rather indirect expressions of task failure, such as vague environmental threat, loss of affiliative objects, legal retaliation, personal reprimand, and major assault on well-being. The German code for scoring FF (Heckhausen, 1963) is a parallel construction to an HS code and emphasizes direct expressions of need to avoid failure, such as anticipation of possible task failure, negative affect about failure, action to avoid or undo failure, failure outcome, negative social consequences as being blamed, and preoccupation with failure as the theme of the story. Finally, there is a new semi-projective device developed by Schmalt (1973a). It consists of depicted achievement situations, sampled across a wide range of activities, and of fixed response-statements taken from TAT scoring codes for HS and FF. This so-called grid test yields, besides intensity scores for both motives, extensity scores indicating the range across situations that elicits HS and FF tendencies. The grid test has a built-in correlation with our TAT measure. With this exception, all measures do not correlate; but they do have a considerable overlap in construct validity. Thus, the measure testifies to the intricacies of the FF motive.

CONSTRUCT VALIDITY RESEARCH

There exist rich nomological networks for the FF motive. They include such diverse indexes as risk-taking, performance, time perspective, volunteering in experiments, conformity, memory, and causal attribution bias (see Atkinson & Feather, 1966; Birney et al., 1969; Heckhausen, 1967, 1968; Meyer, 1973; Schmalt, 1973b). Only the last index, causal attribution, is discussed in this chapter.

The conceptions of an FF motive construct are still far from being unitary. This is no wonder, considering that avoidance tendencies are by their very nature more complicated than approach tendencies. One conception, held by Atkinson (1964), construes FF as a purely inhibitive force. This makes good sense because his risk-taking model is constructed in such a way as to explain why persons in whom FF is stronger than HS prefer low or high risks and avoid intermediate levels of task difficulty. Such a preference is the reversed mirror image of what HS subjects so unshakably keep doing. Research rarely shows the postulated

U-shaped distribution of risk preference (e.g., Heckhausen, 1963; Schmalt, 1973b). From the data it appears that FF subjects, compared with HS subjects, avoid intermediate risks; further, there are constantly two subgroups, one preferring very easy goals and the other very hard goals. With FF as a pure inhibitive force, one wonders why FF subjects engage in achievement activities at all. One has always to assume extrinsic motives, like pleasing the experimenter. Among our students, FF subjects volunteer more readily for experiments than do HS subjects.

It is an oversimplification to conceive of the FF motive solely and always as an inhibitive force in the course of an achievement-related activity. Irrespective of whether a person generally tends to be rather fearful than confident, achievement may rank highly among his salient and current concerns. Depending on situational cues and the anticipation of action-outcome consequences to which these cues give rise, the FF motive may inhibit or may increase the vigor of achievement activity (cf. Birney et al., 1969). Quite in line with this view of motivation, anxiety researchers have begun to emphasize the distinction between trait anxiety and state anxiety (Spielberger, 1966; Wittmaier, 1974).

Performance is a case in point. Not only in easy tasks (Heckhausen, 1967) but also in difficult tasks, anxious subjects have been shown to do better than nonanxious subjects if the task is not presented as a failure threat. This has been demonstrated by Irwin Sarason (1961) using a self-report measure of anxiety and by Weiner (1966) using both a self-report and a TAT measure. Weiner's study, corroborated by Weiner and Schneider (1971), is noticeable because it falsifies the popular interference theory (Spence, Farber & McFann, 1956), according to which high trait anxiety and high task difficulty result in poor performance. It is not task difficulty per se but aroused failure anxiety as a motivating state that causes debilitating effects on performance in FF subjects. If subjects work on paired associates with high intralist competition and if one gives success feedback, FF or high anxious subjects do not worse on these difficult tasks but much better than HS or low anxious subjects.

The FF motive, however, after 20 years of research, poses still more mysteries than does the HS motive. Why is it, for instance, that one FF group constantly chooses extremely high risks instead of interchangeably high and low risks? The nearest explanation we have arrived at is that this FF group has a high total score including both avoidance and approach tendencies. Perhaps this may indicate some proneness to higher activation level in achievement settings or a proneness to some conscious or semiconscious strategy to spur own efforts through high aspirations. Perhaps the FF subject is attempting to impress the experimenter by good will and, at the same time, make clear that a failure is quite natural after having committed himself to such a high goal. All these explanations are far from being conclusive. What we did find, however, is that the direction of the affiliation motive makes a difference. A combination of high FF with high hope of affiliation (in contrast to fear of rejection) is the motivation pattern of the extremely high risk taker in level-of-aspiration experiments (Jopt, 1974; Schneider & Meise, in Schneider, 1973).

Is this an indication that extrinsic motives enter the scene? Not necessarily so. Ordinarly, failure is not only a personal affair, but also a social one. Among the anticipated failure consequences, i.e., among the motivating incentives, one may distinguish between self-reinforcement and external reinforcement, although both go together more often than not. Thus, we may conceive of an intrinsic FF motive system that includes incentives of social devaluation as well as incentives of self-esteem threat or self-punishment. Although I subscribe to an incentive theory of motivation, these distinctions between intrinsic and extrinsic consequences, between self-reinforcement and external reinforcement, or a combination of both, await further empirical clarification. The subcategories of our scoring code for FF, on closer scrutiny, have not turned out to be unitary, as is true with the HS scoring code. The FF code confounds two main factors—one a self-concept of lack of ability combined with a tendency actively to circumvent failure, the other one worry about failure (Schmalt, 1973b). Presently, we are looking for diverging action correlates in our laboratory.

DEVELOPMENT OF THE FEAR-OF-FAILURE MOTIVE

Whatever the dominant incentives in particular FF tendencies may be, we have been attracted by the idea of construing a motive as a self-reinforcing motive system. If the motive construct is justified at all, there must be some processes in the person that stabilize belief systems and action preferences over time and, to some degree, across situations—even contrafactually, i.e., in the face of contradictory facts. The longevity of the motive term as an explanatory construct for individual differences stems from the evidence that people are in some way independent of, and even resistant to, external reinforcement. A long series of successes does not change an FF outlook and behavior into the calm and aspiring confidence typical of HS persons. This holds, vice versa, for HS persons facing a long series of failures. What appears to be a deficient reality orientation and a lack of openness to relearning, is not a simple result of reinforcement history. That is to say, the FF motive is not the outcome of poor ability causing failures, and of failures causing negative external reinforcement by the social and physical environment. There is no notable difference in intelligence test scores, for instance, between FF and HS individuals. The same has been shown for test-anxious subjects (Sarason, Davidson, Lightall, Waite, & Ruebush, 1960).

Motive development is obviously more subtle and complicated than that. Level-of-aspiration research reveals that what defines success or failure—i.e., what constitutes the contingencies for self-reinforcement—is a subjective affair. To experience success or failure is the result of evaluative cognitions which, in their basic patterns, are already established in a person's motive system. If we assume these evaluative cognitions to be motive linked, they have, first, to be biased. Second, they are antecedents for self-reinforcement. Third, self-reinforcement is ultimately the process stabilizing consistency within, and difference between, individuals under comparable circumstances.

Two antecedent processes establish the contingencies for self-reinforcement. First, a comparison process evaluates the result of an action sequence. The actual outcome is compared to a standard or level of aspiration. (I will not go into details of standard setting.) If the outcome exceeds the standard, it is perceived as a success. If it remains below the standard, it is perceived as a failure (see Kanfer, 1971). But this is only half the story. Another process intervenes: causal attribution of success or failure as they are determined by the comparison process.

Causal Attribution

A great deal of data has been accumulated on the impact of causal attribution on affective consequences and expectancy shifts.

This research has mainly been stimulated by Bernard Weiner (1972), who combined Julian Rotter's (1954) distinction between locus of control and Fritz Heider's (1958) distinction between stable and variable forces into a fourfold table of causal factors, as follows: ability, a stable and internal factor; task difficulty, a stable and external factor; effort, a variable and internal factor; and good or bad luck, a variable and external factor (see Weiner, Frieze, Kukla, Reed, Rest, & Rosenbaum, 1971).

Now, if FF persons prefer very low or very high goals, there already are implications for causal attribution and for self-reinforcement. If one chooses low goals, success is easily accomplished; but one can hardly give oneself the credit for success. Retrospectively, the credit goes to facility of the task, an external factor that does not entitle one to self-reward. If one chooses high goals, success is a rare and lucky event, ascribed to good luck, the other external factor. Therefore, by their risk-taking preference, FF people create conditions that minimize their personal responsibility for success.

So far, causal attribution of success appears quite reasonable and realistic. On closer inspection, however, it is somewhat twisted. Even if one controls for individual differences in expectation levels prior to performance and if one, correspondingly, induces success and failure after performance, FF individuals tend to ascribe success more to external (especially good luck) and less to internal factors, compared with HS individuals (Meyer, 1973). The causal attribution bias is still more pronounced in the case of failure. FF subjects tend to ascribe failure more to lack of their own ability than to such external factors as task difficulty and bad luck. Conversely, HS subjects are rather reluctant to ascribe failure to lack of ability. If an external factor does not lend itself readily as an obvious cause, they preferably ascribe failure to a momentary lack of effort which may be compensated for the next time (Weiner & Kukla, 1970; Weiner & Potepan, 1970; Meyer, 1973).

In summary, there is a pervading asymmetry in the motive-linked patterns of causal attribution bias. Under comparable conditions, HS persons credit themselves more for their successes than for their failures, and FF persons credit themselves more for their failures than for their successes. Conceivably, the causal attribution asymmetry leads to a corresponding asymmetry of affective consequences in self-reinforcement. This, in fact, has been confirmed in experiments by Weiner and Potepan (1970), Weiner, Heck-hausen, Meyer, and Cook (1972), and Meyer (1973). The asymmetrical affect balance within and between the two motive groups, based on their preferred causal ascription for success and failure, does not rest on differential bias in the locus of control dimension alone. In reaction to failure, it depends on the stability dimension. FF persons have a bias for lack of ability explanations and HS persons for lack of effort explanations. Within both internal causes, lack of ability leads to more negative affect in self-reinforcement than lack of momentary effort (Meyer, 1973, p. 153).

This, of course, has far-reaching implications for achievement behavior as has been confirmed experimentally. If lack of ability is perceived as the main cause for failing at a new task, then with further trials, subjective probability of success is diminishing rapidly, persistence is low, and affective consequences are rather depressing, as compared with failure ascribed to momentary lack of effort. Moreover, in giving up early, FF persons themselves restrict their opportunities to come up with success in the long run.

I think it is now clear why a motive can and should be conceptualized as a self-reinforcing system. It perpetuates and im-munizes a bias in outlook and action preferences based on the two self-prescriptive contingencies: set standards and causal attribution, as antecedents of self-administration of reward and punishment (or the corresponding feelings of satisfaction vs. dissatisfaction, pride vs. shame, adequacy vs. inadequacy, mastery vs. helplessness etc.). A motive provides the individual with the possibility to condition perpetually his own self-reinforcements—even contrafactually, i.e., in the face of contradictory facts, in resistance to external reinforcements. This raises, of course, the question of how individual differences in contingencies of self-reinforcement have developed. Here, I cannot go into this question and the related empirical evidence (see Heckhausen, 1972).

Perhaps the best opportunity to put our self-reinforcement conception of a motive to empirical test is to take it as a practical lead in trying to alter people's motives. The unhappy self-reinforcing strategy of FF people gives an additional justification for such an attempt. Our targets for motive change, then, should be the two highly biased processes of contingency management: causal attribution and goal setting. As we have seen, the one problem with an FF person is that he neither allows failure experiences to be suspended for awhile nor allows success experiences to make him more confident about his ability because of his unhappy causal attribution bias. The other problem is his unrealistic goal setting through which he shelters himself against probing his ability more closely as well as against weighing appropriately the utility of effort to be expended (the utility of effort output is maximal with moderate goals where the probabilities of success and failure are about equal).

Motive-change Studies

A first motive-change study attempted to alter causal attribution bias in FF students, stimulated by the "Pygmalion in the classroom" paradigm (Rosenthal & Jacobson, 1968). In each of 12 fourth-grade classrooms we selected three to eight underachieving FF students with the typical biased attribution pattern (Scherer, 1972). We invited the teachers of the experimental classrooms to attend a discussion of our theory; i.e., a pronounced change in their causal attributional comments on poor performance in favor of the basic formula "you could do better if you still would expend more effort" might increase the motivation of the target students. The teachers understood quickly and agreed. Then, allowing for a 4-1/2-month treatment period, we took pre-post measures of HS and FF motives (TAT), level of aspiration, causal attribution patterns for success and failure, intelligence (Primary Mental Ability), anxiety (Children's Anxiety Scale, CAS), and scholastic performance in arithmetic.

After the treatment period, results revealed the expected changes in the key indexes for an improved motivation compared with subjects in control classrooms. Failure was more ascribed to lack of effort than to lack of ability. Level of aspiration was more rarely lowered in the face of failure. Anxiety was decreased (although this latter result only approximated level of significance). Even a higher score in Primary Mental Abilities was obtained, due, however, only to improved performance in speed subtests. The results underline the importance of a "causal attribution therapy" for FF persons. Furthermore, the results indicate that the Pygmalion effect, so hotly debated and so often looked for in vain (Elashoff & Snow, 1971), is—where it actually occurs—a motivation effect based on changed causal attribution for student performance and transmitted in teacher-student interaction. What is necessary is some guidance by motivation theory, i.e., to know what to change and where to look, and which individuals will profit from changed attribution patterns (i.e., FF individuals).

In a second study we broadened the line of attack on self-reinforcement contingencies. The main thrust was directed against unrealistic performance standards. Modification of level of aspiration was the main approach of other motive change programs (see deCharms, 1972; McClelland, 1973). Additional targets for our endeavors were other cognitive processes in the motivation sequence, such as goal planning in advance, adequate calculation of effort output, considerate causal attribution, and explicit and properly administered self-reinforcement for attaining a realistic performance standard.

The training program consisted of 10 extracurricular group sessions within 14 weeks. It went through various exercises starting with gamelike activities, such as ring toss and doing mazes, and leading up to school subject matters, such as adding and memorizing sentences (Hanel, 1975). We capitalized on procedures of imitation learning and internal speech as a self-monitoring device elaborated by Meichenbaum & Goodman (1971). The experimenter started to act as a model in doing the single tasks. He spoke out aloud what goes through his mind while setting a standard, planning his actions, calculating effort output, monitoring performance, evaluating performance outcome, weighing causal attributions, and administering self-reward. Then students took turns in going through all these intervening cognitions within a motivated action sequence (see Heckhausen, 1973), first with a loud, then with low, voice and finally with "internal speech." Each student made reports on his progress in adequate standard setting, causal attribution, and self-reinforcement. On the base of these reports there was one personal counseling session for each student. In the last phase of the treatment, transference into real life of what had been exercised was encouraged so that factual contingency experiences would take place. Students were asked to observe their own behavior in the classroom with regard to the exercised contingency aspects and to plan improvements for the next week.

Thirty fourth-grade subjects from three classes were selected. These students had a predominant FF motive and, in addition, a poor school record; but no IQ was below 80. They were assigned to three groups. First, the experimental group went through the motive change program. Second, a pseudoexperimental group had the same number of extracurricular sessions as the experimental group, but their activities were irrelevant for motive change—they simply performed games and scholastic exercises. The rationale for including a pseudoexperimental group was to control for all possible pure expectation effects. The third group was a control with only pretests and posttests. The measurements for inferring motive change included, besides scholastic achievement tests, motive scores for HS and FF (using the semi-projective grid test by Schmalt, 1973), goal-setting variables of a level-of-aspiration experiment, causal attribution and—as the crucial test for change according to our motive conception—self-reinforcement for success and failure in classroom tests.

The obtained results show conspicuous changes in the expected directions for the experimental group as compared with the pseudoexperimental and the control group. The motive scores had changed to a substantial predominance of HS over FF. In the level-of-aspiration test, goal setting had become much more realistic. Typical shifts, i.e., upward after success and downward after failure, increased; and atypical shifts decreased in frequency. Self-reward after success had gone up, whereas there was no difference in self-punishment after failure. The latter result does not disconfirm expectations since we had not encouraged the students to punish themselves for failure. Finally, the gain in scholastic achievement tests exceeded the other two groups. Only one motive index, i.e., causal attribution pattern, showed no differential change between groups. It did show, however, the predicted modification for the experimental group in pre-post comparison: failure is now attributed less to lack of ability and more to insufficient effort.

CONCLUSIONS

To conclude, the reported evidence on motive change supports our conception of fear of failure as a self-reinforcing motive system with its self-perpetuating nature, even in the face of contradictory facts. With theoretically guided interventions aimed at crucial intervening cognitions, it seems possible to break up the unhappy self-prescriptive contingencies by which a fear-of-failure person reinforces his own fear of failure.

REFERENCES

Atkinson, J. W. *Introduction to motivation.* Princeton, N.J.: Van Nostrand, 1964.

Atkinson, J. W., & Feather, N. T. *A theory of achievement motivation.* New York: Wiley, 1966.

Birney, R. C., Burdick, H., & Teevan, R. C. *Fear of failure.* Princeton, N.J.: Van Nostrand-Reinhold, 1969.

deCharms, R. Personal causation training in schools. *Journal of Applied Social Psychology,* 1972, 2, 95–113.

Elashoff, J. D., & Snow, E. *A case study in statistical inference: Reconsideration of the Rosenthal-Jacobson data on teacher expectancy.* Stanford, Calif.: Stanford University Press, 1971.

Hanel, J. Der Einfluss eines Motivänderungsprogramms auf schulleistungsschwache misserfolgsmotivierte Grundschüler der 4. Klasse. Unpublished diploma thesis, Psychologisches Institut der Ruhr-Universität, 1975.

Heckhausen, H. *Hoffnung und Furcht in der Leistungsmotivation.* Meisenheim/Glan: Hain, 1963.

Heckhausen, H. *The anatomy of achievement motivation.* New York: Academic Press, 1967.

Heckhausen, H. Achievement motive research: Current problems and some contributions towards a general theory of motivation. In W. J. Arnold (Ed.), *Nebraska symposium on motivation 1968.* Lincoln, Neb.: University of Nebraska Press, 1968.

Heckhausen, H. Die Interaktion der Sozialisationsvariablen in der Genese des Leistungsmotivs. In C. F. Graumann (Ed.), *Handbuch der Psychologie, Sozialpsychologie.* Vol. 7(2). Göttingen: Hogrefe, 1972.

Heckhausen, H. Intervening cognitions in motivation. In D. E. Berlyne & K. B. Madsen (Eds.), *Pleasure, reward, preference.* New York: Academic Press, 1973.

Heider, F. *The psychology of interpersonal relations.* New York: Wiley, 1958.

Jopt, U.-J. Extrinsische Motivation und Leistungsverhalten. Unveröffentlichte Dissertation, Psychologisches Institut der Ruhr-Universität, 1974.

Kanfer, F. H. The maintenance of behavior by self-generated stimuli and reinforcement. In A. Jacobs & L. B. Sachs (Eds.), *The psychology of private events.* New York: Academic Press, 1971.

McClelland, D. C. What is the effect of achievement motivation training in the schools? In D. C. McClelland & R. S. Steele (Eds.), *Human motivation.* Morristown, N.J.: General Learning Press, 1973.

Mandler, G., & Sarason, S. B. A study of anxiety and learning, *Journal of Abnormal and Social Psychology,* 1952, 47, 166–173.

Meichenbaum, D. H., & Goodman, J. Training impulsive children to talk to themselves: A means of developing self-control. *Journal of Abnormal Psychology,* 1971, 77, 115–126.

Meyer, W.-U. *Leistungsmotiv und Ursachenerklärung von Erfolg und Misserfolg.* Stuttgart: Klett, 1973.

Rosenthal, R., & Jacobson, L. *Pygmalion in the classroom*. New York: Holt, Rinehart, & Winston, 1968.

Rotter, J. B. *Social learning and clinical psychology*. Englewood Cliffs, N.J.: Prentice-Hall, 1954.

Sarason, I. G. The effects of anxiety and threat on the solution of a difficult task. *Journal of Abnormal and Social Psychology*, 1961, 62, 165-168.

Sarason, S. B., Davidson, K. S., Lightall, F. F., Waite, R. R., & Ruebush, B. K. *Anxiety in elementary school children: A report of research*. New York: Wiley, 1960.

Scherer, J. Änderungen von Lehrer-Attribuierungen und deren Auswirkungen auf Leistungsverhalten und Persönlichkeitsmerkmale von Schülern. Unpublished diploma thesis, Psychologisches Institut der Ruhr-Universität, 1972.

Schmalt, H.-D. Die GITTER-Technik—ein objektives Verfahren zur Messung des Leistungsmotivs bei Kindern. *Zeitschrift für Entwicklungspsychologie und Pädagogische Psychologie*, 1973, 5, 231-252. (a)

Schmalt, H.-D. Entwicklung und Validierung einer neuen Technik zur Messung verschiedener Aspekte des Leistungsmotivs—das LM-GITTER. Unpublished dissertation, Psychologisches Institut der Ruhr-Universität, 1973. (b). Universität, 1973. (b)

Schneider, K. *Motivation unter Erfolgsrisiko*. Göttingen: Hogrefe, 1973.

Spence, K. W., Farber, I. E., & McFann, H. H. The relation of anxiety (drive) level to performance in competitional and non-competitional paired-associates learning. *Journal of Experimental Psychology*, 1956, 52, 296-305.

Spielberger, C. Current trends in anxiety research. In C. Spielberger (Ed.), *Anxiety and behavior*. New York: Academic Press, 1966.

Weiner, B. The role of success and failure in the learning of easy and complex tasks. *Journal of Personality and Social Psychology*, 1966, 3, 339-343.

Weiner, B. *Theories of motivation*. Chicago: Markham, 1972.

Weiner, B., Frieze, I., Kukla, A., Reed, L., Rest, S. & Rosenbaum, R. M. *Perceiving the causes of success and failure*. New York: General Learning Press, 1971.

Weiner, B., Heckhausen, H., Meyer, W.-U. & Cook, R. E. Causal ascriptions and achievement behavior: A conceptual analysis of effort and reanalysis of locus of control. *Journal of Personality and Social Psychology*, 1972, 21, 239-248.

Weiner, B., & Kukla, A. An attributional analysis of achievement motivation. *Journal of Personality and Social Psychology*, 1970, 15, 1-20.

Weiner, B., & Potepan, P. A. Personality characteristics and affective reactions towards exams of superior and failing college students. *Journal of Educational Psychology*, 1970, 61, 144-151.

Weiner, B., & Schneider, K. Drive versus cognitive theory: A reply to Boor & Harmon. *Journal of Personality and Social Psychology*, 1971, 18, 258-262.

Wittmaier, B. C. Test anxiety, mood, and performance. *Journal of Personality and Social Psychology*, 1974, 29, 664-669.

II
EMPIRICAL APPROACHES TO STRESS

7

CULTURAL ASPECTS OF STRESS

Richard Trumbull

American Institute of Biological Sciences
Arlington, Virginia
United States

Any orientation or introduction for a significant discussion of stress sooner or later attempts to review its history. It is difficult to ascertain just when the word "stress," from the world of engineering, assumed importance in the world of human factors. It is more difficult to trace the concept under a variety of other names back through history to Hippocrates, to whom Hans Selye gives some credit (Selye, 1952). It was natural for Selye to recognize the roles of suffering (pathos) and toil (panos) in the bodily processes of restoration because he developed his concept within the world of medicine. If we think of Selye as a near contemporary, I would like to trace the changes from his time to the point where we are discussing stress and anxiety in a much broader context today.

There are two progressions that merit attention. The first involves the world of the individual and his reactions to stressful situations. The original emphasis of Cannon (1932), Selye (1952), and Bernard (1945) on systemic equilibrium and adjustment mechanisms had to acknowledge, in time, the importance of personality factors. These, in turn, had to be recognized as developments within certain social contexts, such as family, peer group, and the world of work. Next, we were reminded that *these* contexts were part of larger concepts of mores, customs, and cultures. Thus, cultural factors will determine which conditions or events are perceived as stressful and the degree and type of response to them.

As this concept was being elaborated, it became evident that another one was getting in the way and preventing a clear development of my thesis. This second concept runs from the microworld to the macroworld with the same basic thesis that although there are stresses to which there are specific responses, there also are stresses which elicit a general adaptation syndrome characteristic at each level from cellular to cultural. There are, then, stresses to which whole cultures, nations, or societies respond. There is the characteristic fight—or flight—here just as certainly as there is at the cellular level when a disease is attacking its equilibrium or adaptation. The question that haunted me as I employed various illustrations of motivations for research on our more traditional concept of stress was, Is war part of a general adaptation syndrome at this higher level? I raise this point now only to stimulate some increased sensitivity to this progression.

There is a research history of stress, whether defined as situation, agent, or reaction, which can be followed due to the funding made available under a variety of governmental concerns. Hebb, a physiological psychologist in Canada, provided a natural bridge from Selye's world of medicine to the world of psychology as he became involved in appraising the techniques of "brainwashing" employed in the Korean War. For instance, we find that the study of stress in individuals and groups is inextricably bound to war, its equipments, its operations, and its ramifications through cultures. The isolation of "brainwashing" later had implications for the development and ultimate use of fallout shelters. The same element of space limitation influenced research on submarine space layout; and we find the word "habitability," acknowledging psychological aspects, first appearing in specifications for design of submarines in the 1960's. In the meantime, great concern was expressed over the performance deterioration and potential personality problems that would arise during protracted B-52 bomber operations. When man ventured on into space, much of this research history was of value to those confronted with decisions on space vehicle design, mission assignments, and, especially, mission duration.

Over the years, we have seen a progression in our understanding of stress—the nonspecific response of the body to demands made on it. It appears that there has been some restriction in our definition, for we appear to be concentrating on "distress." Selye made a point of this in *Stress Without Distress* (Selye, 1974). He recalled:

> The greatest handicap of early students of this topic was their failure to distinguish between distress, which is always un-pleasant, and the general concept of stress, which, in addition, also includes the pleasant experiences of joy, fulfillment, and self-expression [p. 34].

There is no problem here so long as we recognize the restriction and the more usual relationship of *distress* to anxiety. In fact, it is far easier to discuss the progressions I have in mind in terms of distress.

There was the original emphasis on bodily reponses that occurred regardless of the nature of the stressor. In time, there was consideration of psychological factors that played a role in the perception of the stressor, the response, and the frequency and nature of report. Frequency and nature of report of stress responses soon were associated with social factors, which, in turn, have their antecedents in cultures. Thus, we find ourselves in an ideal situation for establishing a firmer understanding of some basic aspects for progress into the broader implications of research on *distress* as it is perceived and pursued in different cultures.

There tends to be a natural starting point for a concept, and research in different countries will go through similar sequences. For various reasons, some countries will not begin at the beginning but will come into that same stream later and continue "on-line" from there. Some of this might be attributed to the sharing of scientific literature, and we often find that research in one country *will* parallel that in another just enough out of phase to allow for reading of reports and establishing laboratories and programs. Part of this same sequencing can be the result of training of research personnel in the first country. Upon returning home, they try to reproduce the research and method of attack experienced in their training. Due to their contacts, correspondence, and new interest in research reports from the country of their training, they continue that parallel course. This does make it more difficult to determine just how the research interest and approach would have evolved in their native country in response to more endemic pressures or needs.

Fortunately, although the emphasis remained on the straight mechanical, thermal, pressure, humidity, and other measurable variables, there was an early awareness of personality and social factors that could influence the impact of stressors and its manifestation. There were straightforward measures of this impact on blood pressure, biochemical products, electroencephalogram (EEG), and heart rate; but verbal report continued to be employed without adequate recognition of social pressures to prove oneself, "to be a man." Gradually, we learned that it made a difference who the experimenter was and what relationship existed between the experimenter and the subject. We learned that the orientation talk with the subject could play a part in his anticipation of and ultimate reaction to the stressor under study. Indeed, it was discovered that, quite unwittingly, one could suggest the response to him; and the experimenter's credibility and the subject's desire to cooperate both became important factors in research.

We must recognize and acknowledge that there *was* an earlier definition of personality factors or entities that, in turn, could be related to those responses associated with stress. Thus, the terms of Selye's time, such as neurasthenia and hysteria, described people with sensitivity or overreaction to bodily processes. The first appearance of signs of stress that might have been ignored by most individuals became causes of concern or alarm and actually were augmented by the neurasthenic or hysteric individual. We must recognize the role of anticipation, too, with such people being more apprehensive and predisposed to a higher degree of response to both real and imagined stressors. Years ago, society talked about the "sensitive child," a term that afforded protection in some cases and that resulted in derision and problems in others. In any event, it related reactions to stress to personality.

When we started to consider the psychological components of stress more fully, specialists in personality structure allowed the semipsychiatric terms of neurasthenia and hysteria to pass into history but provided new concepts such as Witkin's "field" versus "body" dependency or orientation which recognized individual differences in responsiveness and sensitivity to the world in which one functioned (Witkin, Lewis, Hertzman, Machover, Meissner, & Wapner, 1954). Notterman and Trumbull (1959) introduced "Radar Robert," characterized by an active radar-like scanning of any new environment to establish a sense of security. The relationships between such personality types and physiological reactions were elaborated by Cohen (Appley & Trumbull, 1967). Today, we seek relationships between anxiety and stress.

In December 1973, Tinbergen shared the Nobel Prize for Physiology or Medicine in recognition for his work on ethology and stress diseases. The lecture he gave on that occasion has been reprinted in *Science* (Tinbergen, 1974). His work appraised autism in the context of psychosocial stress and psychosomatic disease. Of primary interest to me in this detailed discussion and interpretation of behavioral aberrations is the presence of an EEG pattern indicating high overall arousal. To some, this hyperactivity is a possible cause and precursor of the other features of "Kanner's syndrome." He does not elaborate upon this hyperactivity, but the therapies for which Tinbergen is given credit lead me to relate this pattern to "Radar Robert." The issue is whether the hyperactivity reflects a lack of cortical integration which should have been developing or an active searching for sensory input. Is the child mute and "withdrawn" because no connections are available or because his perception or interpretation of sensory input requires a flooding of the system?

At least we know that the "withdrawal" is not a passive reaction in the absence of neural activity. The techniques Tinbergen employed appear to indicate that, at least in some instances, the child recovers by association and meaning of gestures and roles played by the therapist. If we find some of this active seeking for reassurance and meaning in later years, we will recognize autism as something that is not all or none, nor as something that one outgrows. There is a greater need for security or affiliation that can appear later under conditions of stress, reflecting an inadequacy in adjustment. Tinbergen expresses the belief that "[this] inadequacy of adjustment . . . will become perhaps the most disruptive influence in our society."

As we move one step further away from the actual situation and seek predisposing determinants, we must deal with the past experience of the individual and the nature of the social structure into which he was born and in which he is operating. One might ask why there is so much concern about developing such information on prersonality and other correlates with stress response. In the 1950's, we would take a number of subjects and place them in what was believed to be a stressful situation to observe their adjustment or reactions. Our level of sophistication was such that one subject was about as good as another.

Those were the days when we took a subject just like cookbooks say "take an egg." Because availability was a prime consideration, students in classes of the investigator or service personnel at the location of the research laboratory provided our first statistics. Later, when investigators, as well as the area of stress, received more recognition, it became possible to select subjects with some criteria in mind. A sophisticated cook knows that no two eggs are exactly alike and the end product can be influenced by the egg one takes. We ourselves no longer can take a subject without more information on his history and some idea about his sensitivity to the stress or anxiety we have in store for him. We must constantly ask ourselves why a certain situation, event, or change represents stress. There have been instances in which the experimenter defined that which was stressful almost as simply as stating "I do not like riding in roller coasters, so that must be stressful." There have been instances in which correlates with breakdown of personality or performance have been so defined. We find reflections of these situations in what became known as "stress interviews" and situational tests of candidates for positions or employment. The term entered military training camps in the physical proficiency exercises and those trials of endurance and initiative known ingeniously as "survival training." Here, stress was defined as an aggregate or total situation rather than as a specific entity exceeding human tolerance.

It was both inevitable and advantageous that the early concern about and emphasis on the physiological and biochemical indicators of stress gave way to the determination of personality and social factors. Psychology once was described as the science concerned with the description, prediction, and control of behavior. The early years of stress rightfully emphasized that *description*. It was necessary to know just what we were measuring and their correlations with the controlled stressor. Prediction, however, involves antecedents and the determination beforehand of the responses of specific persons as we move from actuarial data on groups to a recognition of individual differences. As is true with much research, the first studies did not pay great attention to variance or acknowledge that there were people who overreacted to the given stressor as well as those who never reacted.

Indeed, a study that always intrigued me was one in which subjects were to be confined for a number of days to note reactions to isolation. The first follow-up test was scheduled for the second day. Unfortunately, a number of subjects were unwilling to tolerate the situation and requested termination at the end of day 1. They never were included in the final report because they had not lasted long enough into the procedure. I say unfortunately because it would appear that they were the most stressed subjects of the study and one tail of the distribution had been eliminated. Any statistical treatment of the remainder would lead to questionable conclusions.

Fortunately, the sociologist, the anthropologist, and specialists in personality and clinical psychology were quick to see implications in the work of Selye, Hebb, and those to follow. As stated before, Hebb's involvement in the analysis of "brainwashing" provided one of the biggest transitions of stress into the nonmedical world. The influence of isolation on personality structure or integrity and ultimate facilitation of imparting new information and concepts was of vital concern to military authorities. It became evident that an enemy already had some crude ideas of the individuals most likely to succumb to such treatment. Some insights were gained as information became available on who was being "brainwashed" and the conditions under which a treatment was terminated. Here was an interesting cultural aspect of stress because any form employed by an enemy must have some significance or implications in his own culture *unless or until he knows his opposition well enough to tailormake the treatment to the subject's own culturally determined weakness.*

From these studies, then, sociologists and anthropologists obtained information. The significance of confinement, or isolation, could be related to Hall's (1959) concept of "space." "The silent treatment," an organized isolation imposed in some schools on a person, as well as an unorganized condition spontaneously appearing in some marriages, had new meaning. It was inevitable that this aspect would receive attention by the military naval services in submarine research. The protracted operations of nuclear submarines and the prospective establishment of truly submarine habitats demanded both new impetus and funding. The recognition of individual and personality differences, however, had been established. From this point on, no matter what the major motivation for "stress" studies might be, there would be evaluations of compatible personnel and the life histories and personality factors that contributed to maintenance of performance. The influence of isolation on personality also had implications for another program that was not so mission oriented—fallout shelters. If people were going to have small personal and neighborhood shelters, there were things that needed additional study beyond the experiences afforded by wartime air raids and brainwashing. It seems that there must be some overall governmental or societal concern about issues such as these to keep the level of funding one desires and needs for interdisciplinary research especially.

We have seen the larger programs sustained by protracted bomber flights and the problems of crew selection and compatibility that paralleled the concerns of the submarine force. Then, there was the space program as the ultimate test of physiological, biochemical, psychological, and social factors. As the Russians join the United States in a first coordinated venture, we will have an opportunity to see how well we understand cultural differences as well.

As the world grows smaller and we share more things across cultures, we will need a clearer picture of these sequences in those cultures. There are many questions yet to be answered. Is there some particular reason why we start with stressors in the environment and then go on to those of a more subtle social nature? What sequence brought the U.S. Navy interest in relationships between stress and disease with the stressors from the personal and military lifestyle? What explains the United Kingdom's interest in meditation or in the concept of lifestyle that involves so many aspects of job satisfaction? Note the growing interest in retirement and aging as periods of unique and increasingly severe distress. Just what are the determinants of those things to which governments finally devote attention and funding once they are considered to be cultural distressors? What are the determinants that direct the next research by the individual researcher who does not have to respond to governmental interests?

It is possible that the next major motivation will come from concern about overpopulation and urban development. Many formerly recognized stresses in their usual form (e.g., noise) and in new forms (proximity and behaviors of others) will receive attention. It is certain that others will appear as secondary byproducts of urban characteristics. In time, we might develop a concept of lifestyle and an expectancy for its realization that will be interfered with to the point of introducing its own stressors.

I have tried to sketch a progression in our understanding of distress research. It is necessary to recognize this progression because the basic concept often is the only thing that supplies motivation for discussion. When one country is so far ahead of others because of its longer history in a field or advanced technology in research organizations, those others have less incentive to participate in the discussion or to return to their laboratories motivated to contribute to the international literature. We have reached a point in distress research where an international literature is worth seeking because each culture's perception of that which is distressful adds something unique. At the same time, we are finding more and more common elements in the distressful; and shared borders also mean shared air, shared water, and shared droughts. New communications and air travel have brought with them a new sharing of disease, social unrest, and worldwide epidemics of a biological and psychological nature. As one specific, the requirement for an international literature in the area of stress and anxiety is evident, especially in urban development and its resource depletion, congestion, and byproduct accretion aspects.

In conclusion, I would like to acknowledge some historical footnotes to my discussion of a progression. Selye's (1974) *Stress Without Distress* provided significant insights. The major point of the book was an explanation of the biological roots of what he called "altruistic egotism." Believing that there is a finite reserve of adaptation energy against which one can draw in meeting the stressful situations in life, Selye recommended more deliberate election of times for fight or flight to husband or conserve that energy. Whereas small distresses can be handled by superficial adaptation energy supplies that can be rebuilt, the greater ones draw on the finite deep adaptation energies.

He finds an example for man in the fact that

. . . the evolution of diverse species was largely dependent upon the development of processes that permitted many cells to live in harmony, with a minimum of stress between them, serving their own best interests by ensuring the survival of the entire complex structure [p. 65].

For man, "The aim of life is to maintain its own identity and express

its innate abilities and drives with the least possible frustration." And
further:

> In interpersonal stress, the gain is the incitement in others of
> friendship, gratitude, goodwill, and love toward ourselves; the
> loss is the creation in others of hatred, frustration, and an urge
> for revenge. This applies both to people around us and to
> ourselves, for our own positive or negative feelings toward
> others respectively benefit or hurt us directly, just as much as
> we are helped or hurt by inciting those feelings in others [p.
> 74].

The basis for this conserving of one's deep adaptation energy pool
and a protracted, meaningful, and enjoyable life he establishes in the
admonition "Earn thy neighbor's love."

Claude Bernard (1945) devoted the last chapter of his book,
Introduction a l'Etude de la Medecine Experimentale to the
philosophical and social aspects of maintaining the stability of the
body's *milieu interieur*, and Walter Cannon (1932), the father of
homeostasis, provided an epilogue for his book, *Wisdom of the Body*,
entitled "Relations of Biological and Social Homeostasis." It seems
that all these men, in developing a finer understanding and definition
of our topic of stress and anxiety, anticipated the progression I have
discussed and also discovered some guidance for personal living as
well. Maybe we can discern similar guidance for nations and cultures.

REFERENCES

Appley, M. H., & Trumbull, R. (Eds.) *Psychological stress: Issues in research*.
New York: Appleton-Century-Crofts, 1967.

Bernard, C. *Introduction a l'etude de la medecine experimentale*. Paris: Editions
Flammarion, 1945.

Cannon, W. B. *The wisdom of the body*. (2nd ed.) New York: Norton, 1932.

Hall, E. T. *The silent language*. New York: Doubleday, 1959.

Notterman, J. M., & Trumbull, R. Note on self-regulating systems and stress,
Behavioral Science, 1959, 4, 324-327.

Selye, H. *The story of the adaptation syndrome*. Montreal: Acta, Inc., 1952.

Selye, H. *Stress without distress*. Philadelphia: Lippincott, 1974.

Tinbergen, N. Ethology and stress diseases. *Science*, 1974, 185(4145), 20-27.

Witkin, H. A., Lewis, H. B., Hertzman, M., Machover, K., Meissner, P. B., &
Wapner, S. *Personality through perception*. New York: Harper & Row, 1954.

8

ELECTRODERMAL LABILITY: A PSYCHOPHYSIOLOGICAL ANALYSIS OF INDIVIDUAL DIFFERENCES IN RESPONSE TO STRESS

Edward S. Katkin

State University of New York at Buffalo
Buffalo, New York
United States

The purpose of this chapter is to present the results of a program of research that began 10 years ago with a primary focus on the effects of individual differences in anxiety on the response to stress, and is now concerned with the relationship of autonomic responsivity to the acquisition and processing of information. The connection between these two different foci and the central link among the studies discussed is the assessment of small-amplitude spontaneous (i.e., nonspecific) fluctuations in skin resistance that occur in the absence of specific stimulation. After a discussion of the measurement and meaning of these spontaneous responses in electrodermal activity, their relationship to anxiety and stress are evaluated. Then the relationships among anxiety, attention, and

Some of the research reported in this paper was supported by Research Grant MH-11989 and Special Fellowship MH-17490 from the National Institute of Mental Health, United States Public Health Service. Research support was also provided by a grant in aid from the Society of the Sigma Xi. The author is deeply indebted to his teachers, Charles D. Spielberger, Richard Hirschman, Herbert Rappaport, Robert McCubbin, Andrew Sostek, and Anita Sostek.

arousal are explored. Finally, some newly acquired data on the relationship of individual differences in electrodermal activity to signal detection and vigilance research are presented.

ELECTRODERMAL LABILITY:
DEFINITION AND MEASUREMENT

The electrodermal response (EDR), more commonly known as the galvanic skin response (GSR), has been the subject of psychological interest since Richter (1927) first demonstrated that its elicitation was a convenient index of sympathetic arousal. Early electrodermal research focused either on the elicited, specific electrodermal response to stimulation, or alternately on basal or tonic levels of skin conductance. More recent research has indicated however, that there are smaller amplitude EDRs that are not elicited by specific stimuli, but appear spontaneously or nonspecifically both during rest and during activity. Mundy-Castle and McKiever (1953), the first investigators to discuss the meaning of spontaneous EDRs, reported that under identical conditions different individuals emitted reliably different numbers of spontaneous responses. Subsequently, Lacey and Lacey (1958), in their pioneering investigations of individual differences in resting autonomic activity, designated subjects showing a great deal of electrodermal activity as "labiles," and subjects showing low amounts of such activity as "stabiles."

Although Mundy-Castle and McKiever's (1953) and the Laceys' (1958) original studies focused on individual differences in resting levels, much of the subsequent research on electrodermal lability concentrated on the overall effects of physiological and psychological stress on electrodermal response rates, irrespective of individual differences. Burch and Greiner (1960), for instance, administered both depressant and activating drugs to human subjects and observed that spontaneous EDRs increased in response to activating drugs and decreased in response to depressant drugs. Burch and Greiner concluded, therefore, that spontaneous electrodermal response rate monotonically reflected CNS activation, and they postulated a link between EDR rate and reticular activity. This suggestion was supported by Silverman, Cohen, and Shmavonian (1959), who also reported a positive correlation between frequency of spontaneous EDR and basal conductance level, a more traditionally established index of arousal. Furthermore, Silverman et al. (1959) reported that spontaneous EDRs increased when subjects were exposed to increasing G forces in a human centrifuge. Following upon these findings on the effects of pharmacological and physical stress on the rate of spontaneous electrodermal responses, my colleagues and I set out to evaluate the effects of psychological stress and its interaction with individual differences in susceptibility to being threatened (i.e., anxiety) on the production of spontaneous electrodermal responses.

TRAIT ANXIETY, STRESS, AND ELECTRODERMAL LABILITY

The first experiment in this series (Katkin, 1965) was based on the notion that most people react with anxiety responses to stressful situations and that such responses are characterized by autonomic arousal. Additionally, it was based on the widely believed notion that there are individual differences in the extent to which people react with anxiety (trait differences, according to Spielberger's trait-state distinction). The purpose of the first experiment, therefore, was to examine the extent to which individual differences in "anxiety-trait," as measured with a questionnaire, affected autonomic responses to a psychologically stressful situation. The autonomic index chosen was electrodermal activity, primarily because the innervation of palmar sweat glands is exclusively sympathetic; inferences about underlying activity derived from electrodermal measurement, therefore, can be related more closely to sympathetic arousal than can inferences derived from any other autonomic index.

Of the many indexes of trait-anxiety used to measure individual differences, the Taylor Manifest Anxiety (MA) scale (Taylor, 1953) had been the most widely known and used at the time this first study was undertaken, having been shown to relate to clinical judgments of anxiety (Buss, 1955; Buss, Wiener, Durkee, & Baer, 1955) and to other scalar indexes of anxiety (Bendig, 1957; Cattell & Scheier, 1958).

The general goals, then, of this first study were to investigate the relationship between measures of individual differences in anxiety and electrodermal indexes of autonomic nervous system (ANS) arousal during both stressful and nonstressful conditions.

Under stressful conditions both high anxious (HA) and low anxious (LA) subjects were expected to show greater autonomic arousal than comparable subjects who were not stressed. It was also expected that HA subjects in a stress condition would show greater ANS arousal than LA subjects who were subjected to stress and, furthermore, that the extent of their arousal would be a positive function of the degree of apprehension experienced during the experiment. On the assumption that trait anxiety, as reflected in MA scores, reflected a tendency to react with anxiety only to *stressful* situations, HA and LA subjects were not expected to differ on electrodermal indexes during a nonstressful condition.

The basic design of the study was as follows: All subjects in an undergraduate subject pool were tested with a modified form of the Minnesota Multiphasic Personality Inventory that included the MA scale and Welsh's (1956) A scale. Those subjects who scored in the upper 20% of the distribution of MA scale scores and in the upper half of the distribution of A-scale scores were designated the HA group; those who scored in the lower 20% of the distribution of MA scores and in the lower half of the distribution of A-scale scores were designated the LA group. All subjects so identified were then assigned on a random basis to experimental or control conditions. The experiment consisted of the measurement of electrodermal activity during three consecutive time periods. For all subjects the first time period and the third time period were nonstressful rest periods, but the middle period was varied for subjects in the experimental and control conditions. For subjects in the control condition the middle period was identical to the first and last periods, consisting of continued rest and relaxation. For subjects in the experimental condition the middle period was a psychologically stressful situation. At the beginning of the second period, subjects in the experimental condition were informed that they would receive painful electric shocks delivered to their ankles and that the shocks would be delivered on a random schedule during the subsequent 10 minutes. The purpose, it was explained, was to compare physiological responses to the stress of extreme pain with the physiological responses already obtained during the rest period. No shocks were actually delivered at any time to any subjects who participated in the experiment. For subjects in the control condition the experimenter did a "checking out" of the apparatus so that the amount of time spent between experimental periods and the amount of physical activity of subjects in the stress and nonstress conditions was equated. Details of the recording apparatus and a technical description of the equipment used can be obtained from Katkin (1965). In summary there were four groups of subjects: HA subjects in stress and nonstress situations and LA subjects in stress and nonstress situations. Electrodermal activity was recorded from all subjects in all four conditions across the three experimental periods, and spontaneous fluctuations in electrodermal activity were counted during each period. A spontaneous fluctuation was defined as a decrease in skin resistance of at least 100 ohms followed by a gradual return to predeflection level. A continuous record of spontaneous fluctuations was obtained for each subject, and subjects' scores on this measure were determined by counting the number of spontaneous responses in each period of the experiment. In this manner three spontaneous response scores were obtained for each subject.

The results of this first experiment consistently showed that individual differences in anxiety, as measured on the MA scale, were *unrelated to any other variable.* Analyses of the data showed that there were no main effects nor any interactions of MA scores with any other experimental treatment. The experimental manipulation of the threat of shock, however, resulted in highly significant experimental effects for both dependent measures. Figure 8-1 shows the effects of experimental conditions on nonspecific electrodermal responses for subjects in the threat and nonthreat conditions collapsed across MA scale scores. Subjects in the two experimental groups showed equal rates of nonspecific electrodermal activity during the initial rest period, and the introduction of the threat of shock caused those subjects who were threatened to show a large increase in the number of small amplitude electrodermal responses emitted. After the threat condition was removed and the subjects were asked to rest again, their spontaneous response rate declined to the same consistently low level that was shown by subjects in the control group. This interaction of Groups × Time Periods was statistically significant ($p < .001$).

It is fairly clear from these results that spontaneous rate of electrodermal fluctuation was a highly sensitive index of a subject's response to the threat of electric shock, irrespective of preexisting individual differences in trait anxiety as measured by the MA scale. This interpretation was supported by the results of an extensive

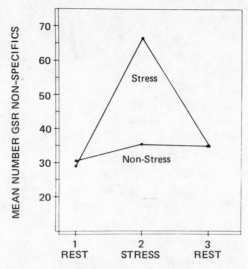

Fig. 8-1. Mean number of nonspecific electrodermal responses (EDRs, or galvanic skin responses, GSRs) for the threatened and nonthreatened groups for the three experimental periods. (From Katkin, E. S. Relationship between manifest anxiety and two indices of autonomic response to stress. *Journal of Personality and Social Psychology*, 1965, 2, 324–333. Copyright 1965 by the American Psychological Association. Reprinted by permission.)

interview conducted at the conclusion of the middle period of the experiment, in which an attempt was made to assess the degree to which subjects were made to feel apprehensive by the threatening instructions. Of the 26 combined HA and LA subjects in the threatened group, 24 reported that they experienced apprehension immediately after being threatened. Of the 26 combined HA and LA subjects in the control group, only 9 reported experiencing any apprehension during the middle experimental period. Thus, it may be concluded that the results of this experiment indicated that spontaneous rate of electrodermal activity is related not only to the experimental induction of stress but also to a subject's self-report of apprehension pursuant to that induction. These results were gratifying and suggested that future research on individual differences on spontaneous activity was in order. However, there was a sense of disappointment at the failure to find the predicted relationship between individual differences in MA scores and electrodermal responsivity to stress. It had been predicted, of course, that subjects with high scores on the MA scale would show greater electrodermal responsivity than subjects with low scores, and this prediction most decidedly was not confirmed. Consequently, a second study (Katkin, 1966) was carried out, this time attempting to assess more closely a subject's experience of apprehension or transitory anxiety in the experimental situation.

STATE ANXIETY, STRESS, AND ELECTRODERMAL ACTIVITY

One possible reason for the failure to obtain a relationship between MA scores and EDR responses to the threat of shock may have been that MA scale items refer to general states of the organism or what we now refer to as trait anxiety rather than to transitory emotional reactions now commonly called state anxiety (Spielberger, 1966). With that distinction in mind, a replication of the first experiment was attempted using an index of state anxiety to be administered at the time of the experiment instead of the MA scale. At the time we began this work, Zuckerman (1960) described an Affect Adjective Check List (AACL) that measured transitory, or state anxiety; and it had been demonstrated that increases in AACL scores were associated with transitory fears of failure on classroom examinations (Zuckerman & Biase, 1962) and with emotional responses to stressful films (Winter, Ferreira, & Ransom, 1963). The goal of the next study (Katkin, 1966), therefore, was to evaluate the relationship between scores on the AACL and nonspecific EDRs during differentially stressful conditions. The paradigm employed was identical to the earlier (Katkin, 1965) study except that subjects were defined as anxious or nonanxious on the basis of scores on an AACL, which was administered after subjects were inside the experimental chamber and connected to the physiological recording apparatus, but before they were told about the threat of electric shock. Thus, individual differences in state anxiety were ascertained at the time the experiment took place and in the experimental laboratory, which is itself moderately stress inducing. Our purpose was to ascertain if differentially anxious subjects, as measured by the AACL, would show differential autonomic arousal during the initial rest period, and furthermore whether subjects scoring high on the AACL would show greater increases in arousal as a function of stress than subjects scoring low on the AACL.

The experiment was carried out in the same manner as the first experiment. Details of the methodology and recording apparatus can be obtained from Katkin (1966). A spontaneous EDR was defined again as a response of at least 100 ohms amplitude. Figure 8-2 contains the mean number of nonspecific EDRs for high and low AACL subjects in both stress and nonstress conditions across all three experimental periods. It may be observed from Fig. 8-2 that these results were strikingly similar to those obtained in the earlier experiment (see Fig. 8-1). In the initial rest period all subjects showed approximately the same number of spontaneous

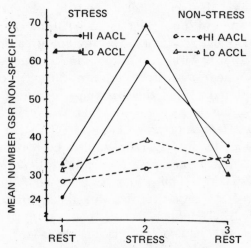

Fig. 8-2. Mean number of nonspecific electrodermal responses (EDRs, or galvanic skin responses, GSRs) for four subject groups across the three experimental periods. Hi AACL = subjects scoring high on the Affect Adjective Check List (AACL); Lo AACL = subjects scoring low on the AACL. (From Katkin, E. S. The relationship between a measure of transitory anxiety and spontaneous autonomic activity. *Journal of Abnormal Psychology*, 1966, **71**, 142-146. Copyright 1966 by the American Psychological Association. Reprinted by permission.)

EDRs, irrespective of differential score on the AACL. During the second experimental period, in which the threat of shock was introduced, subjects who were threatened showed a large increase in number of nonspecific EDRs emitted, whereas subjects who were not threatened showed no increase. These differential responses as a function of experimental threat were, as in the earlier experiment, independent of individual differences in AACL score. Thus it may be seen that these results for the first two experimental periods were essentially identical with the results obtained in the earlier study using Taylor MA scale scores. After the conclusion of the threat period in this experiment, however, subjects who scored high on the AACL showed less of a decline in electrodermal responsivity than subjects who scored low on the AACL. This interaction between AACL score and recovery of electrodermal rate was statistically significant and suggested the possibility that subjects high in state anxiety may have less ability to show sympathetic nervous system quiescence after excitation.

This finding of a differential rate of EDR decline after the cessation of stress was interpreted at the time (Katkin, 1966) to reflect the possibility that the AACL, while unable to differentially predict changes in electrodermal responsivity to severe threat, may have been able to reflect what we called at the time "autonomic recovery rate." That is, it was thought possible that the AACL reflected the degree to which a subject's autonomic activity would return to prestress levels after the removal of severe threat. Two subsequent experiments designed to test this notion led to an abandonment of interest in the problem. Simply stated, what we discovered in these replications was that the "autonomic recovery rate" patterns observed for the third period by Katkin (1966) were not replicable. The clear effects of stress on spontaneous electrodermal activity, however, were replicated almost exactly as they were first reported (Katkin, 1965, 1966).

The finding of these studies that all subjects, regardless of anxiety level, showed higher rates of nonspecific activity under stressful conditions was consistent with the first study and supported the notion that the frequency of spontaneous electrodermal responses could be used as an effective index of emotional response to stress. The findings that there were no differences in response rate for high AACL and low AACL groups, however, was not consistent with the interpretation of the AACL as an index of state anxiety. This finding could be explained only if it were assumed that the threat of shock was sufficiently arousing to evoke greatly increased responses even from relatively nonresponsive subjects. That is, to account for the findings in the second experimental period, it had to be assumed that AACL scores reflected differential tendencies to give autonomic responses only to stresses less intense than the one employed in these two experiments. To elicit differential physiological responses to stress from subjects who are presumed to differ in anxiety, it appeared that we would have to use a stress substantially less severe than the threat of electric shock.

ANXIETY, RESPONSE TO MILD STRESS, AND THE PERCEPTION OF VISCERAL ACTIVITY

The failure to obtain relationships between electrodermal activity and self-report measures in our two earlier studies, along with the frequent reports of similar failures (see Sarason, 1960) could not be dismissed simply by assuming that either of the indexes was invalid, because the self-report scales used in these studies are relatively valid indexes of anxiety (Cattell & Scheier, 1958; Zuckerman & Biase, 1962), and the physiological measures with which they are compared are considered to be useful indexes of ANS activity (Greiner & Burch, 1955; Silverman et al., 1959). Therefore, two possible explanations were proposed to help resolve the problems created by these early failures.

First, "anxiety" could be viewed as a construct composed of both an autonomic component, reflected in ANS responses, and a "perceptual" component, reflected in a subject's ability to recognize his ANS responses and report them accurately. It is possible, according to this distinction, that differential scores on a self-report inventory might reflect no real difference in the autonomic component (that is, the subject's ANS responses to threat) but rather differences in the perceptual component (that is, their ability to recognize and describe their visceral activity). Consequently, an anxious person, according to this view, may be seen as one who perceives and describes his visceral responses readily but not one who is necessarily more active autonomically.

An alternate explanation for the frequent failure to find relationships between autonomic indexes and self-report measures of anxiety holds that anxiety is a response mechanism that may be elicited differentially only by certain specified conditions (Endler, Hunt, & Rosenstein, 1962; Farber & Spence, 1956; Spence, 1958). According to this view, our early failures could be explained in part by the use of inappropriately extreme stressors, since the threat of shock caused *all* subjects, anxious and nonanxious alike, to become quite apprehensive. Conceivably the employment of a more subtle stressor, preferably one that was personally involving (Mandler, Mandler, Kremen, & Sholiton, 1961) rather than physically threatening, would be expected to elicit differential anxiety responses from subjects who differed in self-reported anxiety level.

To test these two alternative explanations of our previous failures, Rappaport and I (Rappaport & Katkin, 1972)[1] set out to repeat the basic design of the earlier two studies using a mild and personally involving threat rather than the threat of electric shock. The "stress" situation employed required the subject to report to the experimenter each time he perceived an "emotional response" within himself. The subject was told that lie detector apparatus enabled the experimenter to verify his reports and that the purpose of the experiment was twofold: to test the subject's "openness" or "honesty" about his own emotional life, and to test him for accuracy of self-knowledge. In this manner both a subject's skill and integrity were placed in a competitive contest with a "sophisticated" machine. This experiment also enabled us to obtain a record of each subject's perception of autonomic responses on the polygraph, which contained his electrodermal activity level record, thus enabling us to analyze the relationship between a subject's electrodermal activity rate and his awareness of it.

On the assumption that there was a "real" relationship between self-report of trait anxiety and physiological response to personally involving stress and that the "anxiety response" was evoked only during the stressful period, the following hypotheses were formulated: (*a*) no differences in frequency of spontaneous EDRs emitted by anxious and nonanxious subjects would be expected during an initial rest period and (*b*) during a subsequent period of

---

[1] Rappaport and Katkin's paper, although published in 1972, was completed and reported on in 1967. An innumerable variety of irrelevant considerations resulted in the publication of some of these studies in a time sequence that bears no resemblance to the sequence in which they were completed.

mild stress those subjects scoring high on the MA scale would be expected to show a greater increase in rate of EDRs than those scoring low.

The alternate view that MA scale scores reflected only differences in autonomic perception but not in actual arousal led to the prediction of no differences between anxious and nonanxious subjects in EDR rate during either the rest or stress period; however, this view also led to the hypothesis that anxious subjects would report a higher frequency of "emotional" responses and would be more accurate than nonanxious subjects in identifying their occurrence.

The experiment was conducted in a manner similar to the two earlier experiments except that the third rest period was omitted. As in the previous experiments, the introduction of the stress-eliciting instructions came at the end of the initial rest period. High and low anxious subjects were selected on the basis of Taylor MA scale scores. High anxious subjects scored in the upper 20% of the distribution of undergraduate students and LA subjects scored in the lower 20% of the distribution. In this experiment 32 subjects were assigned to the experimental group and 16 to the control group; half of each group of subjects were HA and half LA.

The main results of Rappaport and Katkin's experiment are presented in Fig. 8-3, in which it may be seen that the rate of spontaneous electrodermal activity for the last 2 minutes of the initial rest period was compared with the average rate per 2-minute interval of the experimental period.[2] Figure 8-3 shows that during the last 2 minutes of the initial rest period there were no significant differences among the four experimental groups. However, the mean number of spontaneous EDRs for anxious and nonanxious groups who were stressed increased during the second period whereas the mean number for anxious and nonanxious groups who were not stressed decreased. These results were, once

---

[2] Rappaport and I had noticed in the data of the earlier studies and in pilot data for this study that the last 2 minutes of the initial rest period seemed to be a more meaningful measure of resting rates, because the newness and strangeness of the laboratory tended to elevate all subjects' lability levels in the early minutes of the rest period. To reduce the data from the stress period into a comparable mensurational unit, we compressed the data into mean rates per 2-minute units.

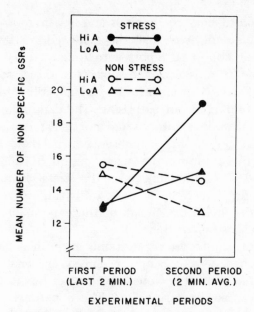

Fig. 8-3. Mean number of electrodermal responses (EDRs, or galvanic skin responses, GSRs) for subjects in the four experimental groups in the two experimental periods. Hi A = high anxious subjects; Lo A = low anxious subjects. (From Rappaport, H., & Katkin, E. S. Relationships among manifest anxiety, response to stress, and the perception of autonomic activity. *Journal of Consulting and Clinical Psychology,* 1972, 38, 219–224. Copyright 1972 by the American Psychological Association. Reprinted by permission.)

again, similar to those reported earlier by Katkin (1965, 1966); however, closer inspection of Fig. 8-3 indicates that among subjects in the stress group those who were designated anxious showed a greater increase in EDR rate than those designated nonanxious. An analysis of variance of these data confirmed the observation of a greater increase in spontaneous EDRs for the anxious subjects in the stress group as compared to nonanxious subjects in the stress group; a similar analysis obtained from the two control groups showed no difference in rate of response as a function of anxiety level.

An inspection of both the anxious and nonanxious groups in the stress conditions indicated that they showed no systematic differences in their ability to report autonomic activity correctly. In light of the fact that 78% of the subjects in these groups reported that they felt unable to perform the experimental tasks successfully, this finding is not surprising. The data indicated that the anxious and nonanxious subjects did not differ in their ability to correctly report autonomic responses nor in their absolute estimates of reactivity during the stress period of this experiment. Furthermore, 81% of the subjects in the stress group, irrespective of anxiety score, perceived the task of having to report internal sensations as the specific element of the experiment that created the most apprehension for them.

The results of Rappaport and Katkin's experiment confirmed the hypothesis we had been chasing for many years—that subjects who differed in trait anxiety would exhibit differential autonomic responsiveness to a stress situation. The experiment showed furthermore that these results were obtainable when the stress situation was relatively mild and geared to be ego involving, although we could not obtain similar results with the threat of electric shock that apparently elicited extreme apprehension from all subjects irrespective of MA scale score or AACL score. The results of Rappaport and Katkin's paper lent no support to the alternative hypothesis that scores on anxiety scales are related only to a subject's perception of his autonomic activity and not to his actual level of activity. First, it was clear that no actual differences in the reports of electrodermal activity could be attributed to individual differences in anxiety scale score. Second, there was a significant interaction of anxiety with stress, confirming the observation of actual differences in autonomic response rate as a function of anxiety score.

The findings of Rappaport and Katkin lent support also to the distinction between trait and state conceptions of anxiety discussed by Spielberger (1966). This distinction suggests that scales such as Taylor's MA scale reflect trait anxiety—a subject's propensity to respond anxiously under specified stress situations. The results of Rappaport and Katkin's experiment supported the notion that subjects with high trait anxiety (high MA scale score) exhibited more state anxiety (spontaneous EDRs) during stress than did subjects with low trait anxiety. In summary the results of this study showed that subjects who identified themselves as anxious on self-report inventories showed greater autonomic activity in response to mildly threatening ego involving instructions than subjects who did not identify themsleves as anxious.

ELECTRODERMAL ACTIVITY AS A PREDICTOR OF ANXIETY RESPONSE: ANXIETY OR ATTENTION?

At about the time that the data from Rappaport and Katkin's study came in, McCubbin and I (Katkin & McCubbin, 1969) began to focus our attention more on the dependent variable than on the independent variable. Just what was this measure of spontaneous electrodermal activity really reflecting? Was it state anxiety? Or was it perhaps an index of vigilance associated with anxiety? That is, was the sympathetic arousal reflected in increased spontaneous electrodermal activity merely efferent outflow serving the exclusive purpose of maintaining homeostasis, or was it perhaps a component of a more complex process related to increased central nervous system alertness or vigilance? One of the major reasons we became so interested in the functional role of spontaneous autonomic activity was that we had observed that during the initial rest periods of the prior three experiments (as well as in others) our subjects showed enormous variability in *resting levels* of spontaneous electrodermal activity. That is, just as Mundy-Castle and McKiever (1953) and the Laceys (1958) had reported, there were stable and reliable individual differences in the rate of spontaneous electrodermal activity among subjects. In our earlier experiments, we had observed that some subjects emitted as many spontaneous EDRs during prolonged relaxation as other subjects did during intense stress. What could such individual differences in activity level mean? If the universal increases observed under stress reflected some homeostatic effort on the part of the organism, then did high rates during rest reflect similar homeostatic effort? Did high resting rates perhaps reflect chronically high states of vigilance or alertness? These issues led to our next study (Katkin & McCubbin, 1969), which was addressed to the relationship of individual differences in electrodermal activity to the habituation of the orienting reflex (OR).

Orienting Reflex

The relationship between higher mental processes and ANS activity was discussed extensively by Sokolov (1960, 1963) in his description of the nature and significance of the OR and its patterns of adaptation and habituation. The OR, as described by Sokolov, is characterized by increased sense organ sensitivity, changes in skeletal muscle tonus, and specific changes in autonomic and CNS activity. Its relevance to higher mental processes is reflected in Pavlov's postulation that the OR had to be elicited before a conditioned reflex could develop.

With respect to parametric studies of the OR, Sokolov has noted that repeated presentations of the same stimulus will cause the OR to habituate; that is, neutral stimuli will fail to elicit an OR if they are presented repeatedly, unless they lose their neutrality by being paired with unconditioned stimuli or by acquiring signal value in some other way. Sokolov noted also that inherently threatening stimuli possess signal value and elicit a defense reflex (DR) rather than an OR. One of the major criteria for discriminating between an OR and a DR, therefore, is the extent to which the autonomic component of the elicited response habituates with repeated presentations. A response that rapidly habituates is presumed to be an OR. A response that resists habituation is presumed to be a DR. It has become traditional in studies of OR and DR elicitation and habituation to assess the autonomic component of these responses by quantification of the magnitude of the specific EDR to auditory or visual stimuli (Lynn, 1966).

Habituation of the OR as a Function of
Individual Differences in Electrodermal Lability

The point of departure for the study by Katkin and McCubbin (1969) was individual differences in the tendency to interpret stimuli as threatening or nonthreatening. It is clear that stimuli can be so intense that most subjects will judge them to be noxious; similarly stimuli can be so weak that few if any subjects will respond to them as if they were noxious. When moderately intense stimuli are used, however, the influence of individual differences becomes crucial; some subjects are likely to respond as if the stimuli were quite intense, and other subjects are likely to respond as if they were not at all intense. With respect to this distinction,

Katkin and McCubbin suggested that anxious subjects would be more likely to interpret moderately intense stimuli as noxious than would nonanxious ones. Thus, anxious subjects would be expected to show autonomic responses characteristic of the DR to moderately intense stimuli, i.e., responses that resist habituation; nonanxious subjects would be expected to show autonomic responses characteristic of the OR to moderately intense stimuli, i.e., those that habituate rapidly. The basic aim of Katkin and McCubbin's study, therefore, was to select subjects presumed to differ in anxiety level and to present them with repeated presentations of moderately intense auditory stimuli. Subjects were selected, as in the earlier studies, on the basis of extreme scores on Taylor's MA scale. However, Katkin and McCubbin also attempted to evaluate individual differences in "anxiety" by using individual differences in the resting level of electrodermal activity as an independent measure of anxiety. The logic behind this decision was roughly as follows: since all subjects tended to show large increases in electrodermal activity level under conditions of stress, perhaps those subjects who showed large levels of electrodermal activity during rest were more likely to perceive environmental stimulation as a stressful condition than those subjects who showed low levels of electrodermal activity. Consequently, Katkin and McCubbin hypothesized that subjects who were *electrodermally labile*, i.e., who showed high resting levels of spontaneous electrodermal activity, would be likely to interpret moderately intense auditory stimuli as threatening and respond with nonhabituating DRs, whereas subjects who showed low levels of spontaneous electrodermal activity would be likely to interpret the repeated auditory stimuli as nonthreatening and respond with rapidly habituating ORs. Subjects were also administered very low intensity stimuli as a control series. It was expected that no subjects in any condition would interpret the very low intensity stimuli as threatening; therefore, all subjects would show equal rates of rapid habituation to the low-intensity stimuli, irrespective of individual differences in anxiety or electrodermal lability.

Subjects were asked to relax during a 10-minute adaptation period, and their resting levels of spontaneous electrodermal activity were recorded. After that all subjects received 15 presentations of a 1000-Hz tone that lasted 2 sec. and was presented at variable intervals ranging from 30 to 90 sec. with a mean of 60 sec. The results of the experiment with respect to individual differences in Taylor MA scores were unremarkable; no significant effects of individual differences in anxiety scale score nor any interactions of anxiety scale score with habituation rate of electrodermal responses was obtained. However, when subjects' responsivity to the tones was evaluated as a function of individual differences in resting level of spontaneous electrodermal activity, highly significant results confirming our hypotheses were obtained. Figure 8-4 depicts the main findings of Katkin and McCubbin's (1969) experiment. In this figure, mean response magnitude is graphed for subjects in the High Nonspecific Activity (HNS) and the Low Nonspecific Activity (LNS) conditions for both moderate intensity (M Int) and low intensity (L

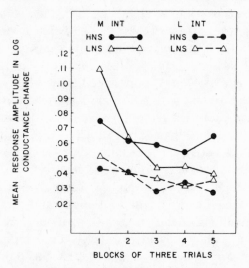

Fig. 8-4. Mean amplitude of response (change in log conductance) for subjects in four groups across five trial blocks of three trials each. HNS = High Nonspecific Activity condition; LNS = Low Nonspecific Activity condition; M Int = stimulation of moderate intensity; L Int = stimulation of low intensity. (From Katkin, E. S., & McCubbin, R. J. Habituation of the orienting response as a function of individual differences in anxiety and autonomic lability. *Journal of Abnormal Psychology*, 1969, 74, 54-60. Copyright 1969 by the American Psychological Association. Reprinted by permission.)

Int) stimulation. The responses to the 15 stimuli were grouped into five trial blocks of three trials each. The data contained in Fig. 8-4 indicated that response magnitudes for subjects in the two M Int groups appeared to be greater than comparable responses for subjects in the two L Int groups for all trials. Figure 8-4 also indicates that the habituation rate for the M Int-LNS group appeared steeper than that for the M Int-HNS group and that the habituation rates for subjects in the two L Int groups were similar. It may also be noted that there were initial differences in response strength among the groups; an analysis of the first trial block indicated a significant difference between the two M Int groups and the two L Int groups but no differences between HNS and LNS groups. More specifically, the initial difference between the HNS and the LNS subjects in the M Int group was not statistically significant.

Analysis of variance of the data for the five trial blocks confirmed that LNS subjects in the M Int group showed significant habituation; at the end of 15 trials their mean response magnitude was essentially identical to that of the subjects in the L Int groups. Mean response magnitude for HNS subjects in the M Int condition, however, followed a pattern expected for the DR; the trend for these subjects from trials 1 through 15 was essentially a flat horizontal curve, indicating no habituation of response magnitude. The finding that autonomic responses typical of the DR were elicited from electro-dermally labile subjects and that autonomic responses characteristic of the OR were elicited from electrodermally stabile subjects confirmed our main hypothesis and enhanced the validity of the use of electrodermal activity level as a reliable index of individual differences in responsivity to environmental stimulation.

The findings of Katkin and McCubbin have been replicated in various forms by Crider and Lunn (1971), Koepke and Pribram (1966), and Johnson (1963). Therefore, after McCubbin and I obtained these data, we went back to data we had collected in other research and proceeded to analyze them on the basis of individual differences in electrodermal lability.

Further Support for the Relationship between Individual Differences in Electrodermal Lability and Habituation of the OR

At the same time Katkin and McCubbin's (1969) study was being conducted, McCubbin and I were also conducting other experiments on the effects of the extent and quality of stimulus change on the magnitude of the orienting response (McCubbin & Katkin, 1971). In the course of that research, which was unrelated to the problem of individual differences in electrodermal lability, McCubbin and I obtained from 48 subjects data that indicated a clear pattern of OR habituation to a series of standard stimuli. These data are presented in Fig. 8-5. Note particularly the data for the first eight trials of what we have called the SS (standard stimulus) series. As is obvious from the data in Fig. 8-5 there was a clear pattern of habituation for all 48 subjects. Having just completed the study in which we had observed that habituation rates were dependent on individual differences in electrodermal lability, McCubbin and I took the data from Fig. 8-5 and subjected them to a reanalysis. We went back and divided the 48 subjects into subgroups based on individual differences in electrodermal

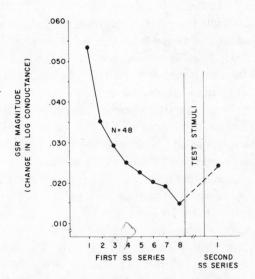

Fig. 8-5. Mean galvanic skin response (GSR) magnitude (change in log conductance) for all subjects ($N = 48$) for eight repetitions of standard stimuli. (From McCubbin, R. J., & Katkin, E. S. Magnitude of the orienting response as a function of extent and quality of stimulus change. *Journal of Experimental Psychology*, 1971, 88, 182–188. Copyright 1971 by the American Psychological Association. Reprinted by permission.)

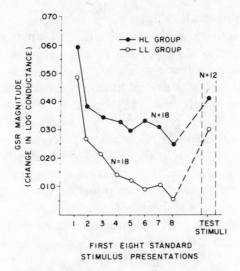

Fig. 8-6. Mean galvanic skin response (GSR) magnitude (change in log conductance) for labile (HL) and stabile (LL) subjects ($N = 36$) for eight repetitions of standard stimuli.

lability and selected the 18 most active and 18 least active subjects. Figure 8-6 contains the habituation curves for these 36 subjects for the same stimuli. The 18 electrodermally labile (HL) subjects showed some response decrement between trial 1 and trial 2, but thereafter showed resistance to habituation. Subjects who were electrodermally stabile (LL) showed consistent habituation across all eight trials. An analysis of variance of these data confirmed that there was a significant difference in rate of habituation; thus the findings of Katkin and McCubbin (1969) were substantiated in an entirely different experiment that was not addressed to the problem of individual differences in electrodermal lability. These data suggest that much of the current research on evaluation of autonomic responses to attention and orientation should take into account the important variable of individual differences in electrodermal lability.

The results of Katkin and McCubbin (1969) and the reanalysis of McCubbin and Katkin's (1971) data led us to the conclusion that high rates of spontaneous electrodermal activity were probably related to states of defensive or anxious-like hyperresponsivity to environmental stimulation. Therefore, McCubbin and I were eager to interpret individual differences in resting level of spontaneous electrodermal activity as a reliable index of what we had begun to think of as state anxiety. No sooner had we begun to feel complacent about our new approach to anxiety research than one of our colleagues, Richard Hirschman, suggested that it was as yet unclear whether individual differences in electrodermal lability represented defensive responsivity or merely some dimension of generalized attentional set. Hirschman suggested that if individual differences in electrodermal lability were merely an index of enhanced attentional capacity, or greater responsivity to stimulation, independent of noxious components, then we should be able to demonstrate increased levels of spontaneous electrodermal activity in nonthreatening environmental situations that might be likely to elicit increased attention. Thus, the next experiment in our series (Hirschman & Katkin, 1971) set out to evaluate the relationship between electrodermal lability and attention in a nonthreatening situation.

ANXIETY OR ATTENTION?
INTERPERSONAL ATTRACTION

The object of Hirschman and Katkin's (1971) study was to present subjects with a series of tape recordings of other students' "self-perceptions." Each subject was asked to listen to four recordings of different types of students and then to answer questions concerning the degree to which they identified with each of the four people that they heard. The assumption underlying the study was that the tape-recorded information could be construed as nonstressful but attention-eliciting stimuli. A further assumption was that subjects would attend most closely to the tape recordings with which they had the greatest degree of identification, and that electrodermal activity levels would be greatest for subjects while they were listening to the tape recording with which they identified most.

The subjects were 48 undergraduate females who listened to four prepared interviews taped by female confederates. Each female portrayed a student with one of the following sets of characteristics concerning academic life: hard work—no success; hard work—a great deal of success; little work—no success; little work—a great deal of success. The confederates on these tape recordings spoke in a normal tone with little emotional inflection. During the "interview" they responded to questions that focused on the work-success dimension. Each tape began with a male interviewer in the process of expressing a thought; thus the impression was created that the tape was an extract from a larger interview. All sessions were improvised and were practiced several times before adequate tapes were prepared. Following are representative samples of the content of the interviews:

Hard work—no success.

I don't like the pressure of having to study very hard and keep up with my grades. I find it difficult to do that. I study a lot but I don't feel I really get that much done. It's more the lack of success after putting in a lot of time that gets me down.

Hard work—a great deal of success.

I worked pretty hard. My school had a lot of pressure. I did pretty well. There's a certain way of taking exams and papers. I've gotten the grades and that's pretty important to me and my parents are pleased with me.

Little work—no success.

School is not very exciting. I am not very much of a student. I guess a lot of it is me. I'm not that involved. I don't do very well. I'm kind of borderline. I guess if I worked harder I might get better grades.

Little work—a great deal of success.

It's just my marks are very good because studying takes up almost no time. Just sort of read it once. I usually study maybe once or twice a week. I'm taking maximum credits. It has never been very much work for me to do so. It's really not that difficult to do well in school.

The presentation of the four tapes was completely counterbalanced for the 48 subjects, and all 24 possible orders of counterbalancing were used so that each order was presented to two individuals. Interspersed between each of the four tapes was a rest period. After hearing each tape, subjects checked one of the following statements: (*a*) this girl sounds a great deal like me; (*b*) this girl sounds somewhat like me; (*c*) this girl sounds very little like me; (*d*) this girl sounds not like me at all. The subjects were then asked to rank the tapes into four categories from most to least like themselves in decreasing order. Electrodermal activity was monitored throughout all phases of the experiment so that spontaneous activity rates could be evaluated as subjects listened to each tape.

The results of this experiment are depicted in Fig. 8-7, in which it may be seen that the mean number of spontaneous or nonspecific EDRs was greatest in response to those tapes with which subjects identified most and least in response to those tapes with which subjects identified least. Analysis of variance of these data confirmed the observation that there was a significant main effect of identification on electrodermal activity, and a posteriori tests indicated further that there were significant differences between the category of greatest identification and the other three categories, but no other significant differences.

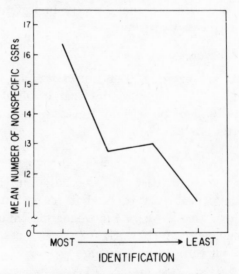

Fig. 8-7. Mean number of nonspecific electrodermal responses (EDRs, or galvanic skin responses, GSRs) for all subjects as a function of degree of identification with tape-recorded voices.

The findings of Hirschman and Katkin's study supported the notion that the process of identifying with another person is associated with differential physiological change. It does not seem reasonable, however, to posit a direct relationship between electrodermal activity and a psychodynamic process such as identification. An alternate and more parsimonious explanation is that attention was the critical mediating variable. It is likely that at the beginning of a presentation subjects would manifest a minimal level of attention to a tape. As a function of the degree to which they identified with a tape, however, attentional activity may have selectively increased or decreased, resulting in differential degrees of arousal and then differential electrodermal activity. Subjects in Hirschman and Katkin's study were told "we will be trying to study students' perceptions of themselves." This instruction may have set them to focus on statements that were meaningful in regard to themselves, thereby increasing the likelihood of differential attention to tapes that were more or less like themselves. At first it seemed obvious to us that the findings of this experiment supported the contention that cognitive activity associated with identification may have influenced ANS functions in this nonstressful paradigm. When we later reflected on this study, however, we began to wonder if we had not concluded too hastily that cognition affected the ANS. How could we be sure that cognitive activity simply elevated electrodermal activity and not that elevated electrodermal activity had a feedback function that subsequently facilitated the attentional or cognitive component? This speculation brought us back once again to a specific research focus on the relationship of electrodermal lability to cognitive behavior. The task seemed clear. It was time now to look closely at the burgeoning experimental literature on the psychology of attention and vigilance and to begin to integrate that literature with our research focus on individual differences in electrodermal lability.

At this point we went back to the earlier work we had done on differential rates of habituation of the OR. Our own research, as well as the studies by Koepke and Pribram (1966), Johnson (1963), and especially Crider and Lunn (1971), indicated to us that there was a clear relationship between activity level of the sympathetic division of the ANS, as represented in electrodermal responding, and the higher mental processes involved in selective habituation to environmental stimulation. Exactly what the nature of the mechanisms or processes underlying this relationship is remains unclear; but Crider and Augenbraun (1973) suggested that the EDR decrement observed in studies of OR habituation represents a decrement in attention, and they have posited that it should be possible to demonstrate differential rates of attentional decrement between fast and slow habituators of the OR. Since fast and slow habituators are also stabile and labile subjects, respectively, it follows that one should be able to observe differential attentional decrement between electrodermally labile and stabile subjects.

ELECTRODERMAL LABILITY, ATTENTION, AND VIGILANCE

The logic for the investigation of the relationship between electrodermal lability and attentional or vigilant behavior was summarized clearly by Crider and Augenbraun (1973). First, it must be noted that since there is a consistent positive relationship between rate of spontaneous EDRs (electrodermal lability) and the rate of habituation of the OR, it is reasonable to use either rate of spontaneous response or rate of habituation as legitimate operational indexes of the construct "electrodermal lability": this point was made clear by Crider and Lunn (1971) as well as by Crider and Augenbraun (1973). Noting this, Crider and Augenbraun suggested:

> If the elicited EDR is regarded as a component of a more generalized attending response to environmental change, then stable individual differences in EDR habituation can be considered to reflect characteristic rates of attentional decrement with repetition of the eliciting event. It should therefore be possible to demonstrate differential rates of attentional decrement between fast and slow EDR habituators on tasks demanding focused attention for extended periods [p. 1].

In fact, there have been demonstrations of just that point. Coles and Gale (1971) reported a positive relationship between rate of EDR habituation and number of correct signal detections in a 1-hour auditory vigilance task, and Siddle (1972) found that decrement in auditory vigilance paralleled decrement in EDR response to moderately intense tones. Crider and Augenbraun correctly noted, however, that neither of these two reports provided crucial evidence that electrodermal lability was related to attentional capacity, because performance in signal detection tasks may be accounted for either by genuine differences in *perceptual* sensitivity, or by differences in response set or bias. In signal detection theory, these two components are usually separated from each other by mathematical manipulation of the ratio of correct detections to false alarms. Perceptual sensitivity, or attentional capacity, is represented by the symbol d', and response bias, or willingness to respond indiscriminately, is represented by the symbol β. To assess the extent to which electrodermal lability was related to d' or β, Crider and Augenbraun ran two experiments in which previously identified labile and stabile subjects were asked to identify three-digit signals against a background of digits presented auditorily at a rate of one per second for 64 minutes. A correct signal was an odd-even-odd combination in which the two odd digits were different from each other. In this experiment, electrodermal lability was defined by the rate of habituation of skin potential responses. As in the reports of Siddle (1972) and Coles and Gale (1971), Crider and Augenbraun found that labile subjects got more correct signal detections than did stabile subjects; however, further analysis of their data led them to conclude that all differences were attributable to β rather than to d'. That is, their data indicated that the greater number of correct detections observed for labile subjects were associated with a greater number of false alarms also, indicating that the labile subjects were merely less cautious in reporting what they believed to be a signal. They concluded that the results of their experiments indicated that electrodermal lability predicted *motivational* rather than perceptual components of the signal detection task, and that those subjects who became "involved" in the habituation task, and thereby habituated slowly, were the same subjects who became "involved" in the signal detection task and adopted a more liberal reporting strategy, resulting in more hits and more false alarms.

In an attempt to manipulate the motivational level of subjects, two of my colleagues and I (Sostek, Katkin, & Sostek, 1972) carried out an experiment using the same stimulus materials employed by Crider and his associates. In our experiment, however, a differential payoff matrix was introduced in an attempt to elevate the risk-taking probability of stabile subjects, thereby equating β for both stabile and labile subjects. It was anticipated that if β could be equated by this experimental manipulation, then differences in d' independent of β would emerge. A detailed description of Sostek et al.'s experiment follows.

Two experimental sessions were carried out approximately 1 month apart. During the first session, subjects were told that they would have a rest period, after which they would hear pure tones presented through a loudspeaker. Each of these tones was 9 sec. long and was presented on a variable interval schedule around a mean of 60 sec. During the 10-minute rest period, skin resistance responses of 100 ohms or more were measured; these data were subsequently used to divide subjects into labile and stabile groups in the manner described previously (Katkin, 1965, 1966; Katkin & McCubbin, 1969). The purpose of the presentation of 20 tones was twofold. First, it was desirable to replicate the well-reported phenomenon of differential rates of habituation to auditory stimuli for labile and stabile subjects. Second, we planned to evaluate the extent to which d' might deteriorate over time during a signal detection task. Since stabile subjects characteristically show habituation of the orienting response to tones whereas labiles do not, we speculated that a parallel phenomenon for higher cognitive activity such as perceptual sensitivity might be discernible. Thus it was decided to compare the habituation curves to the 20 tones with the rate of decrement in perceptual sensitivity (d') during the signal detection task to be administered 1 month later.

Approximately 1 month after this initial session, each subject was asked to participate in the second part of the experiment. When the subjects arrived again at the laboratory they were seated in the same chamber as in the first session, and the same recording procedure was followed. The second experimental session consisted of two parts. The first part was a tone habituation procedure similar to the initial session, but of shorter duration. In the second part of the experiment the vigilance task used by Crider and Augenbraun, adapted from Krupski, Raskin, and Bakan (1971) was presented to the subjects. As described earlier, this task consisted of a series of taped random digits spoken by a male voice at the rate of one per second. The tape was slightly modified so that the entire tape lasted 56 minutes, of which the first 8 minutes were used for a practice session and the remaining 48 minutes for the actual experiment. The subject's task was to detect infrequent odd-even-odd digit combinations that included three different successive digits (e.g., 9-4-3). Such combinations occurred irregularly at the rate of 11 signals per period in each of the three 16-minute time periods of the experimental period. The 8-minute practice period contained signals at approximately the same rate.

Subjects were then divided randomly into three groups. One group was told that they would receive a reward of 9 cents for each correct response, that they would lose 9 cents for an omission or a miss, and that they would lose only 1 cent for a false alarm. This instruction was designed to increase risk-taking behavior, or a risky response strategy. A second group of subjects was told that they would receive 9 cents for a correct hit, lose only 1 cent if they omitted a response, but lose 9 cents if they gave a false alarm. These instructions, of course, were designed to maximize a cautious response set. Neutral subjects were told nothing about payoffs and simply were asked to try to identify signals correctly.

The results of the study were as follows. First, with respect to habituation of the OR, we replicated the common finding that labile subjects and stabile subjects differed in rate of habituation to repeated auditory stimuli. Both labile and stabile subjects initially showed approximately the same magnitude of the electrodermal component of the orienting response to auditory tones; but over trials labile subjects resisted habituation whereas stabile subjects habituated. During the signal detection task, data were analyzed for hits, sensitivity (d') and response bias (β). In general, the analysis of data for the mean number of hits, mean d' and mean β for the entire 48-minute period confirmed Crider and Augenbraun's observation that labile subjects got more correct signal detections than stabiles. It should be noted that in our experiment, as opposed to Crider and Augenbraun's, labile subjects did *not* differ from stabiles on response bias. Furthermore, the payoff matrix and differential instructions resulted in no differences in correct detections or in d'; therefore, the remainder of the data analyses are described for labile and stabile subjects irrespective of payoff condition.

When the data were analyzed as a function of time, it was found that labile and stabile subjects got essentially the same number of correct responses during the first 16-minute period, but that in the next two periods stabile subjects showed a continual decline in number of hits while labile subjects showed a lesser decline. This interaction, which was statistically significant, is depicted in Fig. 8-8. When the data on sensitivity (d') were analyzed, the trend became more clearly pronounced. That is, d' for labile subjects stayed at essentially the same level throughout the 48-minute period, whereas d' for stabile subjects showed a rather clear linear decline from the first 16-minute period to the last 16-minute period. This interaction, which is statistically significant, is depicted in Fig. 8-9. The relationship between labile and stabile subjects across time on the signal detection task parallels the curves reported for habituation of the OR 1 month earlier. Figure 8-9 indicates that the critical difference in perceptual sensitivity between labile and stabile subjects emerges as a function of time on task and is not readily apparent in early stages of the task. Furthermore, the analysis of variance of the six data points in Fig. 8-9 indicated that there was no main effect of labile versus stabile subjects when the three time periods were collapsed, but that there was a significant main effect of time on task.

A close inspection of Crider and Augenbraun's data leads to the conclusion that the current findings from our laboratory are not

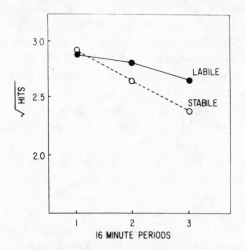

Fig. 8-8. Mean square root of hits for labile and stabile subjects across three trial blocks of 16 minutes each.

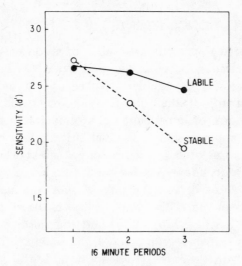

Fig. 8-9. Mean sensitivity score (d') for labile and stabile subjects across three trial blocks of 16 minutes each.

inconsistent with theirs. Crider and Augenbraun also found that hits and d' dropped off as a function of time for stabile subjects, but not labile subjects; however, their results, while entirely consistent with ours, were not statistically significant. There was one clear difference between their procedure and ours that might account for the stronger effects of time in our data. We used frequency of spontaneous responses, rather than rate of habituation, to define subjects as labile or stabile. Although frequency of response and rate of habituation are positively correlated, the relationship is not perfect; and there may be differences among subjects as a function of differences in the procedures employed to label them. All future studies in this area should examine the differences in results that may result from differential use of the frequency-of-response versus rate-of-habituation definition of lability.

At any rate, it seems clear from the significant results in our laboratory and the statistically nonsignificant but similar trend from Crider and Augenbraun's laboratory that electrodermally labile subjects show better performance than electrodermally stabile subjects in an auditory vigilance task.

SUMMARY AND CONCLUSIONS

The cumulative impact of this series of studies seems to be that electrodermal lability is, as Crider and Lunn (1971) suggested, a meaningful personality variable. We began this series of studies with an interest in individual differences in electrodermal lability as a convenient index of *dependent* autonomic responsivity to stress. At present, it appears that individual differences in resting autonomic level, as reflected in electrodermal lability levels, represent an important *independent* variable for future research.

Our studies showed that the rate of spontaneous electrodermal activity increased markedly when subjects were threatened experimentally (Katkin, 1965, 1966) and that individual differences in trait anxiety effectively predicted the extent of responsiveness to mild, ego-involving stress (Rappaport & Katkin, 1972). If the research had stopped there we would have been able to conclude safely that electrodermal lability reflected state anxiety, and this conclusion would have drawn support from the obvious theoretical link between state anxiety and sympathetic arousal, of which electrodermal responsivity is an index.

Our later studies, however, indicated that different levels of electrodermal activity could be elicited from nonstressful experimental manipulations and that these differences were probably related to the attentional demands of our tasks (Hirschman & Katkin, 1971). Subsequent studies showed that resting differences in electrodermal lability could predict differential rates of habituation to repeated stimuli (Katkin & McCubbin, 1969) and could also predict individual differences in sustained perceptual sensitivity. Thus, the most obvious conclusion to be drawn from these studies is that electrodermal activity is a personality variable that reflects individual differences in higher central processes involved in attending to and processing information. To the extent that high rates of electrodermal lability are elicited by the induction of experimental stress, it might be concluded that these increases in electrodermal responsivity serve to increase or enhance attentional and information-processing capacity during such stress. This interpretation is not only consistent with the obtained data, but is consistent with a functional interpretation of the significance of autonomic outflow as a "fight or flight" mechanism during times of emergency. Our data, however, take us a bit beyond the traditional view of "emergency preparedness." The data from our recent work (Sostek, Katkin, & Sostek, 1972), which shows that electrodermal lability is related to perceptual sensitivity, but not to indiscriminate overall responsiveness, suggest that lability reflects a variable that is a selective enhancer of *effective central processes*, rather than merely a generalized arousal mechanism.

FUTURE DIRECTIONS

The observation of a correlation between increased perceptual vigilance and electrodermal lability fails to clarify any questions of cause and effect. It is not obvious from the data we have collected so far whether electrodermal lability serves some facilitative feedback function that enhances central processes, or whether enhanced central processing is merely reflected in some increase in rate of sympathetic outflow. Our current research is attempting to deal with this question by direct experimental manipulation of electrodermal activity rates. The technique to be used involves the instrumental modification of electrodermal activity. If it is true (as it seems to be) that electrodermally labile subjects perform better on vigilance tasks than electrodermally stabile subjects, then the question may be asked whether instrumental elevation of a subject's electrodermal lability level will result in improved vigilance performance. The past decade has witnessed an enormous surge of interest in the conditionability of autonomic nervous system responses by instrumental techniques. Miller and his colleagues (DiCara & Miller, 1968; Miller, 1969; Miller & DiCara, 1968) pioneered the research with animals, and Kimmel (1974) and the Harvard group (Birk, Crider, Shapiro, & Tursky, 1966; Crider, Shapiro, & Tursky, 1966) pioneered the work with humans. Considerable controversy has arisen concerning the theoretically proper interpretation and the ultimate significance of current demonstrations of instrumental modifiability of ANS responses (see Crider, Schwartz, & Shnidman, 1969; Katkin & Murray, 1968; Katkin, Murray & Lachman, 1969), but there is little doubt that under specified conditions it is possible to instrumentally modify autonomically mediated responses such as spontaneous electrodermal activity. Hopefully, the research to be conducted in our laboratory will be able to use this new technique to improve our understanding of the relationship between electrodermal activity and higher cognitive processes.

In addition to this line of research development, we are also busily engaged in a project to develop a predictive measure of individual differences in lability. The aim of this project is to develop a test that has high reliability and validity and that is easy to administer and score, thereby making it particularly useful for screening labile and stabile subjects out of large populations. One immediate advantage of such a test is that it will facilitate future research on labile and stabile subjects by allowing their identification without the need for psychophysiological analysis. If this should successfully come to pass, we will have come full circle (methodologically) back to the investigation of stable personality traits reflected in self-report inventories.

REFERENCES

Bendig, A. W. Extraversion, neuroticism, and manifest anxiety. *Journal of Consulting Psychology*, 1957, 21, 398.

Birk, L., Crider, A., Shapiro, D., & Tursky, B. Operant electrodermal conditioning under partial curarization. *Journal of Comparative and Physiological Psychology*, 1966, 62, 165–166.

Burch, N. R., & Greiner, T. H. A bioelectric scale of human alertness: Concurrent recording of the EEG and GSR. *Psychiatric Research Reports*, 1960, 12, 183–193.

Buss, A. H. A follow-up item analysis of the Taylor Anxiety Scale. *Journal of Clinical Psychology*, 1955, 11, 409–410.

Buss, A. H., Wiener, M., Durkee, A., & Baer, M. The measurement of anxiety in clinical situations. *Journal of Consulting Psychology*, 1955, 19, 125–129.

Cattell, R. B., & Scheier, I. H. The nature of anxiety: A review of thirteen multivariate analyses comprising 814 variables. *Psychological Reports*, 1958, 4, 351–388.

Coles, M. G. H., & Gale, A. Physiological reactivity as a predictor of performance in a vigilance task. *Psychophysiology*, 1971, 8, 594–599.

Crider, A., & Augenbraun, C. B. Auditory vigilance correlates of electrodermal response habituation speed. Unpublished manuscript, Department of Psychology, Williams College, 1973.

Crider, A., & Lunn, R. Electrodermal lability as a personality dimension. *Journal of Experimental Research in Personality*, 1971, 2, 145–150.

Crider, A., Schwartz, G., & Shnidman, S. On the criteria for instrumental autonomic conditioning: A reply to Katkin and Murray. *Psychological Bulletin*, 1969, 71, 455–461.

Crider, A., Shapiro, D., & Tursky, B. Reinforcement of spontaneous electrodermal activity. *Journal of Comparative and Physiological Psychology*, 1966, 61, 20–27.

DiCara, L. V., & Miller, N. E. Changes in heart rate instrumentally learned by curarized rats as avoidance responses. *Journal of Comparative and Physiological Psychology*, 1968, 65, 8–12.

Endler, N. S., Hunt, J. McV., & Rosenstein, A. J. An S-R inventory of anxiousness. *Psychological Monographs*, 1962, 76(17, Whole No. 536).

Farber, I. E., & Spence, K. W. Effects of anxiety, stress, and task variables on reaction time. *Journal of Personality*, 1956, 25, 1-18.

Greiner, T. H., & Burch, N. R. Response of human GSR to drugs that influence the reticular formation of brain stem. *Federation Proceedings, American Society of Experimental Biology*, 1955, 14, 346.

Hirschman, R., & Katkin, E. S. Relationships among attention, GSR activity, and perceived similarity of self and others. *Journal of Personality*, 1971, 2, 277-288.

Johnson, L. C. Some attributes of spontaneous electrodermal activity. *Journal of Comparative and Physiological Psychology*, 1963, 56, 415-422.

Katkin, E. S. Relationship between manifest anixiety and two indices of autonomic response to stress. *Journal of Personality and Social Psychology*, 1965, 2, 324-333.

Katkin, E. S. The relationship between a measure of transitory anxiety and spontaneous autonomic activity. *Journal of Abnormal Psychology*, 1966, 71, 142-146.

Katkin, E. S., & McCubbin, R. J. Habituation of the orienting response as a function of individual differences in anxiety and autonomic lability. *Journal of Abnormal Psychology*, 1969, 74, 54-60.

Katkin, E. S., & Murray, E. N. Instrumental conditioning of autonomically mediated behavior: Theoretical and methodological issues. *Psychological Bulletin*, 1968, 70, 52-68.

Katkin, E. S., Murray, E. N., & Lachman, R. Concerning instrumental autonomic conditioning: A rejoinder. *Psychological Bulletin*, 1969, 71, 462-466.

Kimmel, H. D. Instrumental conditioning of autonomically mediated responses in human beings. *American Psychologist*, 1974, 29, 325-335.

Koepke, J. E., & Pribram, K. H. Habituation of GSR as a function of stimulus duration and spontaneous activity. *Journal of Comparative and Physiological Psychology*, 1966, 61, 442-448.

Krupski, A., Raskin, D. C., & Bakan, P. Physiological and personality correlates of commission errors in an auditory vigilance task. *Psychophysiology*, 1971, 8, 304-311.

Lacey, J. I., & Lacey, B. C. The relationship of resting autonomic activity to motor impulsivity. *Research Publications of the Association for Nervous and Mental Diseases*, 1958, 36, 144-209.

Lynn, R. *Attention, arousal, and the orientation reaction*. Oxford: Pergamon Press, 1966.

Mandler, G., Mandler, J. M., Kremen, I., & Sholiton, R. The response to threat: Relations among verbal and physiological indexes. *Psychological Monographs*, 1961, 75(9, Whole No. 513).

McCubbin, R. J., & Katkin, E. S. Magnitude of the orienting response as a function of extent and quality of stimulus change. *Journal of Experimental Psychology*, 1971, 88, 182-188.

Miller, N. E. Learning of visceral and glandular responses. *Science*, 1969, 163, 434–445.

Miller, N. E., & DiCara, L. V. Instrumental learning of urine formation by rats: Changes in renal blood flow. *American Journal of Physiology*, 1968, 215, 677–683.

Mundy-Castle, A. C., & McKiever, B. L. The psychophysiological significance of the galvanic skin response. *Journal of Experimental Psychology*, 1953, 46, 15–23.

Rappaport, H., & Katkin, E. S. Relationships among manifest anxiety, response to stress, and the perception of autonomic activity. *Journal of Consulting and Clinical Psychology*, 1972, 38, 219–224.

Richter, C. P. A study of the electric skin resistance and psychogalvanic reflex in a case of unilateral sweating. *Brain*, 1927, 50, 216–235.

Sarason, I. G. Empirical findings and theoretical problems in the use of anxiety scales. *Psychological Bulletin*, 1960, 57, 403–415.

Siddle, D. A. T. Vigilance decrement and speed of habituation of the GSR component of the orienting response. *British Journal of Psychology*, 1972, 63, 191–194.

Silverman, A. J., Cohen, S. I., & Shmavonian, B. M. Investigation of psychophysiologic relationships with skin resistance measures. *Journal of Psychosomatic Research*, 1959, 4, 65–87.

Sokolov, E. N. Neuronal models and the orienting reflex. In M. A. B. Brazier (Ed.), *The central nervous system and behavior*. New York: Josiah Macy, Jr., Foundation, 1960.

Sokolov, E. N. *Perception and the conditioned reflex*. New York: Macmillan, 1963.

Sostek, A. J., Katkin, E. S., & Sostek, A. M. Signal detection as a function of electrodermal lability and differential payoffs. Paper presented at meetings of the Society for Psychophysiological Research, Boston, Nov. 1972.

Spence, K. W. A theory of emotionally based drive (D) and its relation to performance in simple learning situations. *American Psychologist*, 1958, 13, 131–141.

Spielberger, C. D. Theory and research on anxiety. In C. D. Spielberger (Ed.), *Anxiety and behavior*. New York: Academic Press, 1966.

Taylor, J. A. A personality scale of manifest anxiety. *Journal of Abnormal and Social Psychology*, 1953, 48, 285–290.

Welsh, G. S. Factor dimensions A and R. In G. S. Welsh & W. G. Dahlstrom (Eds.), *Basic readings on the MMPI*. Minneapolis: University of Minnesota Press, 1956.

Winter, W. D., Ferreira, A. J., & Ransom, R. Two measures of anxiety: A validation. *Journal of Consulting Psychology*, 1963, 27, 520–524.

Zuckerman, M. The development of an affect adjective check list for the measurement of anxiety. *Journal of Consulting Psychology*, 1960, 24, 457–462.

Zuckerman, M., & Biase, B. V. Replication and further data on the validity of the affect adjective check list measure of anxiety. *Journal of Consulting Psychology*, 1962, 26, 291.

9
ANXIETY, STRESS, AND PSYCHOPATHY

Robert D. Hare

Department of Psychology
University of British Columbia
Vancouver, Canada

This chapter discusses two topics that appear to be conceptually related: (*a*) psychopathic or sociopathic behavior and (*b*) the psychophysiological processes involved in responding to anxiety- or stress-inducing stimuli.

Most discussions of anxiety and stress, including the majority of those in the present work, tend to emphasize the negative or unpleasant aspects of these states. Where therapeutic efforts are involved, they are generally geared to reducing anxiety and stress, the assumptions being that the person will thereby be made more comfortable and that his behavioral efficiency will increase. To a great extent, the validity of the latter assumption rests on the theoretical and empirical relationships between arousal (activation) and performance (see Duffy, 1972). To the degree that anxiety or stress contributes to arousal level, their reduction should improve

The research reported herein was supported by grant MA-4511 from the Medical Research Council of Canada and by the Canadian Mental Health Association.

behavioral efficiency on tasks for which high levels of arousal have a disruptive effect. In this regard, it may be worthwhile to recall the right-hand half of the inverted U-curve relating arousal and performance, in which performance drops off as arousal increases beyond some optimal level.

However, there are probably some situations and conditions in which an improvement in behavioral efficiency requires an increase in anxiety rather than a decrease. I am not simply thinking of the left-hand side of the inverted U-curve, since there are obviously several ways of increasing arousal to an optimal level without increasing anxiety.

Rather, I have in mind the propositions that certain minimal amounts of anxiety are required for the acquisition and maintenance of some forms of prosocial behavior, and that even these minimal amounts are lacking in a particular clinical disorder, psychopathy. It can be argued that psychopathic behavior is, at least in part, related to a failure to experience sufficient anxiety or anticipatory fear for the inhibition of behavior likely to lead to punishment or social disapproval.

TWO-PROCESS THEORY OF AVOIDANCE LEARNING

To a large extent, this argument makes use of the well-known two-process theory of avoidance learning in which learning to avoid punishment involves (1) the classical conditioning of fear to cues associated with the punishment and (2) the subsequent reinforcement, by fear reduction, of responses that remove the individual from the fear-producing cues (Mowrer, 1947; Solomon & Brush, 1954). The psychopathic individual is relatively deficient in the acquisition of classically conditioned fear responses and therefore is missing a key element (stage 1) in the avoidance learning sequence (see Hare, 1970, 1974, for reviews of the relevant empirical evidence). In view of this, a reasonable prediction would be that procedures designed to increase the psychopath's capacity for experiencing fear should also increase his ability to inhibit behavior that would otherwise get him into trouble.

I should note here that although two-process avoidance learning theory is able to handle much of the clinical and empirical data on psychopathy, it has been subjected to vigorous attack by several investigators. One result of these criticisms has been the development of several modified versions of the theory, the most promising of which is the cognitive theory of avoidance learning proposed by Seligman and Johnston (1973). Even this theory, however, which emphasizes expectancies about act outcomes and preferences for outcomes, assigns an important role to classically conditioned fear during the early stages of the acquisition of avoidance responses. As a result, we would still expect an increase in anxiety to facilitate avoidance and, by implication, prosocial behavior in the psychopath.

PSYCHOPATHY AND ANXIETY

Before introducing some comments and speculations about the mechanisms that may be responsible for the psychopath's attenuated anxiety, let me explain that by psychopathy I mean that clinical disorder and its various manifestations described by Cleckley (1968) in *The Mask of Sanity*, and referred to by the World Health Organization (1968) and the American Psychiatric Association (1968) as category 301.7, Antisocial personality. The latter suggests that the term be reserved for

...individuals who are basically unsocialized and whose behavior pattern brings them repeatedly into conflict with society. They are incapable of significant loyalty to individuals, groups, or social values. They are grossly selfish, callous, irresponsible, impulsive and unable to feel guilt or to learn from experience and punishment. Frustration tolerance is low. They tend to blame others or offer plausible rationalizations for their behavior. A mere history of repeated legal or social offences is not sufficient to justify this diagnosis . . . [American Psychiatric Association, 1968, p. 43].

Anticipatory Anxiety

Elsewhere (Hare, 1970, 1974) I have reviewed physiological research relevant to the concept of psychopathy. One of the most frequent findings has been the subjects (Ss) defined as psychopathic show relatively little evidence of anticipatory electrodermal activity prior to the onset of painful stimulation. This finding readily fits in with my earlier argument that psychopaths do not experience sufficient anticipatory fear for the instigation of avoidance responses. While most of the available electrodermal data are consistent with this position, some apparent anomalies appear when cardiovascular variables are considered. For example, several years ago we found that although psychopathic inmates gave very small electrodermal (skin conductance) responses to conditioned stimuli (10-sec. tones) prior to electric shock, their cardiovascular responses (heart rate and peripheral vasoconstriction) were just as large as those given by nonpsychopathic inmates (Hare & Quinn, 1971). That is, the psychopaths appeared to be poor electrodermal conditioners but good cardiovascular ones. Consider also a recent study (Hare & Craigen, 1974) in which pairs of Ss (A and B) were required to take turns administering shock to themselves and to one another. A 10-sec. conditioned stimulus (CS) tone preceded each shock, so that it was possible to evaluate physiological responses prior to reception of shock delivered to one's self (direct shock) and to the other S ("vicarious" shock). Shock contingencies were arranged so that if S A chose to give himself a small shock on any given trial, S B would get a large one on that trial. However, S B then was given a chance to retaliate, although his choices of shock intensity were actually overridden by the experimenter. Half the A Ss were psychopathic inmates (Group P) while the other half were not (Group NP). There were no differences between groups in the intensities of shock chosen for themselves and for the other Ss.

However, as Fig. 9-1 indicates, we found that the Ss in Group NP gave much larger anticipatory electrodermal responses (i.e., increases in palmar skin conductance prior to reception of shock) than did those in Group P, particularly when they themselves were about to receive the shock. These results are of course consistent with previous research in which the conditioned response was an electrodermal one.

When cardiac responses were considered, the Ss in Group P turned out to be the better conditioners. Figure 9-2 shows the mean sec.-by-sec. changes in heart rate (HR) following onset of the CS tone preceding shock to self (S) and to the other (O); the data are averaged over the eight trials involved. The anticipatory HR response was primarily accelerative in nature, giving way to a decelerative phase just prior to shock. The size and form of the response were much the same whether shock was about to be

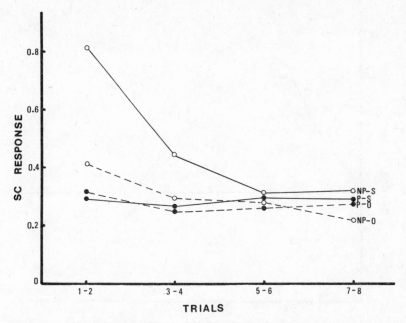

Fig. 9-1. Mean amplitude (in μmhos) of the anticipatory skin conductance response given by psychopathic (P) and nonpsychopathic (NP) Ss to conditioned stimuli preceding shock to self (S) and shock to other (O). Source: Hare, R. D., & Craigen, D. Psychopathy and physiological activity in a mixed-motive game situation. *Psychophysiology*, 1974, 11, 197–206. With permission.

received directly (S) or "vicariously" experienced (O). However, both the accelerative and the decelerative phases were significantly larger in Group P than in Group NP. The most dramatic difference between groups, a difference obscured by the averaging of data across trials, occurred on the first trial. As Fig. 9-3 indicates, the anticipatory HR response of Group P on Trial 1 consisted primarily of marked acceleration during the first 5 or 6 sec. after CS onset, whereas those of Group NP were small and slightly decelerative in nature. On the second trial, Group P developed a secondary decelerative component while Group NP's responses became similar to those given by Group P on the first trial. On subsequent trials, the response patterns of each group became more and more similar to one another.

These findings again suggest that psychopathic inmates may be poor electrodermal conditioners but relatively good cardiovascular ones, at least within the limitations of the procedures used. Though

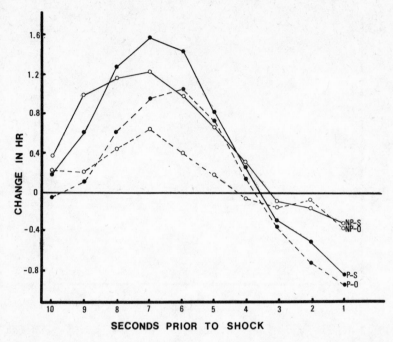

Fig. 9-2. Mean sec.-by-sec. changes in HR (bpm) shown by each group to the conditioned stimuli preceding shock to self (S) and shock to other (O). (Groups are psychopathic Ss, P, and non-psychopathic Ss, NP.) Averaged over 8 trials. Source: Hare, R. D., & Craigen, D. Psychopathy and physiological activity in a mixed-motive game situation. *Psychophysiology*, 1974, 11, 197–206. With permission.

there is no reason why the various components of conditioned autonomic activity should necessarily be highly correlated, either within or between Ss, this dissociation (on a group basis) between electrodermal and cardiovascular activity in a conditioning paradigm is unusual. Whether it is also surprising depends to a certain extent on how comfortable one feels with some of the recent theory and research on the putative role of cardiovascular activity in the modulation of sensory input (e.g., Graham & Clifton, 1966; Lacey, 1967; Sokolov, 1963). Very briefly, integration of Western and Soviet theory suggests that the orienting response (OR) elicited by novel, interesting stimulation should include HR deceleration, an increase in skin conductance, and (according to Sokolov, 1963) peripheral vasoconstriction and cephalic vasodilation.

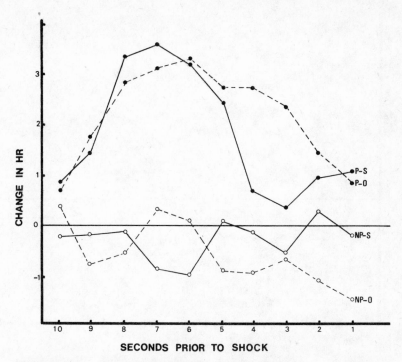

Fig. 9-3. Mean sec.-by-sec. changes in HR shown by each group to the conditioned stimuli preceding shock to self (S) and shock to other (O) on Trial 1. (Groups are psychopathic Ss, P, and non-psychopathic Ss, NP.) Source: Hare, R. D., & Craigen, D. Psychopathy and physiological activity in a mixed-motive game situation. *Psychophysiology*, 1974, 11, 197–206. With permission.

Defensive Responses

On the other hand, the defensive response (DR) to intense or noxious stimulation should include HR acceleration, an increase in skin conductance, and (again according to Sokolov) both peripheral and cephalic vasoconstriction. Some of our recent research supports these predictions rather well. For example, in one study (Hare, 1973) Ss with a phobic fear of spiders (Group SP) and Ss unafraid of spiders (Group NP) were shown a random series of colored slides of spiders and "neutral" objects. Neither group responded much to the neutral slides. However, as Figs. 9-4 and 9-5 indicate, those Ss afraid of spiders responded to the spider slides with simultaneous HR acceleration and cephalic vasoconstriction (a

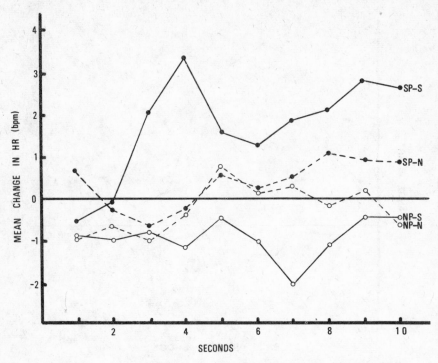

Fig. 9-4. Mean sec.-by-sec. changes in HR shown by Ss afraid (group SP) and unafraid (group NP) of spiders in response to spider (S) and neutral (N) stimuli. Source: Hare, R. D. Orienting and defensive responses to visual stimuli. *Psychophysiology*, 1973, 10, 453–464. With permission.

DR), and those unafraid of spiders responded with HR deceleration and cephalic vasodilation (an OR). We recently replicated these findings (Hare & Blevings, 1975b).

Of more direct relevance to the present topic, we also found that orienting and defensive responses apparently can be anticipatory in nature. Figure 9-6 for example, is from a study (Hare & Blevings, 1975a) in which an 11-sec. CS or warning signal preceded presentation of spider and neutral slides. It is clear that on the first block of trials, the HR of Ss afraid of spiders increased sharply following CS onset, and that by the fourth block of trials this accelerative phase became more prolonged. We suggested that this accelerative response was adaptive and helped S to "tune-out," cope with, or otherwise reduce the emotional impact of the impending aversive slide. We also noted that the resultant attenuation of potentially disturbing stimuli would be adaptive only

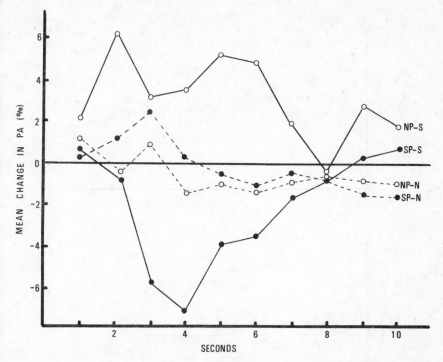

Fig. 9-5. Mean sec.-by-sec. changes in cephalic pulse amplitude (PA) shown by two groups (afraid of spiders, SP, and unafraid, NP) in response to the spider (S) and neutral (N) slides. Responses below the baseline indicate vasoconstriction. Source: Hare, R. D. Orienting and defensive responses to visual stimuli. *Psychophysiology*, 1973, 10, 453–464. With permission.

when the person could not use these stimuli to facilitate avoidance behavior.

Coping Efficiency

If anticipatory HR responses (and the more general DR) do in fact reflect the efficiency with which *S* modulates aversive cues and copes with impending stressors, then the data presented earlier in Figs. 9-2 and 9-3 are consistent with the hypothesis that psychopaths may be particulalry adept at the process. The result would be that situations that have considerable emotional impact on normal people may be of relatively little consequence to psychopathic ones, simply because the latter are better able to attenuate aversive sensory input.

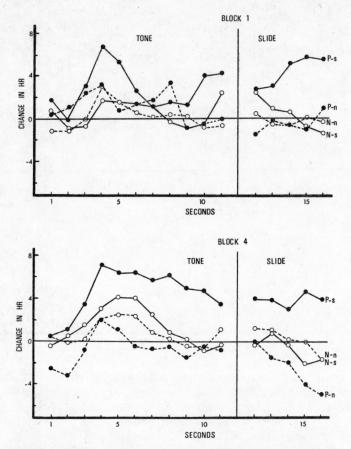

Fig. 9-6. Mean sec.-by-sec. changes in HR shown by Ss afraid (group P) and unafraid (group N) of spiders in response to conditioned stimuli (tones) preceding spider (s) and netural (n) slides. Source: Hare, R. D., & Blevings, G. Conditioned orienting and defensive responses. *Psychophysiology*, 1975, in press. With permission.

This leads to a hypothesis about the psychopath's combination of poor electrodermal and good cardiovascular conditioning. That is, the anticipatory cardiac activity may reflect an adaptive process that serves to reduce the emotional impact of the situation, whereas the small electrodermal responses that precede aversive stimuli reflect the relative absence of fear arousal. Whether the two processes are causally connected, with the former being partly responsible for the latter, is not known, although my feeling is that they are.

NEGATIVE PRECEPTION AND IMPLICATIONS FOR THERAPY

The picture of psychopathy that emerges, therefore, is of a disorder in which there is ready activation of psychophysiological defense mechanisms when aversive stimulation is threatened or anticipated. (We might speculate that if this is true, the psychopath's immediate existence might be made more pleasant for him, but that at the same time, emotional cues would not have the impact required for the instigation and guidance of prosocial behavior.) In a related sense, psychopathy may involve a specific adeptness at "negative preception," a process that involves getting set for a predictable noxious stimulus so as to reduce its subjective impact (Lykken & Tellegen, 1974).

Earlier I suggested that therapeutic efforts with psychopaths might benefit from attempts to increase the capacity for experiencing anticipatory fear. Related efforts might be aimed at reducing the efficiency of their psychophysiological defensive mechanisms. Unfortunately, these suggestions may be more appealing on the theoretical than on the practical level. Although the technical procedures could probably be worked out without too much difficulty, the moral, ethical, and legal problems involved in doing so would be considerable (see Katz, 1973, pp. 1016-1018; Mitford, 1973).

REFERENCES

American Psychiatric Association. *Diagnostic and statistical manual: Mental disorders*. Washington, D.C.: Author, 1968.

Checkley, H. *The mask of sanity*. (4th ed) St. Louis, Mo.: Mosby, 1968.

Duffy, E. Activation. In N. Greenfield & R. Sternbach (Eds.), *Handbook of psychophysiology*. New York: Holt, Rinehart, & Winston, 1972.

Graham, F. K. & Clifton, R. Heart rate change as a component of the orienting response. *Psychological Bulletin*, 1966, 65, 305-320.

Hare, R. D. *Psychopathy: Theory and research*. New York: Wiley, 1970.

Hare, R. D. Orienting and defensive responses to visual stimuli. *Psychophysiology*, 1973, 10, 453-464.

Hare, R. D. Psychopathy. In P. Venables & M. Christie (Eds.), *Research in psychophysiology*. New York: Wiley, 1974, in press.

Hare, R. D., & Blevings, G. Conditioned orienting and defensive responses. *Psychophysiology*, 1975, in press. (a)

Hare, R. D., & Blevings, G. Orienting and defensive responses to visual stimuli: A replication of results. Unpublished manuscript, Department of Psychology, University of British Columbia, 1975. (b)

Hare, R. D., & Craigen, D. Psychopathy and physiological activity in a mixed-motive game situation. *Psychophysiology*, 1974, 11, 197-206.

Hare, R. D., & Quinn, M. J. Psychopathy and autonomic conditioning. *Journal of Abnormal Psychology*, 1971, 77, 223-235.

Katz, J. *Experimentation with human beings*. New York: Russell Sage Foundation, 1973.

Lacey, J. I. Somatic response patterning and stress: Some revisions of activation theory. In M. H. Appley & R. Trumbull (Eds.), *Psychological stress. Issues in research*. New York: Appleton-Century-Crofts, 1967.

Lykken, D. T., & Tellegen, A. On the validity of the preception hypothesis. *Psychophysiology*, 1974, 11, 125-132.

Mitford, J. *Kind and usual punishment*: New York: Alfred A. Knopf, 1973.

Mowrer, O. H. On the dual nature of learning—a reinterpretation of "conditioning" and "problem-solving." *Harvard Educational Review*, 1947, 17, 102-148.

Seligman, M. E. P., & Johnston, S. C. A Cognitive theory of avoidance learning. In F. J. McGuigan & D. B. Lumsden (Eds.), *Contemporary approaches to conditioning and learning*. Washington, D.C.: V. H. Winston, 1973.

Sokolov, E. N. *Perception and the conditioned reflex*. New York: MacMillan, 1963.

Solomon, R. L., & Brush, E. S. Experimentally derived conceptions of anxiety and aversion. In M. R. Jones (Ed.). *Nebraska Symposiuma on Motivation*, 1954, 4, 212-305.

World Health Organization. *International classification of diseases*. (8th rev.) Geneva: Author, 1968.

III
LIFE STRESS
AND ANXIETY

10

TOWARDS A SYSTEMS MODEL OF STRESS: FEEDBACK FROM AN ANTHROPOLOGICAL STUDY OF THE IMPACT OF GHANA'S VOLTA RIVER PROJECT

D. Paul Lumsden

Anthropology Department, York University
Downsview, Ontario, Canada

INTRODUCTION

The concept of stress is one of the most significant and integrative concepts ever developed in the social and biomedical sciences; its potential as a prime intellectual tool for not only understanding but also explaining individual and collective human behaviour and disorders has not yet been fully realized. This chapter has two related aims. The first of these is to describe the impact of one of the world's most mammoth development projects, the Volta River Hydroelectric and Resettlement Project, on the lifestyle of members of a hitherto little-known Ghanaian people, the Nchumuru or N'Chumbulung of Krachi Administrative District.[1] Certain features of this Project and of its intended and unintended social

---

[1] The history and social organization of this people are given in detail by Lumsden (1973-74). This research was funded by the Canada Council, for which I am grateful. Thanks are extended to the Nchumuru for suffering my many questions.

consequences were perceived to be stressors by both the alien anthropologist and many of the affected Nchumuru themselves. The second, and perhaps more important, aim is to present a theoretical model encompassing both individual and group response levels to stressors, a model of "an open system under stress," a model that has evolved from a general systems theory approach to the anthropological data. The concept of stress has already been used by several anthropologists (Beattie, 1964, p. 245; Caudill, 1958; Fortes, 1969, pp. 179, 182, 191; Fortes & Mayer, 1969, pp. 40, 47, 52, 60; Goody, 1956, p. 48; Lewis, 1971; Nadel, 1951, pp. 269, 281, 326-327, 342; Naroll, 1959, 1962; Spencer, 1970; Turnbull, 1972, pp. 175, 230; Wallace, 1956a). In most cases, however, anthropological usage of this key concept is inadequate and somewhat unsophisticated. In many cases, the term "stress" appears in but a descriptive assertion, while the exact definition of the concept and the detailed specification of all the relevant variables involved in the situations discussed seem to be viewed as rather messy tasks that safely can be left to the reader's imagination; seldom is adequate use made of findings from stress research in such fields as neurophysiology, psychosomatic medicine, and psychiatry. Indeed, all too seldom are such findings actively sought out, since for some social anthropologists, those overly influenced by certain pronouncements of Durkheim in his *Rules of Sociological Method* in 1895, there remains something unclean about having truck or trade with anything smacking of "psychology" (cf. Lewis, 1971, p. 178). Such a naive and negative attitude must be expunged from the discipline in favour of developing interdisciplinary conceptual frameworks and research endeavours. In any case, and to the best of my knowledge, the model of "an open system under stress" given here is the most detailed ever presented by an anthropologist. Before considering the development project and its consequences, it first is necessary to specify what I mean by the key terms "system" and "stress," and, as a result of certain recent attacks on it, it is also necessary to defend the continued scientific use of the "stress" concept.

SYSTEM AND STRESS

The research and analysis presented here have been guided throughout by a general systems theory approach to, and model of, systemic organization, persistence, and change. A recent comment by

Straus (1973, p. 107, fn. 2 and n. 116) is pertinent here:

> In one sense, general systems theory is not a theory. It is a
> metatheory or a *conceptual framework* which can be utilized to
> construct a theory. . . . However, in another sense, general
> systems theory is a true theory. That is the sense in which it is a
> theory concerning the operation of complex adaptive systems in
> general. That is, general systems theory is concerned with
> identifying and explaining general features of adaptive systems
> which transcend the peculiarities of any one type of system.

Clearly, such a theoretical approach is the one best suited to
dealing with the concept of stress in all its aspects, a concept that not
only links and draws together the social and biomedical sciences, but
also applies and is evident at the physiological, psychological, and
behavioural response levels (or subsystems) of the individual
considered as a system, as well as at the interpersonal and societal
levels. The fact that several other investigators (Aakster, 1974;
Fabrega, 1974, pp. 47–48, 138–141; Moss, 1973; Straus, 1973; cf.
Kagan & Levi, 1974, p. 226), in addition to myself, have each
independently turned for assistance to systems theory, especially as
it has been formulated by Walter Buckley (1967, 1968), strengthens
the case for its use in developing an integrative, level-embracing
model of stress.

Part of the model, as it evolved after my fieldwork had been
completed, is given in the flowchart presented in Fig. 10-1; the rest of
the model, the specification of the variables and features of the
boxes shown in that flow chart, is given in the section "A Model of
an Open System Under Stress." The fieldwork was guided by a
somewhat simpler version of this model.[2] The model was of an
exogenous (e.g., the Volta Project) stimulus, input or "stressor"
penetrating a "boundary" or passing over a "threshold" and entering
a "system" of somewhat interdependent components (e.g., a social
system of partially interconnected institutions, relationships, beliefs,
sanctions, and customary activities—say, Nchumuru society as a
whole, or the lifestyle in specific villages). These component parts
themselves already were in an ongoing process of "ordinary" or
developmental change, with further changes or readjustments

---

[2] For the record, it should be noted that my copy of Buckley (1967) was with
me throughout my 18-month stay in Ghana in 1968 and 1969, as was Herbst
(1961).

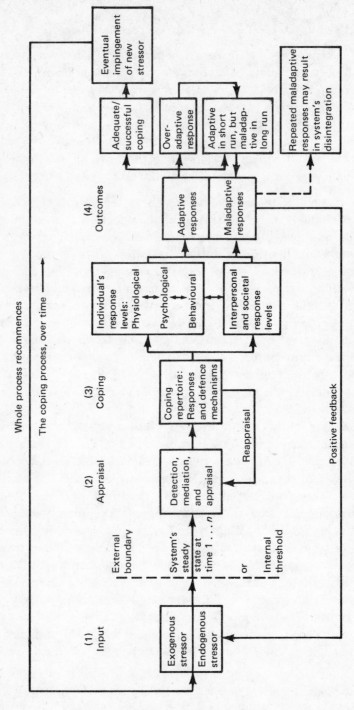

Fig. 10-1. Paradigmatic flowchart of an open system under stress.

(Radcliffe-Brown, 1957, p. 87) in some parts of the system owing to stimuli and "feedback" from their interaction with other components, i.e., from endogenous pressures. This incoming stimulus was conceived of as affecting some, but not necessarily all, of these component parts, while "reverberations" from the original stimulus work their way through the system over time, so that some consequences of the impact of that stimulus occur more quickly and clearly than do others. The incoming stimulus elicits a reaction or "coping responses" (which may turn out to be adaptive or maladaptive responses) from the affected components or from the system as a whole; some of these coping responses themselves set off or necessitate additional internal changes or readjustments.

A key term in both the earlier and more elaborate formulations of the model is the concept of "system" (Buckley, 1967, pp. 5, 41; Hall & Fagen, 1956, pp. 81, 83; Herbst, 1961, p. 71, 1970, pp. 47-48; Miller, 1969, pp. 68 ff.). This concept entails the elements of "self-regulation" (see Buckley, 1967, p. 163) and of a degree of interconnectedness or interdependence between parts of an analytically or otherwise delimited whole (cf. Hall & Fagen, 1956, pp. 84, 85), a whole or system with a "boundary" setting it apart from an "environment" with which it is in "transaction" (i.e., it is an "open" system, with the possibility of material, energy and "information" being exchanged in the transaction: Buckley, 1967, p. 50; Miller, 1969, p. 72; Vickers, 1968, pp. xxi, 135, 165), and a whole with some degree of continuity in, or of the persistence of, its "identity" over time (cf. Lumsden, 1973-74, pp. 9-10). The model employed is homeostatic, rather than a simple equilibrium model. Since the process of "coping" with an input may lead to a major reorganization of the system, to an increase as well as to a decrease of its internal complexity, or even to a change in the whole system's nature or type, the model takes into account Buckley's criticism of homeostatic models and his morphogenic or "structure-elaborating" alternative (Buckley, 1967, pp. 4-5, 40, 58, 128; cf. Frankl, 1973, p. 166; Moore, W., 1963, pp. 10-11; Moss, 1973, pp. 187-197; Vickers, 1968, pp. 170, 194); it is a "complex adaptive system" model.[3] It

---

[3] It is curious to note that, though Aakster (1974) claims to base his theoretical framework on Buckley's formulation, Aakster in fact reverts to a straightforward equilibrium model, thereby ignoring Buckley's critique of such models.

undoubtedly is better to speak of the state of the system as being a "steady state" (Buckley, 1967, pp. 15, 130; cf. Vickers, 1968, pp. 35-36) rather than as being one of "homeostasis" or of "equilibrium." The "steady state" usage better allows for the occurrence of "relatively transient" (Buckley, 1967, p. 35) "new equilibria," as well as for changes of type: a "steady state" system is not one that necessarily tries to maintain a particular level of functioning or coherence, nor one that tries to revert to a prestimulus status quo. However, Buckley pays inadequate attention, as also does von Bertalanffy (1968, p. 192), to developing the second key concept for the present model and approach, that of "stress," which Buckley describes as being a homeostatic tension-reducing and tension-producing process internal to the system (1967, pp. 51-52, 129, 160, 206; an exception is on p. 63).

The adequate use of the "stress" concept is hampered by the fact that different investigators have employed somewhat different referents or meanings for the term "stress" (cf. Appley & Trumbull, 1967, ch. 1; Dodge & Martin, 1970, pp. 30, 32; Kagan, 1971, p. 38; Lazarus, 1966, ch. 1; Levine, S., & Scotch, 1967, pp. 163-165; McGrath, 1970; Moss, 1973, pp. 52, 54, 55; Richter, 1960), and thus have employed different explicit or implicit models, many of these ignoring important variables as well (Scott & Howard, 1970). A seminal influence on the whole field of stress research, of course, has been the work of the eminent Canadian scientist, Hans Selye (1956, 1960, 1974; note Mason, 1971), on the "wear and tear" in biological systems when reacting to a chronic stressor with a "General Adaptation Syndrome" involving the three successive stages of alarm, resistance, and exhaustion. Selye suggested, though not in a detailed fashion, that a somewhat similar process may operate in man at the level of the "nation" (Selye, 1956, pp. 91, 275; in a discussion at York University, Canada, Feb. 11, 1972, and 1974, pp. 17, 53). My own conception of "stress" has also been influenced by the work of A. H. Leighton (1945, pt. II; cf. Smelser, 1968, pp. 222-227, 232), Richard Lazarus, the Dohrenwends, and, to a lesser extent, by Herbst's homeostatic model (1961, pt. I, 1970, pp. 47-51).

Before specifying the present usage, however, it is worth noting that two recent works have called for the total abandonment of the term "stress." Moss (1973, pp. 19, 23, 24, 56, 59, 97)[4] considers

---

[4] I am grateful to Professor Bruce P. Dohrenwend (personal communication, Dec. 11, 1973) for drawing the existence of Moss' book to my attention.

"stress" to be an "intervening variable" similar to "emotion" and to "motivation" (cf. Lazarus, Averill, & Opton, 1970, p. 209) and calls for its replacement and its transcendence by the phrase "biosocial resonation." This is a poorly defined concept, however, (Moss, 1973, pp. 9–10, 132, 185, 192–193, 194, 196, 241), which seems to mean the same as "interaction," especially with respect to information exchange. Moss' suggestion does not seem to be very helpful. The hardest-hitting attack on the continued use of the "stress" concept is that by Hinkle, who remarks that "it is hard to conceive of a 'state of stress' within an organism which is qualitatively different from any other state of being alive [1973, p. 43]. Hinkle does not deign to suggest an alternative, more useful, conceptualization (1973, p. 47). As will become apparent, my own formulation does not see stress as a response state; it does include the provision that coping responses can indeed be purposeful, directed, and specific, and that some stressors actively may be sought out by the system (cf. Hinkle, 1973, pp. 31, 32, 37, 43, 45). I do not conceive of all stimuli or inputs as being stressors nor of all system-environment transactions as being "stressful"; therefore, I do not consider it useful, as Moss and Hinkle would seem to suggest, to try to understand or explain certain transactions by saying that the system is "resonating" or is simply being "alive." It is quite clear that it is possible to specify certain stimuli (whether or not the stimulus is "pleasant" or "unpleasant"— Dohrenwend, B. S., 1973; Seiler, 1973, p. 261; cf. Hinkle, 1973, p. 46) as immediately or eventually having enervating or deleterious consequences for the system in whole or part. It is possible, albeit crudely as yet, to measure the amount of stressor exposure an individual or group has experienced within a set period of time (e.g., Cochrane & Robertson, 1973, pp. 136, 138). It is possible to evaluate certain responses as being maladaptive ones; one needs a specific theory and special concepts for this. Hinkle (1973, p. 47) to the contrary notwithstanding, the investigator cannot simply collect observations and data in a vacuum; a theory is needed for encompassing transactions at all levels, for specifying which variables are more important than others, which object-loss will be more stressful in a matrilineal society than in a patrilineal one, and so on. Moreover, when situations can be specified as potential stressors for particular individuals and certain populations, then this has preventive implications; and opportunities for corrective or supportive intervention are present, which the stress framework does alert one to, and therefore that framework ought not to be abandoned. Some workers have tried to devise a theory of "crisis" (e.g., Kalis, 1970) separate from that of "stress"; this is unacceptable (Eastham, Coates, & Allodi, 1970, p. 470), for a "crisis" is but part of one's overall concern with stressful transactions.

In the present model and analysis, an exogenous or endogenous stimulus is termed a "stressor" when it is a demand on the system and its resources (Herbst, 1961, p. 80; cf. Nadel, 1951, p. 303), either because it is overstimulating or understimulating (cf. Selye, 1974, p. 32); it is a "demand for adaptation" (Wolff, 1968, p. 4). As Lazarus puts it (1971, p. 54), stressors are *any demands which tax the system*, whatever it is, a physiological system, a social system, or a psychological system" (cf. Eastham, et al., 1970, p. 465; Engel, 1960, pp. 473, 480; Fabrega, 1974, p. 140; Freud, 1963, p. 91; Selye, 1974, p. 29). This definition makes it clear that, unlike that of Moss and Hinkle, the present analysis is not concerned here with just any stimulus but only with those that are, or are perceived as being, possible or actual taxing or wearing demands, ones which the system cannot for long safely ignore or speedily and automatically handle. In response to a stressor, the system (as a whole or in part) uses up some of its limited resources or assets; this is analogous to Selye's concept of "adaptation energy" (1956, pp. 65, 88, 274-276, 1974, pp. 38-41). Resources expended by a system in coping with one stressor may render the system vulnerable to, or less immediately effective in successfully coping with, another stressor. Here, the term "coping process" refers to the ongoing set of reactions of the system (in whole or part), whether this be an organ system, an individual, or a society, to a stressor. Each response is thus a "coping response"; i.e., the system's repertoire of (adaptive or maladaptive) responses and defence mechanisms are brought into play, at any and all levels, to somehow deal with the taxing demand (cf. Lazarus, 1971, p. 55). The system or subsystem may not adequately (i.e., too poorly or too successfully) cope with the stressor; this failure itself may then act as a further, endogenous, stressor (by means of "positive feedback"—see later discussions) on the system and its resources (Levi, 1967, p. 43; note also Selye's "diseases of adaptation" concept here, 1956, p. 66). The term "stress" is not applied to the coping process or response state alone; the term "stress" is applied to the total transaction (Lazarus, 1971, p. 54), to both the stressor and the coping responses in interaction together over time, so that one may speak of a system as being "under stress" (cf. Selye,

1974, p. 32) and of a particular situation as being a "stressful" one.

As indicated, not all inputs are perceived as being stressors, but stressors are ubiquitous (Buckley, 1967, p. 51; Selye, 1956, p. 299; Wolff, 1968, p. 4); some are the ingredients of everyday life (Crown, 1970, p. 103; Moore, T., 1969), depending in part on the particular cultural setting. Indeed, some degree of stress is necessary for the system's maintenance of its boundary and for its persistence over time (cf. Herbst, 1961, pp. 71, 89; Levine, S., 1971). With S. Levine and Scotch (1967, p. 164), one does not assume that "stressful events must lead to disruptive or pathological consequences" in every case; some such events may even be desirable (cf. Holmes & Rahe, 1967, p. 217; Paykel & Uhlenhuth, 1972, p. SS98) or may provide "an opportunity for growth" for the system concerned (Tyhurst, in Dohrenwend, B. P., 1969, p. 161; cf. Eastham et al., 1970, p. 464; Kalis, 1970, p. 74; Selye, 1974): as Frankl (1973, p. 162) points out, even unavoidable suffering provides the opportunity for one to create "a human achievement."

Implied here is the notion of there being an internal "threshold" of perception and of tolerance (Appley & Trumbull, 1967, pp. 10, 171-172; Herbst, 1961, p. 229; Vickers, 1960, pp. 4, 10); on the stimulus' passing over this threshold, the system (as a whole or in part) *must* react to a stressor with various coping techniques, to maintain or to achieve some sort of systemic coherence (cf. Vickers, 1968, pp. 41, 44, 129-130), to protect itself against a threat, or to take up a challenge: the stressor can no longer be overlooked or ignored, but it can be sought out. Obviously, some stressors prove to be more "noxious" than are others (Wolff, 1968, p. 6); in any case, limited resources are being tapped by the system. It must be emphasized that the concept is not a mere abstraction or heuristic device; as is well known, certain stressors have been produced in experimental laboratories and have been shown to have observable, and even measurable, effects (or outcomes) on the organisms involved: e.g., the "stress triad" of enlargement of the adrenal glands, shrinkage of the thymus and the deep, bleeding stomach ulcers created in Selye's laboratory rats (1956, pp. 20-21, plate I), and the experiments on human subjects by Levi (1967, chs. 2, 3, 1972; cf. Nadel, 1951, p. 209) which resulted in significant amounts of the "stress hormones" adrenaline and noradrenaline being found in the subjects' urine, and so on. This physiological level of response, however, was not a focus of the present fieldwork, which was more concerned with, and better equipped to deal with, the "sociological" response levels.[5]

Before continuing the discussion of the present model of "an open system under stress," the fieldwork situation and some of the findings that helped generate that model must now be delineated.

THE VOLTA RIVER PROJECT
AND ITS IMPACT

A few years ago, S. Levine and Scotch (1967, p. 171) remarked, "A researcher should seek naturalistic situations where the variables are strongly operative and where, in a sense, the situation for the study of stress is ready-made." This aptly describes the case of Ghana's Volta River Resettlement Project. Indeed, one would suggest that resettlement projects, wherever they may occur, are prime "natural" laboratories in which social and biomedical scientists (and an interdisciplinary team approach is to be preferred) may examine the processes of change and readjustment and the management of stress at all response levels.

Because of the construction of the Akosombo Dam in the early 1960's, which led to the formation of the world's largest man-made lake (Lake Volta, covering some 3,275 square miles), some 80,000 persons had to be evacuated from about 740 villages, and from their ancestral lands, within a very short period of time; most of these were rehoused in 52 government-built resettlement sites. In these Volta Resettlement Authority (VRA) sites, the resettlers found themselves grouped together with old antagonists, new friends, followers of different chiefs, as well as with close kin. In these sites, the resettlers were allocated new styles of housing, housing which often was not sufficient for the present households' needs, nor was the addition of new rooms an easy task in coping with the increasing population and with the wishes of maturing young people to form

---

[5] The field attempt to use Langner's 22-Item Screening Scale (for psychophysiological impairment) had to be abandoned for lack of sufficient time, and also because of difficulties in achieving linguistic equivalency for these items in the Nchumuru language and medical system. In any case, the Langner scale's validity and usefulness have met with serious criticism. For a recent review of the scale, see Seiler (1973). Regrettably, the Ghanaian government did not engage in a before-after mental health study of the resettlers, for lack of funds and trained personnel.

further households. Furthermore, at least in the research area, this housing was the only compensation given for the lost compounds and flooded croplands of those displaced by the government's industrialization strategy. In these new towns, the people were more subject to the scrutiny of the government and its agents, their customs were more exposed to less sympathetic eyes, and the resettlers were subject to certain VRA-imposed constraints on their activities. Plans were also set afoot to change the traditional farming practices of the bulk of the resettler population, but such additional demands have not reached fruition (see Lumsden, 1973). The Volta Project, in fact, was intended to transform the rural heartland and to stimulate further changes in it.

There were five major and related aspects of the Project that seemed likely to be (and which proved to be) exogenous stressors for many persons and groups in the affected area; each would thus elicit a number of adaptive or maladaptive coping responses, and each would result in a number of manifest and latent consequences for the systems concerned over time. These five major aspects were (a) the formation of the new lake itself, which affected more persons and communities than were officially part of the Resettlement Project; (b) the move from an old, familiar village to new surroundings; (c) the rehousing of resettler households in a new and smaller type of housing; (d) the VRA's policy constraints on resettler behaviour; and (e) the fact that most resettlers now found themselves dwelling in a larger, and often a less harmonious, concentration of kin and "strangers" than before. Numerous investigators have pointed to population displacement, resettlement, rehousing, overcrowding, and the attendant lack of privacy as being potentially stressful life-events for some, if not all, of those exposed to such changes. Moreover, the resettlers were not simply faced with the need to cope with but one stressor at a time; rather, several important changes were taking place concomitantly in their way of life within a short period of time. In his discussion of the stressors experienced by a group of Japanese-Americans forcibly relocated during World War II, Leighton mentioned several which were also at work among the resettled Nchumuru: "loss of means of subsistence," "dislike and ridicule from other people," perceived threats to "family unity," "deprivation of sexual satisfaction," "persistent frustration of goals, desires, needs, intentions and plans," and some "confusion and uncertainty as to what is happening in the present and what can be expected in the future [Leighton, 1945, pp. 252, 255, 260, 331, 332]." Such items, and others, were perceived by Nchumuru resettlers themselves as "worries." Of their life in the VRA new town, which was also research headquarters, several informants remarked, "We are like animals," despite the fact that life there did have some recognized or hoped for advantages. Not all such features can be touched on here.

Survey research alone cannot hope to uncover and to assess the full meaning and the significant consequences of a resettlement exercise for those affected; an in-depth study of the particular ethnographic background must also be made. The present research concentrated on several villages of the Nchumuru, and participant observation and a programme of 10 social surveys were the major fieldwork techniques. Since a before-after research design was not possible in this case, VRA-affected villages and non-VRA-affected villages were selected for a comparison and contrast of the details of their respective lifestyles. These were highly comparable sites—all were nearby in the same ecological area, all had the same economic base, and so on. Four sites were examined in detail whose overall Nchumuru population total was 1,457 persons—about 10% of all the Nchumuru in Ghana.

These four sites can be placed along a "continuum of disruption." At one end of such a continuum would be the small village of Kradente (100 Nchumuru in 16 households; of Begyamso *kasuro* or phratry), which almost completely was unaffected by any of the Volta Project's aspects; then would come the village of Akaniem (433 Nchumuru in 69 households; of Sungwae phratry), whose men had lost farmland to the new lake, whose buildings were threatened by its waters, and whose membership was slowly resettling itself in the nearby bush. The third site examined, Papatia, or more correctly New Papatia (259 Nchumuru in 42 households; of Chachiae phratry), originally was supposed to have been resettled by the VRA (as also was Akaniem), but in the end its membership resettled itself along the main road near to the official VRA site in 1966; the houses at all three of these sites largely were of traditional materials (mud and thatch), and so easily could be expanded at need. The fourth site, that at the other end of the continuum, would be the VRA resettlement town of New Grube (665 Nchumuru in 117 households); here were rehoused the members of five formerly separate Nchumuru villages (each possessing its own head, elders, shrines, and traditions). These subsystems represented three of the five or six Nchumuru phratries: Banda (related to Begyamso), Chachiae, and Sungwae; indeed, the fact that members of different phratries were concentrated together (with some residential intermixing) in the one town, a town which had no single, commonly accepted Nchumuru head, was one of the roots of dissension there. Those at New Grube took up residence there from late 1965 to 1967. Since most of these had been at least somewhat prepared for this move and were resettled along with all their village mates rather than being uprooted and bereft of group support, the actual move undoubtedly was not as stressful as it otherwise might have been. There was some evidence that a handful of male resettlers was suffering the "grieving for a lost home" syndrome delineated by Marc Fried (1963). This section discusses some features of the Volta Project's impact on the economic, the politico-jural, the moral or religious, and on the domestic "domains" (Fortes, 1969, pp. 97–99) of the Nchumuru lifestyle at New Grube; some findings and social indicators are noted that suggest or confirm that the Nchumuru at New Grube were at risk for a number of stressors, and that some were in fact under stress (were experiencing "distress" as Selye would term it, 1974) to varying degrees.

Since the formation of the new Lake Volta submerged several hundred square miles of farmland in Krachi District alone, one of the key consequences of the Project was that farmland in the research area was no longer as abundant as it once was. This was an irreversible change that threatened the continuance of the Nchumuru's traditional yam-farming practice of shifting cultivation. Two-thirds of the 201 male household heads in the four sites surveyed recognized that a "scramble" for land had been generated in this area; some men coped with this change by "begging" the use of less fertile land owned by another village or kin group; some in Akaniem tried to prevent phratry-mates from New Grube moving onto their own diminishing land base, partly for political reasons; in other cases, a person's farming area was now a longer walk away. In future, this situation will affect the size and yields of the farm clearings, as well as the likelihood of youths remaining in their paternal village. In addition, the lake's "waters of change" obliterated almost all the many streams in this area, which were owned by the various kin-groups (*mbuno*), and which provided members with needed food and cash from the sale of fish. Today, many men must buy their household's daily fish, a staple food, largely from non-Nchumuru fishermen who are more adapted to the techniques of lake fishing; this purchase is a chronic drain on a household's financial resources. Some men's revenue-producing trees have also been lost to the waters. The formation of the lake also hampered access to the market towns of Salaga and Kete-Krachi, though the markets at Chinderi, Banda, and especially at Borae No. 2 have at least compensated for this reversible change. Furthermore, in a bid to make "model towns" out of their VRA sites, the planners prohibited the resettlers from taking their goats, sheep, and pigs with them into the sites themselves; some men's domestic animals thus were sold off, were put into the care of nonresettlers, were lost, or were stolen. In short, for many persons the Project in its various aspects resulted in their experiencing an economic loss. In a systematic sample survey on economics, only 25% of the New Grube men (as compared to 60% of the combined Akaniem and Papatia men) considered themselves to be "very much satisfied' with their personal economic situation.

The loss of farmland also contributed to an ongoing political "struggle" in the research area, first between most of the Nchumuru and the neighbouring Krachi people over land ownership and taxation, and second between Akaniem (which was then supporting the Krachi claims and putting forward its own) and all the other Nchumuru villages studied, this last being a very fierce factional split. It is conceivable that in some cases factionalism can be creative and in some sense "normal"; but for the Nchumuru as a whole it clearly was maladaptive, since it prevented them from presenting a united front to Krachi demands. The fact that Akaniem was an opponent, however, did give the otherwise somewhat antagonistic groups resettled in New Grube a common cause (as did the mutual performance of the many funeral ceremonies there). In a way too, it seems likely that the resettlers' participation in the wider political movement (with its many meetings, financial demands, perceived threats, and rumours) gave them some welcome distraction from life in the VRA site, or an outlet by means of which they could vent some of their frustrations. As for the New Grube political domain, there was persistent squabbling over which subsystem head could judge law cases and thus over which man should be the head of the whole site; this persisted into 1974. At the same time, the fact that non-Nchumuru agents of the VRA resided in the site and had some legal say in how it was run lessened the authority of the Nchumuru leaders and bred some uncertainty among the people as to what acts and customs "government" would allow there.

In addition, the members of different villages resettled in New Grube and their constituent *mbuno* feared that members of one of the other phratries would learn of their respective, group-defining "secrets"; and efforts were made to control the permeability of group boundaries. One of these village groups had special cause for alarm since it "owned" (and thus profited from) one of the area's most important deities (the *kisi* Nana Kosoe, bringer of children, curer of impotence); hence, this group's elders were faced with having to cope with the twin problems of (*a*) convincing the other people in the site to obey the prescriptions and the taboos enjoined by the deity, especially so at the time of its annual festival, and (*b*) retaining control over their own group's young people, who were now more exposed to competing influences from schoolteachers, Christians, and other nonbelievers. These elders' endeavours generated some intrafamilial altercations within their group. However, traditional religious beliefs and practices were still alive within the new site. Many members of each village group still put their trust in their group's antiwitchcraft deity, and the last of the ancestor and other key shrines were brought to the VRA town in 1969 and 1970 from their old sites. Thus, true believers adequately could manage some of their "worries" by turning to these traditional coping aids, and their attendant libation-prayers, sacrifices, and thanks-offerings: ritual can help an individual or group cope with stressors. Certain significant holy places and objects, however, could not be saved from the lake's embrace. For some persons, resettlement at New Grube meant that their traditional beliefs were called into question; for others, such beliefs may well have become more salient and necessary.

At New Grube, the resettlers found themselves having to act before a larger and less friendly audience: e.g., those women who could not afford to dress up on occasion met with ridicule at the hands of women from one of the other groups; even the coping device of extending classificatory kinship terms (brother/sister) to nonrelatives in the other groups could not entirely smooth the path of social interaction. Studies of certain other resettlement schemes have shown that the new concentration of people can foster an outbreak of infectious disease (e.g., Fernea & Kennedy, 1966); indeed, measles was a dangerous problem threatening the town's children during my stay. It should be added, however, that measles outbreaks were not unknown in previous years when the people lived in their separate, somewhat isolated communities. The Project's impact on the mortality rate and on the incidence of mental disorders is most difficult to assess.

There was much actual overcrowding and a pervasive lack of privacy thanks to the housing provided to the resettlers at New Grube. Each deserving household, regardless of its size and thus of its stage in its developmental cycle, was allocated a "core house"; such a house consisted of one enclosed room, measuring 10 by 12 feet, and a roofed-over, but exposed, space for a second such room. In all cases, two of these houses were attached to each other by a common wall in blocks of four houses; this meant that one's neighbour could overhear the daily joys and passions of one's household. In fact, 49.4% of the 79 married male household heads in New Grube indicated that their sexual activities with their wife or wives had been interfered with by this lack of privacy; moreover, there was evidence to support the hypothesis that household overcrowding would foster or increase the occurrence of domestic quarrels. A major factor behind this situation was the VRA ruling which at first prohibited the enclosing of the second room or the addition of new ones in any materials other than the expensive ones of cement (landcrete) blocks and metal sheet roofing; in 1968, only metal roofing, a very costly item, became the requirement for expansion. This meant that some men were unable to provide separate rooms for their maturing sons, nor a room apiece, as was their right, for each of their wives if polygynously married—and Nchumuru believe, and act on this view of "emotions," that women are more prone to anger than are men, so that several women in the one space is likely to cause quarreling. Lack of room space also interfered with the young people's sex life, since there are strong supernatural and legal sanctions against couples having intercourse "in the bush," which act profanes the land. There were adaptive ways of coping with this situation, of course, such as one's visiting the girls in nearby Papatia; but there was no sign of homosexuality. Many household heads at New Grube had coped with the room shortage, or were about to do so, by building cheap mud-and-thatch rooms a short distance away from the VRA-controlled area. In 1969, the VRA itself sent in masons and supplies to enclose the second room of each of the core houses, though resettlers may be expected to pay for these materials. By then, in any case, some households' members had experienced 1–3 years of cramped living conditions, and some members had slept wherever room space could be found; thus, co-residence was not a defining feature of such households. Many resettlers did perceive advantages to life in New Grube, and undoubtedly most will remain there; however, its disadvantages were clearly recognized and keenly felt.

The difference in the quality of life at the three non-VRA villages from that at New Grube is most striking when one notes the replies given by the 201 male household heads to the question as to the first thing (assumed to be the most personally meaningful thing) each disliked about life in their particular site. The men of Kradente complained about their site's poor water supply; the men of Akaniem were bothered by malarial mosquitoes and by snakes, while 4 (or 7.3%) of the 55 men surveyed there complained of some intravillage quarreling. At Papatia, the third site on the continuum, the men complained of the high cost of living, as did some New Grube men, for resettlement has engendered some new economic wants. However, the striking feature of the New Grube replies to this question is the fact that they provide several indicators which, taken together (and one must examine several indicators, not just one or two), clearly show that the New Grube people as a whole were under some degree of stress, though some stressors probably were transient or were correctable. Of the 95 male household heads at New Grube, 28.4% complained of the fighting in the town, most fights being intervillage group or interphratry. A couple of these donnybrooks involved several hundred swirling, shouting, and shoving persons and sorely strained the regulative activities of the various sets of elders. People at Akaniem and Papatia also recognize that fighting is a feature of New Grube life. A further 20% of the New Grube men expressed concern at the amount of ill health and at the number of funerals at the site; another 8.4% complained of thefts occurring at the site or at their farms, and an additional 4.2% spoke darkly of the number of "back-biters" or gossipers there. In sum, 61% of the male household heads at New Grube gave replies symptomatic of the presence of stress (others complained of not having a wife, of their farm being too far away, etc.).

In attempting to assess cross-culturally what he termed "culture-stress," Naroll (1959, 1962; cf. the crude indicators proposed by Kardiner, 1967, p. 184; LeVine, R., 1961, p. 86; see also Lynn's very debatable study, 1971) constructed a "tentative" index involving four indicators: protest suicide, defiant homicide, drunken brawling, and witchcraft attribution.[6] The first two indicators were completely absent from the New Grube situation; the last two were present. There was a considerable amount of quarreling and fighting at New Grube, and 71.6% of the male household heads there considered this to be a higher amount from that which had been present in their old, preresettlement sites. In part, this fighting reflected the increased production and availability of alcoholic drinks in the area; e.g., at the resettlement site there now is a more concentrated and more accessible consumer population for the wares of local brewers and distillers. Overall, 92.6% of the 189 male respondents at Akaniem, Papatia, and New Grube claimed that people at their particular site were now drinking more often than had been the case 4 years earlier (i.e., preresettlement). At Akaniem, 94.5% of the men gave this answer, this high amount reflecting not just the increased production of drink, but also reflecting in part their coping response to their social ostracism at the hands of all the nearby Nchumuru villages. At the non-VRA-resettled village of Papatia, 76.9% gave this reply, whereas 97.9% of the respondents in the VRA resettlement site considered people there to be drinking more often than before. Taken together with other symptoms of "distress" at New Grube, this drinking must be considered as partly reflecting the fact that people there were under stress. In the early months of the study, almost every Sunday market day at New Grube, with its ready supply of drink, saw its drunken tussle between two or three people; probably there were only seven or eight major intergroup confrontations over the full 18 months, with relations between the New Grube subsystems having improved somewhat in the last few months of that period.

I never heard a New Grube Nchumuru privately or publicly accuse a member of one of the other village groups of witchcraft,[7] though

---

[6] More recently, Naroll (1969) suggested that suicide is the prime, best documented, cross-cultural "culture-stress" indicator. To use only one indicator, however, may be misleading; moreover, his proposed measure—the wordage devoted to suicide in the (published) ethnographic reports on each people—is absurd.

[7] But some Akaniem informants did accuse their Nchumuru political opponents of killing the head of Akaniem in February 1969 by means of witchcraft. It might be added that, for space reasons, data from surveys of Nchumuru wives and youths are not given here.

accusations of theft were so levied. There were persons whose death was caused by witchcraft (discovered because of the sacrifice of numerous chickens at a local Tigare shrine, usually in my presence) or who were supposed to have been killed by one of the gods for being witches (cf. Naroll, 1959, p. 114); but the witchcraft involved was always within the particular village group, not directed outside of it. At least 47.4% of the New Grube male respondents own their own "juju" or "objects of power" (*asibeng*), as do 45.5% of those at Akaniem and 56.4% of those at Papatia. Each village and village group has its own protective deity as well, thus giving some security against culturally engendered threats and fears. Despite this culturally provided protection, though, 36.4% of the Akaniem men, 10.3% of those at Papatia, and 34.7% of the male household heads at New Grube stated their belief that someone "often" or "sometimes" attempted to use such "objects of power" against them. Moreover, 21.1% of these New Grube men, contrasted to only 3.6% of those at Akaniem and 2.6% of those at Papatia, stated that they are "often" worried by witch-craft. These results, together with other indicators, show that many New Grube men were under stress.

Other aspects of coping and of what some might term "social pathology" or "social unease" could be noted here, but enough has been said to support or confirm the hypothesis that New Grube Nchumuru were at risk for a number of stressors, and that many were under stress because of various aspects of the Volta Resettle-ment Project. The research findings, plus an examination of the literature in the field of stress research, led to the development of a theoretical, level-embracing, model. Clearly, not all the variables specified here were of importance, and some were unknown or were not fully examined in my first research period among the Nchumuru. No one empirical study is likely to take all those listed into account (cf. Straus, 1973, p. 107); unless it is a very large research team indeed. Needless to say, stress research and its integrative character will not flourish until all the key variables finally are spelled out in one place (as is attempted here) for testing and their step-by-step linkages with the other variables are charted with more detail and sophistication than is given in Fig. 10-1. It might also be added that stress research programmes must be longitudinal, as the Nchumuru study is intended to be.

A MODEL OF AN OPEN SYSTEM
UNDER STRESS

The reader's attention is called once more to a consideration of the flowchart in Fig. 10-1. This should be compared with the diagrams espoused by a number of other workers; see Aakster (1974, p. 80); Averill, Opton, and Lazarus (1971, p. 111); Coates, Moyer, and Wellman (1969, p. 423); Dodge and Martin (1970, p. 56); B. P. Dohrenwend (1961, p. 295); Kagan and Levi (1974, p. 226); Reeder, Schrama, & Dirken (1973, p. 575); Smelser (1968, pp. 227, 277), and Straus (1973). It remains now to complete the model, as far as it has been developed to date, by commenting on its features and by specifying the contents of the flowchart's key boxes. Future research will suggest additions and modifications to the details presented; the reader is invited to test the hypothesis that the model does take into account, or allows for, what is now known or is now being uncovered in the interdisciplinary field of stress research. The concept of "stress," as it is used here, must be an integral part of any worthwhile, sophisticated theory of social change (a bare beginning has been made along these lines by Moss, 1973, pp. 197ff., especially pp. 203–206; Smelser, 1968), and so of any account of how a system copes with its environment. To put the point very baldly here, for much more research must yet be done, almost all social change arises through a complex adaptive system's coping with exogenous and endogenous stressors.

Throughout the following discussion, a large number of citations have been given; this is done not simply to refer the reader to relevant elaborations, but is also done to subsume the cited authors' works within the framework of the present research. That said, the following comments must be made concerning each numbered section of the flowchart:

Section (1): Stressors

Some recognized examples of exogenous and endogenous stressors, given here to suggest the range of events of interest, are natural disasters (e.g., Wallace, 1956b); culture contact (Caudill, 1958, p. 12); resettlement; "enforced radical change" (Nadel, 1951, p. 326); certain institutional or cultural overemphases in a society (e.g., Aakster, 1974, p. 89, on Western "consumerism"); disconfirmation of a prophecy (Brown, R., 1962); concentration camp internment

(Frankl, 1973); overcrowding (Brown, B., 1974, p. 90); taboo transgression; uncertainty and "subjective information incongruities" (Moss, 1973, pp. 133, 137, 185-186, 247); loss of status (Rahe, Meyer, Smith, Kjaer, & Holmes, 1964, pp. 37, 41, 42); bereavement (Caudill, 1958, p. 15; but cf. Coates et al., 1969, p. 422); role impoverishment; all the stressors for which naval personnel are at risk (Wallis, 1972, pp. 500-502); blocked attainment of a goal (Levine & Scotch, 1967, p. 167); long-lasting preparedness for an action, which cannot be vented (Hamburg, 1961, pp. 284-285); role conflicts (Dodge & Martin, 1970, ch. 3); intrasystem population pressure on scarce resources; long-term imprisonment (Cohen, S., & Taylor, 1972); surgery (Cohen, F., & Lazarus, 1973); sensory deprivation; excessive or unpredictable noise; extreme heat; an examination, or one's being observed and evaluated by psychological experimenters (Lazarus, Tomita, Opton, & Kodama, 1966, p. 63); "nontraumatic but wearing events" (Scott & Howard, 1970, pp. 267, 269), and perhaps "emergent properties of the event" (Moss, 1973, pp. 57, 58). The variables enumerated here must be taken into account to assess the extent to which the previous items are in fact stressors in each particular case; it is suggested here that, in the long run, a system cannot be "neutral" to such inputs or life events. The list could be expanded, but the point is made; it ought to be mentioned that the "worries" of the specific society examined must also be specified (the "emic" level of analysis), in addition to testing and assessing more universal events. Some of the most stimulating work on this topic is that of Thomas Holmes and his coworkers on the Social Readjustment Rating Scale (SRRS) (Holmes & Rahe, 1967; Holmes & Masuda, 1972); they seem to have met with some success in achieving respondent consensus on "the magnitude of change in adjustment required [Masuda & Holmes, 1967, p. 227] " in order for one to cope with each of 43 life events. Holmes' group has carried out studies on the SRRS involving various American minority groups, resulting in "highly concordant" ratings (Masuda & Holmes, 1967, p. 228); and several cross-cultural studies have been done as well (Harmon, Masuda, & Holmes, 1970; Masuda & Holmes, 1967; Rahe, 1969), which in general found "exceptionally high inter-cultural agreement [Rahe, 1969, p. 191] ." It is to be hoped that anthropologists will pursue this and similar work on life events in their diverse fieldwork settings; such work, plus medical anthropology, transcultural psychiatry, and stress research in general will help the anthropologist to develop what can be termed a true "anthropology of suffering."

Section (2): Detection, Mediation, and Appraisal

The list of variables given in this and the following section is not a mere shopping list; each variable must be assessed, weighted, and tested as to its relative importance (e.g., as to its predictive significance) in certain classes of situations or transactions, keeping in mind too the fact that the absence of certain elements may be just as significant as their presence in some transactions (Kagan & Levi, 1974, p. 225).

Detection of a Stressor

First, then, there are certain critical characteristics of a stressor that affect the coping process, and that imply detection of the stressor by the system in whole or part. These characteristics of the stressor are its source, nature (whether bacteriological, etc.), duration (Caudill, 1958, pp. 7-8; cf. Dodge & Martin, 1970, pp. 115, 241, 247-248, 255, 265, 268, on the "accumulation" of demand over time), timing, intensity (Appley & Trumbull, 1967, p. 11; Marmor & Pumpian-Mindlin, 1950, p. 303), frequency (Rahe et al., 1964), rarity (Coates et al., 1969, p. 433), ambiguity (and the system's degree of tolerance thereof), and novelty (cf. Berlyne, 1962).

In addition, the stressor's meaning for the system (Miller, 1969, p. 57; Vickers, 1968, p. 160) must be considered; e.g., whether it is achievement related or security related (Dohrenwend, B. P., & Dohrenwend, B. S., 1969); and this too is related to the degree of the person's "subjective involvement" in that transaction (Moss, 1973, p. 144) and to whether the input is perceived as being "pleasant" or "unpleasant" (cf. Dohrenwend, B. S., 1973, p. 174; Cochrane & Robertson, 1973, p. 138). Other important features of the input that affect the coping process are whether this stressor acts alone or in combination with another stressor (Broadbent, 1971, pp. 405-408; T. Moore, 1969, p. 247; Wilkinson, 1972, on the multiplier effect); whether it is avoidable; whether it is objectively or subjectively controllable (cf. Seligman, 1974, on hopelessness, and Weiss, 1972b, pp. 258, 266, 272, on the pathology of helplessness); whether its occurrence is predictable (Coates et al., 1969, p. 427; Glass, Singer, & Friedman, 1969); whether the system has previously experienced this stressor, and if so, how well it was coped with before—this being the very important variable of past psychological and social experience (cf. Engel, 1960, pp. 466, 477, 483; Hinkle, 1973, p. 41; Kagan & Levi, 1974, p. 227; Lazarus et al., 1966, p. 631; see also Pollin, 1972, pp. 52-53, on enzyme availability and past experience); whether the stressor precipitates a response or simply predisposes the system to that response (e.g., a "disease"); whether the system gets feedback (e.g., by reappraisal) on how well it is coping (cf. Miller, 1969, p. 117; Weiss, 1972a, p. 111, 1972b); whether the stressor impinges on all, or on only some of the system's parts; whether the stressor is an exogenous or an endogenous one (cf. Miller, 1969, p. 106), and whether its impact is directly or indirectly experienced.

Mediating Factors

Mediating factors, between the stressor and the coping response, affect the detection, appraisal, and interpretation of the stressor by the person or the group. These mediating factors are the age (Coates et al., 1969, pp. 432-433; Freud, 1963, pp. 82, 88-89, 1971, p. 552; note Lazarus, 1973, p. 19), sex (e.g., Hamburg & Lunde, 1967, p. 156), birth order, and marital status (Dodge & Martin, 1970, ch. 8) of the person and the stage in his developmental cycle at which he is affected (Lazarus, 1966, p. 22). The individual's and group's race or ethnicity is important at least for the likelihood, degree, and nature of its exposure to discrimination. One's body type may also be an important variable (e.g., Schär, Reeder, & Dirken, 1973, pp. 595, 601, on endomorphy and cardiovascular risk). Child-rearing practices of the individual's group are a mediating factor, one that also partly affects the types of defence mechanisms learned and used by the person in his coping efforts; the family structure (Caudill, 1958, pp. 17, 18), and the nature of family functioning—e.g., the degree of marital satisfaction, the frequency of intrafamilial quarrels, etc. (Pless & Satterwhite, 1973; Pollin, 1972, pp. 52-53), and the features of the communication pattern within the family to an analysis of which the anthropologists Bateson (e.g., 1972) and Henry (1971) have contributed so heavily.

Other mediating factors are the socioeconomic class (Dohrenwend, B. P., & Dohrenwend, B. S., 1969), status, and reference group of the individual; the nature of the role demands on the person, their clarity, and the degree of flexibility in role performance allowed by the group (Kalis, 1970, p. 74); the type and nature of one's occupation (Kagan & Levi, 1974, p. 233; Reeder et al., 1973, pp. 575, 579–580; Schär et al., 1973, p. 597), for example, the ulcer proneness of air traffic controllers (*Time*, 1972, p. 33), and the power relationships involved in the transaction. In addition, coping is affected by culturally-patterned attitudes to threat, injury (Caudill, 1958, pp. 11–12), pain (Zborowski, 1952), illness, "deviance," and so on.

Other mediating factors are the individual's "physical" health and the intactness of his central nervous system prior to the onset of the stressor; hereditary and nutritional factors; and the quality of one's "inborn endocrine equipment" (Tepperman, in Hamburg & Lunde, 1967, p. 156), e.g., the adequacy of one's thyroid hormone secretion (Hamburg & Lunde, 1967, p. 155).

Psychological factors also mediate between stressor and coping: degree of motivation or arousal (Broadbent, 1971, p. 411 ff.; Lazarus, 1966, p. 25, 1973, p. 13; cf. Wallace, 1956a, pp. 265–266); "characteristic level of activity and stimulation" (Scott & Howard, 1970, p. 270); expertise and success in self-regulating emotional reactions (Lazarus, 1973, pp. 11, 12, 17) and capacity to maintain focal attention (Pollin, 1972, p. 53; cf. Moss, 1973, p. 67); the degree of "hypersensitivity" to the demands of everyday life (Dodge & Martin, 1970, pp. 88, 318), and so too the individual's characteristic pattern of threat appraisal (Lazarus, 1973, p. 17). Other considerations are whether the individual is an introvert or an extrovert (Broadbent, 1971, pp. 421–423); the strength of his ego (Levine, S., & Scotch, 1967, p. 168) and superego (Dohrenwend, B. P., 1961, p. 299); the strength and nature of the person's "will-to-meaning," in Frankl's sense (1973, p. 154); the nature of his self-image and degree of self-esteem (Coates et al., 1969, p. 430); and the complexity of his response repertoire (cf. Levine, S., & Scotch, 1967, p. 168). Coping with a stressor also depends on whether there is a family history of vulnerability (Schär et al., 1973, pp. 592–593, 595); the person's degree of closeness to another person who is under stress (Dodge & Martin, 1970, pp. 91–97, 116, 120, on the "social stress contagion process"), e.g., wives of hard-pressed executives (cf. Seiler, 1973, p. 260); the individual's or group's degree of preparedness for the stressor (Fried, 1965, pp. 123, 146–147; Nadel, 1951, p. 390), and whether the stressor was actively sought by the system (acceptance of challenge: cf. Nadel, 1951, p. 347).

Appraisal

B. Brown (1974, p. 54) stated: "Experimental evidence indicates that nonconscious mental activity is often more realistic in its appraisals than is conscious mental activity." Moreover, Lazarus et al. (1970, p. 218) argued that "each emotion involves its own particular kind of appraisal." Appraisal of the input as being a stressor may also be affected by the size, degree of cohesiveness, and degree of factionalism of the group; by the number, strength, and effectivenes of the group's boundary-maintaining mechanisms and of those for internal control (cf. Eisenstadt, 1971, p. 83); and the degree of social mobility fostered by the group. In addition, appraisal is affected by whether the group supports the appraisal and interpretation given the input by the individual member, (as well as the nature and degree of support by the group); the priorities and values of the individual (cf. Caudill, 1958, pp. 8–9) and the group and the amount of discrepancy between these; and the degree to which the group (its institutions and culture) itself is changing and the rate at which this is taking place. Finally, another variable is the amount of time available to the system for careful appraisal to take place.

Sections (3) and (4): Coping and Its Outcomes

As will have been noted, many variables mentioned previously also affect the system's coping responses; detection, appraisal, coping, and reappraisal (itself an ongoing coping device; note Lazarus et al., 1970, pp. 220, 228; Weiss, 1972b, p. 259; Vickers, 1968, pp. 80, 118, 139, 147, 154, 191, on appreciation and reality and value judgments) go hand in hand. Much of this is information-seeking behaviour and is dependent on the receipt of a signal (a passing over of the threshold) to trigger it off. For example, a person may experience Freud's anxiety affective signal (1963, pp. 65, 73, 77, 80, 86, 108–109, 1971, pp. 395, 405, 546, 548, 554, 557, 558–559), which is triggered by the ego and its perception of a danger. Freud distinguished this function of anxiety from "anxiety" as an outcome of a transaction (Freud, 1963, pp. 67, 82, 107, 108–109, 114; cf. Lauer, 1973, p. 173); this is but one example of the importance of cognitive triggers to emotions (Lazarus et al., 1970, p. 223; Pollin, 1972, p. 51). As Lazarus emphasized (1973, p. 2), "Coping is part of the self-regulation of emotional states"; much more needs to be done on the determinants of coping (cf. Lazarus, 1973, p. 18) and on the nature of adaptive as opposed to maladaptive responses.

Coping Repertoire

Thus coping is affected by how quickly the stressor is detected and by whether it is identified (in which cases coping responses can be more specific and "realistic") or is not identified (responses in such cases would be more nonspecific and diffuse, while further reappraisal would be called for, and the uncertainty about the input itself would act as an additional stressor) (cf. Notterman & Trumbull, 1950, p. 352). The amount of knowledge the system has about the stressor is crucial: too much information can be maladaptive (e.g., see Cohen, F., & Lazarus, 1973, pp. 384, 385, 387, on "vigilant" surgery patients; cf. Hinkle, 1973, p. 42; cf. Freud, 1971, pp. 407–408); thus, coping is affected by the degree to which the system is able to engage in "anticipatory coping" (the preparedness factor again: Cohen, F., & Lazarus, 1973; Kalis, 1970, p. 83; Lazarus, 1973, pp. 12–13; Lazarus et al., 1970, pp. 224, 227). Other related determinants of coping are whether the stressor is an overload or an underload (excess or deprivation) for the system's capacities and needs (cf. Miller, 1969, p. 110); whether there are alternative routes, responses, or mechanisms that can be used if one such is blocked by the stressor or "if there are duplicate components capable of performing the same process [Miller, 1969, p. 103]"; and what defence mechanisms have been learned by the system, through child-rearing practices or past experience, and their order of use (the system's "response-hierarchy"). Group support can affect coping by the extent to which the group members share the appraisal and meaning of the stressor and support each other's responses (cf. Marmor & Pumpian-Mindlin, 1950, p. 301); such support is affected by the degree of "stability and durability of social relationships" customary in that particular group (Dodge & Martin, 1970, p. 62) or by what Engel (1960, pp. 477, 481) refers to as the system's "object-relationship capacities." In addition, the nature and extent of the system's coping resources are important—how effective the early coping responses are, and how great the costs of their use are to the system (Miller, 1969, p. 126). The nature and efficacy of the group's medical care system (cf. Dodge & Martin, 1970, p. 232) and when one is culturally expected to seek help (Engel, 1960, p. 467) also affect the coping process and the outcome of the transaction; certain medications (e.g., phenothiazines) can help some individuals cope more successfully (Birley & Brown, 1970, pp. 301–302; Cohen, F., & Lazarus, 1973, p. 376).

Individual's Response Levels and Feedback

The model envisages that, if these early coping responses are ineffective or are overridden by the stressor, then other defences or responses are brought into play from lower down in the system's response hierarchy; such outputs are likely to be less well organized and less "realistic" or pertinent than were the earlier ones, and so themselves add to the demands on the system (cf. Menninger, 1954; Miller, 1969, p. 110). The total set of available responses constitutes a finite repertoire (cf. Vickers, in Miller, 1969, p. 116); as noted earlier, the system's coping resources are limited, and its ability and capacity to cope are also limited (cf. Freud, 1963, p. 91; Vickers, 1968, pp. 129–130). In a way too, there is a "common denominator," a degree of consistency or a "coping style," to a particular system's responses to various stressors (Cohen, F., & Lazarus, 1973, pp. 376, 379, 385; Lazarus, 1973, p. 17; Lazarus et al., 1970, p. 222; Levi, 1967, pp. 34, 80, 167; Martin, 1970, p. 1087; Rioch, 1971, p. 90; Selye, 1956, p. 54, 1974, p. 17) and to certain situations; perhaps some responses are universal ones to certain stressors. There are problems remaining connected with knowing how and when to label a response as definitely being adaptive or maladaptive, since the actors and the observer may not always agree on the validity of the label for a specific response-outcome and since an adaptive response may in time prove to have been ultimately a maladaptive one (note the criteria suggested in Kalis, 1970, pp. 75–76). As noted in Fig. 10-1, maladaptive responses or response-outcomes provide "positive" feedback. "Positive feedback" means that such responses increase, add to, or "amplify" the taxing demands on the system and become internal or endogenous stressors (cf. Miller, 1969, pp. 114–115; Straus, 1973, pp. 105, 113; cf. Aakster, 1974, p. 79, on illness "as a case of positive feedback," though such can also be an adaptive tactic or strategy in some cases). It is "negative" feedback that "dampens" the load. The concept of "feedback" is crucial for a model to be a dynamic one.

Physiological Response-Outcomes

As for response-outcomes at the individual's physiological level or subsystem (cf. Hinkle, 1973, pp. 41, 43; Mason, 1971, p. 331), the verified responses to stressors are too numerous to mention (and clearly the role of one's central nervous system is important here). Some physiological responses are an elevated plasma hydrocortisone level, heightened urinary corticosteroid excretion, and elevated serum cholesterol levels (Hamburg, 1961, pp. 282, 283, 285; Kagan & Levi, 1974, pp. 227-228; Levi, 1967, chs. 2, 3, 1972; Pollin, 1972, p. 53); hyper- and hypothyroidism (Hamburg & Lunde, 1967); profuse nasal secretion (Hinkle, 1973, pp. 39-40, 43) and elevated skin conductance (e.g., in American as opposed to Japanese subjects: Lazarus et al., 1966), while much research has also been done on such responses as ulcers (Kagan & Levi, 1974, p. 234; Weiss, 1972b, p. 259); and essential hypertension (Kagan & Levi, 1974, pp. 232-233; Scotch, 1960, p. 1008) and cardiovascular problems (e.g., Syme & Reeder, 1967). Responses of some organ systems may be more adaptive than, or may conflict with, those made by other subsystems of the one body system (cf. Engel, 1960, pp. 469, 484).

Psychological Response-Outcomes

At the psychological, or "inner-personal" (Nadel, 1951, p. 305) level, Freud's work on such defence mechanisms as symptom formation (1963, p. 86, 1971, pp. 404, 548), projection, rationalization, and repression is highly relevant (see Kline's critical review, 1972, pp. 151-203, especially pp. 181, 192; cf. Lazarus, 1973, p. 9, and Lazarus et al., 1966, p. 630, on "denial" and "intellectualization" as coping devices, as is selective perception, Moss, 1973, p. 45). "Increased intrusive and repetitive thought" is reported to be "a general response tendency in both male and female [American] subjects [Becker, Horowitz, & Campbell, 1973, p. 522; cf. Sandler, in Weiss, 1972b, p. 270]" following mild or moderate stressors, with the possible development of "repetition compulsion" as an outcome of one's experiencing a major stressor (see also Menninger, 1954). Pertinent here also is the early work on the frustration-aggression hypothesis (Dollard, Doob, Miller, Mowrer, & Sears, 1939; Straus, 1973, pp. 108, 119), though "aggression" may cover a multitude of sins and a "variety of response patterns" (Lazarus et al., 1970, pp. 214, 215). See also the work on "cognitive dissonance" (Brown, R.,

1962, pp. 44–59; Dodge & Martin, 1970, pp. 316ff.). Suicide, alcoholism, a neurosis (Marmor & Pumpian-Mindlin, 1950, pp. 301, 303–304; McNeil, 1970b, p. 58; Nadel, 1951, p. 326), or a psychosis (McNeil, 1970a, pp. 59–63, 92) may be an individual's psychological and behavioural response to an intense or prolonged stressor, though the outcome of psychosis, at least, undoubtedly is the result of a number of interacting factors. A good case in point here is that of "schizophrenia" (leaving aside for now the intracultural and inter-cultural problems of diagnostic accuracy); stressors clearly are implicated in the "onset, relapse or exacerbation of schizophrenic states [Birley & Brown, 1970, p. 293; cf. Wallis, 1972, on stressors as "prognostic predictors"]," as are genetic and enzyme factors. The finest recent statement on the pathogenesis of schizophrenia, and the significance of the "stress" concept for integrating and explaining that process, is that by Pollin (1972, especially pp. 49–51, 52; cf. Birley & Brown, 1970, p. 300). Another, culturally patterned, individual response may be the "peripheral spirit possession" discussed by Lewis (1971); one thinks here too of the shivering and shaking response exhibited by East African Samburu young men (the *moran*: Spencer, 1970, pp. 132, 135–136, 139, 151) in stressful transactions. The whole issue of what "emotions" are is involved here, and it is useful to note the statement of Lazarus et al. (1970, pp. 210, 217, 218) that "each emotion [is] characterized by its own specific pattern of response, which includes physiological, behavioural, and cognitive components."

Interaction Between Levels

In man there clearly is some interaction between the physiological and the psychological response levels when a person is under stress (cf. Caudill, 1958, pp. 1–2; Rahe & Arthur, 1968, p. 341, Rahe et al., 1964, p. 42); research and research findings on the "psychosomatic" disorders (Marmor & Pumpian-Mindlin, 1950, pp. 307, McNeil, 1970b, pp. 62ff; Rahe & Arthur, 1968, p. 344, cf. Aakster, 1974, p. 87, also pp. 79, 88–89), so regrettably neglected by anthropologists, are all relevant here, as are findings on at least some of the related "chronic organic diseases" (Dodge & Martin, 1970). However, this interaction or feedback between the two levels does not always operate, nor is it always effective for the coping process (Lazarus, 1966, ch. 10; cf. Sachar, in Weiss, 1972b, p. 272); one may not be conscious of the fact that one's physiological system is under stress for some time, while psychological coping devices may not eliminate a physiological level stressor (Lazarus, 1971, p. 54). Moreover, there may well be a delay of some months before a disease outcome emerges as a result of an earlier cluster of transactions (as noted by Holmes & Masuda, 1972, pp. 71, 106; Rahe & Arthur, 1968, p. 344; Rahe et al., 1964, p. 42). A number of stressors and coping responses may be in transaction at the physiological, psychological, and behavioural levels at the same time in one individual, with varying degrees of interaction between these levels.

Interpersonal and Societal Response Outcomes

On the interpersonal response level, coping responses include co-operation, withdrawal or aggression (Leighton, 1945, p. 263); role changes; marital breakdown; scapegoating, and so on. One man's frustration and defeat is another man's challenge; different people may give different responses to the "same" stressor, this depending on the various characteristics of the stressor, past experience, and the other mediating factors mentioned previously (Dodge & Martin, 1970, pp. 87, 106, 120, 179, 250, 260, 307; Lazarus et al., 1970, p. 225; Pollin, 1972, pp. 50, 51; Selye, 1974, pp. 45–46; Williams, Kopinak & Moynagh, 1972, p. 398). As for coping at the societal level, "Our major instrument of adaptation is government [Vickers, 1968, p. 60]"; i.e., much depends on the nature of the decision-making persons and institutions in the group and on their acts and strategies. Some possible group response-outcomes are revitalization movements (Wallace, 1956a); complete mastery of the stressor; panic; revolution, as an adaptive response; migration; mass apathy and alcoholism; and witch-hunts (see also Barton, 1969). Some of these response-outcomes are temporary or irreversible, limited or all-embracing, in nature. Interaction and feedback between the individual and the societal or group levels when under stress is also not an automatic process in all cases (Dodge & Martin, 1970, pp. 56, 58; Lazarus, 1966, pp. 402, 405); a few group members may be under severe stress, as individuals, yet the system as a whole may well be able to easily carry on. This chapter presents an argument for a general systems theory approach to stressors and coping responses at all levels and for an integrative, level-embracing, dynamic model of such transactions over time. It may well prove true that "some of the rules will be quite different at each level" (R. Lazarus, personal communication, Jan. 9, 1974); however, as was noted near the beginning of this chapter, the present research is *also* concerned with "identifying and explaining general features of adaptive systems which transcend the peculiarities of any one type of system [Straus, 1973, p. 107, fn. 2]," and of any one transactional level.

CONCLUSIONS

This chapter has defended the continued scientific use of the "stress" concept, albeit in a revised form, and has presented a detailed exposition of a model of "an open system under stress," along with some data drawn from ethnographic fieldwork among the Nchumuru people of Ghana, some of whom were found to be under stress as a consequence of the various aspects of the Volta Resettlement Project. During the course of this presentation, I have called for the development of a subfield, "the anthropology of suffering," which is based on stress research and on work in such related fields as medical anthropology and transcultural psychiatry. Social scientists cannot develop an adequate and a sophisticated theory of social change unless the concept of "stress," as defined here, is firmly placed at the very core of that theoretical endeavour. It is to be hoped that this detailed theoretical treatment of that concept will convince workers in other fields that anthropologists, too, have a role to play in ongoing and future stress research programmes. An integrative, level-embracing, general systems theory approach is the one most suited for the furtherance of the field of stress research.

With further knowledge of the significance of the various variables specified in the section, "A Model of an Open System Under Stress," and so with an enhanced knowledge of the stressfulness of certain life-events in Western and non-Western settings, preventive intervention programmes can be developed for individuals or groups at risk—perhaps through the careful monitoring of life-event clusters in the histories of persons participating in improved community health clinics (e.g., by the use of the Subjective Stress Scale by general practitioners, too: Reeder et al., 1973, p. 578), by the development and administration of hormone secretion-adjusting pills, or through the restructuring of the wider society for the benefit of its members. More academically, such knowledge should help in the development of an adequate, etic (cross-cultural) disease nosology (cf. Kagan, 1971, p. 45; Moss, 1973, p. 11).

Finally, through increased knowledge of, and participation in, the endeavours of the field of stress research, and through the elaboration of an anthropology of suffering, social scientists may soon be able to satisfy the terms of the programmatic statement made over 20 years ago by the great anthropologist S. F. Nadel (1951, p. 377):

But surely we wish to say more than merely that each mode of behaviour has its utility; we wish to say that the people buy their pleasures and integration *at a price.*

REFERENCES

Aakster, C. W. Psycho-social stress and health disturbances. *Social Science and Medicine*, 1974, 8, 77-90.

Appley, M., & Trumbull, R. (Eds.) *Psychological stress: Issues in research.* New York: Appleton-Century-Crofts, 1967.

Averill, J., Opton, E., & Lazarus, R. Cross-cultural studies of psychophysiological responses during stress and emotion. In L. Levi (Ed.), *Society, stress and disease.* Vol. I. *The psychosocial environment and psychosomatic diseases.* London: Oxford University Press, 1971.

Barton, A. H. *Communities in disaster: A sociological analysis of collective stress situations.* Garden City, N.Y.: Anchor Books, 1970. (Originally published 1969.)

Bateson, G. *Steps to an ecology of mind.* New York: Ballantine, 1972.

Beattie, J. *Other cultures.* London: Routledge & Kegan Paul, 1964.

Becker, S., Horowitz, M., & Campbell, L. Cognitive responses to stress: Effects of changes in demand and sex. *Journal of Abnormal Psychology*, 1973, 82, 519-522.

Berlyne, D. E. New directions in motivation theory. In T. Gladwin & W. Sturtevant (Eds.), *Anthropology and human behavior.* Washington, D.C.: Anthropological Society of Washington, 1962.

Bertalanffy, L. Von *General system theory.* New York: G. Braziller, 1968.

Birley, J., & Brown, G. Crises and life changes preceding the onset or relapse of acute schizophrenia: Clinical aspects. In R. Cancro (Ed.), *Annual review of the schizophrenic syndrome.* Vol. I. New York: Brunner/Mazel, 1971. (Originally published 1970.)

Broadbent, D. *Decision and stress.* London: Academic Press, 1971.

Brown, B. B. New mind, new body. *Psychology Today*, 1974, 8(3), whole issue.

Brown, R. Models of attitude change, In T. Newcomb (Ed.), *New directions in psychology.* New York: Holt, Rinehart, & Winston, 1962.

Buckley, W. *Sociology and modern systems theory.* London: Prentice-Hall, 1967.

Buckley, W. (Ed.) *Modern systems research for the behavioral scientist.* Chicago: Aldine, 1968.

Caudill, W. *Effects of social and cultural systems in reactions to stress.* (Social Science Research Council, pamphlet 14), New York: Social Science Research Council, 1958.

Coates, D., Moyer, S., & Wellman, B. The Yorklea study of urban mental health: Symptoms, problems and life events. In C. Boydell, C. Grindstaff, & P. Whitehead (Eds.), *Deviant behaviour and societal reaction.* Toronto: Holt, Rinehart, & Winston, 1972. (Originally published 1969.)

Cochrane, R., & Robertson, A. The life events inventory: A measure of the relative severity of psycho-social stressors. *Journal of Psychosomatic Research*, 1973, 17, 135-139.

Cohen, F., & Lazarus, R. Active coping processes, coping dispositions, and recovery from surgery. *Psychosomatic Medicine*, 1973, 35, 375-389.

Cohen, S., & Taylor, L. *Psychological survival: The experience of long-term imprisonment.* London: Penguin, 1972.

Crown, S. *Essential principles of psychiatry.* London: Pitman Medical Books, 1970.

Dodge, D., & Martin, W. *Social stress and chronic illness: Mortality patterns in industrial society.* London: University of Notre Dame Press, 1970.

Dohrenwend, B. P. The social psychological nature of stress: A framework for causal inquiry. *Journal of Abnormal and Social Psychology*, 1961, 62, 294-302.

Dohrenwend, B. P. Social status, stress and psychological symptoms. *Milbank Memorial Fund Quarterly*, 1969, 47(1, part 2), 137-150.

Dohrenwend, B. P., & Dohrenwend, B. S. *Social status and psychological disorder: A causal inquiry.* New York: Wiley, 1969.

Dohrenwend, B. S. Life events as stressors: A methodological inquiry. *Journal of Health and Social Behavior*, 1973, 14, 167-175.

Dollard, J., Doob, L., Miller, N., Mowrer, O., & Sears, R. *Frustration and agression.* New Haven: Yale University Press, 1963. (Originally published 1939.)

Durkheim, E. *The rules of sociological method* (G. Catlin, Ed.) Toronto: Collier-Macmillan, 1964. (Originally published, 1895.)

Eastham, K., Coates, D., & Allodi, F. The concept of crisis. *Canadian Psychiatric Association Journal*, 1970, 15, 463-472.

Eisenstadt, S. Problems in theories of social structure, personality and communication in their relation to situations of change and stress. In L. Levi (Ed.), *Society, stress and disease.* Vol. 1. *The psychosocial environment and psychosomatic diseases.* London: Oxford University Press, 1971.

Engel, G. L. A unified concept of health and disease. *Perspectives in Biology and Medicine*, 1960, 3, 459-485.

Fabrega, H. *Disease and social behavior: An interdisciplinary perspective.* Boston: Massachusetts Institute of Technology Press, 1974.

Fernea, R., & Kennedy, J. Initial adaptations to resettlement: A new life for Egyptian Nubians. *Current Anthropology*, 1966, 7, 349-354.

Fortes, M. *Kinship and the social order.* London: Routledge & Kegan Paul, 1970. (Originally published 1969.)

Fortes, M., & Mayer, D. Psychosis and social change among the Tallensi of northern Ghana. In S. Foulkes & G. Prince (Eds.), *Psychiatry in a changing society*. London: Tavistock, 1969.

Frankl, V. E. *Man's search for meaning*. (rev. ed.) New York: Pocket Books, 1973.

Freud, S. *The problem of anxiety*. (Trans. by H. Bunker) New York: Norton, 1963.

Freud, S. *The complete introductory lectures on psychoanalysis*. (Trans. by J. Strachey) London: Allen & Unwin, 1971.

Fried, M. Grieving for a lost home. In A. Kiev (Ed.), *Social psychiatry*. Vol. 1. London: Routledge & Kegan Paul, 1970. (Originally published 1963.)

Fried, M. Transitional functions of working-class communities: Implications for forced relocation. In M. Kantor (Ed.), *Mobility and mental health*. Illinois: Charles C Thomas, 1965.

Glass, D., Singer, J., & Friedman, L. Psychic cost of adaptation to an environmental stressor. *Journal of Personality and Social Psychology*, 1969, 12, 200-210.

Goody, J. R. *The social organization of the LoWiili*. London: Oxford University Press, 1967. (Originally published 1956.)

Hall, A., & Fagen, R. Definition of system. In W. Buckley (Ed.), *Modern systems research for the behavioural scientist*. Chicago: Aldine, 1968. (Originally published 1956.)

Hamburg, D. The relevance of recent evolutionary changes to human stress biology. In S. Washburn (Ed.), *The social life of early man*. Chicago: Aldine Press, 1961.

Hamburg, D., & Lunde, D. Relation of behavioural, genetic, and neuroendocrine factors to thyroid function. In J. Spuhler (Ed.), *Genetic diversity and human behavior*. (Viking Fund Publications in Anthropology, No. 45), New York: Wenner-Gren Foundation, 1967.

Harmon, D., Masuda, M., & Holmes, T. The social readjustment rating scale: A cross-cultural study of Western Europeans and Americans. *Journal of Psychosomatic Research*, 1970, 14, 391-400.

Henry, J. *Pathways to madness*. New York: Random House, 1971.

Herbst, P. G. A theory of simple behaviour systems. *Human Relations*, 1961, 14, 71-94, 193-239.

Herbst, P. G. *Behavioural worlds: The study of single cases*. London: Tavistock, 1970.

Hinkle, L. E. The concept of "stress" in the biological and social sciences. *Science, Medicine and Man*, 1973, 1, 31-48.

Holmes, T., & Masuda, M. Psychosomatic syndrome. *Psychology Today*, 1972, 5(11), 71-72, 106.

Holmes, T., & Rahe, R. The social readjustment rating scale. *Journal of Psychosomatic Research*, 1967, 11, 213-218.

Kagan, A. Epidemiology and society, stress and disease. In L. Levi (Ed.), *Society, stress and disease*. Vol. 1. *The psychosocial environment and psychosomatic diseases*. London: Oxford University Press, 1971.

Kagan, A., & Levi, L. Health and environment—psychosocial stimuli: A review. *Social Science and Medicine*, 1974, 8, 225-241.

Kalis, B. L. Crisis theory: Its relevance for community psychology and directions for development. In D. Adelson & B. Kalis (Eds.), *Community psychology and mental health*. Scranton, Pa.: Chandler, 1970.

Kardiner, A. Models for the study of collapse of social homeostasis in a society. In S. Klausner (Ed.), *The study of total societies*. New York: Anchor Books, 1967.

Kline, P. *Fact and fantasy in Freudian theory*. London: Methuen, 1972.

Lauer, R. H. The social readjustment scale and anxiety: A cross-cultural study. *Journal of Psychosomatic Research*, 1973, 17, 171-174.

Lazarus, R. S. *Psychological stress and the coping process*. New York: McGraw-Hill, 1966.

Lazarus, R. S. The concepts of stress and disease. In L. Levi (Ed.), *Society, stress and disease*. Vol. 1. *The psychosocial environment and psychosomatic diseases*. London: Oxford University Press, 1971.

Lazarus, R. S. The self-regulation of emotion. Paper presented at the symposium on Parameters of Emotion, Stockholm, Sweden, June 4-6, 1973.

Lazarus, R., Averill, J., & Opton, E. Towards a cognitive theory of emotion. In M. Arnold (Ed.), *Feelings and emotions*. New York: Academic Press, 1970.

Lazarus, R., Tomita, M., Opton, E., & Kodama, M. A cross-cultural study of stress-reaction patterns in Japan. *Journal of Personality and Social Psychology*, 1966, 4, 622-633.

Leighton, A. H. *The governing of men*. Princeton: Princeton University Press, 1968. (Originally published 1945.)

Levi, L. *Stress: Sources, management and prevention*. New York: Liveright, 1967.

Levi, L. (Ed.) *Stress and distress in response to psychosocial stimuli*. (International Series of Monographs in Experimental Psychology, No. 17), New York: Pergamon Press, 1972.

LeVine, R. Africa. In F. Hsu (Ed.), *Psychological anthropology*. Homewood, Ill.: Dorsey, 1961.

Levine, S. Stress and behavior. *Scientific American*, 1971, 224(1), 26-31.

Levine, S., & Scotch, N. Toward the development of theoretical models: II. *Milbank Memorial Fund Quarterly*, 1967, 45(2), 163-174.

Lewis, I. M. *Ecstatic religion: An anthropological study of spirit possession and shamanism*. London: Penguin, 1971.

Lumsden, D. P. The Volta River Project: Village resettlement and attempted rural animation. *Canadian Journal of African Studies*, 1973, 7, 115-132.

Lumsden, D. P. Nchumuru social organization and the impact of the Volta River Project. Unpublished doctoral dissertation, University of Cambridge, U.K., 1973-74.

Lynn, R. *Personality and national character*. (International Series of Monographs in Experimental Psychology, No. 12) New York: Pergamon Press, 1971.

Marmor, J., & Pumpian-Mindlin, E. Toward an integrative conception of mental disorder. In W. Gray, F. Duhl, & N. Rizzo (Eds.), *General systems theory and psychiatry*. Boston: Little, Brown, 1950 (1969).

Martin, R. Social stress. *New Society*, 1970, 1086-1088.

Mason, J. W. A re-evaluation of the concept of "non-specificity" in stress theory. *Journal of Psychiatric Research*, 1971, 8, 323-333.

Masuda, M., & Holmes, T. The social readjustment rating scale: A cross-cultural study of Japanese and Americans. *Journal of Psychosomatic Research*, 1967, 11, 227-237.

McGrath, J. E. A conceptual formulation for research on stress. In J. McGrath (Ed.), *Social and psychological factors in stress*. Toronto: Holt, Rinehart, & Winston, 1970.

McNeil, E. B. *The psychoses*. Toronto: Prentice-Hall, 1970. (a)

McNeil, E. B. *Neuroses and personality disorders*. Toronto: Prentice-Hall, 1970. (b)

Menninger, K. Psychological aspects of the organism under stress. *General Systems*, 1957, 2, 142-172. (Originally published 1954.)

Miller, J. G. Living systems: Basic concepts. In W. Gray, F. Duhl, & N. Rizzo (Eds.), *General systems theory and psychiatry*. Boston: Little, Brown, 1969.

Moore, T. Stress in normal childhood. *Human Relations*, 1969, 22, 235-249.

Moore, W. *Social change*. Toronto: Prentice-Hall, 1963.

Moss, G. E. *Illness, immunity, and social interaction*. Toronto: Wiley, 1973.

Nadel, S. F. *The foundations of social anthropology*. London: Cohen & West, 1963. (Originally published 1951.)

Naroll, R. A tentative index of culture-stress. *International Journal of Social Psychiatry*, 1959, 5, 107-116.

Naroll, R. *Data quality control: Prolegomena to a cross-cultural study of culture-stress*. Toronto: Collier-Macmillan, 1962.

Naroll, R. Cultural determinants and the concept of the sick society. In S. Plog & R. Edgerton (Eds.), *Changing perspectives in mental illness*. Toronto: Holt, Rinehart, & Winston, 1969.

Notterman, J., & Trumbull, R. Note on self-regulating systems and stress. In W. Buckley (Ed.), *Modern systems research for the behavioural scientist*. Chicago: Aldine Press, 1968. (Originally published 1950.)

Paykel, E., & Uhlenhuth, E. Rating the magnitude of life stress. *Canadian Psychiatric Association Journal*, 1972, 17, SS93-SS100.

Pless, I., & Satterwhite, B. A measure of family functioning and its application. *Social Science and Medicine*, 1973, 7, 613-621.

Pollin, W. The pathogenesis of schizophrenia: Possible relationships between genetic, biochemical, and experimental factors. In R. Cancro (Ed.), *Annual review of the schizophrenic syndrome*. Vol. 3. New York: Brunner/Mazel, 1974. (Originally published 1972.)

Radcliffe-Brown, A. R. *A natural science of society*. Toronto: Collier-Macmillan, 1964. (Originally published 1957.)

Rahe, R. Multi-cultural correlations of life change scaling: America, Japan, Denmark and Sweden. *Journal of Psychosomatic Research*, 1969, 13, 191-195.

Rahe, R., & Arthur, R. Life-change patterns surrounding illness experience. *Journal of Psychosomatic Research*, 1968, 11, 341-345.

Rahe, R., Meyer, M., Smith, M., Kjaer, G., & Holmes, T. Social stress and illness onset. *Journal of Psychosomatic Research*, 1964, 8, 35-44.

Reeder, L., Schrama, P., & Dirken, J. Stress and cardiovascular health: An international cooperative study. I. *Social Science and Medicine*, 1973, 7, 573-584.

Richter, D. Some current usages of the word "stress" in different fields. In J. Tanner (Ed.), *Stress and psychiatric disorder*. Oxford: Blackwell, 1960.

Rioch, D. McK. Transition states as stress. In L. Levi (Ed.), *Society, stress and disease*. Vol. 1. *The psychosocial environment and psychosomatic diseases*. London: Oxford University Press, 1971.

Schar, M., Reeder, L., & Dirken, J. Stress and cardiovascular health: The male population of a factory at Zurich. *Social Science and Medicine*, 1973, 7, 585-603.

Scotch, N. A preliminary report on the relation of sociocultural factors to hypertension among the Zulu. *Annals of the New York Academy of Sciences*, 1960, 84, 1000-1009.

Scott, R., & Howard, A. Models of stress. In S. Levine & N. Scotch (Eds.), *Social stress*. Chicago: Aldine Press, 1970.

Seiler, L. H. The 22-item scale used in field studies of mental illness: A question of method, a question of substance and a question of theory. *Journal of Health and Social Behavior*, 1973, 14, 252-264.

Seligman, M. Submissive death: Giving up on life. *Psychology Today*, 1974, 7(12), 80-85.

Selye, H. *The stress of life*. Toronto: McGraw-Hill, 1956.

Selye, H. The concept of stress in experimental physiology. In J. Tanner (Ed.), *Stress and psychiatric disorder*. Oxford: Blackwell, 1960.

Selye, H. *Stress without distress*. Toronto: McClelland & Stewart, 1974.

Smelser, N. Toward a general theory of social change. In N. Smelser, *Essays in sociological explanation*. Toronto: Prentice-Hall, 1968.

Spencer, P. The function of ritual in the socialization of the Samburu Moran. In P. Mayer (Ed.), *Socialization: The approach from social anthropology*. London: Tavistock, 1970.

Straus, M. A. A general systems theory approach to a theory of violence between family members. *Social Science Information*, 1973, 12, 105-125.

Syme, S., & Reeder, L. (Eds.) Social stress and cardiovascular disease. *Milbank Memorial Fund Quarterly*, special issue, 1967, 45(2, part 2).

Time, June 26, 1972, 33.

Turnbull, C. *The mountain people*. New York: Simon & Schuster, 1972.

Vickers, Sir G. The concept of stress in relation to the disorganization of human behaviour. In J. Tanner (Ed.), *Stress and psychiatric disorder*. Oxford: Blackwell, 1960.

Vickers, Sir G. *Value systems and social process*. London: Tavistock, 1968.

Wallace, A. F. C. Revitalization movements. *American Anthropologist*, 1956, 58, 264-281. (a)

Wallace, A. F. C. *Tornado in Worcester*. (National Research Council, Pub. No. 392, Disaster study No. 3) Washington, D.C.: National Research Council, 1956. (b)

Wallis, G. Stress as a predictor in schizophrenia. In R. Cancro (Ed.), *Annual review of the schizophrenic syndrome*. Vol. 3. New York: Brunner/Mazel, 1972 (1974).

Weiss, J. M. Psychological factors in stress and disease. *Scientific American*, 1972, 226, 104–113. (a)

Weiss, J. M. Influence of psychological variables on stress-induced pathology. In Ciba Foundation Symposium, n.s. 8, *Physiology, emotion and psychosomatic illness*. Amsterdam: Associated Scientific Publishers, 1972. (b)

Wilkinson, R. One stress on top of another. *New Society*, 1972, 72, 74–75.

Williams, J., Kopinak, K., & Moynagh, W. Mental health and illness in Canada. In C. Boydell, C. Grindstaff, & P. Whitehead (Eds.), *Deviant behaviour and societal reaction*. Toronto: Holt, Rinehart, & Winston, 1972.

Wolff, H. G. Stressors as a cause of disease in man. In J. Tanner (Ed.), *Stress and psychiatric disorder*. Oxford: Blackwell, 1960.

Wolff, H. G. *Stress and disease*. (rev. ed.) Illinois: Charles C Thomas, 1968.

Zborowski, M. Cultural components in response to pain. In E. G. Jaco (Ed.), *Patients, physicians and illness*. Glencoe: Free Press, 1958. (Originally published 1952.)

11

THE PUEBLO INCIDENT: PSYCHOLOGICAL RESPONSE TO SEVERE STRESS

Charles V. Ford

University of California, Los Angeles
United States of America

The capture, imprisonment in North Korea, and en bloc return to the United States of 82 surviving crew members of the USS *Pueblo* allowed for a systematic study of the psychological responses to severe stress. Reports from World War II and the Korean conflict indicated that the experience of being an occidental POW in an oriental country is extremely stressful and associated with high mortality (Mayer, 1956; Nardini, 1952). Although no mortality occurred with the Pueblo crew during imprisonment (one man was killed during capture) the uncertainty of their fate made this an extremely stressful event for all men involved. This communication reports the men's reaction to the stress, compares methods of coping, and includes some follow-up over a period of time. Aspects of this work have been reported in detail previously (Ford & Spaulding, 1973; Spaulding & Ford, 1972).

HISTORICAL SUMMARY OF THE "*PUEBLO* INCIDENT"

There have been numerous reports both via the news media and accounts of various crew members in books that they have written

229

(Brandt, 1969; Bucher, 1970; Murphy, 1971; Schumacher, 1971). The following summary, abstracted from these accounts, appears to be generally agreed upon by all crew members.

On January 23, 1968, the small intelligence ship USS *Pueblo* (AGER-2) was attacked in international waters off the Pacific Coast of North Korea. One crew member was killed; two others sustained substantial injuries. The ship was then boarded, captured, and sailed into Wanson Harbor. The crew was then transferred to Pyongyoung by railroad, where they were imprisoned in a building known to the crew as "the barn."

The commanding officer was isolated from the others, who were quartered three or four to a room. Crew members were threatened with death and interrogated; some were severely beaten. Forced "confessions" about "criminal aggressive acts" were obtained from all crew members as a result of these threats and ill treatment. Possession of the men's service records gave the North Koreans a strong position in their interrogations. Later, in March 1968, the crew was transferred to other accommodations near military installations, where officers had their own rooms and enlisted men generally were housed eight to a room.

Their treatment by the North Koreans varied, but in general the living quarters, sanitation facilities, and medical care were unsatisfactory by Western standards. Food was a particular difficulty, since it was deficient both in quantity and quality. The attitudes of the captors seemed capricious; the crew members began to associate improved food and a decrease in physical maltreatment with hopes for imminent release and the converse as a sign that negotiations were going poorly. Despite the "confessions," members of the crew attempted to communicate to the free world their lack of sincerity. These actions included references to dead relatives and awkward and uncharacteristic phrasing in letters. Propaganda photographs often showed smiling faces in association with obscene gestures.

The North Koreans attempted through lectures, field trips, and written material to convince crew members of the injustices of their "imperialist" government.

In the fall of 1968 there were signs of increased friendliness by the Koreans, which was interpreted by the crew as an indication of increasingly good prospects for release. However, this turn of attitude changed abruptly in the first week of December and was supplanted by "Hell Week." It became apparent that the Koreans had learned the meaning of the obscene gestures, as well as the meaning of some details in the letters. Physical maltreatment increased to its most intense level since their capture, and there were extensive efforts to force information from the crew as to which of its members had collaborated in the efforts to foil the propaganda plans of the North Koreans.

Suddenly and unexpectedly on December 19, the maltreatment was reversed. On December 23 the crew was returned to South Korea; they walked across a bridge connecting the Koreas. Each man received a screening physical examination, was provided with an American uniform, and had a holiday meal. The crew was then flown to San Diego Naval Hospital for a more intensive evaluation and intelligence debriefing. They arrived on Christmas Eve into an emotional scene provided by welcoming relatives.

METHODS OF STUDY

Initial Evaluation

The *Pueblo* crew members returned to the Naval Hospital, San Diego, within 48 hours of their release from North Korea. Detailed physical examination and psychiatric consultation preceded debriefing procedures. The psychiatric evaluation consisted of at least one individual private interview with one of the six psychiatrists who were part of the medical team. Each man also completed a questionnaire concerning demographic information, a Sentence Completion Test, and the Minnesota Multiphasic Personality Inventory (MMPI).

Each interviewer was requested to complete a detailed protocol on each man that he evaluated. This protocol documented whether (in the evaluator's clinical judgment) the man had suffered any significant anxiety or depression during the crew's period of incarceration. Methods of defending against anxiety or depression were documented and recorded at the time of the interview. Information also recorded included demographic information, impression of character structure, ego-defense mechanisms, and other coping devices used during imprisonment. In addition, notations were made of the man's opinions of how he had fared during the time of captivity and his opinion concerning those men he felt had done well and those who had done poorly.

Selection of Comparison Groups

The definition of "success" in coping with the stress is obviously subjective. An arbitrary definition was established that incorporated the individual's reaction to stress as well as his function as a part of a military group. This reflects a value judgment that mental health reflects one's social relationships as well as personal comfort. The definition of success consisted of the ability to (a) defend against excessive anxiety or depression; (b) contribute to group support and morale; and (c) provide realistic resistance to demands of the captors. Lack of success was defined as the presence of psychiatric symptoms, behavior detrimental to morale, and excessive co-operation with the captors as reported by the crew member or his peers.

Two of the psychiatrists independently reviewed all the protocols and ancillary material for the factors of success listed previously and rated each of five factors by assigning it a score of +1, 0, or −1. The five factors were (a) the man's opinion of how well he had done, (b) the crewmates' opinion of how well he had done, (c) the examining psychiatrist's opinion of how well the individual had defended against anxiety and depression, (d) the examining psychiatrist's opinion of how well the man had supported group morale, and (e) the examining psychiatrist's opinion of how well the man had resisted cooperation with the captors.

The scores of independent raters were added together and the resultant scores ranged from −10 to +10 (distribution of scores is listed in Table 11-1). It was decided to compare the approximate upper third with the approximate lower third, and cutoff points were so determined. Interrater reliability was high. A rank-order correlation coefficient was computed ($r = .786$) and found significant at the .001 level. No man was placed in the upper group by one rater and in the lower group by the other rater.

Method of Comparison

The evaluation protocols were used in analyzing factors for comparison, which included age, martial status, length of military service, education, history of psychiatric consultation or treatment, and history of legal problems. In addition, all ego defenses listed or described by the examining psychiatrist were compared, as well as the personality diagnoses. The MMPI T scores were averaged and

Table 11-1

Distribution of Rating Scores

Rating score[a]	Number of men
Upper group (N = 24)	
+10	2
+9	0
+8	5
+7	3
+6	6
+5	3
+4	5
Middle group (N = 31)	
+3	10
+2	8
+1	9
0	4
Lower group (N = 27)	
−1	3
−2	6
−3	4
−4	8
−5	2
−6	1
−7	0
−8	1
−9	2
−10	0

[a] Explained in text.

compared. The man's average weight losses were computed from medical records, averaged and compared.

RESULTS

Clinical Observations

When the men of the *Pueblo* were first seen, they generally appeared subdued and voiced concern about wanting to see their families. However, there was a major contradiction between the verbalized affect and that which the examiners observed. Such comments as "This is the happiest day of my life" were *not* associated with euphoria. Quite the contrary, the majority of the crew seemed mildly depressed or anxious, although, almost to a man, they denied such feelings.

The men were characterized by a willingness to talk freely and to discuss their feelings toward their captors and fellow crew members. Expressions of overt hatred toward the North Koreans were common and there were many spontaneous comments denying that they had had any success in "brainwashing" crew members. At times the protests were so insistent as to suggest a reaction formation. There were concerns of guilt about the capture and subsequent "confessions," but serious statements of this type were limited to a minority and most men had ready rationalizations, such as "We really screwed them over" (in reference to widely publicized pictures in which the crew members were making an obscene gesture).

There was in general a willingness to talk about other crew members and to describe those who had done well and those who had tolerated the stress poorly. The descriptions were fairly unanimous in singling out the ones who had done poorly as well as those who had done well. In both instances the feelings were strongly expressed but did not seem to us as intense as those reported following the Korean conflict in similar circumstances. The consistency of the crew's reports permitted the examiners to believe that the physical and emotional experiences the men had endured during the preceding 11 months were accurately reported.

The crew as a whole had experienced anxiety and apprehension during the first days immediately following their capture. Feelings of guilt that followed the "confessions" for the most part were transitory and were ameliorated by shared rationalizations with other crew members. Many men, initially encouraged by rumors of imminent release in October, ascribed their lowest period to the disappointment and despair that followed the failure of repatriation at that time. Anxiety again increased in response to "Hell Week" prior to their actual release in December.

However, there were some men who had more striking reactions than these generalized ones. Forty men admitted experiencing significant anxiety, but all attributed this to the unpredictability of their treatment by the North Koreans. Sixteen men gave a history of subjective depression, often accompanied by feelings of despair, hopelessness, and suicidal ideation. An attempt was made to define the nature of the object loss(es) that were thought to be responsible for the depressive reactions. For 11 men this was separation from family. Four men stated that their failure to live up to personal ideals in regard to the "confessions" was a significant factor. For seven men the anticipated loss of their Navy careers was important. One man worked through a transient depression secondary to traumatic castration by shrapnel. (Some men experienced more than one significant loss.) Suicidal ideation was uncommon, but six admitted this and two actually made three attempts; two of these, however, seemed to be more manipulative than serious. One man did make an attempt to end his life, but the degree of despair that he was suffering at that time probably precluded his effectively killing himself.

Food was monotonous, limited in quantity, and prepared with less than usual Western standards of sanitation. Despite this, the majority of men ate what was available. Significant weight losses, the average being 30 pounds, were reported by most crew members. Twenty-seven men complained of anorexia during their confinement. Of these, 9 were anorexic throughout their stay, 15 were anorexic early during internment but later regained their appetite, and 3 who originally ate well became anorexic at a later time. The anorexia that was reported was not clearly related to anxiety or depression. Discussion of food was a favorite subject during the internment. In fact, one of the ship's cooks kept himself busy by planning menus.

Disturbances of sleep patterns were more clearly related to feelings of depression or anxiety, and most of those who complained of a change from their usual sleep pattern admitted to feelings of depression or anxiety. One man was hypersomnic, 10 complained of difficulty falling asleep, and 3 men were bothered with early wakening. Dreams were common and a variety of themes were presented, including wish-fulfillment dreams ("fishing back home with Dad"), dreams of abandonment ("I returned home and everyone had left"), and sexual dreams. Dreams of retaliation were rare; however, many of the men fantasized that the United States would strike with vengeance at the *Pueblo* and possibly at the area where the crew was interned, killing them all for their breach of conduct and loss of ship. Several men reported dreaming about escape.

When crew members were asked about the methods they used to cope with their incarceration, they frequently stated that they maintained a faith in their commanding officer, religion, and country. It became apparent that there was considerable group support provided by the natural leaders who emerged in each of the rooms in which they had been randomly billeted. Crew members referred to their room as a "haven" and convinced themselves that it was not bugged since they talked freely about their captors.

Many of the rooms apparently operated like leaderless group therapy; there was ample time for extended review of their individual lives, hopes, aspirations, and accomplishments. Sexual topics for discussion were common and often quite candid, although some men denied any sexual libido during their captivity. There was no report of any homosexual activity. Many of the crew members commented that they felt that they had gained from the experience through increased understanding of themselves and others. Furthermore, there were statements reflecting a belief in increased maturity on the part of the individual, greater appreciation for the American way of life, and a firm resolve for meaningful application to a purposeful life in the future.

Comparison of Factors Relating to Coping Ability

Two groups, the upper third and lower third, chosen as to their coping abilities (see "Methods of Study") were compared in a number of different demographic and psychological variables. There were no significant differences in age, length of military service, educational level, and history of psychiatric treatment or legal difficulty (Table 11-2). Marital status was not remarkably different, although the lower group revealed three who were divorced or separated as opposed to none of the upper group for that category.

Table 11-2

Comparison of Personal History Information

Personal data	Upper group (N = 24)	Lower group (N = 27)
Average age (years)	29.1	27.9
Average education (years)	12.8	11.5
Average military service (years)	8.3	8.5
Marital status (number of men)		
Married	13	14
Single	11	10
Divorced	0	3
Positive psychiatric history (number of men)	0	2
Positive legal history (number of men)	6	6

The average weight loss of the upper group (13.34 kg) did not differ significantly from that of the lower group (14.06 kg).

Marked differences between the groups occurred in the distribution of personality diagnoses. Passive-dependent personality was the predominant diagnosis in the lower group (10 men, 36%). In the upper group the predominant personality type was identified as healthy (11 men, 46%); the second most prevalent personality diagnosis in the upper group was schizoid personality (5 men, 21%). A comparison of personality diagnoses is listed in Table 11-3.

Evaluation of ego-defense mechanisms used by both groups revealed both qualitative and quantitative differences. An average of five mechanisms were listed for each man in the upper group, compared with an average of 2.4 in the lower group. The most remarkable difference was in the increased frequency of the upper group's use of reality testing, rationalization, "faith," denial, and humor. The lower group reported more obsessive ideation. Table 11-4 compares the frequency of defense mechanisms employed by the two groups. It must be noted that the six different psychiatrists may have used the terms somewhat differently; but, generally, terminology follows the descriptions in standard references.

Altruism was listed as a defense by several psychiatrists, but was not included in the comparison because qualities related to altruism were used in defining the two groups. Two other common defense mechanisms were not recorded because they were uniformly present

Table 11-3

Comparison of Personality Diagnoses

Diagnosis	Number of men	
	Upper group (N = 24)	Lower group (N = 27)
Healthy	11	0
Schizoid	5	2
Passive-aggressive	2	2
Obsessive-compulsive	1	3
Immature	1	1
Passive-dependent	0	10
Paranoid	0	1
Emotionally unstable	0	1
Inadequate	0	1
Not specified	4	6

Table 11-4

Comparison of Ego Mechanisms Used During Imprisonment

Ego mechanism	Upper group (N = 24)	Lower group (N = 27)
Faith	15	4
Reality testing	13	0
Denial	12	5
Rationalization	12	2
Humor	11	2
Religion	9	7
Fantasy	7	7
Repression	7	2
Sublimation	5	4
Suppression	5	0
Reaction formation	5	5
Intellectualization	5	4
Obsessive thinking	3	6
Acting out	3	3
Isolation	3	4
Somatization	2	2
Compulsive rituals	1	2
Other[a]	3	4

[a]"Other" includes displacement, counterphobic mechanisms, avoidance, identification with the aggressor, and passive-aggressive behavior.

in the crew due to the reality situation: one was projection and the other anticipation. The presence of a real external persecutory agent provided all the men with a logical source of projection of difficulties. Also plans for activity and life goals after release provided for anticipation of life change related to a real event.

Comparison of MMPI data from the two groups was generally unremarkable.

A review of characteristics of the middle group indicated that although it was an admixture of the two groups, in general the men comprising this group were more typical of the upper group rather than the lower group.

Follow-up

The crew initially remained a very well integrated group. Individuals remained identified with the crew as a whole, and daily military routine was maintained. After 3 weeks most were found fit for limited duty and were scheduled for reevaluation 3 months later, at which time it was anticipated that a Board of Inquiry would have completed its investigation and recommendations.

At the time of reevaluation, the difference in the crew was striking. In contrast to the initially bland cooperative demeanor observed, many men were openly antagonistic and hostile toward both the Navy and their fellow crew members despite the fact the findings of the Board of Inquiry were more benign than initially anticipated by the crew. At this time there was evidence of considerable acting out with alcohol and drugs, minor traffic violations, and squandered back pay.

During the succeeding 5 years, a number of other problems surfaced. Despite the lack of a systematic follow-up study, it is known that there was one suicide. In addition to this, there has been a psychotic depression, a paranoid reaction, an incapacitating obsessive-compulsive neurosis, an incapacitating psychosomatic pain syndrome, and a hospitalization for newly developed alcoholism. To investigate this apparent increase of psychiatric symptoms, a systematic study of all crew members is planned and a control group will be used for comparison.

DISCUSSION

The comparison of what factors were associated with better adjustment to the acute distress confirms some psychiatric prejudices and raises other interesting questions. Men defined as "healthy" possessing a number of defensives could react with flexibility and adaptability to marked changes in environment and the anxiety of indeterminate fate. Schizoid men also did well, apparently able to emotionally isolate themselves from the immediate situation. Passive-dependent men, who on first impression might have been thought to tolerate imprisonment well, did quite poorly. One explanation could be that these men were in intense conflict between giving in to their dependency wishes by cooperation with the captors and at the same time trying to please their military authorities who demanded resistance.

The degree of psychological distress during imprisonment, as reported by the crew members, does not seem dramatic when measured by reports of the extent of the stress experienced by the men. An objective measure that indicates the degree of stress is the high average weight loss (30 pounds). There appears to have been sufficient stress to evoke massive repressive defenses, and these account for the somewhat bland and apathetic appearance of the men upon release (Greenson, 1949). Similar findings have been reported previously in describing prisoners of war released from oriental POW camps (Lifton, 1954; Segal, 1954; Wolf & Ripley, 1947). Further evidence that massive repression was evoked as an acute defensive mechanism is suggested by the observation that several weeks after the men's return there was considerable expressed anger and acting out. This can be seen as a release phenomenon where the repressed emotion is expressed and worked through. There is the suggestion, however, that a least for some of the men the stress was not mastered easily. The reports of a suicide, psychotic depression, etc., suggest that the long-range psychological response to severe stress may be much greater than the acute response.

An important question yet to be answered is to what degree this acute stress effected psychological functioning on a long-term basis. A theoretical question is whether those men who apparently did well during the acute situation continue to do well over a long period of time. It is possible that adjustment on the short term basis was due to marked repression and denial and that the price must be paid later. Plans for an extensive follow-up program, with comparison to a control group of Navy men on sea duty at the same time, are now being formulated.

REFERENCES

Brandt, E. *The last voyage of USS* Pueblo. New York: Norton, 1969.

Bucher, L. M. *My story*. Garden City, N.Y.: Doubleday, 1970.

Ford, C. V., & Spaulding, R. C. The *Pueblo* incident: A comparison of factors related to coping with extreme stress. *Archives of General Psychiatry*, 1973, 29, 340–343.

Greenson, R. R. The psychology of apathy. *Psychoanalytic Quarterly*, 1949, 18, 290–302.

Lifton, R. J. Home by ship: Reaction patterns of American prisoners of war repatriated from North Korea. *American Journal of Psychiatry*, 1954, 110, 732–739.

Mayer, W. E. Why did so many GI captives cave in? *U.S. News & World Report*, Feb. 24, 1956, 56–72.

Murphy, E. R. *Second in command*. New York: Holt, Rinehart, & Winston, 1971.

Nardini, J. E. Survival factors in American prisoners of war of the Japanese. *American Journal of Psychiatry*, 1952, 109, 241–248.

Schumacher, F. C. *Bridge of no return*. New York: Harcourt Brace Jovanovich, 1971.

Segal, H. A. Initial psychiatric findings of recently repatriated prisoners of war. *American Journal of Psychiatry*, 1954, 111, 358–363.

Spaulding, R. C., & Ford, C. V. The *Pueblo* incident: Psychological reactions to the stresses of imprisonment and repatriation. *American Journal of Psychiatry*, 1972, 129, 17–26.

Wolf, S., & Ripley, H. S. Reactions among Allied prisoners of war subjected to three years of imprisonment and torture by the Japanese. *American Journal of Psychiatry*, 1947, 104, 180–193.

12

THE STRESS OF COPING WITH THE UNKNOWN REGARDING A SIGNIFICANT FAMILY MEMBER

Yona Teichman

Tel-Aviv University
Tel-Aviv, Israel

This chapter is based on observations accumulated while working with families who had a relative—father, son, or husband—missing in action during the October 1973 Middle East war. These families were deprived of information about the fate of a significant member for different periods of time, which varied from a few days to a few months. The inferences from these observations may be integrated within the increasing body of research which concerns families' reactions to stressful situations like separation (Bell, 1971, Steinzor, 1969), illness (Heimlich & Kutscher, 1970; Kastenbaum & Aisenberg, 1972; Walker, 1970), or death (Kastenbaum & Aisenberg, 1972; Kubler-Ross, 1969; Walker, 1970). It is also interesting to discuss them in terms of the nature of psychological help that may be offered in this kind of situation.

The work with the families of soldiers missing in action was organized by the Israeli Psychologists' Association. Twenty senior psychologists supervised the work of two-person teams who did the actual fieldwork. The team members were junior psychologists, social workers, students, and nonprofessionals. Most of the work was done on a voluntary basis. This report is based on supervision sessions conducted by the author with six teams who worked with 20 families.

The guiding philosophy of this work was that of passive intervention. Although the families who were approached were under extreme objective and subjective stress, we felt that they should be left to deal with the crisis on their own, and that their privacy should be respected. However, where help was needed it was promptly provided. Help was defined as practical assistance in dealing with formalities; psychological support; and when detecting signs of a severe crisis, reference to a mental health, medical, or community agency.

GENERAL PATTERNS OF REACTION

The psychological reactions of relatives of front-line soldiers and POW's were sporadically studied (Hall & Simmons, 1973; Parker, 1972). The systematic assistance and study of families of missing soldiers has apparently not been done before. In Israel it emerged from a war reality; because of the intensive manifestation of the problem, the "helping professions" were forced to focus on it.

The situation of doubting the existence of a significant family member is a uniquely stressful one. Because the situation occurred during a war, the probability of death was heightened, yet many other possibilities might have been true as well. The situation thus was undefinable, and the family faced an acute emotional experience with no predetermined reaction patterns. Bereavement could not be accepted, and hope was mixed with anxiety. Suddenly people found themselves in a cognitive and emotional state of unclarity with undefined behavioral implications—a situation that clearly represents a crisis as defined by Caplan (1956).

Because the soldiers' ages ranged from 18 to 36 years, parents, wives, and children were encountered. This enabled, on one hand, the identification of general, cross-generation reaction patterns, and, on the other hand, specific patterns that characterized one generation rather than the other. Patterns of interaction among generations and between the family and outsiders were also observed.

The general reaction patterns discussed are (a) defensive resignation, (b) defensive optimism, and (c) search for objective information.

Defensive Resignation

There were families who, from the very beginning, prepared themselves for the worst; negated any hope of seeing their missing member again; started to refer to him in the past tense; and, without spelling it out, engaged in socially accepted bereavement behaviors. A similar kind of reaction was previously described by Lindemann (1944). He described an anticipatory grief reaction in wives and daughters of soldiers who had been sent overseas. According to Lindemann, this reaction was adapted as a safeguard against the impact of a sudden death. These women went through the grief process and reached a state of mental separation from the loved person to such an extent that when a reunion was necessary it was impossible.

In the few families in which reunion occurred, we noticed no problems. This most probably was due to the fact that the fate of soldiers who were captured prisoners at least on the Egyptian front became clear pretty soon, and reunions were actualized after 4 months. Apparently, the prospect of the reunion and, shortly later, its actualization prevented the initiation of a grief-separation experience.

Many families, however, were officially informed that their missing relative was dead. Observation of these families clearly indicated that their prior resignation reaction was merely a defensive guise. When death became a reality, the crisis was extreme. The previously manifested acceptance did not ease the experience of facing reality; occasionally, reactions were very severe, like threats of suicide or temporal disorientation. As a matter of fact, when death had to be faced, the reaction of those who had manifested resignation did not differ from the reaction of people who had adopted the opposite mode of defense.

Defensive Optimism

Other families, on receiving the message that their husband or son was missing in action, reacted by expressing extreme optimism and hope. They concentrated on the fact that definitely fatal information was not delivered to them and chose to deny the pessimistic aspect of the ambiguous situation. The denial reaction was prompt and forcefully expressed. As time passed, they accumulated selective information to strengthen their convictions.

The missing person was identified in the most unclear newspaper photographs or on the basis of unreliable information. The compulsive character of the optimism and its extremity pointed to its defensive properties. Indeed, when people who had adopted this kind of reaction had to face the confrontation with death, the crisis that followed was acute. The acute cognitive and emotional dissonance caused the adjustment to be long and painful.

Previous works dealing with reactions to crisis situations did not identify this kind of reaction. This suggests that the uniqueness of the situation at hand, namely its ambiguity, brought it about and that it may appear in other crisis situations with similar properties like premature childbirth and illness.

Although optimism expressed by people in crisis and personal stress tends to encourage us, it is advisable to assess the degree of the defensiveness in it. The need for intervention in these cases may be as strong as in cases of defensive resignation. It is also worth considering the possibility that some of the cases described in the literature as "delay reactions" (Lindemann, 1944) actually began as defensive optimists.

Search for Objective Information

Another way of coping with the unknown, observed very early in our contacts with the families, was a tremendous craving for objective information. Many requested to meet with army officials; others initiated visits at the places where the lost member was last seen and looked for people who had any kind of information about him. The teams were urged to help in acquiring any kind of information about the lost man and every bit of such information was greatly appreciated and helped in increasing emotional closure.

Another pattern of search for clarification was the search for contact of people in the same situation. Meetings of families who shared the same fate were often initiated and actively attended. The craving for objective information could hardly be satisfied. It caused a remarkable level of activity, which on the one hand increased the tension, but, on the other hand, offered distraction from the mental pain and anguish.

The fact that people in a cognitively or emotionally unclear situation tend to reach out for clarification was recognized by Festinger (1954) and Schachter (1959) and proved in many of the laboratory and field studies that dealt with social affiliation

(Gerard, 1963; Gerard & Rabbie, 1961; Latane & Wheeler, 1966; Rabbie, 1963; Strumpfer, 1970; Teichman, 1973; Zucker, Manosevitz, & Lanyon, 1968). Generally, these studies demonstrated that people who experience emotional arousal due to crisis or because of being in an ambiguous, unclear situation manifest a need for social affiliation. The motivation to affiliate was interpreted as a need to engage in social comparison to acquire more information about personal beliefs or feelings.

Of the three described reactions, it was especially difficult to deal with the first two. We did not want to break defenses; yet, being personally less involved, we could anticipate the approaching turning point, especially in the optimistic defense pattern. The course of action that was adopted was that of mild and gradual introduction of a realistic approach. This, however, was a moderate intervening step that only seldom bore any results. The main help was to be present and offer support whenever reality proved to be tragic. Two main variations of support were used: (*a*) justification of the agony, grief, and disorganization that was felt and (*b*) expressing belief in the person's ability to handle the emotional and situational difficulties.

THE THREE GENERATIONS IN CRISIS

Because we dealt with families of soldiers whose ages ranged from 18 to 36 years, we encountered parents, wives, and children (mainly young children). First, some cross-generation general reaction patterns were described; next, a more specific look at the three generations, as well as some interactions among generations, are presented.

Parents

Three main modes of reaction were reported as characterizing this generation: (a) personal grief, (b) heroism, and (c) bitterness.

Personal Grief

This reaction is a highly personal way of experiencing grief and a refusal to share it with others. Behaviorally, it was expressed by an almost complete withdrawal from the environment and personal neglect. Where partial approach was possible, but mainly later on, those parents said that they had been occupied with memories about the missing son, recounting their last encounters together, visualizing him, and trying to remember every detail of their recent mutual activity or conversation. This intensive kind of grief did not last long; after a week or two it began to fade gradually. In general, the parents started to open up first towards other family members, then to strangers; but sometimes the sequence was reversed. It is worth mentioning that despite the extreme withdrawal that worried the family and looked very acute, no perpetuation into a pathological, long-lasting withdrawal was reported. This apparently was due to the fact that the intensified personal grief was a first step in a process of separation from a love object in which the individual built up personal resources to cope with the threatening reality.

In keeping with our philosophy of passive intervention, the person's preference to be left alone was always respected, and no relationship was imposed. In those instances where we were concerned about serious psychological deterioration, we kept the person under close observation. In most instances the passive standby during this period of grief helped to establish trust and facilitated the formation of a meaningful relationship at a later time.

Heroism

The heroic attitude toward a personal tragedy was intensified because it occurred during a national emergency. It was most frequent among parents (fathers and mothers alike), and usually they tried to impose it on other family members, mainly on wives, but even on children. The motto of the heroic response was that of "being strong." These people felt that they had to conform with a socially expected stereotype of emotional restraint and endurance; expressing relevant emotions was taboo. The emotional pressure was indirectly discharged by holding long and calm conversations about the lost son. They liked to show his letters, photographs, belongings, and achievements, yet all in a matter-of-fact sterile atmosphere. In some instances, the identification with the heroic pattern was deep and true, in others it was superficial and an additional burden. This could be inferred from their frequently expressed need for self-reassurance, e.g., "We have to be strong," or search for social reassurance, e.g., "Aren't we strong?" and by occasional emotional outbursts that were promptly arrested and followed by self-reproach. In contrast to those who identified fully with the norm, these people were tense and nervous. The pressure due to lack of congruency between feelings and behavior could be sometimes alleviated by offering justification, acceptance, and understanding of the concealed feelings or by reflecting them. Such intervention usually helped to initiate an overt expression of the suppressed emotion, especially if no other people were around. The expression granted the individual some calmness and relief; but whenever it occurred, more frequent visits to the family were planned. It was felt that a person who admitted feelings that were censored by him and by his family would need further support.

Bitterness

In cases of personal loss, negativistic reactions are well known (Lindemann, 1944). Occasionally they may reach a level of furious hostility. Although a systematic comparison is impossible, it seems that in social crises this kind of reaction would have even a more salient manifestation. In the families which were seen by us, many parents found relief in extreme expression of hostility and criticism toward people whom they held responsible for their situation. The volunteers who visited these families had to endure a lot of the bitterness and criticism. In most of the families a gradual reduction of the bitterness was reported. Some of the parents started to feel shame and self-reproach; others could not break away from this pattern, and hostile generalizations built up. In these cases a more active intervention was recommended, the aim of which was to break the vicious circle of bitterness, negativism, and pessimism, to pull together strength and positive resources.

Wives

Two of the previously described reactions could be identified in wives as well, but less frequently and in a milder form. Bitterness was expressed only occasionally, heroism more so. The fact that heroism was identified in two generations suggests that it stems from a widely accepted norm that cuts through generations.

Unique modes of reactions seen only in wives were (*a*) compulsive preoccupation with practical problems and (*b*) dependency.

Compulsive Preoccupation with
Practical Problems

Many of the teams who met with women whose husbands were missing in action were surprised to find them busy with very practical, material things. Sometimes these were major concerns like unfinished business, or housing problems; but more often the problems looked trivial, like choosing a carpet or paying a phone bill. Whether the problem was major or minor, the women were compulsively preoccupied with it and this preoccupation gave us the insight that it had an emotional meaning and goal. It postponed confrontation with the emotional stress, and it was a way of self-reassurance of being able to cope with realistic problems. Women who unexpectedly found themselves alone assumed the role of their missing husbands and maintained a grasp on reality by trying to struggle with what represented to them realistic problems. This way of coping reduced the intensity of the emotional experience and stress and the immediate confrontation with it. Some of these women gave up the defense gradually, others did not. The latter ones, we suspected, might go through a crisis later in life. In these cases we looked for a contact between them and existing community agencies for a close follow-up and possible intervention in the future.

Dependency

Many wives manifested strong dependency on old or new supporting figures. Actually some loss of independence was to be expected, but the variations in degree were remarkable. While some gave up periodically chores they usually fulfilled and expected others to take over, others reached the stage of stopping to function and avoiding decisions. In this kind of situation, overlooking the danger of dependency development is a common hazard. Relatives, neighbors, and professionals want to help; often, the help is functional for them as well. When one side wants heavily to lean and the other to support, an ideal background for the formation of dependency occurs. This dependency, however, may be resented later by both sides.

Due to close supervision and group work we were able to monitor and control quite successfully the development of dependency between the women and the team members. Our contact with the women aimed to strengthen their own resources. Thus, as much as possible we avoided doing things for them, but rather encouraged them to be active. This model was applied to resuming or finding jobs, monetary problems, housing problems, legal rights, and interpersonal relationships.

Occasionally we witnessed an obvious formation of a dependency relationship with a figure within or outside the family, but very little could be done about it. An active interference with ongoing relationships should by all means be avoided in this kind of situation.

Children

Generally speaking, we found that children, especially the young ones, reacted to the general stress atmosphere at home rather than to the specific loss. Young children up to the age of 7 years do not grasp the impact of death (Furman, 1970), and even less so of a sudden disappearance. On the other hand, dependency on their immediate environment makes them sensitive to the mood that prevails. Many of the children we met displayed the well-known regressive reactions to stress. Mothers complained of sleep and eating disturbances, fears, excessive dependency, refusal to leave for kindergarten, school, etc. Other children became compulsively conformative, they tried to please as much as they could, and they were referred to as "little angels." Although people usually take the positive for granted, it is advisable to consider the "little angel" no less in need of help than the regressive child.

Working with the whole family gave us the opportunity to attend to the children, but also to focus on the relationships within the family. When the orientation is one of prevention, the attitudes that develop toward children in families under stress and the interactions between mothers and children are of special interest.

One of the first things we noticed was that mothers tended to overprotect their children in different ways. The most extreme protections were avoiding and postponing communication about the stressful event or planning to send the child away from home, at least for a while. In these instances we tried by means of a gentle intervention to strengthen the tie between mother and child. The main objective was to increase the mother's confidence in her own ability to deal with the situation and to bring her to share it with her child or children as a mutual experience. Under no circumstances did we assume the role of mother substitutes. In most instances, it was enough to give mothers the legitimation to act congruently with their feelings even in the presence of young children. By means of modeling we tried to help mothers to relate to their children. We started with simple things such as establishing eye contact (Satir, 1972), then relating feelings and fantasies through verbal communication, role-playing, painting, or other creative activities.

A potential source of conflict between adults and children was the fact that children even as old as 7 or 8 years did not express grief continuously. Mothers and other relatives were amazed to see their children resuming usual activities. Resentment and even hostility started to build up toward the noisy "unfeeling" child. Bringing this point up, especially, with mothers showed that they felt shame at the child's inconsiderate behavior and insult at his lack of empathy. In these instances intervention was very important. Usually a short conversation helped the mother to view the child more realistically and to differentiate between a child's and an adult's ability to grasp implications. The mere information that most normal kids react this way would alleviate the disappointment and reproach from the mother and potential guilt feelings in the child.

Instances where strong denial or identification started to build up were few. We met one boy of 6 and a girl 8 years old who continuously claimed that since father had promised them personally to come back, nothing could have happened to him. Another boy 3 years old started to behave toward his mother as his father would. He stopped playing with friends and toys, refused to go to kindergarten, was constantly with his mother, and changed his manner and topics of conversation. In these cases, a need for more systematic professional help was recommended.

ENVIRONMENTAL REACTIONS

In the term "environment," nonfamily members, neighbors, friends, and community settings are included. In our observations of friends, neighbors, and distant family members, we noted two forms of behavior: encouragement of culturally accepted norms and avoidance of the family in crisis. Our main interest, however, was directed at searching for ways in which the environment may be facilitated in helping the crisis.

In most of the cases that were observed, nonfamily members or distant relatives tended to encourage culturally accepted behaviors and emotional reactions. The heroistic approach, for instance, was often praised or demanded. This kind of pressure offered a well-defined behavioral code and was often accepted. In general, we noticed that families under stress were eager to comply. Compliance offered a structured behavioral repertoire and brought forth sympathy and acceptance from the environment. On the other hand, reactions according to individual judgment or preference were often a cause of tension among family members and between the family and its environment.

The length and intensity of visitation during the crisis closely resembled mourning customs and thus depended on the culture of the family. However, visitation decreased with time, sometimes to a stage of avoidance. There were families who complained of loneliness and attributed it to the environment's lack of knowledge how to deal with them. Loneliness in a stressful situation is difficult to endure, and in many instances it was a cause of aggravation and bitterness, which led at least to a temporal break in long-lasting relationships. It is also interesting to note that in this kind of atmosphere new friendships may emerge. Thus, personal stress situations prove to be from the beginning a socially dynamic period. This fact may explain why in most of the cases the team members had been so warmly accepted and their help appreciated. Being less involved, they could help people who were unaware of the ongoing interpersonal processes to react insightfully to their new circumstances. Yet, bearing in mind that the intervention should be limited in time and preferably short, team members were urged not to establish deep personal relationships with the family in crisis, but rather to facilitate contacts with different community settings. Where children were involved, educational settings were approached. The purpose of these approaches was either to arrange places for preschool children or to bring the family's problems to their attention and if possible to involve them as help agents. When a job was a problem, interviews and consultations were arranged. Welfare agencies, mental health agencies, and medical agencies, as well as community clubs and organizations, all were approached. We have seen how problems like refusal go to school, lack of jobs, or social solitude, which could have developed into symptoms, were relatively smoothly resolved.

REFERENCES

Bell, R. R. *Marriage and family interaction*. Homewood, Ill.: Dorsey, 1971.

Caplan, G. An approach to the study of family mental health. (Public Health Reports, Vol. 71, No. 10) Washington, D.C.: U.S. Government Printing Office, 1956.

Festinger, L. A theory of social comparison processes. *Human Relations*, 1954, 7, 117–140.

Furman, R. A. The child's reaction to death. In B. Shoenberg, A. C. Carr, D. Peretz, & A. H. Kutscher (Eds.), *Loss and grief: Psychological management in medical practice*. New York: Columbia University Press, 1970.

Gerard, H. B. Emotional uncertainty and social comparison. *Journal of Abnormal and Social Psychology*, 1963, 66, 568–673.

Gerard, H. B., & Rabbie, J. M. Fear and social comparison. *Journal of Abnormal and Social Psychology*, 1961, 62, 586–592.

Hall, L. C., & Simmons, W. C. The POW wife: A psychiatric appraisal. *Archives of General Psychiatry*, 1973, 29, 690–694.

Heimlich, H. J., & Kutscher, A. H. The families' reaction to terminal illness. In B. Shoenberg, A. C. Carr, D. Peretz, & A. H. Kutscher (Eds.), *Loss and grief: Psychological management in medical practice*. New York: Columbia University Press, 1970.

Kastenbaum, R., & Aisenberg, R. *The psychology of death*. New York: Springer, 1972.

Kubler-Ross, E. *On death and dying*. London: MacMillan, 1969.

Latane, B., & Wheeler, L. Emotionality and reaction to disaster. *Journal of Experimental and Social Psychology*, 1966 (suppl. 1), 95–102.

Lindemann, E. Symptomatology and management of acute grief. *American Journal of Psychiatry*, 1944, 101, 141.

Parker, R. S. (Ed.) *The emotional stress of war, violence, and peace*. Pittsburg: Stanwix House, 1972.

Rabbie, J. M. Differential preferences for companionship under threat. *Journal of Abnormal and Social Psychology*, 1963, 67, 643–648.

Satir, V. *Peoplemaking*. New York: Bruner/Mazel. Inc., 1972.

Schachter, S. *The psychology of affiliation*. Stanford: Stanford University Press, 1959.

Steinzor, B. *When parents divorce: A new approach to new relationships*. New York: Pantheon Books, 1969.

Strumpfer, D. J. Fear and affiliation during a disaster. *Journal of Social Psychology*, 1970, 82, 263–268.

Teichman, Y. Emotional arousal and affiliation. *Journal of Experimental Social Psychology*, 1973, 9, 591-605.

Walker, K. *The circle of life.* College Park, Md.: McGarth Publishing Company, 1970.

Zucker, R. A., Monosevitz, M., & Lanyon, R. Birth order, anxiety and affiliation during crisis. *Journal of Personality and Social Psychology*, 1968, 8, 354-359.

13
NATIONAL DIFFERENCES IN ANXIETY, 1935-65

Richard Lynn

University of Ulster
County Londonderry
Coleraine, Northern Ireland

The thesis presented in this chapter is that there are differences in the levels of anxiety among the populations of different nations and that it is possible to measure these from the prevalence rates of a number of epidemiological and demographic phenomena, e.g., alcoholism, suicide, accidents, cigarette smoking, caffeine intake and so forth. The work to be discussed falls into two parts: first, an analysis of national differences in anxiety at a particular date and, second, an analysis of fluctuations in national anxiety levels over the period 1935-65.

NATIONAL DIFFERENCES IN ANXIETY

Probably the idea that national differences in certain epidemiological and demographic phenomena could be due to differences in the underlying level of anxiety in different populations will not seem to many psychologists altogether implausible. Take, for instance, alcoholism. It is fairly well established that alcoholics tend to be anxious; and it is perfectly intelligible why this should be so, since it is well known that alcohol reduces anxiety and it is easy to envisage highly anxious people turning to alcohol to reduce their anxiety, and the drinking habit becoming reinforced by drive reduction. These mechanisms are familiar to us all from the classical experiments of Masserman on the cat.

Thus, when the psychologist is asked to consider the fact that the prevalence of alcoholism in, say, France is approximately five times as great as in Britain, it will probably not seem completely unacceptable to suggest that the explanation could be that the French have a higher level of anxiety than the British. If this were true, there would be proportionately more Frenchmen at the high level of anxiety at which people tend to turn to alcohol for relief, and hence more French alcoholics.

So much by way of illustration of the theory. In itself, the explanatory power of the illustration is of course weak and needs considerable strengthening if it is to become in any way convincing. Our method of strengthening the thesis is as follows. First we assemble a number of other epidemiological and demographic variables which we think could also be plausibly explained in terms of national differences in anxiety. Second, these variables are factor analysed, and the presence of a strong first factor is revealed. The loadings of the variables on this factor are all in the direction presupposed by our initial knowledge of them, so this factor is interpreted as anxiety.

The variables used were the national rates of alcoholism, suicide, accidents, crime, murder, illegitimacy, coronary heart disease, calorie intake, caffeine intake, chronic psychosis, cigarette smoking, and divorce. These variables were selected because their relationship with anxiety has already been established (except for the last two). The evidence for the substantiation of this claim is presented in the following sections. A fuller review of the literature is given in other publications (Lynn, 1971; Lynn & Hampson, 1975).

Suicide

There are several lines of evidence to indicate that people who commit suicide tend to be characterised by a high level of anxiety. In the first place, it has often been found that such people are frequently in a state of anxiety as a result of stresses of various kinds, such as bereavement, bankruptcy, and so forth and have turned to suicide as a way out of their stressful situation (e.g., Roberts & Hooper, 1969; Stengel, 1964). It is probably reasonable to assume that such people would score high on a test of anxiety.

Probably the most satisfactory study of the personality of those who commit suicide is that of Paffenbarger and Asnes (1966). They took 50 graduates of the University of Pennsylvania who committed suicide and determined their anxiety level as students from college case records, matched against a control group. Those who committed suicide scored higher on anxiety than the controls.

Another approach to the suicidal personality is to measure by questionnaire the personality structure of those who attempt suicide but fail. A study along these lines was made by Philip (1970) in Edinburgh, and the result showed that the attempted suicides scored highly on the anxiety factor of Cattell's 16 PF test. A similar study using Eysenck's neuroticism (which is highly correlated with anxiety) scale was carried out by Colson (1972) on 72 students at the University of Illinois who had attempted suicide or seriously considered suicide. He found that their neuroticism scores were considerably above the mean for American students. National rates of suicide are therefore taken as a positive index of the level of anxiety in the population.

Accident Proneness

The relationship between accident proneness and anxiety has frequently been reported. One of the earliest findings was that of Biesheuval and White (1949) in South Africa on accident-prone pilots, who were found to be more emotional than those who were accident free. Many similar studies have been published and the literature has been well reviewed recently by Shaw and Sichel (1971). Hence national rates of accidents are taken as a positive index of national anxiety levels.

Crime

There is a good deal of evidence that criminals tend to have high levels of anxiety. The earlier literature pointing to this conclusion was reviewed by Eysenck (1964). This has subsequently been confirmed in several studies in which questionnaires of anxiety or neuroticism have been given to criminals. Representative reports have been published by H. J. Eysenck and S. B. G. Eysenck (1964), Burgess (1972 a, b), Iwawaki, Sujiyama, and Nanri (1964),

Cattell, Eber, and Tatsuoka (1970), Pierson and Kelly (1963), Warburton (1965), Sanocki (1969), Hoghugi and Forrest (1970), and Little (1963). A high crime rate is therefore taken as a positive index of national anxiety levels.

Murder

There is rather little evidence on the personality characteristics of murderers. Some murderers were present in the groups of criminals characterised by high anxiety reported by Iwawaki et al. (1964) and by Warburton (1965). There are also a number of studies showing that murderers have a high propensity to commit suicide (reviewed in Lynn, 1971), which also argues for an anxious personality. It cannot be suggested that the evidence for an association between murder and anxiety is strong. Nevertheless, bearing in mind the well-established association between crime and anxiety, perhaps it seems reasonable to suppose that murderers probably have a higher-than-average anxiety level. For this reason national rates of murder have been included in the analysis as a probable positive index of national anxiety levels.

Caffeine Consumption

Caffeine is a drug that has a stimulating effect on the nervous system (e.g., Gooch, 1963). This leads to the expectation that caffeine would be taken in larger quantities by people who are low on anxiety. The reason for this is that stimulants activate the sympathetic nervous system. Anxious people tend to have a sympathetic nervous system that is easily activated and hence require less stimulation to obtain the sympathetic arousal which we all enjoy in moderation. Anxious people, therefore, should tend to take less caffeine. Direct evidence showing that caffeine consumption is negatively associated with anxiety has been reported previously (Lynn, 1973). We are therefore led to the prediction that national per capita consumption of caffeine should be a negative function of national levels of anxiety.

Alcoholism

Alcohol is a drug that has broadly the opposite properties of caffeine. Where caffeine stimulates the sympathetic nervous system, alcohol sedates it. Hence, whereas people who are low on anxiety apparently tend to take larger quantities of caffeine, those high on anxiety would be expected to take larger quantities of alcohol.

The effects of alcohol on sedating the sympathetic nervous system and reducing the emotions of anxiety and fear are well established. At the physiological level, it is known that alcohol has depressant effects on the nervous system, dampening down the system as a whole and the sympathetic system in particular (e.g., Block, 1962; Rosen & Gregory, 1965). At the psychological level, the best known classical experiments are probably those of Masserman and his colleagues on cats (Masserman & Yum, 1946). They subjected cats to frightening stresses and found that they developed a taste for alcohol and that the alcohol reduced the cats' phobias.

It is not only cats whose anxiety level can be reduced by alcohol. The same is true of human beings and there is a good deal of evidence that people who suffer from excessive anxiety are prone to alleviate their condition by consuming alcohol. For instance, Vallance (1965) has reported a study of 65 male alcoholic patients admitted to Glasgow General Hospital in which he found that a substantial proportion of the patients had a history of neurotic symptoms and took alcohol as a means of relief. Other studies finding a high level of anxiety in alcoholics have been reported by Rosenberg (1969) in Sydney, Hoy (1969) in Britain, and Golightly and Reinehr (1969) in the United States. This leads us to the prediction that among nations the prevalance of alcoholism is a positive function of the national level of anxiety.

Illegitimacy

Are people who procreate illegitimate children anxious? There appears to be only one study on this question, namely the investigation of S. B. G. Eysenck (1961) of 100 unmarried mothers admitted to a maternity hospital in London and compared with 100 matched married mothers. The unmarried mothers proved to be somewhat higher than the normal population on anxiety, so that we are led to the prediction that among nations the illegitimacy rate should be a positive function of the anxiety level of the population.

Chronic Psychosis

There are several sources of evidence to indicate that the level of anxiety tends to be low among chronic psychotics. Many chronic psychotics are cases of simple schizophrenia and Bleuler's classical description of these patients as emotionally blunted or unreactive continues to stand in psychiatric descriptions of the condition. For instance, Hofling (1963) writes of "pervasive apathy" as the commonest symptom of these patients. This lack of emotional reactivity is suggestive of a low level of anxiety.

Such psychiatric opinion has been confirmed by the more objective studies of psychologists. The simplest and most straight-forward evidence of a low level of anxiety in the chronic psychotic probably comes from questionnaire data. It is important here to distinguish the questionnaire results of chronic psychotics from those of other kinds of psychotic patients, and reports on chronic patients as a distinct category are rare. But at least two have been published. The first is by Al-Issa (1964) and reports the mean scores of 34 chronic psychotics with an average stay in hospital of 14.2 years; these patients had a mean score on Eysenck's neuroticism scale at approximately a third of a standard deviation below the mean of the normal population.

A similar result has been reported in the United States by Farley (1970). He tested 20 chronic psychotics who had been in hospital for an average of 14.9 years. The test used was the Maudsley Personality Inventory, and the psychotics obtained a mean neuroticism score approximately half a standard deviation below the mean of the normal population. These results are corroborated by the work of Cattell (1957). In Cattell's personality system the psychoticism factor (U.I.T. 25) is negatively correlated with the anxiety factors 0 (Guilt) and Q4 (Ergic Tension).

In addition to these questionnaire results, there is an extensive physiological literature indicating that typically there is a low level of sympathetic reactivity in chronic psychotics. The most well-known studies in English are probably those of Gellhorn (1957; Nelson & Gellhorn, 1957) showing that the majority of chronic psychotics show little sympathetic nervous reactivity to stimulation, e.g., a poor generation of heat following exposure to cold, low psychogalvanic reactions and reduced desynchronisation of the EEG alpha rhythm.

The same conclusion has been reached in a considerable Russian literature. This originates from Pavlov's observations of the apathy of many chronic psychotics and his theory that protective inhibition has spread from the cerebral cortex to the subcortical centres and reduced the reactivity of the nervous system. Russian experimental studies of sympathetic reactivity have confirmed that it is low in chronic psychotic patients. The Russian work is reviewed in some detail in Lynn (1971).

Coronary Heart Disease

There is some evidence that coronary heart disease is related to low anxiety. This may be surprising in view of the common supposition that coronary disease is associated with stress, and hence possibly with a high level of anxiety, but this belief has been discredited by the research on approximately a quarter of a million Bell Telephone Company employees which showed that coronaries are less prevalent among managers than among blue-collar workers (Hinkle, Whitney, Lehman, Dunn, King, Plankun, & Flehinger, 1968).

One of the problems in evaluating the personality of coronary patients is that of obtaining a control group. The coronary patient has the stress of the illness, and the most satisfactory controls are probably other patients. Three studies of this kind have been published. One reported that coronary patients were "more cheerful and better socialisers" (O'Leary, Schwab, John & McGinnis, 1968), suggesting a low level of anxiety. This was also found by Bendien and Groen (1963) and Sainsbury (1950) in investigations using neuroticism questionnaires. The coronary patients had lower mean neuroticism scores than did the control group. Thus we are led to the prediction that the prevalence of coronary heart disease in nations should be associated with a low level of anxiety.

Calorie Intake

There are theoretical reasons for regarding calorie intake as a negative function of anxiety. These lie in the reciprocally inhibiting relationship between the parasympathetic nervous system, which is involved in the ingestion of food, and the sympathetic system, which mediates fear and anxiety. If one system is active, it tends to suppress the other (Morgan, 1965). An early demonstration of the reciprocally inhibiting relationship between fear and eating was given in the studies carried out in John Watson's laboratory on the counterconditioning of infants' phobias by the use of sweets (Jones, 1924).

More recently, experimental evidence demonstrating the inverse relation between calorie intake and anxiety has been published by Schachter, Goldman, and Gordon (1968). They stressed subjects in an experimental situation and obtained a reduction in eating. Questionnaire results showing an inverse relation between neuroticism and calorie intake have been reported by Silverstone (1968) and Kalucy and Crisp (1974).

There is corroboratory evidence from a variety of other sources. For instance, damage to the frontal lobes has the effect both of reducing anxiety and nervous tension and of increasing the appetitie (e.g., Hofling, 1963). Conservely, stimulant drugs increase anxiety and nervous tension and reduce appetite. Although it is sometimes maintained that anxiety can motivate eating, a large scale study of normal eaters and overeaters among 1,000 children carried out by Brandon (1968) in Newcastle showed that the emotionally disturbed had poor appetites rather than large ones and also had lower body weights; there was no evidence of emotional disturbance among voracious overeaters. We are therefore led to the prediction that there should be an inverse relation between national levels of calorie intake and of anxiety.

Cigarette Smoking

The most extensive study of the relationship of cigarette smoking to anxiety appears to be that of Eysenck (1965) on a sample of 2,400 subjects in Britain. In this study there was no significant relationship between cigarette consumption and neuroticism, and this was subsequently confirmed by Smith (1967) and Cattell and Krug (1967). On the basis of these three large-scale studies it would appear that cigarette consumption is unrelated to anxiety and these findings lead to the prediction that cigarette smoking among nations will be unrelated to national levels of anxiety. This variable was included because of its known relationship with extraversion, but this is not our present concern.

Divorce

Like cigarette smoking, divorce has no known relationship with anxiety, but it does have an association with extraversion (Cattell & Nesselroade, 1967); for this reason, it was included in the analysis. Since it is a function only of extraversion, we are not concerned with it in the present study.

A description of the data and its sources is given as follows:

1. Cigarette consumption: Number consumed per capita aged 15 years and over,, per annum. Source: Tobacco Research Council (London).
2. Crime: The number of prisoners per 10,000 population. Source: Government Statistical Offices of the individual nations. Missing data: Switzerland does not record the information.
3. Divorce: Number per 10,000 population. Source: U.N. Demographic Yearbooks. Missing data: Ireland and Italy do not permit divorce.
4. Illegitimacy: Percentage of live births that are illegitimate. Source: U.N. Demographic Yearbooks.
5. Accidents: Number of deaths from all accidents per 100,000 population. Source: U.N. Demographic Yearbooks.
6. Coronary heart diseases: Deaths from ischaemic heart disease per 100,000 population. Source: U.N. Demographic Yearbooks.
7. Suicide: Number of deaths per 100,000 population. Source: U.N. Demographic Yearbooks.
8. Caffeine consumption: Kilograms of coffee and tea imports retained for home consumption per annum, per capita; the index of caffeine consumption was derived by weighting tea consumption twice that of coffee because tea has approximately twice the caffeine content of coffee per unit weight. Source: Pan American Coffee Bureau, New York, and International Tea Committee, London.
9. Alcoholism: Number of deaths from liver cirrhosis per 100,000 population. Source: U.N. Demographic Yearbooks.
10. Calorie intake: Daily intake of calories per capita. Source: U.N. Statistical Yearbook.
11. Chronic psychosis: Number of psychiatric patients per 1,000 population. (Because of the relatively rapid turnover of acute psychiatric patients, the number of patients in mental hospitals at any one time is heavily weighted in favour of chronic cases.) Source: World Health Statistics Annual and Government Publications from the individual nations.
12. Murder: Number of deaths from murder per 100,000 population. Source: U.N. Demographic Yearbooks.

Factor Analysis

The variables were factored by principal components analysis. In this study, component analysis is not being employed in its most common use as a method of classifying data, but for its less common function as a device for confirming or rejecting a model of interrelationships among variables that has been built from other evidence.

The measures are taken from the 18 major economically advanced Western nations.

The results of the principal components analysis are shown in Table 13-1. The first factor is apparently anxiety, since all the variables are loaded on it in the predicted direction. The second factor is interpreted as introversion-extraversion. Thus we may regard the nations as varying along the two dimensions of anxiety and introversion-extraversion, and most of the epidemiological and demographic variables are joint functions of these underlying personality dimensions. However, as in this volume we are concerned with anxiety, this second factor of introversion-extraversion will not be considered further.

Table 13-1

Principal Components Analysis of the 12 Variables for 1960

Variables	Factor loading		
	I	II	III
1. Chronic psychosis	76	33	07
2. Calorie intake	65	35	34
3. Caffeine consumption	67	31	28
4. Coronary heart disease	61	65	18
5. Suicide	−78	01	20
6. Alcoholism	−70	22	35
7. Murder	−36	62	−61
8. Crime	−56	57	32
9. Divorce	−14	72	01
10. Cigarette smoking	24	63	−54
11. Illegitimacy	−32	51	71
12. Accidents	−69	40	30
Variance	4.03	2.85	1.75
Percent variance	33.56	23.73	14.62

Note: There are three factors with eigenvalues greater than unity. The first factor is interpreted as anxiety; the signs require reversal to make the factor positive for high anxiety.

Table 13-2

Factor Scores of the Nations on the First
Component Interpreted as Anxiety

Nation	Anxiety factor scores
Australia	−0.75
Austria	3.73
Belgium	0.15
Canada	−0.29
Denmark	−0.55
Finland	0.61
France	2.37
Germany	2.11
Ireland	−4.58
Italy	1.05
Japan	2.95
Netherlands	−1.52
New Zealand	−1.61
Norway	−0.86
Sweden	−0.86
Switzerland	0.28
United Kingdom	−2.41
United States	0.18

Note: Signs are reversed to make high
positive scores represent high levels of anxiety.

The nations are of course being treated as subjects, and the epidemiological and demographic variables are treated as the subjects' scores in a conventional psychometric analysis. This being the case, we can use these variables to calculate our subjects' scores on the anxiety factor. This is done by computing each nation's factor score on the first factor. The results are shown in Table 13-2. Here we see that the most anxious of this group of nations in 1960 was Austria and the second most anxious was Japan; the least anxious nations were the United Kingdom and Ireland.

Let us now consider a further question. All the data so far analysed are derived from 1960. It is possible that this was some kind of freak year? Obviously our general thesis would be stronger if it could be shown that the factor structure remained stable over a number of years.

A convenient and tidy way of going about this would seem to be to take the data at five yearly intervals. We can start at 1935. Unfortunately there are gaps for 1940 and 1945 because many of our subjects were too preoccupied during these years to collect

Table 13-3

Coefficients of Factor Similarity for Factor I

Year	1935	1950	1955	1960	1965
1935	(1.00)				
1950	0.89	(1.00)			
1955	0.90	0.98	(1.00)		
1960	0.83	0.96	0.97	(1.00)	
1965	0.84	0.93	0.95	0.96	(1.00)

Note: The values are high enough to show the essential identity of the factor, and thus the essential identity of the statistical solutions.

epidemiological and demographic information. So we have to jump to 1950, and thereafter we can take the years 1955, 1960, and 1965.

The data for the 12 variables have been collected and factored for these 5 years separately, and the results show that the same first factor is present in all 5 years. The coefficients of factor similarity are shown in Table 13-3.

FLUCTUATIONS IN NATIONAL ANXIETY LEVELS, 1935-65

We have advanced the thesis that national variations in a number of epidemiological and demographic phenomena are to a considerable extent caused by variations in the underlying anxiety level of the populations. The reader may perhaps take the view that the thesis is, up to a point, plausible. But the theory could certainly do with further substantiation, and it would gain in credibility if more evidence could be advanced in its support. The marshalling of such additional evidence is the problem to which we now turn.

If we consider the period 1935-65, one major event occurred which must surely have affected anxiety levels in some of the advanced Western nations. This is the Second World War. This event subjected some of the populations to the stresses of military defeat, occupation by foreign armies, the fear of death, the loss of their loved ones, and so forth. It might reasonably be predicted that anxiety levels would increase in these nations, and would then decline as the war years receded. If such a rise in anxiety level from the prewar to the war years and a subsequent decline could actually be shown, then the theory would be strengthened.

It is fortunate that the trauma of the war was escaped by some of the nations, such as Switzerland, Sweden, and Ireland, so that these can be regarded as a control group in which we should expect expect neither an increase in national anxiety level nor a decline. Actually, it so happens that the 18 nations can be split into two equal groups of 9 each on the basis of whether or not they suffered military defeat and occupation, so that the most sensible way of considering the data seems to be to predict a rise in anxiety levels in the nations that experienced military defeat and occupation (e.g., Japan, Germany, France, etc.), and a less marked rise or perhaps no rise at all in the nations that escaped these traumata (e.g., Switzerland, Ireland, New Zealand, etc.) This is therefore the prediction to be examined.

In order to quantify the fluctuations of the national anxiety levels, we need to obtain a score for each nation for each of the 5 years. The procedure adopted for this has been to treat each nation at each year as an independent subject, so that there are 18 X 5 = 90 subjects. Then the data are factored for the 90 subjects. The next step is to calculate the factor scores of each subject on the first (anxiety) factor, and these give us an index of the anxiety level of each nation in each year. By examining these we can see the secular trends in the anxiety level in each nation over the period.

Let us turn straight away to the question of whether the Second World War had the effect of raising the anxiety levels in the defeated nations. First, the nine nations that experienced military defeat and occupation are shown in Fig. 13-1. Examining the anxiety levels over the 5 years, we can see that in all nine of these nations the anxiety level rose from 1935 to 1950 and declined thereafter. (It may be noted that the rank order of the nations in 1960 in this analysis has slight differences from that presented in the first part of this chapter. The reason for this is that the variables have slightly different loadings in the two analyses and the factor scores, being derived partly from the factor loadings, are themselves slightly different.)

The remaining nations are the control group, which escaped military defeat and occupation. The results for these nine nations are shown in Fig. 13-2. It will be seen that in seven nations

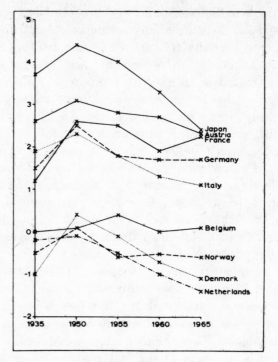

Fig. 13-1. Anxiety levels in the nations suffering military defeat in the Second World War.

anxiety levels fell from 1935 to 1950. In the United Kingdom there was a slight increase, which is probably quite understandable in view of the considerable involvement of the U.K. in the war. The only anomalous case is Sweden, which also apparently experienced some increase in anxiety. There seems no obvious explanation for this discrepant phenomenon.

Is the rise in anxiety level in the nine defeated nations significantly different from the fall in anxiety in seven of the nine victorious or neutral nations? This is probably an inappropriate question. We are not dealing here with samples of the populations of the advanced Western nations but with total populations. Nor are our nations samples of some larger universe of nations, since they are themselves the universe of advanced Western nations. Hence, our results can hardly have arisen from chance sampling errors. Thus there is much to be said for the view that it is simply a fact that anxiety levels rose more from 1935 to 1950 in the

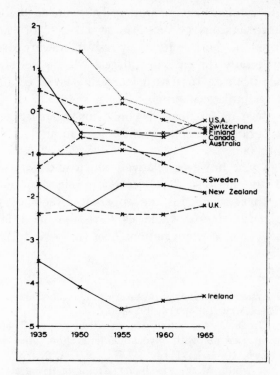

Fig. 13-2. Anxiety levels in the nations that escaped military defeat and occupation in the Second World War.

defeated nations than they did in the victorious and neutral nations (assuming of course that the first factor among the variables is correctly interpreted as anxiety).

Perhaps some readers will be unpersuaded by this view and would prefer to see a statistical evaluation. The initial difference between the mean levels of anxiety in the two groups in 1935 was controlled by an analysis of covariance. The F ratio using the adjusted means for 1950 is 16.8, which is statistically significant at $p < .01$.

There is another trend in the results that may be worth mention. This is that if the 18 nations are considered as a whole, it is apparent there has been little overall change in anxiety levels from 1935 to 1965. In 12 nations anxiety has fallen, and in the remaining 6 it has risen. This result tells against the proposition not infrequently advanced by doomcasters to the effect that the populations of the economically advanced democracies are becoming more anxious or neurotic as a result of the increasing stress and strain of modern life. Our results indicate that this is by no means universally the case and suggest what is perhaps the more common-sense position that with increasing levels of affluence and medical and technological progress the populations of many of the advanced Western nations have become somewhat less stressed over this 30-year period and consequently that mean levels of anxiety have tended to fall.

This tendency is however relatively slight and does not hold for one-third of the nations. The clearest implication of the results seems to be that except for the apparent effects of the Second World War, national anxiety levels have remained fairly steady among the advanced Western nations over the period 1935-65.

REFERENCES

Al-Issa, I. The Eysenck Personality Inventory in chronic schizophrenia. *British Journal of Psychiatry*, 1964, 110, 397-400.

Bendien, J., & Groen, J. A psychological-statistical study of neuroticism and extraversion in patients with myocardial infarction. *Journal of Psychosomatic Research*, 1963, 7, 11-14.

Biesheuval, S., & White, M. E. The human factor in flying accidents. *South African Air Force Journal*, 1949, 1, 25-31.

Block, M. A. *Alcoholism*. London: Day, 1962.

Brandon, S. Eating disorders in a child population. *Acta Paedopsychiatrica*, 1968, 35, 317-23.

Burgess, P. K. Eysenck's theory of criminality: A new approach. *British Journal of Criminology*, 1972, 12, 74-82. (a)

Burgess, P. K. Eysenck's theory of criminality: A test of some objections to disconfirmatory evidence. *British Journal of Social and Clinical Psychology*, 1972, 11, 248-256. (b)

Burney, W. E., & Fawcett, J. A. Possibility of a biochemical test for suicide: An analysis of endocrine findings prior to three suicides. *Archives of General Psychiatry*, 1965, 13, 232-239.

Cattell, R. B. *Personality and motivation structure and measurement*. New York: World Book, 1957.

Cattell, R. B., & Krug, S. Personality factor profile peculiar to the student smoker. *Journal of Counseling Psychology*, 1967, 14, 116-121.

Cattell, R. B., Eber, H. W., & Tatsuoka, M. M. *Handbook for the 16 P.F. Questionnaire*. Champaign, Ill.: Institute for Personality and Ability Testing, 1970.

Cattell, R. B., & Nesselroade, J. R. Likeness and completeness theories examined by 16 P.F. measures on stably and unstably married couples. *Journal of Personality and Social Psychology*, 1967, 7, 351-61.

Colson, C. E. Neuroticism, extraversion and repression sensitization in suicidal college students. *British Journal of Social and Clinical Psychology*, 1972, 11, 88-89.

Eysenck, H. J. *Crime and personality*. London: Paladin Books, 1964.

Eysenck, S. B. G. Personality and pain assessment in childbirth of married and unmarried mothers. *Journal of Mental Science*, 1961, 107, 417-430.

Farley, F. H. Moderating effects of psychopathology on the independence of extraversion and neuroticism. *Journal of Clinical Psychology*, 1970, 26, 298-99.

Golightly, C., & Reinehr, R. C. The 16 P.F. profiles of hospitalized alcoholic patients: Replication and extension. *Psychological Reports*, 1969, 24, 543-545.

Gooch, R. N. The influence of stimulant and depressant drugs on the central nervous system. In Eysenck, H. J. (Ed.), *Experiments with drugs*. Oxford: Pergamon Press, 1963.

Hinkle, L. E., Whitney, L. H., Lehman, E. W., Dunn, J., Benjamin, B., King, R., Plakun, A., & Flehinger, B. Occupation, education and coronary heart disease. *Science*, 1968, 161, 238-46.

Hofling, C. K. *Textbook of psychiatry for medical practice*. Philadelphia: Lippincott, 1963.

Hoghugi, M. A., & Forrest, A. R. Eysenck's theory of criminality. *British Journal of Criminology*, 1970, 10, 240-254.

Hoy, R. The personality of inpatient alcoholics in relation to group psychotherapy as measured by the 16 P.F. *Quarterly Journal of Studies on Alcohol*, 1969, 30, 401-407.

Iwawaki, S., Sujiyama, Y., & Nanri, R. *Japanese manual of the Maudsley Personality Inventory*. Kyoto: Kyoto University Press, 1964.

Jones, M. C. The elimination of children's fears. *Journal of Experimental Psychology*, 1924, 7, 383-390.

Kalucy, R. S., & Crisp, A. H. Some psychological implications of massive obesity. *Journal of Psychosomatic Research*, 1974, 18, 465-473.

Little, A. Professor Eysenck's theory of crime: An empirical test on adolescent offenders. *British Journal of Criminology*, 1963, 4, 152-163.

Lynn, R. *Personality and national character*. Oxford: Pergamon Press, 1971.

Lynn, R. National differences in anxiety and the consumption of caffeine. *British Journal of Social and Clinical Psychology*, 1973, 12, 92-93.

Lynn, R., & Hampson, S. L. National differences in extraversion and neuroticism. *British Journal of Social and Clinical Psychology*, 1975.

Masserman, J. H., & Yum, K. S. An analysis of the influence of alcohol on experimental neurosis in cats. *Psychosomatic Medicine*, 1946, 8, 36-52.

Morgan, C. T. *Physiological psychology*. New York: McGraw-Hill, 1965.

Nelson, R., & Gellhorn, E. The action of autonomic drugs on normal persons and neuropsychiatric patients. *Psychosomatic Medicine*, 1957, 19, 486-494.

O'Leary, J. P., Schwab, R. L., John, J., & McGinnis, N. H. Anxiety in cardiac patients. *Diseases of the Nervous System*, 1968, 29, 443-8.

Paffenbarger, R. S., & Asnes, D. P. Chronic disease in former college students. *American Journal of Public Health*, 1966, 56, 1026-1036.

Philip, A. E. Traits, attitudes and symptoms in a group of attempted suicides. *British Journal of Psychiatry*, 1970, 116, 475–482.

Pierson, G. R., & Kelly, R. F. Anxiety, extraversion and personality idiosyncrasy in delinquency. *Journal of Psychology*, 1963, 56, 441–445.

Roberts, J., & Hooper, D. The natural history of attempted suicide in Bristol. *British Journal of Medical Psychology*, 1969, 42, 303–312.

Rosen, E., & Gregory, J. *Abnormal psychology*. Philadelphia: W. B. Saunders, 1965.

Rosenberg, C. M. Young alcoholics *British Journal of Psychiatry*, 1969, 115, 181–188.

Sainsbury, P. Psychosomatic disorders and neurosis in outpatients attending a general hospital. *Journal of Psychosomatic Research*, 1960, 4, 261–273.

Sanocki, W. The use of Eysenck's personality inventory for testing young prisoners. *Przeglad penitencjarny*, 1969, 7, 53–68.

Schachter, S., Goldman, R., & Gordon, A. Effects of fear, food deprivation and obesity on eating. *Journal of Personality and Social Psychology*, 1968, 10, 91–7.

Shaw, L., & Sichel, H. *Accident proneness*. Oxford: Pergamon Press, 1971.

Silverstone, J. T. Psychosocial aspects of obesity. *Proceedings of Royal Society Medicine*, 1968, 61, 371–380.

Smith, G. M. Personality correlates of cigarette smoking in students of college age. *Annals of the New York Academy of Science*, 1967, 142, 308–21.

Stengel, E. *Suicide and attempted suicide*. Harmondsworth: Penguin Books, 1964.

Vallance, M., Alcoholism: A two-year follow-up study of patients admitted to the psychiatric department of a general hospital. *British Journal of Psychiatry*, 1965, 111, 348–56.

Warburton, F. W. Observations on a sample of psychopathic American criminals. *Behaviour Research and Therapy*, 1965, 3, 129–135.

14
ON ANXIETY IN
THE SCANDINAVIAN
COUNTRIES

Keijo Kata

Research Group for Comparative Sociology
University of Helsinki
Helsinki, Finland

INTRODUCTION

This study is part of the Scandinavian survey on welfare, need satisfaction, and mental health in Denmark, Finland, Norway, and Sweden. The data were collected by means of a survey conducted in the spring of 1972 by the Research Group for Comparative Sociology headed by Professor Erik Allardt. The interviews were carried out by the leading opinion research institutes in each country. More detailed information on the theoretical background and the questionnaire can be found in Allardt (1973). The data, sampling, and representativeness are discussed in detail in Kata and Uusitalo (1974). The samples, approximately 1,000 persons in each country, are intended to be representative of the populations between the ages of 15-64 years in these countries.

The term "welfare" is conceived broadly as being composed of matters related both to the level of living and to what currently has been called "quality of life." The researchers related to the project have a somewhat different foci of interest. Erik Allardt is concentrating on the relationships between different dimensions of welfare and their relations to social structure; Hannu Uusitalo is focusing on problems related to income formation and income distribution; Keijo Kata is studying mental health and its relation to other indicators of welfare and need satisfaction; and Magdalena Jaakkola is studying social networks and the Finnish immigrant population in Sweden.

The study of psychological well-being or of problems related to mental health is not the only concern of the survey but is a part of it. This fact is not without consequences for the study of mental health, both positive and negative. Due to increasing pressure for minimizing the number of questions, the coverage of various aspects of the rich field of mental illness is not as comprehensive as one might hope. The limitations are not absent among the explanatory variables, but they are compensated by good coverage of variables indicating various aspects of social position of individuals. Hence it is possible to locate psychological well-being in the social structure.

The present study is restricted in its coverage of psychological well-being. Only one indicator, anxiety, is discussed.

The main method used in the study was the Multiple Classification Analysis (MCA) (see Andrews, Morgan, & Sonquist, 1971). It is impossible to describe it here thoroughly, but it is necessary to explain the general features of the method. It can be used in studying the relationship between one dependent variable and several independent variables. In essence, MCA permits one to compare averages of dependent variables when other variables have been taken into account.

The empirical and adjusted means are the most useful statistics of MCA. The empirical mean is the mean of respondents who belong to a certain category of an independent variable. The adjusted mean is a theoretical construct that should indicate what the mean would be if the effects of other independent variables were eliminated. Only three of the other useful statistics will be taken up here. These are eta^2, beta, and R^2. The value of eta^2 describes how much the variable in question alone can explain the variance of the dependent variable. It has the usual interpretation as the proportion of explained variance. Beta describes how good an explainer the variable is after the effects of other variables have been taken into account. It may not be interpreted, however, as the proportion of explained variance. Hence, comparing the coefficients of variables, one can say which is the best predictor; but one cannot say how much a given variable can explain. R^2 is analogous to the square of multiple correlation and it has the usual interpretation of proportion of variance explained. It tells how much the independent variables together can explain the variance of the dependent variable.

Anxiety is the dependent variable of this study.

Independent variables can be classified into two broad groups. First, there are variables intended to measure various aspects of social status and stress factors or pressures associated with it, and, on the other hand, resources that can help in coping with stressors. The second group of independent variables is more heterogenous, but perhaps one can describe these as more psychological, indicating number and quality of social contacts, pressures on the individual, as well as need satisfaction and personal resources.

MEASUREMENT OF ANXIETY

Anxiety was measured by a set of 10 selected questions, which had been previously used by the research group of World Health Organization in the International Collaborative Study of Medical Care Utilization (Kalimo, Bice, & Novosel, 1970).[1] The wording of the questions is as follows:

Next we have some personal questions. Please say "yes" or "no" on the basis of how you feel.

a. Do you often get spells of complete exhaustion or fatigue?
b. Do you usually feel unhappy or depressed?
c. Do you wear yourself out worrying about your health?
d. Are you often bothered by the thumping of your heart?
e. Does your heart often race like mad?
f. Do you often suffer from pressure or pain in the head?
g. Does your thinking get completely mixed up when you have to do things quickly?
h. Do you often shake or tremble?
i. Are you constantly keyed up and jittery?
j. Do frightening thoughts again come back in your mind?

Because the question "Do frightening thoughts keep coming back in your mind?" was considered to intrusive in Norway, it was dropped from the Norweigian questionnaire. To obtain convenience

[1] The questions can be divided by their content into two parts: psychological (b, c, g, i, and j) and psychosomatic (a, d, e, f, and b), but the correlation of these parts is so high that this division is not necessary in all cases (Kalimo et al., 1970; Kata, K. On anxiety measurements in a comparative survey. Unpublished manuscript, 1973).

in comparisons between countries, a shorter 9-item index, where this particular item is omitted, is used in the analysis in this chapter (unless otherwise indicated). The anxiety-index score is obtained simply by adding up the number of affirmative replies, with a high score indicating high level of anxiety. Distributions, standard deviations, means and reliability estimates of the anxiety index are given in Table 14-1. Affirmative answers to almost all the individual items are rare; hence, the skewness of the summated scale is unavoidable. Although the skewness is apt to lower proportion of explained variance, the anxiety index was left untransformed.

The reliability estimate used here is Cronbach's alpha coefficient, which is very sensitive to the possible heterogeneity of the test (Magnusson, 1961; Valkonen, 1971). The alpha coefficient was considered appropriate because of the possibility of a homogeneity check. Alpha coefficients of the anxiety index range from 0.66 to 0.76.

Measured by the anxiety index, the psychological well-being seems to be highest in Sweden and least in Finland, with Denmark and Norway falling in between. This result also appears when other indicators of well-being are compared (Allardt, 1974). It is not possible here to discuss the problems of comparative international research, but one must keep in mind that regardless of the similarity of the Scandinavian countries, different cultural norms and languages may effect the responses of the survey (Kalimo et al., 1970). Although caution is necessary in interpreting the differences between countries, difficulties are not so great if one is focusing on relationships between anxiety and other variables within nations.

Table 14-1

Percentage Distribution of Anxiety-index Scores, Means, Standard Deviations, and Alpha Coefficients by Country

Country	Scores				Mean	Standard deviation	Alpha coefficient
	0	1–2	3–4	5+			
Denmark	43.4	38.0	13.5	5.1	1.3	1.60	0.68
Finland	34.5	39.7	14.5	11.3	1.7	2.03	0.76
Norway	44.0	40.7	10.0	5.4	1.2	1.55	0.70
Sweden	51.4	37.1	7.6	3.9	0.96	1.42	0.66

Note: These statistics are based on the full 10-item scale, except in Norway.

RELATIONSHIPS OF ANXIETY WITH SOCIAL AND PSYCHOLOGICAL VARIABLES

Social class differences in mental health are clearly demonstrated and are consistent from one study to another. Members of the lowest strata, in particular, seem to have more than their share of mental health problems; and it is here assumed that anxiety is no exception to the rule (Kohn, 1972).

There are numerous possible indicators of social status and only a few are discussed here. Educational level, occupational prestige, occupational status, income, marital status, age, and sex are the main indicators of social status, but some other indicators will also be referred to.

Age and Anxiety

Age of the respondent seems to be one of the best predictors of anxiety. That older people have higher anxiety scores is no surprise; it is known that physical and mental health declines with increasing age (Gaitz & Scott, 1972). Kalimo et al. (1970, p. 237) reported correlations up to 0.34 (median 0.10) between age and anxiety. This general trend can clearly be seen in the data of every country in the Scandinavian survey, but the gap between the youngest and the oldest age group is not the same everywhere. The difference is 0.9 points in Denmark, 1.9 in Finland, 1.2 in Norway and 1.0 in Sweden; in other words, the gap between young and old is greatest in Finland and the smallest in Denmark (Table 14-2).

In Denmark the anxiety scores increase more smoothly with increasing age than in the other Nordic countries. There are no great thresholds between consecutive age groups; although the oldest age group (60-64 years) differs from the next younger age group (55-59 years), this difference is not so great as the corresponding thresholds in the other countries. Table 14-2 shows that there is an exception to this general trend: between the ages of 30 and 44 the increase is not linear, with older groups having lower scores than the next younger age groups in the data from Denmark. Examples of the same phenomenon can also be found in the other countries; however, these cases of inverse order of the scores of consecutive age groups do not disturb the general trend.

Table 14-2

Mean Anxiety Scores in Different Age Groups

Age in years	Denmark Class	Denmark Adjusted	Denmark N	Finland Class	Finland Adjusted	Finland N	Norway Class	Norway Adjusted	Norway N	Sweden Class	Sweden Adjusted	Sweden N
15–19	0.82	0.71	94	1.11	1.33	139	0.60	0.45	96	0.79	0.78	95
20–24	1.10	0.99	80	1.14	1.23	114	0.73	0.66	96	0.63	0.62	83
25–29	1.11	1.14	119	1.06	1.21	93	0.79	0.86	107	0.68	0.76	127
30–34	0.80	0.81	79	1.13	1.36	96	0.98	1.11	111	0.83	0.89	99
35–39	1.23	1.34	91	1.46	1.60	93	1.10	1.16	79	0.84	0.96	80
40–44	1.03	1.13	93	1.86	1.89	85	1.25	1.39	92	0.61	0.66	106
45–49	1.25	1.24	94	1.84	1.93	87	1.22	1.38	94	0.91	0.95	104
50–54	1.30	1.40	99	2.27	2.14	81	1.69	1.66	116	0.95	0.99	108
55–59	1.45	1.47	98	2.56	2.18	75	1.69	1.60	70	1.26	1.20	85
60–64	1.69	1.53	99	2.97	2.32	89	1.81	1.57	96	1.84	1.44	84
Total			946			952			957			971
eta^2		0.029			0.110			0.069			0.065	
beta		0.171			0.210			0.255			0.173	

In Finland the increase of the anxiety level with age is great, and there seem to be two thresholds, the first in the age group 40–44 years and the second in the age group 50–54 years. The increase of anxiety seems not only to be greater but also to begin earlier in Finland than in the other Scandinavian countries.

In Norway there is a threshold in the age group 50–54 years. It is in the same age group as the second threshold of Finland. Up to this point the increase is almost linear, and the threshold is not as great as in Finland.

In Sweden the threshold occurs later in the age group 55–59 years. The scores of the oldest age group of Sweden are high, especially compared with middle-aged Swedish. The conclusions are not different if one looks at adjusted means.

Sex and Anxiety

Sex of the respondent is not a good predictor of the anxiety level although there are differences in mean scores between sexes (Table 14-3). Males have lower scores than women, as was true in the earlier survey by Kalimo et al. (1970, p. 237). Sex differences are greatest in Denmark, next highest in Norway, quite negligible in Sweden and very small in Finland. The "equality" of Finnish women can be seen in the hospital statistics, too. Both the rates of neuroses and of the functional psychoses are more nearly equal in Finland than in Sweden (Haavio-Mannila & Stenius, 1974).

Marital Status and Anxiety

Caution is necessary when one is discussing relationships between marital status and anxiety because two groups—divorced (or separated) and widowed—are small and hence there is risk of chance errors.

In all countries single people are least anxious, followed in order by married people and divorced, with widowed constituting the most anxious groups. These results are in accordance with one's intuitive expectation, but adjustment levels these group differences. This implies that there are other factors besides or in addition to marital status, per se, that play a role here. One—probably the most important—factor is age. Married people, on the average, are older than single people and widowed are again older than married; and, as stated before, older people are more anxious than younger ones (Table 14-4).

Table 14-3

Mean Anxiety Scores According to Sex

Sex	Denmark			Finland			Norway			Sweden		
	Class	Adjusted	N	Class	Adjusted	N	Class	Adjusted	N	Class	Adjusted	N
Male	0.87	0.90	491	1.53	1.64	477	0.92	0.95	496	0.76	0.81	497
Female	1.57	1.54	494	1.78	1.67	516	1.44	1.42	509	1.08	1.03	507
Total			985			993			1,005			1,004
eta²		0.052			0.004			0.027			0.014	
beta		0.209			0.009			0.150			0.080	

Table 14-4

Mean Anxiety Scores According to Marital Status

Marital status	Denmark			Finland			Norway			Sweden		
	Class	Adjusted	N	Class	Adjusted	N	Class	Adjusted	N	Class	Adjusted	N
Single	0.98	1.09	195	1.24	1.48	306	0.79	1.00	196	0.79	0.89	208
Divorced or separated	2.67	2.30	24	2.52	2.52	31	2.53	2.31	15	1.26	1.33	34
Widowed	1.91	1.23	33	2.45	1.19	38	2.95	2.37	38	1.76	1.08	25
Married (or living together)	1.21	1.22	736	1.78	1.74	619	1.18	1.15	755	0.91	0.90	737
Total			988			994			1,004			1,004
eta²		0.033			0.030			0.071			0.014	
beta		0.115			0.113			0.178			0.061	

Education Level and Anxiety

Education seems to have a favourable effect on the level of anxiety, the better educated in general being less anxious (Table 14-5).

In particular, groups with elementary school education or less have high scores in all countries, especially in Finland and Norway. The effects of other factors, e.g., age, do not eliminate the difference between these and other groups. Moreover, these groups are relatively large.

There are some exceptions to the general rule, however. For instance, in the Finnish and Danish data, the group with matriculation examination plus 1 year's vocational schooling has higher scores than the group completing only the matriculation examination, but not in Norway and Sweden.[2] Nevertheless, there is no reason to reject the general conclusion that anxiety decreases with increasing education.

The greatest intergroup differences appear in the Finnish data, the least in the Danish data, with Norway and Sweden falling in between.

Occupational Status and Anxiety

Occupational status describes a person's position in the productive system. The classification is described in detail by Pöntinen and Uusitalo (1974, pp. 22-28). The categories used are farmers, entrepreneurs, upper white collar, lower white collar, skilled workers, unskilled workers, housewives, and persons without occupation. The average proportion of explained variance is about 3%. The differences between various groups in the four countries, however, are more interesting than the slight differences in the variance explained (Table 14-6).

In Denmark and Norway the anxiety level of farmers is lower compared with the average of the whole population aged 15–64 years, whereas in Finland their empirical mean is higher. This is especially clear in the Danish data. In Denmark and Norway adjustment does not eliminate these differences, but in Finland

[2] These groups are rather small, and it is possible that the "wrong order" of groups is due to statistical error or unreliability of educational classification. Yet one possibility—if one does not dislike speculation—is that the situation of these groups is different in Finland and Denmark compared with Norway and Sweden.

Table 14-5

Mean Anxiety Scores According to Education Level

Education	Denmark			Finland			Norway			Sweden		
	Class	Adjusted	N	Class	Adjusted	N	Class	Adjusted	N	Class	Adjusted	N
Less than elementary school	1.70	1.24	10	3.61	2.59	46	1.44	1.26	25	1.21	0.95	28
Elementary school	1.34	1.25	493	1.96	1.75	477	1.58	1.40	313	1.20	1.09	386
Elementary school + 1 year's vocational school	0.99	1.14	171	1.38	1.51	177	1.06	1.11	243	0.71	0.80	147
Middle school	1.10	1.20	108	0.88	1.23	102	1.15	1.17	113	0.87	0.88	129
Middle school + 1 year's vocational school	0.93	0.99	98	1.05	1.59	80	0.82	1.01	134	0.73	0.85	139
Matriculation examination	0.88	0.90	25	0.94	1.42	16	0.87	0.94	32	0.48	0.64	29
Matriculation examination + 1 year's vocational school	1.47	1.61	17	1.21	1.90	19	0.76	0.90	58	0.53	0.63	64
University examination	0.87	0.94	24	0.83	1.54	35	0.67	0.97	39	0.45	0.67	49
Total			946			952			957			971
eta²		0.015			0.103			0.042			0.042	
beta		0.077			0.141			0.111			0.120	

Table 14-6

Mean Anxiety Scores in Different Occupational Status Groups

Occupational status	Denmark			Finland			Norway			Sweden		
	Class	Adjusted	N	Class	Adjusted	N	Class	Adjusted	N	Class	Adjusted	N
Farmers	0.84	0.85	134	1.94	1.56	163	1.10	0.94	91	0.97	1.04	34
Entrepreneurs	0.94	1.02	53	1.71	1.62	38	0.74	0.73	39	0.79	0.89	57
Upper white collar	0.82	1.15	62	1.14	1.69	49	0.82	1.27	95	0.40	0.69	94
Lower white collar	1.20	1.15	181	1.07	1.20	160	1.03	1.14	173	0.79	0.74	244
Skilled workers	1.11	1.36	184	1.51	1.57	202	1.06	1.11	145	1.01	1.06	207
Unskilled workers	1.25	1.25	65	2.25	2.17	96	1.50	1.11	46	0.90	0.73	73
Housewife	1.61	1.23	169	1.71	1.34	93	1.46	1.11	276	1.23	1.01	167
No occupation	1.58	1.58	140	1.90	2.15	193	1.32	1.74	139	1.05	1.20	128
Total			988			944			1,004			1,004
eta^2		0.033			0.036			0.022			0.028	
beta		0.137			0.182			0.156			0.133	

adjustment reduces it. It is likely that this is due to the relatively high average age and low educational level of the farmers.

Finnish entrepreneurs differ from their Scandinavian counterparts: their anxiety level is above the national average, whereas in the other countries it is below average.

As a group, skilled workers are less anxious than unskilled ones, with the exception of Sweden, where the order of groups is reversed. In Finland and Norway adjustment lessens differences between the two groups and alters the order of groups in Denmark. This implies that the groups also differ in other respects that affect the anxiety index. One such variable is age, which is a powerful predictor of anxiety level; in every country the proportion of young people (15-24 years) among skilled workers is higher than in the whole population. In Norway and Sweden unskilled workers are often older people (Pöntinen & Uusitalo, 1974).

Prestige of Occupation and Anxiety

Because prestige of occupation and education level are correlated, it is no surprise that the relationship of both variables to anxiety is similar: more educated and more prestigious people are less anxious (Table 14-7). Compared with level of education, prestige has almost the same predictive power, with the proportion of explained variance being the same in all countries. The prestige classification is based on the Finnish study basing a rating method in the ranking of occupations (Rauhala, 1966).

Economic Resources and Anxiety

If one looks at the proportion of explained variance, income level of the family—and income of respondent—is clearly a weaker predictor of anxiety level than is age, but not so much weaker than education level. A part of this weakness is due to technical reasons: respondents with zero income often are economically dependent on their parents; in their case, the classification does not tell enough about their economic position.

With the exception of the group with zero income, anxiety level decreases consistently with increasing income level in Finland and Denmark; in Sweden only the highest income group is an exception. The pattern in the Norwegian data is most inconsistent, but even there the two lowest income groups have the highest anxiety scores (Table 14-8).

Table 14-7

Mean Anxiety Scores According to Prestige of Occupation

Prestige	Denmark			Finland			Norway			Sweden		
	Class	Adjusted	N	Class	Adjusted	N	Class	Adjusted	N	Class	Adjusted	N
High: 1	1.50	2.09	2	—	—	—	0.00	0.36	1	2.00	2.04	1
2	0.60	0.92	15	0.75	1.26	8	0.86	1.19	22	0.62	0.84	24
3	0.71	0.92	28	1.10	1.50	29	0.82	1.18	57	0.46	0.58	63
4	0.78	0.91	74	1.37	1.42	109	0.86	1.07	100	0.49	0.58	93
5	1.00	1.12	250	1.35	1.46	236	0.79	0.94	178	0.67	0.75	249
6	1.27	1.22	366	1.52	1.52	283	1.29	1.20	442	1.16	1.14	338
7	1.71	1.55	199	2.09	1.90	246	1.64	1.48	165	1.18	1.06	181
8	0.90	1.06	31	2.19	2.18	48	1.20	1.00	25	1.18	1.04	34
Low: 9	1.67	1.39	15	3.07	2.92	29	2.18	1.80	11	0.82	0.59	17
Total			980			988			1,001			1,000
eta^2	0.040			0.048			0.040			0.047		
beta	0.128			0.166			0.114			0.165		

Table 14-8

Mean Anxiety Scores According to Family Income

Family income	Denmark			Finland			Norway			Sweden		
	Class	Adjusted	N	Class	Adjusted	N	Class	Adjusted	N	Class	Adjusted	N
Low: 1	1.52	1.37	166	2.43	2.27	183	1.54	1.35	198	1.47	1.31	187
2	1.35	1.32	185	1.90	1.85	199	1.35	1.32	191	0.91	0.82	185
3	1.28	1.30	154	1.43	1.43	158	1.00	1.02	183	0.79	0.81	182
4	1.03	1.11	165	1.21	1.22	157	1.03	1.13	192	0.71	0.79	181
5	1.02	1.23	156	1.20	1.38	162	0.89	1.03	185	0.75	0.91	181
High: 6	1.11	1.00	162	1.65	1.71	135	1.53	1.44	55	0.86	0.83	88
Total			988			994			1,004			1,004
eta^2	0.014			0.054			0.026			0.041		
beta	0.083			0.189			0.095			0.145		

In addition to income, property is an important resource which is apt to add to the sense of economic security. In the Scandinavian survey the measurement of ownership was somewhat crude, and it is impossible to form a firm opinion about the quantity or value of property because the monetary value of it is unknown. Nevertheless, a crude index was constructed, which was intended to indicate the amount of property and thus called an ownership index.[3]

As regards the ownership index as a predictor of anxiety, in terms of proportion of explained variance it is clearly weaker than income level although the general pattern of empirical means seems to be quite consistent: the anxiety scores decrease with increasing property. In other words, the more wealthy people are less anxious.

Housing density or living density was also examined as a predictor, but this aspect of economic welfare seems to be an inefficient predictor of anxiety and does not provide a consistent picture about the relationship. According to earlier studies, one can not expect a strong relationship between living density and psychological symptoms, but one can expect some effect (Mitchell, 1971). Perhaps housing conditions in the Nordic countries are so good that they no longer have any effect on the psychological well-being of people.

The questionnaire included a question concerning income satisfaction and the reason for possible dissatisfaction. A plausible hypothesis is that those who say that they are dissatisfied because they need more money are experiencing more severe economic pressure and would therefore be more anxious than those who think that they are worth more pay. The data, however, do not support this hypothesis. It is true that in Denmark and in Finland the group means are in accordance with expectations, but in Norway and in Sweden exactly the opposite is true. One must conclude that income satisfaction does not significantly increase the predictive power over family income alone. Among the indicators of economic resources discussed here, family income seems to be the most powerful predictor of anxiety level.

[3] The ownership index was constructed so that one point was added for each of the following items: (a) shares in a bank or company; (b) enterprise, business or corresponding; (c) land of a farm; (d) building site; (e) flat or flats; (f) house; (g) summerhouse or summer cottage. Then the resulting measure was trichotomized: 0, owns none of the above items; 1; owns one to two of the above items; and 3, owns three to seven of the above items.

Physical Strenuousness of the Occupation and Anxiety

It has been shown that morbidity is related to the physical strenuousness or strain of the occupation and to the skill and training required by the occupation, despite the fact that morbidity varies greatly within occupational groupings independently of occupation and age. Especially among the older age groups, the relationship of physical strain to morbidity is clear (Happonen, 1968; Purola & Kalimo, 1970).

To study the effect of physical strain on anxiety, working persons were divided according to the classification by Happonen (1968) into six classes. Despite the fact that physical strain is an apparent stressor, the results did not conform to expectations. Only in the Swedish data did the anxiety scores increase with assumed strain; in the other data there are no systematic differences.

Regrettably, the conclusions remain indecisive; despite our efforts, the strain classification remained crude and hence one cannot decide whether the lack of a relationship is real or only due to the invalidity of the independent variable.

Political Resources and Anxiety

An index called "political resources" was used as an indicator of political power. The index is based on the following three items: if the respondent had voted or not, if he had asked for the floor in a meeting or not, and if he had tried to influence a decision in a community or political question. In this order, the items form a Guttman scale.

Table 14-9 shows that political resources do not have a consistent relationship with anxiety level; therefore, one must conclude that other aspects of social status or closely related factors are more important for the individual's mental health.

Size of Community and Anxiety

Regional differences did not appear clearly in the Scandinavian survey; anxiety is no exception to the rule. Type of living community does not predict the level of anxiety, this being particularly true in Norway and Sweden. In Finland and in Denmark, however, one can see some differences in anxiety scores along the urban rural dimension, but the relationship between anxiety level

Table 14-9

Mean Anxiety Scores According to Political Resources

Political resources	Denmark			Finland			Norway			Sweden		
	Class	Adjusted	N	Class	Adjusted	N	Class	Adjusted	N	Class	Adjusted	N
Low: 0	1.16	1.36	176	1.45	1.84	220	0.95	1.24	215	0.77	0.93	144
1	1.31	1.15	523	1.96	1.79	415	1.38	1.23	402	1.15	1.01	397
2	1.08	1.27	152	1.42	1.41	214	1.09	1.06	214	0.73	0.76	298
High: 3	1.10	1.28	134	1.44	1.38	144	1.15	1.18	174	0.85	1.00	165
Total			985			993			1,005			1,004
eta²		0.004			0.018			0.012			0.021	
beta		0.053			0.105			0.045			0.082	

Table 14-10

Mean Anxiety Scores According to Community Type

Community type	Denmark			Finland			Norway			Sweden		
	Class	Adjusted	N	Class	Adjusted	N	Class	Adjusted	N	Class	Adjusted	N
Countryside	1.11	1.16	411	1.86	1.78	397	1.20	1.17	407	0.90	0.87	233
Densely populated area, 1,000–10,000	1.08	1.08	122	1.91	1.93	144	1.07	1.14	181	1.01	0.98	167
Town over 10,000	1.20	1.20	167	1.35	1.43	265	1.29	1.30	191	0.88	0.90	356
City	1.45	1.38	285	1.49	1.52	186	1.17	1.16	226	0.93	0.97	247
Total			985			992			1,005			1,003
eta²		0.010			0.016			0.002			0.002	
beta		0.069			0.098			0.035			0.034	

and community size is not the same in these countries. In Finland the most anxious people are living in the countryside or in densely populated areas with a population between 1,000 and 10,000 people, whereas in Denmark people living in settings of this kind are least anxious. Perhaps only the mean of the three largest cities is significantly different from the others (Table 14-10).

These results are in accordance with the views of some urban sociologists who contend that urban-rural differences, including psychological ones, vary according to the character of the entire society, particularly its level of modernization. It is in the transitional societies where major urban-rural differences should occur (Fischer, 1973).

Community Cohesion and Anxiety

As stated previously, the type of living community is not strongly related to anxiety. Subjective community cohesion (willingness to move, question 22) is not a better predictor, the proportion of explained variance from it being almost nil in all countries (Table 14-11).

Physical Health and Anxiety

On the basis of common sense, one can expect that good physical health has a favourable effect on a person's anxiety level, and earlier studies have confirmed this expectation (Bradburn, 1969, pp. 117–120). The Scandinavian survey includes only one question indicating subject's physical condition (question 37: Do you suffer from some kind of chronic illness or some impairment which has compelled you to change your occupation?).

Health is the best single predictor of anxiety; in all countries, those suffering from chronic illness or impairment suffer also from anxiety more often than do healthier people. In the Finnish data the proportion of explained variance is greatest; in the other countries there are not significant differences in this respect (Table 14-12).

There is a possibility, however, that the relationship between health and anxiety is partially trivial. The problem is due to the anxiety measurement, which includes psychophysiological symptoms and also a question concerning worry about health. Even allowing for the reality of neurotic complaints, at least a part of worry has to be considered realistic. It is no surprise that the people suffering from ill health also care about it. The effect of the health-worry item can

Table 14-11

Mean Anxiety Scores According to Community Cohesion (Willingness To Move)

Willingness to move	Denmark			Finland			Norway			Sweden		
	Class	Adjusted	N	Class	Adjusted	N	Class	Adjusted	N	Class	Adjusted	N
Would rather move	1.36	1.43	190	1.71	1.78	337	1.18	1.23	247	0.90	0.91	301
Unwilling to move	1.13	1.11	547	1.62	1.57	425	1.22	1.19	448	0.95	0.94	518
eta^2		0.004			0.001			0.000			0.000	
beta		0.093			0.054			0.010			0.011	

Table 14-12

Mean Anxiety Scores According to Physical Health

Health	Denmark			Finland			Norway			Sweden		
	Class	Adjusted	N	Class	Adjusted	N	Class	Adjusted	N	Class	Adjusted	N
"Healthy"	1.03	1.05	856	1.24	1.34	769	0.99	1.05	876	0.76	0.81	877
Ill, impaired	2.40	2.26	136	3.12	2.78	225	2.52	2.16	128	2.02	1.72	127
Total			992			994			1,004			1,004
eta^2		0.094			0.171			0.105			0.098	
beta		0.269			0.316			0.237			0.228	

easily be seen by dropping it away and checking the proportion of explained variance. The decline is less than 1% in every country. One can conclude that the substantial part of the explanatory power of the health variable remains even without this particular item.

Childhood Pressures and Anxiety

There are two indicators of quality of childhood or of pressures experienced during childhood based on questions 70 and 71. The first one concerns whether respondent had been living with both real (biological) parents during his childhood, with the assumption that the broken home is apt to induce more pressure than the unbroken. The other one consists of the presence of the following five troubles during the childhood: (a) family had economic troubles, (b) serious arguments occurred in family, (c) respondent was afraid of some member of family, (d) serious illness in family, and (e) some member of family had troubles because of alcohol. The items are positively correlated with each other.

Knowing whether a person has been living with both parents does not substantially add to the precision of the prediction of the anxiety level. Instead, the predictive power of the trouble index is greater (proportion of explained variance from 2% to 5.5%). Anxiety rises with the increasing number of troubles. Partial exception from the general trend is the Finnish data, where the relationship seems to be slightly curvilinear (Table 14-13).

Need Satisfaction and Anxiety

The questionnaire includes 15 questions aimed at measuring need satisfaction in the Maslowian sense. Other variables may also be useful as indicators of needs, of course; in some instances, these other variables are even better. The specific need queries can be grouped by factor analysis into three groups: a first factor representing satisfaction of cognitive and self-actualization needs, a second factor termed "security," and a third factor that is difficult to interpret but that has high loading on questions measuring aesthetic and physiological needs. Four variables with highest loadings were selected to represent each factor, and summated scales were constructed.

The scales representing lower needs to not predict the anxiety level very well, but the scale of cognitive and self-actualization needs is a more effective predictor: people who are better satisfied in this

Table 14-13

Mean Anxiety Scores According to the Number of Childhood Troubles

Number of Troubles	Denmark			Finland			Norway			Sweden		
	Class	Adjusted	N	Class	Adjusted	N	Class	Adjusted	N	Class	Adjusted	N
No troubles	0.99	1.08	395	1.15	1.39	303	0.88	1.01	442	0.60	0.68	460
1 trouble	1.23	1.21	317	1.76	1.70	352	1.26	1.18	328	1.07	1.04	311
2 troubles	1.38	1.25	184	2.14	1.94	201	1.58	1.45	142	1.34	1.21	161
3 troubles or more	1.80	1.79	96	1.86	1.78	138	1.82	1.64	92	1.39	1.30	72
Total			992			994			1,004			1,004
eta^2	0.024			0.037			0.042			0.055		
beta	0.128			0.106			0.131			0.175		

Table 14-14

Mean Anxiety Scores According to Satisfaction of Cognitive and Self-actualization Needs

Need satisfaction	Denmark			Finland			Norway			Sweden		
	Class	Adjusted	N	Class	Adjusted	N	Class	Adjusted	N	Class	Adjusted	N
Low: 1	1.75	1.49	129	2.24	1.97	240	1.69	1.49	287	1.55	1.36	147
2	1.29	1.21	166	1.74	1.59	244	1.17	1.12	276	1.06	1.02	257
3	1.32	1.31	277	1.55	1.71	295	0.88	0.14	276	0.78	0.82	347
High: 4	0.96	1.08	420	1.10	1.34	215	0.85	1.03	165	0.60	0.71	253
Total			992			994			1,004			1,004
eta^2	0.029			0.042			0.047			0.054		
beta	0.090			0.116			0.122			0.161		

respect are less anxious. The proportion of explained variance is least in Denmark (Table 14-14).

Insubstitutability and Anxiety

In an earlier analysis by Allardt, an insubstitutability scale based on four questions (19, 21, 23, and 27) explained about 3% of variance of anxiety (Allardt, 1973, pp. 55–58). Allardt's scale included the following items: insubstitutability in duties, in groups, in organizations, and whether one's occupation required particular personal qualities. If we add two items, one concerning the possibility that another person could learn one's tasks in a week (question 12) and another specifying that the occupation required special schooling or examination (question 20), and treat each question as separate predictor variables, the proportion of explained variance increases by about 1% (except in Norway, where it almost doubles). Special schooling seems to be particularly important in Norway in this connection.

Possibilities to Influence and Anxiety

Persons who report that they have many possibilities of making decisions in matters concerning their personal lives are less anxious than those who have fewer possibilities to influence. The result is the same in all four countries. In terms of proportion of explained variance this variable is one of the best single variable predictors of the anxiety level, with only age and health exceeding it in predictive power (Table 14-15).

Conformity Pressure and Anxiety

Those people who more often have felt compelled to repress their opinion (question 16) are more anxious than those who have felt this kind of pressure only occasionally or never. Although the proportion of explained variance varies from country to country the results are otherwise very consistent: groups with greater conformity pressure are more anxious (Table 14-16).

Contacts, Contact Possibilities, and Anxiety

The individual's own subjective estimate of his opportunities to make contacts with persons with whom he could have a real feeling of companionship predicts his anxiety level quite well. The exception is Denmark, where there are relatively few people who report that

Table 14-15

Mean Anxiety Scores According to Possibilities To Influence in Matters Concerning Personal Life

Possibilities to influence	Denmark			Finland			Norway			Sweden		
	Class	Adjusted	N	Class	Adjusted	N	Class	Adjusted	N	Class	Adjusted	N
Great	1.03	1.09	651	1.28	1.41	488	1.00	1.07	650	0.78	0.86	760
Small	1.58	1.44	158	1.90	1.82	357	1.72	1.46	151	1.42	1.12	154
Not at all	2.21	1.85	39	3.89	2.89	35	2.87	2.16	15	2.00	1.43	16
Total			848			880			816			930
eta^2		0.043			0.087			0.056			0.044	
beta		0.133			0.175			0.131			0.090	

Table 14-16

Mean Anxiety Scores According to Conformity Pressure

Feelings of conformity pressure	Denmark			Finland			Norway			Sweden		
	Class	Adjusted	N	Class	Adjusted	N	Class	Adjusted	N	Class	Adjusted	N
Often	2.08	1.64	62	2.34	1.96	157	1.72	1.42	71	1.92	1.69	52
Sometimes	1.22	1.20	385	1.54	1.65	554	1.18	1.24	495	0.88	0.91	446
Never	1.02	1.11	401	1.28	1.27	169	0.98	0.95	250	0.81	0.82	432
Total			848			880			816			930
eta^2		0.032			0.035			0.015			0.035	
beta		0.089			0.113			0.099			0.147	

their opportunities for contacts are small or that they have no opportunities at all (Table 14-17).

Although these results seem to indicate that a person's subjective estimate about his possibilities to make contacts is related to the amount of his anxiety, the more objective matters, which should also indicate frequency of human contacts, do not have a similar or as strong a relationship (Tables 14-18 to 14-20). Questions concerning number of friends and frequency of meeting relatives are of this kind.

The opportunity to make contacts is perhaps not the only motivating factor when a person is seeking membership in an organization; nevertheless, such activities often offer good possibilities for human contacts as well. Hence memberships in organizations are referred to here.

The number of friends seems to be completely unrelated to anxiety. According to the present data, the relationship of the frequency of meeting relatives is modest. In all countries, however, the group that never meets relatives is the most anxious, pointing to the significance of contacts with relatives for psychological well-being. A similar conclusion is also possible with respect to the number of the organizational memberships. The specific number of membership affiliations does not matter otherwise; but, again, those who are totally outside organizations are most anxious.

All the results reported here are *not* based on the same MCA. Hence, caution is necessary in interpreting adjusted means. Because of limited space, full reporting is not feasible; to have an idea of the common predictive power of variables, however, some comments on further analyses will follow. In the first MCA, anxiety is the dependent variable and the following seven status variables are predictors: educational level, occupational status, prestige of occupation, family income, marital status, age, and sex. In addition to the status indicators, the second MCA includes the following "psychological" predictors: childhood troubles, cognitive and self-actualization needs, physical health, possibilities to influence, conformity pressure, contact possibilities, number of friends, contacts with relatives, and number of organization affiliations. Proportion of explained variation and beta coefficients of these 16 predictors are given in Table 14-21. (Beta coefficients of Table 14-21 are comparable with each other.)

Table 14-17

Mean Anxiety Scores According to Contact Opportunities

Contact opportunities	Denmark			Finland			Norway			Sweden		
	Class	Adjusted	N	Class	Adjusted	N	Class	Adjusted	N	Class	Adjusted	N
Good opportunities	1.13	1.17	779	1.46	1.58	690	1.06	1..3	737	0.83	0.86	877
Small opportunities	1.82	1.41	56	2.10	1.79	179	2.24	1.57	76	1.98	1.58	45
No opportunities	1.69	1.30	13	4.64	2.66	11	0.67	0.54	3	3.00	2.01	8
Total			848			880			816			930
eta²		0.015			0.052			0.050			0.056	
beta		0.041			0.078			0.087			0.140	

Table 14-18

Mean Anxiety Scores According to Number of Friends

Number of friends	Denmark			Finland			Norway			Sweden		
	Class	Adjusted	N	Class	Adjusted	N	Class	Adjusted	N	Class	Adjusted	N
No friends	1.30	1.13	165	1.81	1.50	222	1.29	0.97	119	0.91	0.89	76
1 friend	1.30	1.12	37	1.63	1.63	115	1.67	1.17	42	1.17	0.91	47
2 friends	1.27	1.15	121	1.63	1.62	131	1.22	1.20	125	0.85	0.72	71
3 friends or more	1.13	1.22	525	1.54	1.71	412	1.08	1.20	530	0.90	0.93	736
Total			848			880			816			930
eta²		0.003			0.003			0.008			0.002	
beta		0.027			0.044			0.051			0.041	

Table 14-19

Mean Anxiety Scores According to Frequency of Contacts with Relatives

Frequency	Denmark Class	Denmark Adjusted	Denmark N	Finland Class	Finland Adjusted	Finland N	Norway Class	Norway Adjusted	Norway N	Sweden Class	Sweden Adjusted	Sweden N
Twice a week or more often	1.42	1.34	145	1.46	1.46	142	1.20	1.11	216	1.03	0.98	214
About once a week	1.03	1.12	207	1.56	1.69	211	1.06	1.17	185	0.85	0.89	254
2 or 3 times in a month	1.17	1.26	169	1.61	1.67	133	1.24	1.22	156	0.88	0.87	138
About once a month	1.13	1.12	162	1.74	1.67	182	0.86	1.03	98	0.72	0.74	130
About every second or third month	1.05	0.93	77	1.55	1.53	99	1.36	1.39	69	0.76	0.88	95
Less than 4 times in a year	1.27	1.16	81	1.78	1.63	106	1.31	1.16	91	1.13	0.98	93
Never	3.57	3.07	7	3.86	2.97	7	3.00	2.20	1	3.00	2.90	6
Total			848			880			816			930
eta^2		0.029			0.015			0.010			0.026	
beta		0.138			0.079			0.062			0.134	

Table 14-20

Mean Anxiety Scores According to Number of Organization Memberships

Organization memberships	Denmark Class	Denmark Adjusted	Denmark N	Finland Class	Finland Adjusted	Finland N	Norway Class	Norway Adjusted	Norway N	Sweden Class	Sweden Adjusted	Sweden N
No organization	1.59	1.43	237	1.90	1.78	329	1.31	1.25	223	1.18	1.01	179
1 organization	1.05	1.00	297	1.63	1.64	321	1.22	1.26	268	0.87	0.89	301
2 organizations	1.02	1.16	175	1.27	1.33	136	0.98	1.03	180	0.78	0.89	227
3 organizations	1.07	1.18	85	1.26	1.55	57	1.16	1.09	95	0.84	0.95	139
4 organizations	0.95	1.33	37	0.72	1.21	18	0.94	1.01	33	0.72	0.90	47
5 organizations or more	0.94	1.25	17	1.63	1.70	19	0.82	0.62	17	0.41	0.50	37
Total			848			880			816			930
eta^2		0.028			0.021			0.008			0.019	
beta		0.117			0.087			0.085			0.072	

Table 14-21

Proportion of Explained Variance and Beta Coefficients of Selected Predictors of Anxiety

Predictor	Proportion of explained variance				Beta			
	Denmark	Finland	Norway	Sweden	Denmark	Finland	Norway	Sweden
1. Educational level	1.1	7.5	4.6	4.1	.078	.070	.099	.127
2. Prestige	3.8	5.0	4.6	5.0	.086	.089	.084	.122
3. Occupational status	2.7	3.4	2.7	2.8	.083	.091	.194	.099
4. Family income	1.7	6.3	2.6	3.2	.070	.145	.060	.080
5. Marital status	3.0	3.3	6.1	1.4	.095	.126	.153	.072
6. Age	2.3	10.9	7.5	5.3	.068	.116	.177	.092
7. Sex	5.1	0.8	2.0	1.2	.168	.060	.086	.090
8. Childhood troubles	3.8	3.6	4.7	5.8	.146	.099	.146	.128
9. Cognitive self-actualization needs	2.4	4.4	4.7	5.1	.065	.079	.059	.108
10. Health	8.3	17.0	9.5	8.5	.232	.258	.207	.176
11. Possibilities to influence	4.3	8.7	5.6	4.4	.133	.175	.131	.089
12. Conformity pressure	3.2	3.5	1.5	3.5	.089	.113	.099	.147
13. Contact possibilities	1.5	5.2	5.0	5.6	.041	.078	.087	.140
14. Number of friends	0.3	0.3	0.8	0.2	.027	.044	.051	.041
15. Contacts with relatives	2.9	1.5	1.0	2.6	.138	.079	.062	.134
16. Number of organization affiliations	2.8	2.1	0.8	1.8	.117	.087	.085	.072
Proportion of variance explained					.261	.366	.317	.302
Multiple R					.451	.565	.511	.503
N					848	880	816	930

Proportion of explained variation of anxiety by the seven status variables is 12%, 20%, 18%, and 14% in Denmark, Finland, Norway, and Sweden, respectively. When "psychological" predictors are added to the model, the proportion of explained variation increases substantially: to 26%, 37%, 32%, and 30%. Although there are differences in proportions of explained variation between countries, one can nevertheless argue that, in general, the same variables are effective predictors in all countries, the pattern of explanations being very similar.

If one looks at the strength of relationship between psychological well-being (or anxiety) and the very variables which can be taken as the most pure indicators of human relations, a curious phenomenon appears in pattern of proportion of variance explained. "Perceived contact possibilities" is clearly a better predictor of anxiety than the number of friends and frequency of contacts with relatives. In the view of the writer this result should not be interpreted as evidence of the irrelevance of human relations for mental health or psychological well-being; but it emphasizes qualitative aspects before quantity. The fact that possibilities to influence and conformity pressure are also related to anxiety is in accordance with this interpretation.

REFERENCES

Allardt, E. *About dimensions of welfare: An exploratory analysis of a comparative Scandinavian survey.* Research Reports, Research Group for Comparative Sociology, University of Helsinki, No. 1, 1973.

Allardt, E. Public policy and dimensions of welfare. Paper presented at the CPS/Polska Akademia Nauk conference on Comparing Public Policy in Jablonna Palace, Poland, May 14–19, 1974.

Andrews, F., Morgan, J., & Sonquist, J. *Multiple Classification Analysis.* Institute for Social Research, The University of Michigan, Ann Arbor, Mich., 1971.

Bradburn, N. M. *The structure of psychological well-being.* National Opinion Research Center Monographs in Social Research. Chicago: Aldine, 1969.

Fischer, C. S. Urban malaise. *Social Forces*, 1973, 52(2), 221–235.

Gaitz, C. M., & Scott, J. Age and the measurement of mental health. *Journal of Health and Social Behavior*, 1972, 13(3), 55–67.

Haavio-Mannila, E., & Stenius, K. *The social construction of psychiatric diagnoses and the rates of mental illness in Finland and Sweden.* Research Reports, Institute of Sociology, University of Helsinki, No. 201, 1974.

Happonen, M-L. *Ammattialoittainen sairastavuus eläkeiän porrastuksen perustana.* Publications of the National Pensions Institute, Finland, Series M:11/1968. Helsinki: Research Institute for Social Security, 1968.

Kalimo, E., Bice, T. W., & Novosel, M. Cross-cultural analysis of selected emotional questions from the Cornell Medical Index. *British Journal of Preventive and Social Medicine*, 1970, 24, 229-240.

Kata, K., & Uusitalo, H. *On the data, sampling and representativeness of the Scandinavian survey in 1972*. Research Reports, Research Group for Comparative Sociology, University of Helsinki, No. 4, 1974.

Kohn, M. L. Class, family, and schizophrenia: A reformulation. *Social Forces*, 1972, 50(3), 295-304.

Magnusson, D. *Testteori (Theory of Testing)*. Stockholm: Almqvist & Wiksell, 1961.

Mitchell, R. E. Some social implications of high density housing. *American Sociological Review*, 1971, 36(2), 18-22.

Pöntinen, S., & Uusitalo, H. *Household incomes in the Scandinavian countries: A multivariate analysis*. Research Reports, Research Group for Comparative Sociology, University of Helsinki, No. 3, 1974.

Purola, T., & Kalimo, E. *Sairastavuuden ammattialoittainen vaihtelu työvoima-ja eläkepoliittisena ongelmana. (English Summary: Occupation and Morbidity)*. Publications of the National Pensions Institute, Finland, Series M:14/1970. Helsinki: Research Institute for Social Security, 1970.

Rauhala, U. *Suomalaisen yhteiskunnan sosiaalinen kerrostuneisuus (The social stratification in Finnish society)*. Porvoo, 1966.

Sievers, K., Koskelainen, O., & Leppo, K. *Suomalaisten sukupuolielämä (The sexual life of the Finns)*. Porvoo: WSOY, 1974.

Valkonen, T. *Haastattelu- ja kyselyaineiston analyysi sosiaalitutkimuksessa (Analysis of Survey Data in Social Research)*. Ylioppilastuki ry, 1971.

IV
COPING WITH STRESS
AND ANXIETY

15
STRATEGIES FOR COPING WITH STRESS

Walter D. Fenz

University of Waterloo
Waterloo, Ontario, Canada

The study of man's reactions to conditions of intense psychological stress has been a major concern of psychological investigators for a long time. More recently, the emphasis in research has shifted to the study of the psychological mechanisms that affect the control of involuntary reactions to stress. In our own research we have tried to identify some of these mechanisms, to document how they are learned, and to find out how they relate to performance.

In our investigations, which have extended over the last 15 years, we have used a field/laboratory setting, with sport parachuting as the source of stress. We have found parachuting to be an ideal situation for studying stress, in that it combines the intense involvement and high degree of stress usually found only in field studies, with the stringent controls that can be obtained only in the laboratory. The intensity of stress experienced by a novice jumper often rivals and even exceeds that encountered in behaviour disorders. As a novice parachutist continues jumping, the investigator is able to study what happens as he gains experience and mastery.

The research has shown that there are marked individual differences in the reactions to the parachuting stress situation, in the strategies parachutists develop for coping with stress, and in the rate at which they learn the type of controls associated with experience and mastery. For some, the parachuting experience is too stressful, and they leave the situation; others learn to cope, first defensively, then gradually more realistically, and become skillful masters of the sport. This chapter documents some of our empirical findings and shows how one study grew out of the other and how our thinking developed over time.

REVIEW OF THE RESEARCH PROGRAMME

In the laboratory, usually a research trailer set up at an airport, we administered a word-association test and recorded responses of novice and experienced sport parachutists to words scaled along a dimension of increasing relevance to parachuting (Epstein & Fenz, 1962; Fenz, 1964, 1971, 1973). In the laboratory we also administered a specially constructed thematic apperception test, which contained pictures varying in degrees of relevance to parachuting; and we analyzed the content of the stories parachutists made to them (Fenz, 1973; Fenz & Epstein, 1962). In real life we recorded the autonomic activity of novice and experienced parachutists during the ride up in the aircraft and after landing (Fenz & Epstein, 1967) and related their response patterns to performance in parachuting (Fenz, 1973; Fenz & Jones, 1972a). The results, in most cases, were extremely reliable, and we developed a theoretical framework to interrelate the findings from the various studies and thus have laid the basis for a theory of stress and its mastery (Epstein, 1967; Fenz, 1969).

Among some of our most interesting findings were changes in cognitive and physiological responses of sport parachutists as a function of experience. These changes were consistent and reliable in responses to stimulus dimensions in both longitudinal and cross-sectional studies (Fenz, 1968, 1971). They also appeared in fear ratings as a function of a time dimension in relation to a jump (Epstein & Fenz, 1965) and in physiological reactions during ascent in the aircraft (Fenz & Epstein, 1967). In studies using a stimulus dimension of words scaled for increasing relevance to parachuting, we were able to show, with a high degree of reliability, that the peak in reactivity becomes displaced towards the low-relevance end of the dimension as a function of increasing parachuting experience and mastery of fear. The emerging response pattern along the stimulus dimension is that of an increasing monotonic gradient for novice jumpers and an inverted V-shaped curve for experienced parachutists (Fenz, 1968, 1971). Fear, or avoidance, responses were also seen to become increasingly anticipatory as a function of experience, producing a similar inverted V-shaped curve (Epstein & Fenz, 1965). Finally, physiological recordings, taken during ascent in the aircraft, showed a continuous increase in reactivity right up to the time of the jump for the novice parachutists, whereas for experienced parachutists there was a sharp increase in reactivity early in the jump sequence, which was followed by a decline, so that arousal at the moment of the jump was at nearly normal levels (Fenz & Epstein, 1967). More recent studies have shown that quality of performance in parachuting, both in novice and in experienced jumpers is related to a well-defined inverted V-shaped pattern of electrodermal reactivity and reaction time to words along the stimulus dimension of increasing relevance to parachuting, as well as a more pronounced inverted V-shaped pattern of autonomic reactivity during the jump sequence (Fenz, 1973; Fenz & Jones, 1972a).

What is the meaning of the gradual development of the anticipatory V-shaped curve of physiological arousal, which becomes established through repeated, successful exposure to a source of stress? In a number of papers (Epstein, 1967; Fenz, 1964, 1969), we elaborated on the traditional approach-avoidance conflict model (Lewin, 1931; Miller, 1944) and equated approach with anxiety, or arousal, and avoidance with inhibition. Following the traditional model, we hypothesized that in relation to a goal that has both positive and negative valence, there develops a gradient of anxiety and a gradient of inhibition of anxiety; the gradient of inhibition of anxiety is assumed to be steeper than the gradient of anxiety itself and becomes increasingly more so with repeated, successful exposure to a source of stress. The interaction between the two gradients causes the peak in arousal to shift to cues increasingly more remote from the source of stress, forcing the individual to attend to low relevant cues, which act as "get ready" or "warning" signals for the forthcoming danger. The ability to respond to these "warning" signals, and to be able to initiate and carry through mechanisms responsible for the inhibition, or control of anxiety, is adaptive and is related to performance.

WHEN COPING MECHANISMS FAIL

If I am taking a student up, I like to see him a little uneasy; it is natural that he should be. I had one particular chap one day, he was too relaxed. . . he jumped into the airplane, and when he got up there, he said "no, I am not going". Now, I knew before he even got up there that he was not going to jump. . . . if this fellow does jump, and he hasn't got this, well, uneasiness, you know, he makes a jump and might kill himself.

Comment made by an experienced jumpmaster

A number of parachutists who were unable to cope with the stress of parachuting stand out among the many successful jumpers we have observed over the years. It is not infrequent that a jump is aborted because a parachutist at the last moment changes his mind. One such "would-be" parachutist—an extreme case, I should add— was a subject in one of our experiments. We recorded his physiological and behavioural responses in the laboratory and observed him during the jump sequence. Although the symptomatology of such cases varies, this represents a good example of a complete breakdown of coping mechanisms and a flight into a psychotic-like withdrawal from the threats of the situation. The case was documented in some detail in a recent study (Fenz, 1974), and I am relating at this time only some of the salient features that are relevant to this chapter.

The case report. While recruiting inexperienced, student parachutists for our research at a parachuting center, we were approached by a man, about 35 years of age, who said he wanted to take part in our study; he said: "this might help me to understand myself better." We accepted him into our sample, and on a control day, 2 weeks before the intended jump, we administered our word-association test (Fenz, 1964); this test has a built-in dimension of words scaled for relevance to parachuting. Among our dependent measures were the galvanic skin response (GSR), heart rate, and reaction time. Two weeks after the initial testing, on the morning in which he planned to make his first jump, he was tested a second time with a parallel set of tests. Our studies in the past had consistently shown that for both autonomic and performance measures the response gradients are steeper on the day of a jump than on a control day; these findings are highly reliable, and are interpreted to represent the combined effects of stimulus and time dimensions. All 27 subjects showed this response pattern for both the GSR and reaction time in the Fenz (1964) study, and similar findings have been replicated in a number of other experiments.

Figure 15-1 presents group data derived from the earlier study and the responses of the present subject. Note the near total absence in autonomic responding by this subject on the day of the jump as compared to the group; in addition, his performance, as measured by reaction time to the stimulus words, shows much greater deficit, especially in response to words highly relevant to parachuting on the day of the jump.

His basal electrodermal level wavered around 25K ohms 2 weeks before the jump, but rose from an initial 12K ohms to over 155K ohms from the beginning to the end of testing on the day of the jump. The group data showed opposite trends in basal levels throughout testing, especially on the day of the

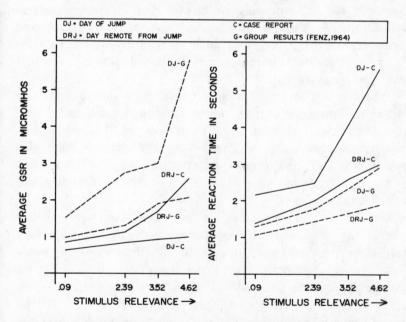

Fig. 15-1. Average galvanic skin response (GSR) and reaction time of a group of novice parachutists (Fenz, 1964) and a subject who could not cope with stress (Fenz, 1974), recorded on the day of a jump and on a day remote from a jump.

jump, namely a continuous decrease from the beginning to the end of the testing session (Fenz, 1964). We then suggested that the change in basal resistance during testing may represent an indication of the degree of active involvement on the part of the jumper in the testing situation, and for that matter, in the jump itself. For the same reason, the sharp rise in resistance throughout testing, shown by the present subject, suggests a gradual passive withdrawal from anxiety-provoking cues, associated with parachuting. Continuous recordings of heart rate, scored during the intervals between words, as well as at the beginning and the end of testing, showed a sharp increase, from 83 bpm (with an average cyclic range of 17.4 beats) prior to testing, to 144 bpm (with an average cyclic range of 1.7 beats) at the end of testing on the day of the jump, while it remained more or less constant around 80 bpm (with an average cyclic range of 18.4 beats) on the control day. These findings lend validity to the above observations made in connection with results on basal skin resistance. Verbal associations indicated response deficit, especially on the day of the jump, such as repetition of stimulus words, the use of neologisms, and perseveration of a response, such as "skydiver-jump; hungry-jump; radiator-heat; happy-parachute; bicycle-jump, damn it, I can't get away from it."

When this subject first came for testing, he did not look like the typical student jumper, he was older than most, and clearly not the athletic type; he was short, about 30 pounds over-weight, and perspired a great deal. The experimenter also remembers him for the many questions he asked about the test and the instruments, especially as to what we would find out about him.

On the day of the jump, his behaviour was clearly patho-logical: he displayed odd mannerisms, and, at first, was very talkative; as testing began, he seemed to withdraw, so that every word, when presented, seemed to catch him by surprise. He perspired profusely and had a somewhat vacant stare in his eyes. Following testing, the experimenter suggested to him that he leave jumping for another day; the subject nevertheless regained some composure, and since his whole family had come to see him jump, he felt he could not let it go. To avoid an additional source of stress, we did not test him during the ride up in the plane; he was sitting next to the open door, and as the plane took off, and gained altitude, he first developed a mild tremor, then assumed catatonic-like rigidity; when talked to, he did not respond, but just stared as into a vacuum. The pilot was asked to land the aircraft, and the jump was aborted. During a therapeutic interview with the experimenter the subject volunteered to talk about many of his personal, psychological problems; he was advised to seek psychiatric help, and to give up the idea of parachuting for a while.

The case history was introduced with the comment that for this "would-be" parachutist adaptive coping mechanisms failed, and that his reactions, temporarily, resembled those of a psychotic individual. In the laboratory he became increasingly less capable to meet appropriately the task demands, while fear about his forthcoming jump increasingly seemed to dominate his fantasy. Later, in the aircraft, there was a total severance of communication, and he became immobile and rigid. We may conclude that in the sequence of events throughout the day, a catatonic-like state was triggered into existence, with less and less reactivity to increasingly more powerful, threatening stimuli, in an attempt to exclude reality, and to isolate himself, psychologically, from the stress-provoking experience.

The psychophysiological responses of this parachutist, though not consistent with expectations derived from previous studies, which had used the same experimental manipulations, were unwittingly replicated in a recent laboratory experiment (Fenz, 1974). This study was designed to answer the following question: To what extent can the stress of parachuting be affected by sources of stress and conflict unrelated to parachuting? Although not previously anticipated, the study also lends itself to the question as to what happens when adaptive coping mechanisms fail.

The research instrument included the usual dimensions of words related to parachuting as well as dimensions of taboo, sexual-emotional words; in addition, subjects were told that they would receive a number of painful electrical shocks throughout the testing session, whenever they did not reach a criterion of performance set for each word. The instructions were sufficiently vague to maximize uncertainty. The design was carefully counterbalanced, and each subject was tested on a control day and on a day of a jump, on both occasions with and without threat of shock.

The findings on reaction time followed the expectations from our earlier work, and added one important new finding. Replicating earlier findings (Epstein & Fenz, 1962; Fenz, 1964), gradients of reaction time to words scaled on dimensions of increasing relevance to parachuting, were steeper on the day of a jump than on a day remote from a jump; threat of shock raised the steepness of the gradients on both days of testing. Thus, threat of shock, an added source of stress, accentuated performance deficit. This could have been predicted from previous studies. The new findings in reaction time relate to the emotional, taboo word dimensions: these followed the same patterns observed for the parachute relevant words, at least insofar as both sets of gradients were steeper on the day of a jump than on a day remote from a jump. Thus, stress associated with parachuting generalizes to other sources of conflict and stress. The case history presented previously suggests that it works the other way around as well; i.e., personal conflicts unrelated to parachuting contribute to the amount of stress experienced in parachuting. This had also been suggested in the case of a chronic stutterer whose symptoms became accentuated preceding a jump, and who experienced an alleviation of symptoms following the jump (Epstein & Fenz, 1962).

The findings on the GSR were unexpected. The same generalizing effect of stress and conflict that was observed for reaction time was also found for the GSR, except that the relative positions of the gradients were a near perfect reversal from the gradients for reaction time. How is one to account for these data?

One of our previous findings, which originally was a source of serious puzzlement to us, concerned the response pattern of experienced parachutists (Fenz, 1971). One might have predicted that their response would be similar to those of novice parachutists, only less pronounced; on the other hand, it has since been reliably shown, in cross-sectional and longitudinal studies, in the laboratory as well as in real life, that experienced parachutists show a different pattern of autonomic responding than novice jumpers. Whereas the mechanism of control for experienced jumpers is selective (Fenz & Epstein, 1968) and highly adaptive in that it is directly related to performance (Fenz & Jones, 1972a), the control mechanism of novice jumpers, under conditions of intense stress, as was attained in the present study, is indiscriminate. The data suggest that under conditions of intense stress, with which a person cannot cope, he withdraws from active participation in the threatening world around him. This seems to have been the "strategy" employed by the man in our case history, and it may be the explanation for the findings in the present study.

A word of caution should be raised. The previous study raises serious ethical considerations, especially if the interpretations of the findings are correct. Nobody was hurt in his jump, but this post facto comment does not justify the procedure; but neither does the post facto awareness of the intensity of the stress induced in the experiment justify its omission from the literature. It may well make a contribution, and it also serves as a warning that the experimenter may not always be aware of the full impact of his manipulations.

DEFENSIVE COPING WITH STRESS

I was not afraid at all, until I looked down and saw my knees trembling. Then I realized how scared I really was.

Comment made by a novice jumper

An analysis of the content of stories to a thematic apperception test, which we administered to novice parachutists before the jump, produced valuable clinical information on defensive strategies that our subjects used to cope with stress in parachuting; in addition, responses on the thematic apperception test were related to physiological reactions on the word-association test, and to performance in parachuting (Fenz, 1964; Fenz, 1973; Fenz & Epstein, 1962). Two of the pictures are reproduced in Fig. 15-2.

Denial of fear was the predominant defense mechanism in novice parachutists. In our first study with the thematic apperception test (Fenz & Epstein, 1962), we examined the unidentified pool of stories and noted eight extreme examples of denial of fear of parachuting. Denial was indicated either by emphasis on how calm and relaxed the hero was, or by an explicit statement that he was not afraid; e.g., "He is not afraid at all, just looks that way, because of the wind that is blowing in his face. He will have a wonderful jump. It will be great, just great!" All eight stories were in response to the high-relevant picture, and were produced on the day of the jump.

This study included 16 novice parachutists, who were tested twice: on the day of a jump and on a day remote from a jump. In addition to the thematic apperception test, we also administered

Fig. 15-2. Thematic picture stimuli: left, slight relevance; right, high relevance. (From "Conflict and stress as related to physiological activation and sensory, perceptual and cognitive functioning" by W. D. Fenz, *Psychological Monographs*, 1964, 78, 1–33. Copyright 1964 by the American Psychological Association. Reprinted by permission.)

parallel forms of the word-association test and recorded GSR and reaction time to each stimulus word. The results for the GSR, shown in Fig. 15-3, were unequivocal: denial of fear on the thematic apperception test was reflected in reduced reactivity to fear-provoking cues on the word-association test; this suggests that denial can serve as an effective defense mechanism to contain anxiety. Of special significance was the fact that the two groups did not differ in their physiological responses on the day remote from the jump, when neither group had denied fear, and that the reduction in physiological reactivity was cue specific; i.e., it did not occur in response to neutral words. The word-association test also included a number of situation-relevant anxiety words, such as "malfunction" and "killed." A less pronounced physiological responsiveness to anxiety words by those who denied fear suggests that it is the anxiety component in the parachute-relevant words against which novice parachutists are defending. Reaction time did not yield significant differential results between subjects who denied and subjects who did not deny fear, although the trend was in the opposite direction to the results in GSR.

We also investigated defense mechanisms of stimulus and drive displacement, which were suggested to us by behavioural observations. It might be argued that inhibited fear of parachuting would be displaced to cues not associated with parachuting. Two neutral pictures elicited a sufficient number of fear responses to warrant investigation. One of the pictures depicted a young man standing in front of a house; this picture elicited a number of fear responses, e.g., "The door is an omen of disaster" and "The boy is scared; he is picking up his girl, and wonders." The other picture was of two boys running; it also elicited fear responses; e.g., "He is scared stiff of being beaten up" and "He is running away from danger which he cannot escape." Parachutists on the day of the jump produced significantly more fear responses that were not associated with parachuting than did a comparable group of nonparachuting control subjects. As a more specific test of displacement, parachutists were divided into two groups: those who did, and those who did not deny fear of parachuting on the picture of high relevance; it was found that subjects who denied fear in response to the picture of

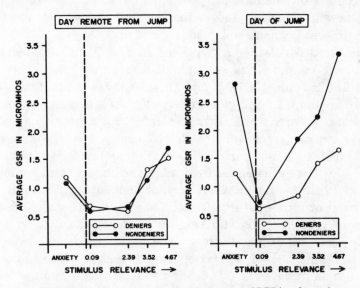

Fig. 15-3. Average galvanic skin response (GSR) of novice parachutists who denied fear about jumping and parachutists who did not deny fear, recorded on a day remote from a jump and on the day of a jump.

parachuting produced significantly more fear responses to pictures unrelated to parachuting.

It was further noted that the picture of the young man in front of the house elicited a few unexpected hostile responses; e.g., "The fellow is looking at the window of his girl friend's house. They had a fight and now he is angry that he got angry, and also angry that she got angry, and also angry that she is in bed now." A careful analysis of the records led us to the conclusion that hostility increases on the day of a jump and is not simply a personality characteristic of parachutists. The findings suggest that expression of hostility, like displacement of fear, might be related to denial of fear of parachuting. Dividing the parachutists into eight deniers and eight nondeniers, it was found that only one of the five subjects who gave a hostile response was a denier, suggesting that the two responses, if anything, represent alternate defense mechanisms. Support for viewing expression of hostility as well as denial of fear as a defense mechanism is again provided by GSR gradients on the word-association test. The composite gradient for eight deniers of fear on the day of the jump was similar to the one for the four expressers of hostility who did not deny fear, with gradient ranges, respectively, of 1.09 and 1.02 micromhos, as compared with 3.86 for the four subjects who demonstrated neither defense and who produced the three steepest gradients obtained in the study.

The word-association test yielded some evidence for perceptual sensitization and a classic example of perceptual defence (Epstein & Fenz, 1962; Fenz, 1964). Figure 15-4 illustrates the findings. On the day of a jump, novice parachutists exhibited a general perceptual deficit for neutral words, a greater deficit for anxiety words, and a relative sensitivity for words related to parachuting. The same results were obtained when parachutists served as their own controls as when they were compared to nonparachutists, and cannot be accounted for by general frequency, or familiarity with words, or by interserial or intraserial set effects. To evaluate the anxiety-reducing effect of misperceptions further, we examined the GSR to anxiety words that were misperceived. Where an innocuous word was perceived in place of an anxiety word (e.g., "chilled" instead of "killed") the GSR was significantly reduced. The findings indicate selective perceptual deficit and an effort to defend against anxiety-provoking cues. Anxiety was contained at the expense of performance.

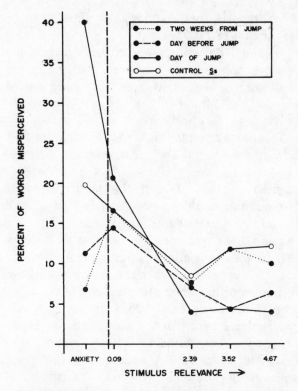

Fig. 15-4. Percentage of misperceptions by parachutists and control subjects of words on a stimulus
dimension and anxiety words. (From "Conflict and
stress as related to physiological activation and sensory, perceptual and cognitive functioning" by W. D.
Fenz, *Psychological Monographs*, 1964, 78, 1–33,
Copyright 1964 by the American Psychological Association. Reprinted by permission.)

DEVELOPING MORE EFFECTIVE STRATEGIES FOR COPING WITH STRESS

As our empirical investigations shifted from the study of novice to
the study of more experienced parachutists, we began to learn more
about the psychological mechanisms that facilitate the adaptive
control of involuntary stress reactions, and which enhance performance. In this, and the next section of this paper, I shall report in
some detail the empirical development of these findings and refer to

other published reports that discuss their theoretical implications (Epstein, 1967; Fenz, 1969).

The developmental pattern associated with increased experience and mastery does not indicate a general decrease in physiological reactivity to all parachute-relevant cues, but rather a gradual shift in responsivity from high-relevant to more low-relevant cues. In the word-association test, this shift was observed in both longitudinal and cross-sectional experiments. Figure 15-5 illustrates these findings.

In addition, it was found that this inverted V-shaped curve in autonomic responding, which is consistently produced by experienced parachutists on the day of the jump, is specific to the parachuting dimension and does not generalize to other dimensions of emotional stimuli unrelated to parachuting. The findings were conclusive: not a single experienced parachutist produced an inverted V-shaped GSR pattern to a nonparachuting, emotional word dimension, whereas 15 out of 16 experienced jumpers showed such a pattern in response to the parachuting dimension when tested on the day of a jump (Fenz & Epstein, 1968). It was concluded that the inhibitory process responsible for the controlled, autonomic response pattern of experienced parachutists is selective and cue specific.

Following a series of laboratory experiments, the critical question arose whether results obtained by testing parachutists with a word-association test, which only symbolically confronts them with

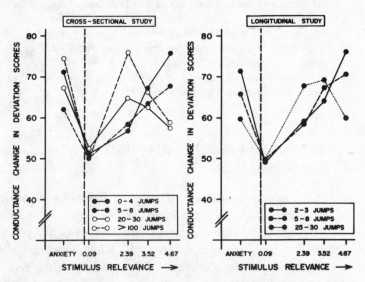

Fig. 15-5. Gradients of galvanic skin response in deviation scores in response to words scaled along a dimension of increasing relevance to parachuting and to anxiety words.

the real-life stressful event, had any real relevance to how they would respond during the event itself. At first (Fenz & Epstein, 1967) we recruited, more or less indiscriminately, novice and experienced parachutists. We recorded their physiological reactions at various intervals while they made preparations for the jump and then continuously in the aircraft itself—as it taxied to the end of the runway, during take-off, while gaining altitude, and finally, during the jump run. We disconnected the recording devices just before the jumper exited the aircraft. As noted earlier, laboratory findings were replicated in real life. To provide comparisons between physiological measures, values are presented as percentages of the total range; the range was calculated by taking the lowest and the highest average values obtained by either group. For respiration rate, these were 15.5 and 31.5 cpm; for heart rate, 73.3 and 146.5 bpm; and for basal conductance, 7.5 and 55.4 micromhos. The difference at each period between the score and the lowest score obtained by either group at all points is represented as the percentage of the total range. The results, thus transformed, are shown in Fig. 15-6. Novice parachutists produced the expected increase in all three physiological measures right up to a few seconds before the jump, when the recording devices were disconnected; in experienced parachutists an early increase in physiological activity was followed by a decline. Note the hierarchy between the time when the decline in reactivity was initiated: first was respiration rate, which produced its first reversal following the end of taxiing, during engine warm-up, and maintained a steady decline after take-off. Next was heart rate, with its first decline one period later than respiration rate, and its continuous decline once airborne. Finally, electrodermal conductance, which did not drop until the very end of the jump sequence. Data obtained in a separate study (Epstein & Fenz, 1965) showed that when experienced jumpers were asked to rate their subjective feelings of fear at various times throughout a sequence of events leading up to a jump, they indicated, on the average, that their greatest fear was on the morning of the jump, even before reaching the airport. If the subjective ratings are viewed in connection with the physiological responses, the hierarchy suggests an orderly progression directly related to the amount of control a person has over a response. It also suggests that one variable, higher on the hierarchy, may act a mediator to facilitate control of the other.

At about this time in our research with sport parachutists, an unrelated laboratory experiment indicated that the cognitive variable of certainty/uncertainty about a forthcoming stressor was critical in

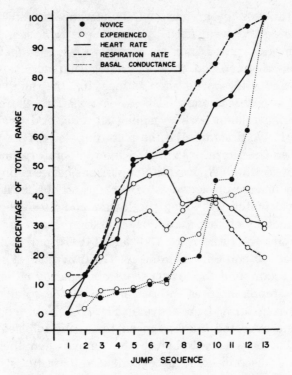

Fig. 15-6. Heart rate, respiration, rate and basal conductance, expressed in percentage scores of total range, for novice and experienced parachutists throughout a sequence of events leading up to a jump.

developing the adaptive anticipatory control in the aversive classical conditioning situation (Shapiro & Fenz, 1969). In our parachuting research we introduced such a variable first in the laboratory (Fenz, Kluck, & Bankart, 1969) and then in real life (Fenz & Jones, 1972b). But first, some anecdotal information. Mishaps, or prolonged absence from jumping, were observed to reverse the direction of development of the curve in experienced parachutists. A well-documented case of one highly experienced jumper illustrates this point. After having been tested on the word-association test as part of an earlier study, this jumper went ahead with his prescheduled jump during which he experienced a malfunction of his main canopy and broke an ankle while landing with the use of his emergency parachute. He was asked to contact us before his next jump for retesting. Figure 15-7 presents responses during the two testing sessions, about 6 months apart, the one preceding the jump during which he had the accident, the other preceding the first jump following the accident. Empirically, the inverted V-shaped curve obtained during the first testing corresponds to results consistently found for experienced jumpers, while the monotonic gradient obtained during the second testing corresponds to the results obtained by novices.

The first experiment (Fenz, Kluck, & Bankart, 1969) tested the hypothesis that the process responsible for the backward shift in responsivity, which occurs along the stimulus dimension as a function of experience, is reversible, and that by introducing a variable of uncertainty and threat, experienced jumpers would

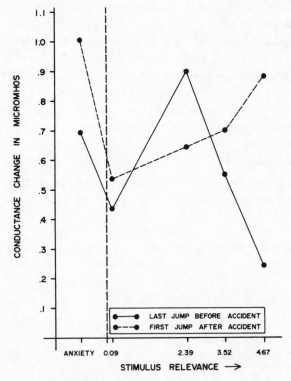

Fig. 15-7. Galvanic skin response of an experienced parachutist tested on the day of a jump before an accident and again on the day of a jump following an accident. (From "The effect of threat and uncertainty on mastery of stress," by W. D. Fenz, B. L. Kluck, and C. P. Bankart, *Journal of Experimental Psychology*, 1969, 79, 473–479. Copyright 1969 by the American Psychological Association. Reprinted by permission.)

produce monotonic gradients, similar to those obtained by novice jumpers, rather than the typical inverted V-shaped curve, on the same stimulus dimension. Threat and uncertainty were created through instructions that subjects would receive a painful electric shock every time they would produce a poor-quality response, without being told, nevertheless, what a poor-quality response was. Shocks were administered randomly throughout the experiment. The findings supported the hypothesis: when tested under conditions of threat and uncertainty, experienced jumpers showed a reversal in response pattern, i.e., monotonic gradients of both GSR and reaction time to the same stimulus dimension. Table 15-1 summarizes the results. Control subjects were experienced jumpers who were tested with two parallel word association tests before two subsequent jumps without threat of shock; experienced subjects were tested first without threat of shock and the second time with threat of shock. It was concluded that the processes responsible for the backward shift as a function of experience are indeed reversible.

The real-life experiment (Fenz & Jones, 1972b) involved a highly experienced parachutist who, just prior to our testing, had celebrated his 1,000th freefall. Let me present the findings in the form of another case report.

The case report. The subject was a 25-year-old Canadian skydiver, who while being a student at a local university also

Table 15-1

Number of Subjects Showing Peak Reactions to Low-, Medium-, and High-relevance Words

Condition	Relevance		
	Low	Medium	High
Control (galvanic skin response, GSR)			
First testing (no shock)	6	2	2
Second testing (no shock)	6	4	0
Experimental (GSR)			
First testing (no shock)	5	5	0
Second testing (shock)	0	2	8
Control (reaction time, RT)			
First testing (no shock)	7	2	1
Second testing (no shock)	5	5	0
Experimental (RT)			
First testing (no shock)	4	6	0
Second testing (shock)	1	0	9

operates a successful parachuting center. Parachuting is very much part of his life. After being told what our study was all about, he volunteered to take part as a subject in the experiment. He was scheduled to make 10 test jumps and three control jumps on two consecutive days; the control jumps were scheduled at the beginning, half-way through, and at the end of the experiment. Test jumps differed from control jumps in that a licensed rigger packed the main parachute for these jumps. The subject was told that for one of the test jumps the rigger would purposely build a total malfunction into the canopy, which would require him to "cut away," i.e., throw off the main canopy, and deploy the reserve chute. The rigger was actually instructed not to cause a malfunction on any of the jumps, but this was kept a closely guarded secret; the experimenters were well satisfied that the subject actually expected the malfunction on one of his 10 jumps. As a special safety precaution, the subject carried two reserve parachutes as well as the main chute; the subject had many times in the past, as part of his training, or for exhibition purposes, "cut away" from his main canopy, and deployed his reserve parachute.

Recordings of heart rate and respiration rate were obtained throughout the jump sequence, as in previous studies (Fenz & Epstein, 1967); all jumps were from an altitude of 12,500 feet, which allowed for a 60-sec. delayed free-fall before pulling the ripcord. The experimenter jumped with the subject on all 13 jumps.

Figure 15-8 (left) presents findings on respiration rate in anticipation of the 10 test jumps. The heavy line represents the average for the 10 jumps. Findings for the three control jumps are illustrated on the right. A comparison of the two parts of this figure shows similarities as well as differences. The overall pattern of the curves is similar, especially if we look at the averaged scores: there is a rise in respiration rate early during the jump sequence, followed by a decline. But note the orderliness of the individual scores shown on the right: on all three control jumps the peak in respiration rate occurred just prior to take-off, which was followed by a gradual and steady decline right up to the jump time. This orderliness was disrupted during the anticipation of the 10 test jumps: the marked fluctuations suggest not completely successful attempts

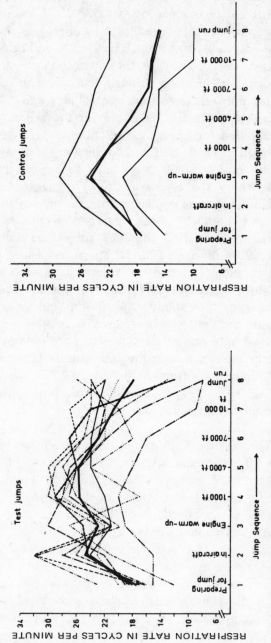

Fig. 15-8. Left: Respiration rate throughout 10 test jumps. Right: Respiration rate through three control jumps. Heavy lines indicate average. (From "The effect of uncertainty on mastery of stress: A case study," by W. D. Fenz and G. B. Jones, *Psychophysiology*, 1972, 9, 615–619. Reprinted with permission of the publisher, The Society for Psychophysiological Research.)

324

at control. During the last four test jumps, the respiration rate in the final phases of the anticipatory period was very low, and the records bear the notation by the examiner that the subject was hyperventilating. This further suggests that the subject consciously was trying to achieve control over his autonomic responses, which under normal jumping conditions occurs without his having to make the special effort.

The data for heart rate complement the data for respiration rate. Figure 15-9 (left) illustrates the anticipatory cardiac activity during the 10 test jumps; it may be seen that the overall pattern is one of cardiac acceleration, but the individual records demonstrate a great lability in responding. The heart rate pattern during each of the three control jumps, on the other hand, is an orderly increase followed by a decrease, so that during the jump run, just prior to exiting the aircraft, heart rate is at normal levels.

A comparison of respiration rate and heart rate suggests that "uncertainty" about the jump had a greater debilitating effect on heart rate than on respiration rate; consistent with previous findings, the peak in respiration rate preceded the peak in heart rate.

This section of the paper demonstrated that cognitive and somatic mediators are responsible for the inverted V-shaped pattern in response to the symbolic stimulus dimension, when subjects are tested before the jump in the laboratory, and throughout a sequence of events leading up to the jump itself. This response pattern is learned, cue specific, and reversible through the introduction of a new source of stress and uncertainty. The next section will show how anticipatory, physiological response patterns are related to performance.

COPING MECHANISMS AND PERFORMANCE UNDER STRESS

Up to this point it had been assumed that anticipatory autonomic response patterns are somehow related to performance in parachuting. We now selected good and poor performers, both novice and experienced parachutists, and observed their respective autonomic responses during the jump sequence (Fenz & Jones, 1972a);

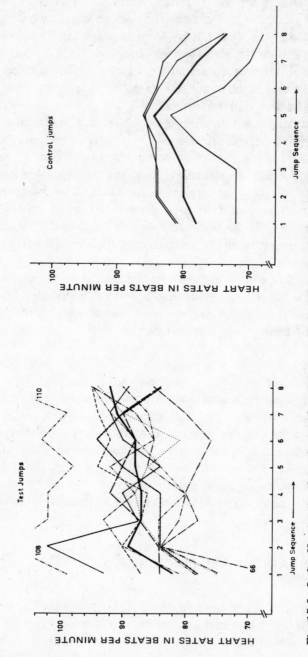

Fig. 15-9. Left: Heart rate throughout 10 test jumps. Right: Heart rate through three control jumps. Heavy lines indicate average. (From "The effect of uncertainty on mastery of stress: A case study," by W. D. Fenz and G. B. Jones, *Psychophysiology*, 1972, 9, 615–619. Reprinted with permission of the publisher, The Society for Psychophysiological Research.)

later, this study was replicated and related to results obtained in the laboratory (Fenz, 1973; Fenz & Jones, 1974).

Obviously, highly experienced parachutists perform better than novice parachutists, but the relevant question is whether it is possible to measure differences in performance between subjects who are equally experienced jumpers and, then, whether a subject's level of performance is related to his autonomic reactivity pattern during the jump sequence.

Novice parachutists were evaluated by the jumpmaster on the jump in which the physiological recordings were taken. The jumpmaster was asked to take careful notes on the performance of each jumper relative to specific aspects of the jump which he had previously discussed with the experimenters. At the end of the experiment, he was asked to rank order the performance of all novice jumpers who had taken part in the experiment.

It is more difficult to evaluate meaningfully the performance of experienced parachutists, especially on any one given jump; even the very best at times end up on top of a tree or in some cow pasture, well beyond the airport. To evaluate the performance of the experienced jumpers, a slightly modified version of a performance rating scale, developed as part of an earlier study (Fenz & Epstein, 1967) was used. Jumpers were rated on two 7-point scales—first, on overall performance compared with other jumpers of equal experience and, second, on the consistency of performance, i.e., the degree to which his performance varies and is erratic as compared to his level of ability. Two highly experienced jumpers, who knew each of the jumpers taking part in the experiment, were asked to rate independently each of the experienced jumpers. In each study that used this rating method, the correlation between the two raters on summed scores of the two scales was high and significant. Since a good number of subjects in the median range received the same scores, only the highest and the lowest in performance were selected for comparisons on the dependent measures. With this we were satisfied that we had valid performance measures.

The study showed that quality of performance in parachuting is related to autonomic arousal during the jump sequence (Fenz & Jones, 1972a); it lent support to the earlier suggestion that the most adaptive response pattern consists of an increase in autonomic arousal during the early phases of the jump sequence when this is followed by a sharp decrease, so that at the time of the jump, arousal is at close to normal levels. This pattern in respiration rate and in heart rate responding was most closely followed by the good performers who were experienced parachutists, and not at all by poor performers who were novices, who showed linear increases in reactivity throughout the jump sequence, with maximum reactivity just prior to the jump; poor, experienced jumpers and good, novice jumpers occupied in-between positions. Inspection of the individual records indicated little overlap, both for respiration rate and heart rate, between good and poor performers in the respective groups, especially in experienced jumpers. Analyses of variance indicated that the observed differences were reliable.

Figure 15-10, derived from the second study in this series (Fenz, 1973), illustrates these findings. This study included 14 novice and 16 experienced parachutists, half of them good and half of them poor performers. The same subjects were also administered, prior to the jump in a research trailer at the airport, the word-association test and the specially constructed thematic apperception test, both used in previous studies. The findings for GSR and reaction time to words scaled along the stimulus dimension of increasing relevance to parachuting are shown in Fig. 15-11. Both good and poor performers who were novices produced monotonic gradients in response to the stimulus dimension, but the gradient of poor performers was steeper than the gradient of good performers. Reaction time of novice jumpers indicated a linear gradient for poor performers, and an inverted V-shaped curve for good performers, with the longest reaction time to medium-relevant words. Five out of seven good performers produced inverted V-shaped curves, while all seven poor performers produced monotonic gradients. Differences in GSR and reaction time patterns between good and poor performing experienced parachutists were statistically significant.

The typical response pattern for both good and poor experienced parachutists was that of an inverted V, namely, an increase in reactivity to cues of low relevance, and a decrease to high-relevant cues. The difference between the two groups was in the location of the two peaks: for both GSR and reaction time, the peak of good performers occurred to cues of low relevance, and of poor performers to cues of medium relevance. Again, differences in response patterns between the two groups of highly experienced parachutists were significant for both measures.

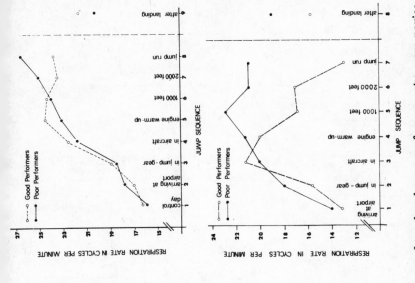

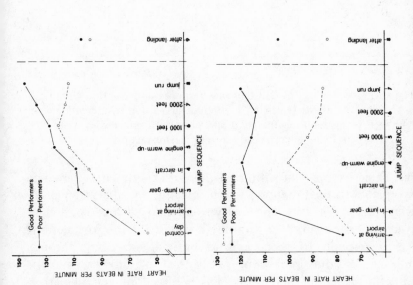

Fig. 15-10. Heart rate and respiration rate during a jump sequence of good and poor performers who were novice (top half) and experienced (bottom half) parachutists. (Figures 15-10 and 15-11 are from "Stress and its mastery: Predicting from laboratories to real life," by W. D. Fenz, *Canadian Journal of Behavioural Sciences*, 1973, 5(4), 332–346. Copyright 1973 by the Canadian Psychological Association. Reprinted by permission.)

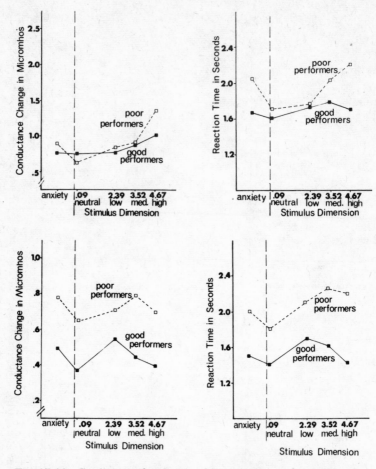

Fig. 15-11. Gradients of galvanic skin response and reaction time in response to words scaled on a stimulus dimension of increasing relevance to parachuting for good and poor performers who were novice (top half) and experienced (bottom half) parachutists.

It may be said, then, that within the present experimental paradigm it was possible to relate laboratory to real life, a goal so frequently missed in clinical research. The ability to attend to low-relevant cues, which act as "get ready" or "warning" signals for the forthcoming danger, to respond to them and to initiate and carry through mechanisms for the inhibition, or control of anxiety and its concomitant physiological arousal, has a direct impact on performance. This process of inhibition, or control, is a learned process, and the data show that some subjects learn better than others.

Responses to our thematic apperception test give us some insight into what may be going on in the mind of parachutists about to make a jump, and may help us to further understand what is involved in this learning process. It seems clear that the experienced jumper becomes increasingly more externally task oriented, whereas the novice jumper ruminates on his own fears or expends much of his energy defending against them. Let me cite, verbatim, some comments by good, experienced jumpers:

> There's the jumpmaster, from the looks of it he is determining the exit point. . . . He is probably at this point thinking of the exit procedures, commands, the problems that could arise with students.

> We see the jumpmaster here, riding up; obviously noting that they are heading out towards the lake; he is probably a little bit concerned over this, and will turn to the pilot, to instruct him to make corrections.

In contrast, here are some comments made by poor, novice jumpers:

> A parachutist is sitting in an airplane thinking about what it's going to be like to go out for the first time—kind of anxious, kind of wondering, looking at the ground so far below, and praying to God that he is going to make it, and wondering whether he is going to have the nerve once he gets out on the step to push himself off, and waiting for the chute to open.

> This is the parachutist just about to jump, and he has his pack on; frightened, but confident, but I guess every time you jump you get anxious and up-tight.

Summarizing the findings on the thematic apperception test, the need most frequently expressed by the good, experienced jumpers was *n-cognizance*, which was defined as follows: To be curious, inquisitive, to search, to want to know or see, to think about a problem, to plan; to strive for knowledge and wisdom; to attempt to solve one's problem by thinking about it." The other needs of this group all reflected activities in which the hero plays the dominant part. This was in contrast to the other three groups. Another marked difference was the reluctance of the good, experienced jumpers to express emotions, except for acknowledging mild fear. The poor, inexperienced jumpers frequently used denial as a defense mechanism against fear, as had been observed in an earlier study (Fenz & Epstein, 1962); when not denying fear, they acknowledged it with great intensity, more so than the other groups. Emotions for poor, novices jumpers were clearly dominant over needs, and *n-cognizance* was represented least in this group. Generally speaking, the other groups followed in-between positions on most scores. The good, inexperienced parachutists stood out in the variety of defense mechanisms used.

CONCLUDING REMARKS AND
SOME NEW FINDINGS

The research programme has progressed primarily on its own momentum; one study has lead into the other, and the meaning of some of the findings has at times escaped us, other times not been immediately clear. Some of the theoretical positions we took during the early years of our work have been discarded, most have been revised. This paper presents primarily the empirical progression of the research programme, without elaborating on the theoretical implications of the findings.

Of special puzzlement has been the inverted V-shaped curve of physiological arousal in response to the symbolic word dimension and during the jump sequence which, as has been seen, develops as a function of experience, and which is related to performance and mastery. At first we disgarded the findings, not knowing what to do with them, but their consistency continued to intrigue us.

Concurrent to the research on real-life stress, my students and I have been conducting a series of laboratory studies to investigate some of the parameters of cardiac conditioning (Dronsejko, 1972; Fenz, 1972; Laird & Fenz, 1971; Shapiro & Fenz, 1969; Stephens & Fenz, 1971). The two areas of research were combined in a recent study (Fenz & Jones, 1974) in which we asked the following questions: (a) Do parachutists who differ in their heart rate patterns in anticipation of the jump also differ in their laboratory-conditioned, heart rate response? and (b) May mechanisms shown to account for the laboratory response also account, at least in part, for the anticipatory heart rate response reported in our work on stress in parachuting?

Continuous recordings of heart rate during the jump sequence replicated earlier findings: good, experienced parachutists showed an early rise in heart rate during the early phases of the jump sequence, followed by a steady decline, so that at the time of the jump, heart rate was at close to normal levels. The poor, experienced parachutists, on the other hand, showed a steady rise from an average of 92 bpm when first arriving at the airport to an average of 122 bpm just before exiting the aircraft. Once again we were able to say that in the parachuting situation, skill is directly related to the way in which a person has learned to control his autonomic responding.

The same parachutists were also tested in the laboratory in a reaction time task. The conditioned stimulus–unconditioned stimulus (CS–UCS) interval was defined by delivery of an 8-sec. 2000 Hz tone at an intensity of 53 dB, 20 dB above the background noise. Termination of the sound was the signal for a subject to respond as quickly as possible in the reaction time task, by depressing a standard telegraph key. Heart rate was scored for second-by-second changes during the critical CS–UCS interval. The effect of *time* was highly significant; when averaged over 30 trials, both groups showed the typical cardiac response: accelerated response to the conditioned stimulus followed by deceleration in anticipation of the unconditioned stimulus. More important, though, were differences between the two groups: for poor parachutists the acceleratory phase of the response was more pronounced than the deceleratory phase, but the opposite could be said for good parachutists. This difference between the two groups was reliable. When measured in raw scores, the average increase in heart rate for poor performers was 4.3 bpm, as compared with 2.3 bpm for good performers, while the average amount of anticipatory deceleration was 5.2 bpm for good performers, and 2.0 bpm for poor performers. Finally, the reaction time of good parachutists, averaged over 30 trials, was 237 ms as compared to 278 ms for the poor parachutists; this difference, although small, was significant.

The process of cardiac conditioning involves the gradual, adaptive control of an involuntary response in anticipation of the stressor; the conditioned response, or the central processes that determine it, enhance performance in cases where the unconditioned stimulus has demand characteristics (Obrist, Webb, Stutterer, & Howard, 1970; Stephens & Fenz, 1971). The experimental paradigm has an analogy with real life in situations in which a person learns to recognize signals of a forthcoming and, for all practical purposes, unavoidable source of stress and learns to prepare himself to meet it in an effective manner. Such a source of stress is well represented in the parachuting situation. This study shows that analogies can be drawn from real life to laboratory, and vice versa. Experiments conducted in other psychophysiological laboratories have shown that central processes are mediating the cardiac response and performance; similar processes are likely to be responsible for the control of the heart rate and other physiological variables, and the facilitation of performance, in more complex, real-life situations as well.

The question may be asked as to whether we may generalize from findings on stress in sport parachuting to other stress situations and whether the study of reactions to one source of stress allows us to make formulations about the nature of stress and its mastery, in general. It seems reasonable to assume that findings on sport parachuting are relevant to other sources of stress in proportion to similarities which these have with sport parachuting. What, then, are the relevant features of sport parachuting?

Parachuting is an intensely stressful situation, where concern is over life itself. It demands great ego involvement; it is not entered into casually; and even as the parachutist gains skills as a skydiver, the sport continues to demand a great deal of personal commitment. It seems reasonable to suspect that given such a high degree of stress and ego involvement, incidental variables become relatively unimportant; that is, a common denominator is reached with other areas where stress is equally intense.

Sport parachuting also has some very specific characteristics: it is engaged in voluntarily, and the jumper is an active participant; in addition, the jumper's proficiency affects his outcome, in that competence reduces danger. In such respects sport parachuting differs from activities such as military jumping, where strong pressures are applied to the individual to keep on jumping, or experiences such as surgery, where the person's fate depends upon the skill of others. It will be necessary to determine what formulations, if any, derived from work with parachuting, hold for the nonvoluntary exposure to stress, and for stressful situations for which no adaptive instrumental activity is possible.

REFERENCES

Dronsejko, K. Effects of CS–UCS duration and instructional set on cardiac anticipatory responses to stress in field dependent and independent subjects. *Psychophysiology*, 1972, 9, 1–13.

Epstein, S. Toward a unified theory of anxiety. In A. Maher (Ed.), *Progress in experimental personality research*. Vol. 4. New York: Academic Press, 1967.

Epstein, S., & Fenz, W. D. Theory and experiment on the measurement of approach-avoidance conflict. *Journal of Abnormal and Social Psychology*, 1962, 64, 97-112.

Epstein, S., & Fenz, W. D. Steepness of approach and avoidance gradients in humans as a function of experience: Theory and experiment. *Journal of Experimental Psychology*, 1965, 70, 1-12.

Fenz, W. D. Conflict and stress as related to physiological activation and sensory, perceptual and cognitive functioning. *Psychological Monographs*, 1964, 78(8), 1-33.

Fenz, W. D. A longitudinal and cross-sectional study of conflict. *Studia Psychologica*, 1968, 10, 284-292.

Fenz, W. D. Die Funktion der Erfahrung bei der Kontrollierung der inneren Erregung. *Psychologische Beiträge*, 1969, 11, 588-594.

Fenz, W. D. Eine Querschnitts- und Longituden-Untersuchung über Angst und ihre Beherrschung. *Zeitschrift für angewandte und experimentelle Psychologie*, 1971, 75, 189-203.

Fenz, W. D. The effect of augmented feedback on cardiac conditioning in the rhesus monkey. *Conditional Reflex: A Pavlovian Journal of Research and Theory*, 1972, 7, 164-169.

Fenz, W. D. Stress and its mastery: Predicting from laboratory to real life. *Canadian Journal of Behavioural Sciences*, 1973, 5(4), 332-346.

Fenz, W. D. Arousal and performance of novice parachutists to multiple sources of conflict and stress. *Studia Psychologica*, 1974, 16(2), 133-144.

Fenz, W. D., & Epstein, S. Measurement of approach-avoidance conflict along a stimulus dimension by a thematic apperception test. *Journal of Personality*, 1962, 30, 613-632.

Fenz, W. D., & Epstein, S. Changes in gradients of skin conductance, heart rate and respiration rate as a function of experience. *Psychosomatic Medicine*, 1967, 29, 33-51.

Fenz, W. D., & Epstein, S. Specific and general inhibitory reactions associated with mastery of stress. *Journal of Experimental Psychology*, 1968, 77, 52-56.

Fenz, W. D., & Jones, G. B. Individual differences in physiological arousal and performance in sport parachutists. *Psychosomatic Medicine*, 1972, 34(1), 1-8. (a)

Fenz, W. D. & Jones, G. B. The effect of uncertainty on mastery of stress: A case study. *Psychophysiology*, 1972, 9, 615-619. (b)

Fenz, W. D., & Jones, G. B. Cardiac conditioning in a reaction time task and heart rate control during real life stress. *Journal of Psychosomatic Research*, 1974, 18, 199-203.

Fenz, W. D., Kluck, B. L. & Bankart, C. P. The effect of threat and uncertainty on mastery of stress. *Journal of Experimental Psychology*, 1969, 79, 473-479.

Laird, G. S. & Fenz, W. D. Effects of respiration on heart rate in an aversive classical conditioning situation. *Canadian Journal of Psychology*, 1971, 25, 395-411.

Lewin, K. Environmental forces in child behavior and development. In C. Murchison (Ed.), *A handbook of child psychology*. Worcester, Mass.: Clark University Press, 1931.

Miller, N. E. Experimental studies of conflict. In J. McV. Hunt (Ed.), *Personality and the behavior disorders*. Vol. 1. New York: Ronald Press, 1944.

Obrist, P. A., Webb, R. A., Stutterer, J. R., & Howard, J. L. Cardiac deceleration and reaction time: An evaluation of two hypotheses. *Psychophysiology*, 1970, 6(6).

Shapiro, A. H., & Fenz, W. D. Changes in heart rate as a function of an unconditional stimulus presented under varying conditions of certainty. *Psychonomic Science*, 1969, 16, 177–179.

Stephens, W. J., & Fenz, W. D. The effect of motivation on cardiac activity in a reaction time task under conditions of augmented feedback. *Psychophysiology*, 1971, 8(2), 264.

16

THE NATURE OF
COPING WITH STRESS

Donald Meichenbaum
Dennis Turk
Sam Burstein

University of Waterloo
Waterloo, Ontario, Canada

The complexity of the coping process has been discussed by many writers. Lois Murphy's (1962) book *The Widening World of Childhood* provides a good illustration of this complexity. Murphy and her colleagues studied children's coping strategies as employed in a variety of threatening situations. She indicated that when a situation involves some threat, the child's actions in relation to the threat may move in a variety of different directions.

The child may attempt to reduce the threat, postpone, bypass it, create distance between himself and the threat, divide his attention, and the like. He may attempt to control it by setting limits, or by changing or transforming the situation. He might even try to eliminate or destroy the threat. Or he may balance the threat with the security measures, changing the relations of himself to the threat or to the environment which contains it, but which also includes sources of reassurance. Instead of dealing with the actual threat itself, he may deal primarily with the tension aroused by the threat: discharging tension by action, or by affect release displacement into fantasy, dramatizing activities or creative work. Or he may attempt to contain the tension via insight, conscious formulation of the nature of the threat, defense maneuvers such as being brave, reassuring himself that he would be able to deal with it [p. 277].

Murphy indicated that the sequence of steps that characterize the act of coping with stressors includes (a) preparatory steps toward coping, (b) the coping acts themselves, and (c) secondary coping efforts required to deal with the consequences of the first two steps. A similar analysis of the coping pattern in adults was offered by Lazarus (1966). For Lazarus, the coping process involves primary and secondary appraisal and specific coping behaviors that in turn produce a new stimulus configuration, which is appraised once again. Many other investigators (Arnold, 1970; Ax, 1964; Glass & Singer, 1972; Mandler, 1962; Schachter, 1966) offered similar analyses of the coping process.

This chapter has two purposes: first, to review the stress literature in order to summarize our knowledge about the three phases of the coping process that Murphy, Lazarus and others described (i.e., preparing for stressors, coping acts, and secondary coping efforts). From this literature review, a number of guidelines for enhancing the coping process are suggested. The second part of this chapter illustrates how these guidelines can be incorporated into a training regimen to teach both clinical and nonclinical populations to cope more effectively with stress. The potential uses of behavior-therapy techniques to teach cognitive and behavioral coping techniques are illustrated.

PREPARING FOR STRESSOR

Much of the coping process is anticipatory in nature and is initiated before a confrontation with a threat or stressor. Coping processes also follow a situation of threat or harm; these are discussed in turn. But first, an examination of the data from both naturalistic and laboratory studies on the preparation for stress.

Two general research strategies have been employed in the naturalistic studies. The first strategy makes use of correlational procedures, whereby the investigator notes the relationship between individual-difference variables and the adequacy of the coping response. Illustrative of the approach is the work on surgical patients (Andrews, 1970; Cohen & Lazarus, 1973; Janis, 1958), military combatants (Grinker & Spiegel, 1945), and parents of children dying of leukemia (Chodoff, Friedman, & Hamburg, 1964; Wolff, Friedman, Hofer, & Mason, 1964). A second research approach within the naturalistic setting is experimental, whereby the investigator manipulates the input to subjects prior to the onset of the stressor. Usually the input is some form of information concerning the forthcoming stressor.

The most salient observation of such studies is the marked variability in subjects' ability and coping style in managing the variety of stressors. A person's coping skills are neither specific to situations nor uniformly successful. The same device used successfully in one situation may be quite unsuccessful in another setting or even in the same situation at another time. Thus, for example, Chodoff et al. (1964) reported that many parents of children dying of leukemia profited from avoidant-denial defenses prior to the child's death, but suffered more afterwards; whereas Hamburg (1953) found with severely burned patients that temporary denial served to reduce the impact of what had to be faced until some aspects of the reality had been sufficiently modified to make the actuality more bearable. Murphy (1962) made a similar point about individual variability in her study of children's coping styles across stressors.

Thus, the search for guidelines for teaching coping techniques is marked by a great deal of subject, situational, and subject-by-situational variance. What's new! However, despite these initial qualifications, perhaps some patterns may emerge that can be put forth as appropriate guidelines for training.

Janis's (1965) review of the characteristics of people who fail to adequately cope with stress provides some suggestions. In summarizing the naturalistic research on stress reactions, Janis noted that the absence of cognitive preparation in the form of the "work of worrying" characterizes persons who fail to cope adequately with stress. Janis proposed that the psychological sequence leading to *failure* in coping with stress includes the relative absence of the anticipatory fear and mental rehearsal that are essential for developing self-delivered reassurances. The absence of such cognitive rehearsal leads to feelings of helplessness when the danger materializes, and often a sense of disappointment in protective authorities and increased expectation of vulnerability.

A major construct underlying Janis's analysis is the "work of worrying." Both Marmor (1958) and Breznitz (1971) also conceptualized the work of worrying as a form of inner preparation increasing the level of tolerance for subsequent threats. Each of these authors distinguished between worrying over a realistic threat, which serves to ward off an anticipated trauma or to overcome the painful effects of a recent trauma, and neurotic worrying. In neurotic worrying the person is unable to attain emotional mastery of the threat. He may be hypervigilant, and his ideas tend to be more catastrophizing and self-deprecative.

The work-of-worrying process was illustrated in a recent study by Burstein and Meichenbaum (1974). What was unique about this study was that the work-of-worrying process was studied in 20 normal children, 4-9 years of age, who were about to undergo surgery (e.g., tonsillectomy, adenoidectomy). In studies with adults, the processes of preparation and resolution are inferred from the content of the person's thoughts, fantasies, dreams, and behavioral and psychophysiological reactions. A child, however, has more limited abilities of verbal communication; therefore, it becomes necessary to use another medium of communication. The child's disposition to engage in the work-of-worrying was inferred from his play behavior with hospital- versus nonhospital-related toys. The play assessments were conducted at home 1 week prior to surgery, the night before surgery while in the hospital, and at home 1 week following surgery. In addition, the children were assessed prior to the initial play assessment on the Wallach and Kogan (1965) defensiveness questionnaire, which measures the tendency to deny common weaknesses. The defensiveness scale was included because Janis (1958) noted that surgery patients with a highly defensive or denial-avoidance disposition tended not to experience presurgical anxiety. This absence of anxiety failed to elicit stress-related thoughts, leaving the defensive patient unprepared for the distress of surgery and causing poorer postsurgical adjustment.

In the Burstein and Meichenbaum (1974) child study, a similar relationship between defensiveness and postsurgical anxiety was found ($r = .52$; $p < .05$). Also of interest was the negative relationship between defensiveness and play with stress-related toys prior to hospitalization ($r = -.46$; $p < .05$). In other words, high-defensiveness children tended not to play with the hospital-related toys prior to hospitalization and also manifested most postsurgery distress. Indeed, what seemed to emerge from the correlational analysis was a group of children who were high in defensiveness, who avoided playing with stress-related toys prior to hospitalization, and who reported most anxiety and manifested most distress following surgery. In contrast, there was another subgroup of children who were low in defensiveness, who actively played with the stress-related toys prior to hospitalization, and who manifested minimal distress and anxiety following surgery. Further evidence for these two differential patterns of "deniers" and "work of worriers" was evident in a 7-month follow-up assessment of the two extreme subgroups of four subjects each. In response to an interview of what they recalled of their hospital experiences, the children who seemed to engage in the work-of-worrying recalled significantly ($p < .05$) more instances of medical and hospital procedures (e.g., "They took some blood from me; I got a big needle") than did the denial group, who focused on medically irrelevant events (e.g., "I played with ducks; my roommate's name was Steven"). These differential styles of recall were evident even though the two groups did not differ in total number of remembrances.

Also administered to the children was a projective test consisting of eight sketches depicting a child during various hospital experiences (e.g., entering the hospital doors, mother departing, child lying on a stretcher, etc.). In guessing what the child in each sketch was thinking, the work-of-worrying group offered significantly more instances of specific threats and self-delivered reassurances, whereas the deniers' answers were much more global and included less well-defined reassurance mechanisms. The following illustrative responses show the two styles.

Illustrative Responses from Follow-up Assessment

Work of worriers	Deniers
Q. What do you remember about going to the hospital?	
A bath, going to the operating room, going to the playroom, going in the stretcher to the operating room, going to the hospital with my mother, making in the cup near the nurses room, nurse giving me needle. She took me to the weighing room. That little ice thing on my neck.	I got nice food; I got my tonsils out; I got a good bed; that's all.
	I went to sleep, started having something to eat, started playing with a truck from the other room. A girl came in and we played with the teddy bear. I went back to bed again.

Q. Suppose that a friend of yours was going to have to go to the hospital for the same thing you went for. What would you tell him (her)?

You should know everything before. It calms you down, doesn't make me scared. If you expect them then you don't get scared, like the nurse coming to give a blood test.

Well, when you first get in and your mom leaves, you might be a bit scared, but then when you meet somebody it's not as scary.

I would tell her that her throat would be sore after she came up from the operation. That when she got a needle it would hurt a lot. They are nice nurses and doctors there.

It's better that you don't have to know everything because they will make you so afraid, you wouldn't want to go.

I wouldn't tell him what happens about the big needle because he'll be so frightened. The only thing I'd say was the needles didn't hurted and when they take blood it doesn't hurt.

You'll like it. That it'll be lots of fun and you'll get drinks.

Projective task: This is a picture of a boy lying in bed getting ready to go to sleep. Tomorrow morning he will have to go into the hospital to have his tonsils fixed. What do you think he is going to dream about tonight.

Maybe he tries to dream about something good, but WHAM! it keeps coming back to the hospital. Something like that happens to me sometimes.

What's going to happen in the hospital when he has to go up to the floor where he has his tonsils out. That he's going to get a blood test before he gets his tonsils out.

Dream about going to the doctor.

What he can do tomorrow. Play in the playing room.

Interestingly, interviews with the children's parents yielded no differences between the two groups in what they had told their children or how they had prepared them for surgery. In light of this fairly uniform reported parental preparation, the striking difference between the number of parental preparatory statements recalled by the two groups of children is especially significant, with the work-of-worrying group recalling significantly more ($p < .001$). Only two of the four children who engaged in denial recalled their parents' advice, and for them it mainly involved playing with toys. On the other hand, all four work-of-worrying children recalled specific parental statements that were relevant to medical procedures and the consequences of these procedures.

The follow-up assessment provides further evidence that some children are disposed to engage in the work of worrying. This cognitive preparation group recalled more of their parents' preparatory statements and seemed more disposed to develop an articulated and specific conception of what were the fearful experiences that had to be dealt with when hospitalized and what were the reassurances to be invoked in coping with these threats.

The Burstein and Meichenbaum study raises a host of researchable questions ranging from children's characteristic coping styles across situations to potential treatment interventions. For the purpose of this chapter, the study underscores the potential value of cognitive preparation in handling stress.

Many field studies (Andrews, 1970; Egbert, Battit, Welch, & Bartlett, 1964; Healey, 1968; Lindeman & Aernan, 1971), especially with hospitalized patients, demonstrated the potential value of preparatory communications in reducing the distress of surgery. Such preparatory communication gives the individual an opportunity to "prelive" an experience, or to conduct the work of worrying to cope vicariously, developing an image of being able to cope with the situation before the actual surgery.

It should be noted that the relationship between the patient's preoperative anxiety level and his postoperative adjustment has not been uniformly observed (Johnson, Leventhal, & Dabbs, 1971; Levy, 1959; Vernon, 1967). For example, Vernon and Bigelow (1974) failed to find evidence that cognitive preparation among adult hernia-repair patients was related to anticipatory fear or to the work of worrying as Janis proposed.

In the different stress-inducing situation of combat, however, Haggard (1949) concluded that prestress information was indeed helpful in fostering cognitive preparation with the resultant reduction in stress reactions. Haggard found that when enlisted men were told the purpose and risk involved in a particular operation, there was both an improvement in performance and a corresponding decrease in breakdowns and general friction among the men. Such preparatory information provided the soldiers with a cognitive structure or a mental picture of forthcoming events. As Haggard stated:

A person is able to act realistically and effectively in a stressful situation only if he knows the nature and seriousness of the threat, knows what to do, and is able to do it.

Haggard points out that one way to develop maximal protection against emotional stress is for the person to experience similar but less extreme versions of the stress. The importance and potential of such inoculation training is underscored in the second part of this chapter.

It is also relevant to note that in each of the field studies concerning information giving, the informational contact was mainly factual and concerned the external situation (i.e., the circumstances of the operation; the sequence of events; and, to a lesser extent, the possible side effects the patient may experience). Little or no information was given to the patient concerning how he might differentially attend to, interpret, appraise, or, in short, cope with the feelings and thoughts he would experience. Minimal emphasis was placed on the variety of self-delivered reassurance mechanisms the patient could employ. The informational manipulation rarely provided or modeled for the patient a plan or strategy for coping with the physiological arousal and cognitive distress he might experience. The therapeutic potential of teaching such coping strategies is discussed later, but for now a recent study by Langer, Janis, and Wolfer (1973) suggests how such coping procedures may be provided.

Langer et al. (1973) successfully trained surgery patients to use coping devices such as cognitive reappraisal of anxiety-provoking events, calming self-talk, and cognitive control through selective attention. The surgery patients were told that people are somewhat anxious before an operation, but that people can often control their own emotions if they know how to. It was explained that it is rarely events themselves that cause stress, but rather the views people take of them and the attention they give to these views. Consistent with these introductory remarks, patients were given several examples from everyday life of alternative ways of viewing negative events, including undergoing surgery. Patients were asked to rehearse realistic, positive aspects of the surgical experience. Such reappraisal training, combined with preparatory information concerning post-surgery discomforts and operative care resulted in significant reduction of postsurgical distress, as indicated by nurses' observations and and requests for sedatives.

A similar pattern for the important role of cognitive preparation in dealing with stress is evident in the laboratory studies. This literature was reviewed in some detail by Averill (1973) and Lazarus, Averill, and Opton (1974), and it was shown that a number of different aspects of the cognitive preparation process are important in the experience of stress and the reduction of its aftereffects. Lazarus' (1966) work with stress-inducing films demonstrated that one can short circuit or reduce the subject's stress reaction by manipulating the prestress input (e.g., exposure to denial or intellectualization passages). Similarly, Glass and Singer (1972) demonstrated that if subjects believe they have control over the onset and offset of aversive stimuli, deleterious aftereffects of stress arousal are reduced. The full practical value and clinical potential of these laboratory studies, however, have not been assessed. In each of the laboratory studies, the subject's cognitive set and appraisal system were modified only within the context of a brief laboratory experiment. Training procedures that can be used to directly influence and manipulate the subject's sense of control, self-attributions, and cognitive appraisal are described in the following section.

Coping Acts

As the initial quote by Lois Murphy indicates, a plethora of coping acts is available to the subject. A useful, but rudimentary, classification scheme of such coping acts was offered by Lazarus et al. (1974). They differentiated between *direct action* coping modes and *intrapsychic* or cognitive coping modes.

These may be viewed as representing, respectively, (*a*) the physical acts one can engage in to prepare for stressors, and the physical manipulation of the environment (e.g., building physical defenses, arranging escape routes) and (*b*) cognitive manipulation to create an impression of safety, security, or gratification, which includes what the person attends to, how he interprets both the external and internal environments, and how he assesses his own capabilities of coping.

There are a number of stressful situations in which direct action modes are limited (e.g., the case of severe injury, terminal illness, death of loved one). Averill (1968) indicated how various cultural rituals such as mourning rites channel cognitive distress such as grief into direct action modes.

Another source of information concerning coping techniques comes from popular "psychology" books for the general public.

The advice offered by these publications for coping with stress seems to fall into three categories: (*a*) physiological exercises (relaxation, breathing, isotonic exercises); (b) cognitive control (positive thinking in one form or another); and (c) the acquisition of interpersonal skills and the accompanying manipulation of the environment.

The "relaxation" procedures recommended are somewhat divergent in that some call for passive, while others call for active relaxation. Coue (1927), Baudouin (1920), and the Nancy school required their clients to relax completely, largely as a means to "becoming receptive." "The key word of this procedure is 'relax', not 'concentrate,' for concentration induces strain, not relaxation [Barksdale, 1972]." Through relaxation one opens his mind, lets his defenses down, and becomes receptive to suggestions of how to deal with the stressor, as well as not feeling stress as much. In opposition to this approach is that which is perhaps best typified by yoga and by the Lamaze preparation for childbirth. These two methods involve very conscious and deliberate relaxation of body muscles, often one muscle group at a time: "You must not think of it as taking it easy. That would be too passive. . . . Instead of 'relaxing,' you must learn to let go of your muscles consciously and actively, so that *they* are at rest, but your mind is not [Karmel, 1965]." The point of this is to occupy one's attention entirely in the active process of relaxation, so that anxiety-producing thoughts may not occur. These two opposing procedures can be recognized, for instance, albeit in somewhat modified forms, in psychoanalytic and systematic desensitization procedures.

The technique best known as "positive thinking" deserves particular attention, since it is close to the coping strategy, the work of worrying that has received much research attention. Dornbusch (1965) indicated, "It is easy to look at the positive thinking notion as a childish American attempt to impose the search for happiness as a perceptual category upon the unyielding objects of man's environment [p. 130]." William Miller (1955) in an excellent article on some negative thinking about Norman Vincent Peale, made a similar point. However, a case can be made for a distinction between the global role of positive thinking and the manipulation of cognitive appraisal or the work of worrying (Meichenbaum, in press). Some of the major differences have to do with the style, type, and timing of the cognitive material that is mentally rehearsed. Whereas the work of worrying deals with each specific stressful situation and task-relevant coping techniques, the positive thinking approach is "formula" based. Excessive generality is a pitfall of Coue and his followers, as well as of more modern writers such as Norman Vincent Peale and W. Clement Stone. The self-statements they recommend often have minimal impact because they are so general. The idea is: "the general formula leaves every mind free to unfold and develop in the manner most natural to itself [Brook, 1922]." However encouraging, the use of a formula or "psychological litany" tends to lead to rote repetition and emotionless patter that has been found ineffective as a coping tool (Meichenbaum & Cameron, 1973).

It is interesting to note some of the similarities between the methods for coping with stress presented in the lay literature and those recommended in clinical practice. For example, Stone, in urging the repetition of "good thoughts" to oneself, says, "You will keep your thoughts off the things you should not want by keeping your thoughts on the things you should want," with a resulting change in one's behavior. The same idea is presented in the Lamaze exercises: the client is urged to occupy herself with thinking about relaxing specific muscles and performing somewhat complicated breathing exercises during labour contractions so that the pain is not experienced as intensely. The Nancy method also comes at times very close to modern systematic desensitization. An especially interesting passage is to be found in a book written by Bonnet *in 1911*, in which he described a treatment for stage fright that could have been a 1970 desensitization protocol. Bonnet advised the patient:

> Isolate yourself in a room where no one will come to disturb you. . . . Lie down on a sofa, close your eyes. . . . Relax your body to the utmost, for this physical inertia favours mental passivity, and renders the mind more accessible to suggestion. . . . At the outset, endeavour to stop thinking altogether. Try to think of nothing at all for a time. Then direct your thoughts toward the idea which is worrying you, and counteract it by its converse, saying to yourself: "I don't suffer from stage fright; I sing well; I am perfectly easy in my mind."
>
> Repeat the process several times according to the amount of leisure at your disposal. Have a number of such sessions. . . . If you carry out this plan with assurance and conviction, success is certain [reproduced in Baudouin, 1920, p. 154].

A rejection of the positive-thinking approach, Coueism, and the Nancy school tradition on the whole should not lead us to overreaction and thus neglect of systematic exploration of how cognitive control could be employed successfully in learning how to cope with stress, as illustrated in the Langer et al. (1973) study with surgery patients.

Guidelines for Training Coping Skills

The concept of coping that emerges from both the research and lay literature is one that emphasizes cognitive processes and adaptive behavioral response mechanisms. There is a great diversity of coping activities a person may employ in meeting a threat or challenge.

From such a viewpoint a number of guidelines for training adaptive coping mechanisms are suggested:

1. Coping devices are complex and need to be flexible. Murphy (1962) suggested that such flexibility of coping styles seems to be a keynote for adaptation. As already indicated, coping devices used successfully in one situation may be quite unsuccessful in another situation or even in the same situation at another time.

2. Consistent with a call for flexibility is the need for any training technique to be sensitive to individual differences, cultural differences and situational differences. This is well illustrated in the research on cultural differences in emotion and on the "meaning" of painful experiences (Zborowski, 1969).

3. Successful coping processes involve strategies and devices for dealing with challenges from the environment: incorporating potentially threatening events into cognitive plans tends to reduce anxiety and lead to more adaptive coping responses; and information that stimulates mental rehearsal or the work of worrying may short circuit the experience of stress or reduce its aftereffects.

4. Actual exposure, during training, to less threatening stressful events has a beneficial effect and can be employed in training.

Thus, the coping processes involve both direct action modes of active preparation and cognitive coping modes. The availability of a variety of such alternative responses in one's repertoire engenders a self-concept that includes a sense of self-control, or what Meichen-baum (1973) called "learned resourcefullness." This is to be contrasted with the sense of "learned helplessness" that Seligman (1973) has described.

STRESS INOCULATION TRAINING

Each of the guidelines from the stress literature was incorporated into a training program, which we have come to call *stress inoculation* training (Meichenbaum & Cameron, 1973). As the name of the training procedure implies, subjects are provided with a prospective defense or set of skills to deal with future stressful situations. As in medical inoculations, a person's resistance is enhanced by exposure to a stimulus that is strong enough to arouse defenses without being so powerful as to overcome them.

Operationally, the stress inoculation training involves three phases. The first phase, educational in nature, is designed to provide the subject with a conceptual framework for understanding the nature of stressful reactions. From such a conceptual framework, a number of behavioral and cognitive coping skills are offered for the subject to rehearse during the second phase of training. During the third phase, the subject is given an opportunity to practice his coping skills while he is exposed to a variety of stressors.

The remainder of this chapter describes each phase of the stress inoculation package, indicating how the guidelines derived from the stress literature were implemented. Two studies in which the training procedure was used are described. Finally, the implications of the stress inoculation training paradigm are considered.

Phase I—Educational Phase

The first phase of stress inoculation training is designed to provide the subject with a conceptual framework for understanding the nature of his response to stressful events. The most important aspect of this phase is that the conceptual framework should be plausible to the subject and that the acceptance of such an explanatory scheme should naturally lead to the rehearsal or practice of specific cognitive and behavioral coping techniques. Thus, the logic of the training paradigm is more comprehensible to subjects in light of the conceptualization offered.

The scientific validity of the conceptualizations offered is less essential than the face validity or air of plausibility of the conceptualization for the subject. In the stress inoculation training studies reported here, the first conceptualization was Schachter's (1966) theory of emotion that was offered to multiphobic clients; and in the second study on the treatment of experimentally induced pain, Melzack and Wall's (1965) theory of pain was offered. Indeed, both Schachter's and Melzack's theories have been subjected to theoretical and empirical criticisms (e.g., Averill & Opton, 1968; Chaves & Barber, 1973; Plutchik & Ax, 1967). The validity of these criticisms does not detract from the usefulness of the theories in helping subjects acquire a new understanding of stress reactions and in the acquisition of new coping skills.

For example, in treating multiphobic clients the stress inoculation therapist, consistent with Schachter's theory, reflected that the client's fear reactions seemed to involve two major elements, i.e., (a) his heightened arousal (e.g., increased heart rate, sweaty palms, rapid breathing, bodily tension) and, (b) his set of anxiety-engendering avoidant thoughts, images, and self-statements (e.g., disgust evoked by the phobic objects, a sense of helplessness, catastrophizing thoughts, etc.). The therapist then indicated that treatment would be directed toward (a) helping that client control his physiological arousal and (b) substituting positive coping self-statements for the anxiety-engendering self-statements that habitually occupied his mind under stress conditions.

The educational phase concluded with a discussion centering on the client's viewing of his phobic or stress reaction as a series of phases, rather than as one massive panic reaction. Four phases were suggested: preparing for a stressor, confronting or handling a stressor, possibly being overwhelmed by a stressor, and finally reinforcing oneself for having coped.

This initial educational phase of the stress inoculation training provided the phobic client with a cognitive framework to better understand his stress reaction. It provided for the transition into the second, rehearsal phase of training.

Phase II—Rehearsal Phase

The second phase of the stress inoculation training was designed to provide the subject with a variety of coping techniques he could employ at each of the various phases of the coping process. The coping techniques included both direct action and cognitive coping modes. Direct action modes included collecting information about the phobic objects, arranging for escape routes, and learning physical relaxation exercises. The cognitive coping modes were treated by viewing such processes as sets of self-statements that the client says to himself. Thus, such constructs as appraisal, attribution, and self-perception were translated into specific self-statements. The modification of the clients' internal dialogue was accomplished by having them become aware of and self-monitor the negative, anxiety-engendering, self-defeating self-statements they emitted in phobic situations. This recognition was the occasion for producing incompatible coping self-statements.

In collaboration with the therapist, the phobic clients were able to generate sets of coping self-statements that encouraged them to (a) assess the reality of the situation; (b) control negative thoughts and self-statements; (c) acknowledge use, and possibly relabel the arousal they were experiencing; (d) "psych" themselves up to confront the phobic situation; (e) cope with the intense fear they might experience; and (f) reinforce themselves for having coped.

Phase III—Application Training

Once the client had become proficient in employing such coping skills (usually in 3 hours of training) the therapist suggested that he should test out and practice his coping skills by actually employing them under stressful conditions, other than the phobic situation. At this point the therapist could expose the client to a variety of ego-threatening and pain-threatening laboratory stressors (e.g., unpredictable electric shocks, cold pressor test, stress-inducing films, and failure and embarrassment situations).

Thus, the application training phase permitted the rehearsal and implementation of the skills that were acquired during the first two phases of training.

In summary, stress inoculation training involved discussing coping skills, and testing these skills under actual stress conditions. The preliminary research (Meichenbaum & Cameron, 1973) suggests that such a skills-oriented inoculation therapy procedure is successful in treating multiphobic patients relative to even such successful treatment procedures as systematic desensitization. Further evidence for the clinical potential of the procedure is offered in a more recent study on pain.

APPLICATION OF STRESS INOCULATION TRAINING TO EXPERIMENTALLY INDUCED PAIN

Picture the following scene. You are a volunteer subject for a pain experiment. With an appropriate amount of trepidation you watch as a blood pressure cuff is inflated around you upper left arm. You are asked by the experimenter to tolerate as long as possible the pain you will experience.

Indeed the ischemic pain you are experiencing is the closest to clinical pain that can be produced in the laboratory (Beecher, 1966). The submaximum effort tourniquet procedure induces a dull, aching, slowly mounting pain (Smith, Egbert, Markowitz, Mosteller, & Beecher, 1966). How long will you tolerate the pain? Five minutes, 20 minutes, 40 minutes? What coping techniques will you employ to tolerate and endure the pain? How would you train someone to cope more adequately with such an experimentally induced stressor?

Turk (1974) successfully applied the stress inoculation training procedure to such an ischemic pain situation. As in the stress inoculation training study with phobics, the training procedure began with an educational phase. Whereas in the treatment of phobics the subjects were given a Schacterian explanation of emotion in order to conceptualize their stress reactions and the treatment procedures, in the Turk study Melzack and Wall's (1965) gate control theory of pain was offered. The gate control theory of pain suggests that the pain experience consists of three different components, i.e., sensory-descriminative, motivational-affective, and cognitive-evaluative. Although Melzack (1973) indicated that the three components interact in a complex fashion, the components were presented separately to the subject so that he could better appreciate the nature of pain and the stress inoculation training procedures.

Following a discussion of how the subject felt and what he thought about during the preassessment phase, the trainer then described the various coping techniques the subject could employ to deal with each of the various aspects of the pain experience as described by Melzack and Wall's theory.

First, the subject was shown that he could control the sensory input or *sensory-discriminative* components of pain by such means as physical and mental relaxation and by attending to slow, deep breathing. The work on natural childbirth (Dick-Read, 1959) was offered as an illustration of how subject's expectations concerning pain increases anxiety, which in turn fosters muscle tension, leading to more pain and consequently more anxiety. This cycle can be interrupted by the use of relaxation procedures. At this point the subjects were given relaxation exercises (e.g., Meichenbaum, 1973; Paul, 1966).

According to Melzack, the *motivational-affective* component includes the feelings the subject has while experiencing pain. Such feelings as helplessness and the absence of control exacerbate the painful experience. To counteract such feelings, the therapist discussed with the subject the strategies he had employed in the preassessment situation and then offered a variety of other strategies that have been shown to be of help to subjects in pain. These strategies included the following:

1. Attention diversion—focusing attention on things other than experimentally induced pain. For example doing mental arithmetic or attending to cues in the environment such as counting ceiling tiles, studying one's clothes.
2. Somatization—focusing attention on bodily processes or bodily sensations including the experimentally induced pain. For example, watching and analyzing the change in the arm and hand.
3. Imagery manipulations—changing or transforming the experience of pain by means of fantasy. The more elaborate, detailed, and involved the fantasy, the greater the amount of pain tolerance. A number of different imagery manipulations were offered. These included imaginative inattention where the subject ignores the experimentally induced pain by excluding it from fantasy, for example, imagine lying on the beach. A second manipulation was imaginative transformation of pain in which the subject includes the experiences of pain in the fantasy, but transforms or interprets these sensations as something other than pain or minimizes the sensation as unreal or trivial, for example, imagining the arm as only cold and not painful, thinking of the arm as being numb as if injected with novacaine. A third imaginative transformation of context is one in which the subject also includes the pain in the fantasy, but now transforms the context or setting in which the pain occurs, for example, imagining that one is a spy who has been

shot in the arm and who is being chased by enemy agents by car down a winding mountain road.

Thus, the subject is exposed to a variety of different coping strategies that he can choose from in "cafeteria style." The subjects were encouraged to develop a plan to deal with the pain and especially to use such coping techniques at "critical moments" when the pain seemed most unbearable and when the subject would like to give up. The availability of such strategies would help control the motivational-affective components of pain.

The present stress inoculation strategy of exposing subjects to a host of different coping techniques that they can tailor to their own needs and styles is to be contrasted with most studies of experimentally induced pain. The pain literature is replete with examples of studies in which the investigator chooses one specific coping strategy and then compares its effectiveness versus a no-treatment control group. In the stress inoculation procedure, the subject, from the outset, becomes a collaborator, helping to generate from his own experience and with the advice and support of the trainer an individually tailored coping package that he can employ on the postassessment.

One way to deal with the *cognitive-evaluative* component of pain was to conceptualize the painful experience as consisting of several phases such as preparing for the painful stressor, confronting and handling the stressor, coping with feelings at critical moments, and self-reinforcement for having coped. In collaboration with the trainer the subject generated a list of self-statements that he could emit at each phase of the stress reaction (for example, see the following list).

**Examples of Self-statements That Stress Inoculation
Ss Practiced To Cope with Pain**

Preparing for the painful stressor:

What is it I have to do?
I can develop a plan to deal with it.
Just think about what I have to do.
Just think about what I can do about it.
Don't worry, worrying won't help anything.
I've got lots of different strategies I can call upon.

Stage of confronting and handling the pain:

I can meet the challenge.
One step at a time; I can handle the situation.

Just relax, breathe deeply and use one of the strategies.
Don't think about the pain, just what I have to do.
This tenseness can be an ally, a cue to cope.
Relax. I'm in control; take a slow deep breath. Ah. Good.
This anxiety is what the trainer said I might feel. That's right; it's the reminder to use my coping skills.

Stage of coping with feelings at critical moments:

When pain comes just pause; keep focusing on what I have to do.
What is it I have to do?
Don't try to eliminate the pain totally; just keep it manageable.
I was supposed to expect the pain to rise; just keep it under control.
Just remember, there are different strategies; they'll help me stay in control.
When the pain mounts I can switch to a different strategy; I'm in control.

Reinforcing self-statements:

Good, I did it.
I handled it pretty well.
I knew I could do it!
Wait until I tell the trainer about which procedures worked best.

As in the treatment of phobic patients, the cognitive processes of work of worrying were made explicit in the form of self-statements, thus conveying to the subject a sense of control over his own thoughts and feelings.

In summary, the stress inoculation subjects were given a conceptualization of pain (i.e., Melzack and Wall's theory) and information as well as an opportunity to rehearse a variety of behavioral and cognitive coping techniques to be employed as the subject saw fit during the various phases of the painful experience. Thus, the educational and rehearsal phases of stress inoculation training were completed and the last application phase remained before the postassessment began.

Whereas in the stress inoculation training with phobics the application phase included exposure to real-life stressors, the pain study application phase was conducted by means of imagery rehearsal and role playing, two widely used behavior therapy procedures. To review and consolidate the training procedures, subjects were asked to imagine themselves in stressful situations including the ischemic pain situation. They were to imagine how they would use the variety of coping techniques (e.g., statement of stages, self-statements, relaxation). Initially, the subjects verbalized aloud the sequence of strategies they were imagining, but with the development of proficiency, verbalizations were faded until the imagery process was engaged in without verbalizations.

Such imagery procedures can be viewed as the subject's providing himself with a model of how he should behave in a stressful situation. Prior research (Kazdin, 1974; Meichenbaum, 1971, 1972) indicated that one can enhance the therapeutic value of such covert modeling procedures by having the subject imagine himself faltering, experiencing anxiety, and then coping with these inadequacies. In this way the therapist anticipates the thoughts and feelings his client is likely to experience in the real-life situation and, by including them in the imagery process, they take on a *deja vu* quality for the client. The client's anxiety, tenseness, negative self-statements, and self-doubts become something the therapist said he might experience: they are the cues; the reminders, to use the coping procedures. Thus, in the imagery procedure, the stress inoculation subjects were encouraged to include any failings, self-doubts, or anxiety and to then see themselves coping with these.

To further consolidate the coping strategies, the subjects were asked to role play giving advice to a novice subject on how to cope with stress and specifically with the experience of pain. The trainer in this instance played the role of the novice subject, while the subject readily took on the role of the trainer.

Thus prepared with 1 hour of stress inoculation training, eight male volunteer college students underwent a postassessment on the ischemic test. On the preassessment the subjects were able to tolerate the pain for a mean of 17 minutes; on the posttest they tolerated the ischemic pain for a mean of 32 minutes, a highly significant difference ($p < .002$). Interestingly, the stress inoculation subjects not only endured the pain longer, but their verbal pain reports, which were collected throughout the assessment, indicated that they subjectively perceived the arm pressure as less painful on the postassessment. Subjects who were remaining twice as long in the postassessment offered pain ratings as the same as or lower than their preassessment ratings. In other words, the pain rating offered by a subject at 40 minutes on the posttest was the same rating as the subject offered at 20 minutes on the preassessment.

The effectiveness of the stress inoculation training takes on added significance when compared to a "strong" attention placebo control group who received both the pre and postassessments as well as exposure to a pseudotraining package. This group controlled for such influences as expectation and placebo factors. The pseudotraining included a general statement that cognitive preparation by way of work of worrying facilitates the coping process. The major difference between the control group and the stress inoculation group was the absence of specific coping techniques. The control group demonstrated minimal change in tolerance time from the preassessments to postasessments, i.e., 18–19 minutes. There were no significant differences in pain ratings on the two occasions for the control group.

The stress inoculation procedures, as applied in both the phobic and pain experiences, raise many researchable questions. The stress inoculation training procedure is complex and multifaceted, and research is underway to discern the necessary and sufficient treatment elements. However, the training package was designed to include each of the guidelines suggested by the stress literature.

To recall, these guidelines included tailoring the coping techniques to individual styles, providing and fostering flexibility, training cognitive and direct action coping skills, and providing prior application training to less intense and varied stressors. The stress inoculation package takes into account each of these suggestions. Elsewhere, Meichenbaum has discussed how one can best accomplish such training (Meichenbaum, 1973, 1975, in press). For now, it is important to appreciate that such a systematic training approach is quite different from how subjects now haphazardly learn to cope with stress. Given the increasing demand for people to deal with stress, the possibility of using stress inoculation training for prophylactic purposes is most exciting, especially with high risk populations.

The time seems at hand to combine the research findings concerning stress with the growing armamentarium of therapy procedures, especially behavior therapy techniques, to develop new training procedures. It is suggested that when such techniques are successfully developed they will include (a) an educational phase concerning stress reactions; (b) training and rehearsal of direct action and cognitive coping skills, the latter of which may be most productively viewed as packages of self-statements; and, finally (c) exercising these new coping skills under a variety of actual stress conditions. Perhaps trying to teach such coping skills will help us to better understand the nature of stress.

REFERENCES

Andrews, J. Recovery from surgery, with and without preparatory instruction, for three coping styles. *Journal of Personality and Social Psychology*, 1970, **15**, 223-226.

Arnold, M. Perennial problems in the field of emotion. In M. Arnold (Ed.), *The Loyola Symposium: Feelings and emotion.* New York: Academic Press, 1970.

Averill, J. Grief: Its nature and significance. *Psychological Bulletin*, 1968, **70**, 721-748.

Averill, J. Personal control over aversive stimuli and its realtionship to stress. *Psychological Bulletin*, 1973, **80**, 286-303.

Averill, J., & Opton, E. Psychophysiological assessment: Rationale and problems. In P. McReynolds (Ed.), *Advances in psychological assessment.* Vol. 1. Palo Alto, Calif.: Science and Behavior Books, 1968.

Ax, A. Goals and methods of psychophysiology. *Psychophysiology*, 1964, **1**, 8-25.

Barksdale, L. Building self-esteem. Los Angeles: Barksdale Foundation, 1972.

Baudouin, C. *Suggestion and autosuggestion.* London: Allen & Unwin, 1920.

Beecher, H. Pain: One mystery solved. *Science*, 1966, **151**, 840-841.

Breznitz, S. A study of worrying. *British Journal of Social and Clinical Psychology*, 1971, **10**, 271-279.

Brook, C. *The practice of autosuggestion.* London: Allen & Unwin, 1922.

Burstein, S., & Meichenbaum, D. The work of worrying in children undergoing surgery. Unpublished manuscript, University of Waterloo, 1974.

Chaves, J., & Barber, T. Acupuncture analgesia. *Human Behavior*, 1973, **2**, 19-24.

Chodoff, P., Friedman, S., & Hamburg, D. Stress, defenses, and coping behavior: Observations in parents of children with malignant disease. *American Journal of Psychiatry*, 1964, **120**, 743-749.

Cohen, F., & Lazarus, R. Active coping processes, coping dispositions, and recovery from surgery. *Psychosomatic Medicine*, 1973, **35**, 375-389.

Coue, E. *The practice of autosuggestion.* New York: Doubleday, 1927.

Dick-Read, G. *Child birth without fear.* New York: Harper & Row, 1959.

Dornbusch, S. Popular psychology: A content analysis of contemporary inspirational nonreligious books. In S. Klausner (Ed.), *The quest for self-control.* New York: Free Press, 1965.

Egbert, L., Battit, G., Welch, C., & Bartlett, M. Reduction of postoperative pain by encouragement and instruction. *New England Journal of Medicine.* 1964, **270**, 825-827.

Glass, D., & Singer, J. *Urban stress: Experiments in noise and social stressors.* New York: Academic Press, 1972.

Grinker, R., & Spiegel, J. *Men under stress.* New York: McGraw-Hill, 1945.

Haggard, E. Psychological causes and results of stress. In D. Lindsley (Ed.), *Human factors in undersea warfare.* Washington, D.C.: National Research Council Press, 1949.

Hamburg, D. Adaptive problems and mechanisms in severely burned patients. *Psychiatry*, 1953, **16**.

Healey, K. Does preoperative instruction make a difference? *American Journal of Nursing*, 1968, **68**, 62-67.

Janis, I. *Psychological stress*. New York: Wiley, 1958.

Janis, I. Psychodynamic aspects of stress tolerance. In S. Klausner (Ed.), *The quest for self-control*. New York: Free Press, 1965.

Johnson, J., Leventhal, H., & Dabbs, J. Contribution of emotional and instrumental response processes in adaptation to surgery. *Journal of Personality and Social Psychology*, 1971, **20**, 55-64.

Karmel, M. *Thank you Dr. Lamaze*. New York: Doubleday, 1965.

Kazdin, A. Covert modeling, model similarity, and the reduction of avoidance behavior. *Behavior Therapy*, 1974, 5, 325-340.

Langer, E., Janis, I., & Wolfer, J. Effects of cognitive devise and preparatory information on psychological stress in surgical patients. Unpublished manuscript, Yale University, 1973.

Lazarus, R. *Psychological stress and the coping process*. New York: McGraw-Hill, 1966.

Lazarus, R., Averill, J., & Opton, E. The psychology of coping: Issues of research and assessment. In G. Coelho, D. Hamburg, & J. Adams (Eds.), *Coping and adaptation*. New York: Basic Books, 1974.

Levy, E. Children's behavior under stress and its relation to training by parents to respond to stress situations. *Child Development*, 1959, **30**, 307-324.

Lindeman, C., & Aernan, B. Nursing intervention with the presurgical patient: The effects of structured and unstructured preoperative teaching. *Nursing Research*, 1971, **20**, 319-334.

Mandler, G., Emotion. In R. Brown (Ed.), *New directions in psychology*. New York: Holt, Rinehart, & Winston, 1962.

Marmor, J. The psychodynamics of realistic worry. *Psychoanalysis and Social Science*, 1958, 5, 155-163.

Meichenbaum, D. Examination of model characteristics in reducing avoidance behvior. *Journal of Personality and Social Psychology*, 1971, 17, 298-307.

Meichenbaum, D. Cognitive modification of test anxious college students. *Journal of Consulting and Clinical Psychology*, 1972, **39**, 370-380.

Meichenbaum, D. Therapist manual for cognitive behavior modification. Unpublished manuscript, University of Waterloo, 1973.

Meichenbaum, D. A self-instructional approach to stress management: A proposal for stress inoculation training. In C. Spielberger & I. Sarason (Eds.), *Stress and anxiety*. Vol. 1. Washington, D.C.: Hemisphere Publishing Corp., 1975.

Meichenbaum, D. *Cognitive behavior modification*. Morristown, N.J.: General Learning Press, 1974.

Meichenbaum, D., & Cameron, R. Stress inoculation: A skills training approach to anxiety management. Unpublished manuscript, University of Waterloo, 1973.

Melzack, R. *The puzzle of pain*. Ringwood, Australia: Penguin Books, 1973.

Melzack, R., & Wall, P. Pain mechanisms: A new theory. *Science*, 1965, **150**, 971.

Miller, W. Some negative thinking about Norman Vincent Peale. *The Reporter*, Jan. 13, 1955.

Murphy, L. *The widening world of childhood.* New York: Basic Books, 1962.

Paul, G. *Insight vs. desensitization in psychotherapy: An experiment in anxiety reduction.* Stanford: Stanford University Press, 1966.

Plutchik, R., & Ax, A. A critique of "Determinants of emotional states" by Schachter and Singer (1962), *Psychophysiology*, 1967, 4, 79-82.

Seligman, M. Fall into helplessness. *Psychology Today*, June 1973.

Schachter, S. The interaction of cognitive and physiological determinants of emotional state. In C. Speilberger (Ed.), *Anxiety and behavior.* New York: Academic Press, 1966.

Smith, G., Egbert, L., Markowitz, R., Mosteller, F., & Beecher, H. An experimental pain method sensitive to morphine in man: The submaximum effort tourniquet technique. *Journal of Pharmacology and Experimental Therapeutics*, 1966, 154, 324-332.

Turk, D. Cognitive control of pain: A skills training approach. Unpublished manuscript, University of Waterloo, 1974.

Vernon, D. The roles of anticipatory fear and information in tuberculosis patients' responses to hospitalization and illness. Unpublished doctoral dissertation, University of Chicago, 1967.

Vernon, D., & Bigelow, D. Effect of information about a potentially stressful situation on responses to stress impact. *Journal of Personality and Social Psychology*, 1974, 29, 50-59.

Wallach, M., & Kogan, N. *Modes of thinking in young children.* New York: Holt, Rinehart, & Winston, 1965.

Wolff, C., Friedman, S., Hofer, M., & Mason, J. Relationship between psychological defenses and mean urinary 17-hydroxycortiosteroid excretion rates: I. A predictive study of parents of fatally ill children. *Psychosomatic Medicine*, 1964, 26, 576-591.

Zborowski, M. *People in pain.* San Francisco: Jossey-Bass, 1969.

17

STRESS REDUCTION THROUGH SENSATION INFORMATION

Jean E. Johnson

Center for Health Research, College of Nursing
Wayne State University
Detroit, Michigan, United States

Cognitive processes involved in emotional response to threatening stimuli have recently received a great deal of attention in the psychological literature. The research reported in this chapter tested a hypothesis about cognitive processes that affect emotional response during a threatening event. The hypothesis that congruency between expected and experienced physical sensations during a threatening event reduces distress was tested in the laboratory and in selected health care settings.

One of the purposes of this research was to explore the effectiveness of various methods of influencing patients' cognitive processes during selected health care procedures. The effects of various cognitive mediating processes on emotional response have been tested in the laboratory (e.g., Lazarus, 1968; Schachter & Singer, 1962; Zimbardo, Cohen, Weisenberg, Dworkin, & Firestone, 1966). Serious problems were anticipated, however, when applying

The research reported was supported by grant NU00430 from the Division of Nursing, Bureau of Health Manpower Education, National Institutes of Health.

some of the proposed methods of influencing cognitive processes to the health care setting. For example, the Nisbett and Schachter (1966) hypothesis that information that leads subjects to attribute their sensations of physiological arousal to a neutral source reduces their emotional behavior, suggests two problems to be considered before applying that hypothesis to health care settings.

First, in the Nisbett and Schachter experiment, the hypothesis was not supported under high-threat conditions; many health care procedures are considered to be highly threatening. Second, in a situation where the health care worker manipulates a patient's interpretation of the source of threat, he may jeopardize his most important relationship to the patient, that of trust. An examination of the experiments that tested the attribution hypothesis (Nisbett & Schachter, 1966; Ross, Rodin, & Zimbardo, 1969) revealed that description of sensations frequently experienced when emotionally aroused and attribution to source of the arousal were confounded. Accurate description of sensations experienced during a threatening event may be the factor associated with reduced emotional response instead of attribution of source of sensations. An accurate description of sensations allows the subject to form accurate expectations about the sensations he will experience. Since intensity of emotional response during a threatening event may be in part determined by the degree of congruency between expected and experienced sensations, accurate descriptions of sensations that typically occur should reduce emotional response. That hypothesis is consistent with theories suggesting that negative affect is a product of discrepancies between what was expected and what is experienced (e.g., Hebb, 1946; McClelland, 1951). There are many factors about which expectations could be formed; the hypothesis makes explicit the critical expectations relevant to emotional response.

ISCHEMIC PAIN STUDIES

The hypothesis that incongruency between expected and experienced sensations produces distress was tested in a series of laboratory experiments. The threatening event that subjects experienced was ischemic pain of the arm (pain caused by lack of oxygen).

The pain experience was conceptualized as consisting of two components; sensory-discrimination component and reactive component (Beecher, 1959; Casey & Melzack, 1967; Melzack & Wall, 1965). Casey and Melzack (1967) suggested that the primary sensory output from a painful stimulus need not have a one-to-one relationship to the reactive component, which has emotional properties. Thus, it was anticipated that only the emotional component of the pain experience would be affected by congruency between expected and experienced physical sensations. To test the congruency hypothesis, separate measurement of the two components of the pain experience was necessary, and it was also necessary to vary expectations about the sensations caused by the painful stimulus without suggesting either the magnitude of those sensations or the degree of emotional response.

Subjects in the laboratory experiments with ischemic pain were all male college students whose age ranged from 18 to 27 years of age. Subjects were studied individually by female experimenters. Ischemic pain was produced by a modification of the submaximum effort tourniquet technique (Smith, Egbert, Markowitz, Mosteller, & Beecher, 1966). The tourniquet was a blood pressure cuff, which was applied to the nondominant arm and inflated to 250 mm of pressure. To reduce the amount of oxygen in the arm and stimulate ischemic pain, the subject exercised his arm by squeezing a hand dynamometer 20 times. Duration of the contraction, duration of relaxation, and pressure applied to the dynamometer were controlled.

The subjects' expectations about the sensations experienced during ischemic pain were manipulated by varying the type of preparatory information given. One message described the five typical sensations subjects experience, i.e., pressure, tingling, aching, numbness, and paleness or blueness of the fingernails.[1] The other message described the procedure used to produce ischemic pain.

Subjects rated the intensity of the physical sensations they were experiencing and how distressing those sensations were periodically during the 5 minutes they endured the effects of tourniquet pressure. Subjects were asked to think of sensations and distress as separate things that could vary independently, and were given separate scales upon which to rate the two components of the pain experience.

A Mood Adjective Check List was used to assess the subject's moods before the preparatory information, after the information but before the tourniquet was inflated, and after the tourniquet was removed. A questionnaire at the end of the experiment provided data about the effectiveness of the information manipulations and

---

[1] "Typical" sensations were determined by exposing subjects to ischemic pain of the arm and are defined as those sensations the majority of the subjects reported experiencing.

information relevant to cognitive processes activated during the painful experience.

The hypothesis that a description of typical sensations experienced would reduce distress ratings and have no significant effect on intensity of physical sensations was supported in the first experiment (Johnson, 1973). As can be seen in Fig. 17-1, the distress ratings of subjects who had received preparatory information that described typical sensations reported lower distress than subjects who received a description of procedure ($F = 5.59$; $df = 1/18$; $p < .05$). The mean ratings of intensity of sensations for the information groups were not significantly different ($F = 0.83$).

This initial experiment demonstrated that subjects could make ratings of the intensity of physical sensations separate from the ratings of how distressing those sensations were. And, the finding that preparatory information affected distress ratings and not sensation ratings supports the notion that the components of the pain experience are not completely dependent.

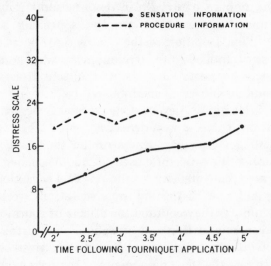

Fig. 17-1. Mean distress ratings for information conditions over time for Experiment I. (Figures 17-1 and 17-2 from "The effects of accurate expectations about sensations on the sensory and distress components of pain" by J. E. Johnson. *Journal of Personality and Social Psychology*, 1973, 27(2), 261–275. Copyright 1973 by the American Psychological Association. Reprinted by permission.)

Alternative Explanations

Subjects' reports in the initial experiment suggested that the amount of attention paid to the sensations may be an important factor in the perception of the pain experience. Subjects who had received a description of typical sensations reported that they attended to their arms throughout the experience. Thus, attending to the sensations in the arm could have reduced the distress.

A second experiment (Johnson, 1973) manipulated the amount of attention subjects could pay to their arms as well as the information from which they could form accurate expectations about sensations. Attention was manipulated by giving subjects tasks that either directed their attention to or away from the sensations in their arm during the intervals between pain ratings. The attention task consisted of asking subjects to look at and think about their arm and hand and then check "yes" or "no" to indicate the presence or absence of each sensation listed. The list of sensations included the five typical sensations plus two atypical sensations (burning and cramping). The distraction task consisted of working multiplication problems.

Figure 17-2 shows that the subjects who had received information that described typical sensations reported lower distress ratings than those who had received a description of procedure (Information: $F = 5.38$; $df = 1/44$; $p < .025$). Both distress and sensation ratings were not significantly different for attention and distraction conditions. Nor was there a significant interaction between the two levels of attention and the two levels of information.

The second experiment replicated the two basic findings from the first experiment, which were that subjects could rate the two components of pain separately and that information describing typical sensations resulted in a reduction of distress during the experience. The second experiment also demonstrated that the act of attending to the sensations by itself did not reduce distress during the experience.

There were data from the questionnaire and Mood Adjective Check Lists from both experiments related to three additional explanations of the results other than the hypothesized process. First, Lazarus' (1968) theoretical position suggests that the low distress ratings of the sensation information group could have resulted from those subjects appraising the situation to be less

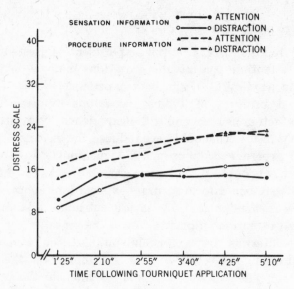

Fig. 17-2. Mean distress ratings for conditions over time for Experiment II.

dangerous than subjects who received a description of the procedure used to produce ischemic pain, but this interpretation was not supported. On a postquestionnaire, subjects were asked their perception of the degree of danger of injury they had been exposed to while the cuff was inflated. The mean level of perceived danger of injury was low, and the reports did not systematically vary by information groups. Therefore, it is unlikely that subjects' perception of danger of injury was the mediating factor that reduced distress.

Second, Janis (1958, 1967) maintained that information about an impending threatening event can arouse an optimum amount of fear and that an optimum amount of fear motivates the subject to develop strategies for coping during the event. Fear was one of the moods measured on the Mood Adjective Check List, which was administered before and after the preparatory information. In both experiments, the changes in reported fear from before to after the information manipulation were not significant for any group of subjects. In fact, there were no significant changes from before to after the information manipulation for any of the five moods measured (well being, fear, anger, helplessness, and depression) in either experiment. Third, the lack of influence of the sensory preparatory information on feelings of helplessness lends no support to the interpretation that subjects' distress varied systematically with feelings of helplessness (Mandler & Watson, 1966).

Congruency Between Expectations and Experience

There was evidence to support the notion that preparatory information that describes typical sensations experienced during a threatening event reduces incongruency between expectations and experience. In both experiments, subjects in the sensory information condition reported that they expected more of the sensations they actually experienced than did subjects in the procedure information condition. Even though statistically significant, however, the differences were small. The average difference in both experiments was equal to only about one sensation. Because subjects were asked to recall their expectations after the tourniquet was removed, recall of expectations could have been affected by the actual experience. Assessment of expectations after preparatory information had been given, but before the pain was experienced, would provide a more direct examination of subjects' expectations.

A third experiment was conducted to explore the effects of information on subjects' expectations about (a) sensations to be experienced, and (b) anticipated intensity of sensations and distress. The procedures of the previous experiments were followed to the point of inflation of the blood pressure cuff. At that time, subjects were told that there were two paper-and-pencil tasks for them before the tourniquet was inflated. First, subjects were asked to indicate on the sensation and distress scales the level they "thought" each would be at the time of the first rating and the last rating. Second, subjects were asked to indicate the likelihood of feeling each of nine sensations (the five typical sensations and four other plausible, but rarely experienced sensations) on a 100-point rating scale representing percent. After the ratings were made, the blood pressure cuff was removed.

The sensation and procedure information groups did not differ significantly on the level of anticipated intensity of either the physical sensations or distress the sensations would cause. Thus, it is unlikely that the sensory information reduces distress during the experience by suggesting that the experience is not very distressing or that the sensations will be of low intensity.

The data supported the notion that preparatory information that describes typical sensations increases accurate expectations by increasing expectations about sensations likely to occur and by decreasing expectations about sensations unlikely to occur. Subjects in the procedure information condition reported lower probability of experiencing typical sensations and higher probability of experiencing rarely experienced sensations than did the subjects in the sensation information condition. In the procedure information condition, subjects' expectations of unlikely sensations was the greater contributing factor to the inaccuracy of expectations.

To further investigate the relationship between degree of accuracy of expectations about sensations and the emotional response during a threatening event, a fourth ischemic pain experiment was conducted (Johnson & Rice, 1974). The degree of accurateness and completeness of the description of sensations given to subjects was varied. Four preparatory messages were used: (*a*) a description of all five typical sensations, (*b*) a description of two of the five typical sensations, (*c*) a description of two false or atypical sensations, and (*d*) a description of the procedure used to produce ischemic pain. This experiment included two types of information (conditions *b* and *c*) not previously studied. Subjects in all conditions were instructed to focus their attention on the sensations they were experiencing while the blood pressure cuff was inflated, by repeatedly indicating the presence or absence of sensations on a list that included both typical and atypical sensations.

Again, subjects who were given a description of five typical sensations reported lower distress than subjects who were given a description of the procedure (Fig. 17-3). But, description of only two typical sensations was as effective in reducing subjects' reported distress as a description of all five typical sensations. Description of false or atypical sensations and description of the procedure (conditions *c* and *d*) resulted in similar elevated levels of distress. Thus, the degree of inaccurate expectations about sensations appears to be more important in producing distress than the degree of accurate expectations is in reducing distress. In agreement with the findings of the second experiment, attending to sensations without preparatory information from which to form accurate expectations was not effective in reducing distress.

The experiments have repeatedly demonstrated that when subjects are given preparatory information that describes the typical physical sensations produced by ischemic pain they report lower distress

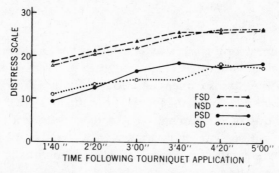

Fig. 17-3. Mean distress scores for information groups by ratings. FSD = False sensory description, which was a description of plausible but unlikely sensations; NSD = Nonsensory description, which was a description of procedure that was used to produce ischemic pain; PSD = partial sensory description, which was a description of only two sensations; and SD = Sensory description, which was a description of five sensations. (From "Sensory and distress components of pain: Implications for the study of clinical pain" by J. E. Johnson and V. H. Rice. *Nursing Research*, 1974, 23(3), 203–209. Reprinted by permission.)

during the painful experience. Cognitive processes involving expectations about sensations to be experienced appears to be the factor associated with distress. Expecting to experience atypical sensations seems to increase distress, whereas expecting to experience typical sensations decreases distress.

HEALTH CARE SETTINGS STUDIES

The laboratory studies contributed to the understanding of the subjects' cognitive processes that mediate the effects of preparatory information on the emotional response to a threatening event, but that body of research may not generalize to patients in health care settings. In health care settings, there are numerous factors that could affect reaction to a threatening event that cannot be rigorously controlled by the researcher. Subjects will be heterogeneous and the impact of the treatment or diagnostic examination on their lives will vary. The treatment or diagnostic examination will usually not consist of one isolated event, but is instead a series of events; often there are variations in the procedures from one subject to the next.

Endoscopy Studies

A gastroendoscopy clinic was selected as the health care setting in which to test the hypothesis that congruency between expected and experienced sensations reduces emotional response during a threatening event (Johnson, Morrissey, & Leventhal, 1973). The gastrointestinal endoscopic examination is a diagnostic test involving the visual examination and photography of the upper gastrointestinal tract. The examination involves a series of potentially threatening and unpleasant steps: throat swabbing to achieve local anesthesia, intravenous puncture, tube passage, retention of the tube for 15-30 minutes, and tube removal. Patients are sedated with a narcotic and a tranquilizer, and the throat is numbed by swabbing before the tube is passed through the mouth into the stomach. The tube is a flexible fiber optic tube that is 12 mm (width of an index finger) in diameter and about 90 cm (about 1 yard) in length.

Patients were randomly assigned to one of three preparatory information conditions, i.e., (a) a description of the sensations patients typically experience (what is seen, felt, tasted, smelled, and heard during the examination), (b) a description of the steps or procedure of doing the examination, and (c) a control condition consisting of no experimental information.

The sample consisted of 99 inpatients and outpatients who had had no more than two previous endoscopy examinations and were no more than 60 years old. All patients in the study were visited by a physician from the clinic who gave an explanation of the purpose of the examination, an explanation of the procedure, and answered patients' questions. This was the control group's primary source of information about the examination. About an hour before the examination, all patients received injections of a narcotic (meperidine) and atropine. Inpatients received a narcotic potentiator (promethazine) in addition to the other two drugs.

The experimental information was recorded by the chief physician in the clinic and played back to patients via a tape recorder. The inpatients heard the recordings between 5 and 7 p.m. the day prior to the examination, and outpatients heard the recordings after they arrived in the clinic the morning of the examination. Each tape was 7-1/2 minutes long and was accompanied by its special set of 11 photographs.

The physicians, nurses, and observer of the patients' behavior were not informed of patients' experimental conditions. Behavioral indicators of distress and fear were observed and recorded during the examination as well as the amount of tranquilizer required to sedate the patient. The tranquilizer flowed slowly into a vein, and administration was discontinued when the physician judged the patient was at the desired level of sedation.

Patients in both experimental message conditions required significantly less tranquilizer to achieve the desired state of sedation than did those in the control condition ($p < .05$; see Fig. 17-4). The patients who had heard the sensation message displayed significantly fewer signs of tension in hands and arms during the tube passage than did the patients in either the procedure or control condition ($p <$

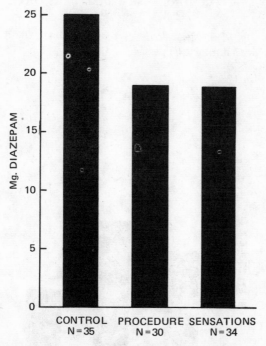

Fig. 17-4. Mean milligrams diazepam (adjusted for age) required for sedation. (Figures 17-4, 17-5, and 17-6 from "Psychological preparation for an endoscopic examination." *Gastrointestinal Endoscopy*, 1973, 19, 180–182. Reprinted by permission.)

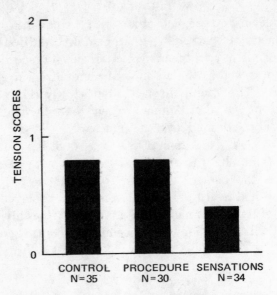

Fig. 17-5. Mean score of tension in hands and arms during tube passage.

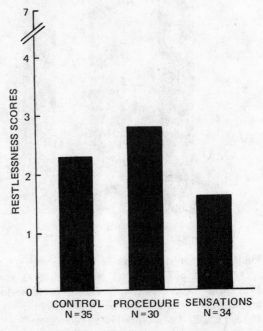

Fig. 17-6. Mean score of restlessness during the first 15 minutes of the examination.

.02; see Fig. 17-5). Signs of restlessness for the first 15 minutes after the tube was in place were lowest in the patients in the sensation condition and highest for the patients in the procedure condition ($p < .02$, see Fig. 17-6). Restlessness in the control condition could have been reduced by the high amount of tranquilizer that group received. Since the sensation and procedure conditions had the same mean amount of tranquilizer, we concluded that sensation information resulted in reduced distress while the tube was in

The experiment demonstrated that a preparatory message describing the sensations patients typically experience during a diagnostic procedure resulted in a significant reduction of emotional response. Although both the procedure and sensation messages resulted in lower doses of tranquilizer required for sedation, only the sensation group of patients maintained a low level of distress behavior during both tube passage and the examination. These findings have been essentially replicated in another study in the same setting (Johnson & Leventhal, 1974).

There were variations between the two messages that suggest alternative explanations for the observed effects of the messages on endoscopy patients' emotional response. The sensation message was more person oriented than was the procedure message. Personal pronouns were used and patients and staff appeared in the photographs that accompanied the message. This contrasts with the procedure message, which was void of personal pronouns; and no people were in the photographs. The personal orientation may have influenced the patients' perception of the examination. In addition, the patients in the photographs could have served as models of low-distress behavior which patients imitated. The sensation message also compared aspects of the procedure to familiar nonthreatening objects or experiences. For example, the message included the statement that the tube was smaller in diameter than a thimble and larger than a pencil. The full feeling after air was pumped into the stomach was described as being similar to the feeling one has after eating a large meal. These analogies to nonthreatening past experiences may have conveyed that the examination was not very threatening.

Cast Removal Study

To rule out alternative explanations of the results of the endoscopy study, and to determine if the congruency hypothesis was relevant to children under threat, another experiment was conducted (Johnson, Kirchhoff, & Endress, Altering children's distress behavior during orthopedic cast removal, in press, 1975). An orthopedic cast removal clinic was the health care setting selected. Orthopedic casts are removed with an oscillating saw in an approximately 2-minute procedure that can be frightening.

Children 6–11 years of age who had had a cast applied following an injury were the subjects. The 84 children studied were randomly assigned to one of three preparatory information conditions: (a) a description of sensations typically experienced during cast removal, (b) a description of the steps or procedure of cast removal, and (c) a no-experimental-information control condition. Children assigned to an experimental information condition listened to the taped message over headphones in an examining room before being taken to the cast removal room. Each message was 2-1/2 minutes long, was recorded by the same woman, began with the same introductory remarks, and contained personal pronouns. No photographs accompanied the messages.

The procedure message told the child that he (or she) would go to different rooms, would sit or lie down on a large table, and the doctor would use a circular saw to cut two sides of the cast. It was emphasized that the child would not be hurt and that the saw would not cut him. The use of spreaders and scissors to finish removing the cast was described. The need for an X-ray following cast removal was explained, and the child was told he could go home after the doctor had checked the X-ray.

The sensation message included a few seconds of the noise of the saw, told the child that the cast would be cut on two sides and that the saw would not cut his skin. In addition, the message told the child that when the cast was cut, he would feel vibrations or tingling, feel warmth, and see chalky dust fly. The child was told that his skin where the cast had been would be scaly and look dirty, that his arm or leg might be a little stiff when he first tried to move it, and that the arm or leg would seem light because the cast had been heavy.

During cast removal, the child was observed by an observer uninformed of the child's experimental information condition. The observer watched the child's face, hands, and feet for signs of tension such as facial grimace, and flexion of hands or feet. She also observed for such behaviors as pulling away, kicking, whining, calling out commands such as "stop," crying, and screaming. The behavior was scaled on a 3-point distress scale ranging from 0, or no signs of distress, to 2, indicating a high amount of distress behavior. .

The children in the control condition had the highest mean distress score (1.00); the procedure condition, the next highest mean (0.7); and the sensation condition mean was lowest (0.5). Only the sensation condition mean differed significantly from the control condition mean (Dunnett's $t = 2.44$; $p < .025$).

The children in the control condition may have been more distressed because they perceived that the saw would cut them. This seems unlikely because the clinic staff consistently told all the children that the saw would not cut them, and often the physician demonstrated this by placing the operating saw against his own skin. The messages in the cast removal study differed only in type of content (sensation description vs. procedure description), thus reducing the confounding present in the endoscopy study were the messages differed on factors in addition to type of content.

CONCLUSIONS AND DISCUSSION

The hypothesis that preparatory information describing the sensations typically experienced reduces the emotional response during a threatening event has been demonstrated to be robust. It has received support not only in the controlled conditions of the laboratory but also in health care settings where experimental control of a host of potentially relevant factors is difficult, if not impossible to achieve. It is hypothesized that a description of typical sensations leads the subject to form accurate expectations about sensations to be experienced and to give up expectations about the occurrence of rarely experienced sensations. Congruency between expected and experienced sensations results in low emotional response during the encounter with the threatening event.

The question of why that congruency reduces distress remains. Information that oriented subjects to the environment, phases of the experiences, and the equipment did not significantly reduce distress. Accurate expectations about those aspects of the experience must not be as important in distress reduction as accurate expectations about sensations. Accurate expectations about sensations to be experienced did not reduce subjects' estimate of how distressing those sensations would be before experiencing the painful sensations. Therefore, a description of the sensations to expect does not appear to lead subjects to appraise the impending event as less threatening. Sensation expectations appear to have their effect at the time the sensations are experienced, and confirmation of those expectations about the objective sensations appears to be the critical factor in lowering distress.

The notion that the intensity of physical sensations and the emotional response need not have a one-to-one relationship received support from the ratings indicating that emotional response was affected without significant effect on sensations. Certainly there was a strong association between the intensity of the sensations and the magnitude of the response to those sensations, and there probably is a limit to the amount of independence that can be achieved psychometrically. Hebb (1946), nearly three decades ago, emphasized that analysis of the physical characteristic of the stimuli would not lead to an understanding of the emotional responses. Beecher (1956) observed that the characteristics of a soldier's wound did not predict his pain experience. Melzack and Wall (1965) postulated a neural mechanism to explain discrepancies between sensory discrimination on several dimensions and the emotional response. There are still many problems to be explored in the assessment of the quality and magnitude of both the sensation and emotional components of the pain experience. The efforts reported here are only a beginning.

The research points up some practical considerations. The compatibility of psychological and physical management of patients was demonstrated by the delivery of the experimental information to patients with a minimum of interruption of ongoing care activities. The briefness of the psychological management technique and the delivery of the message by mechanical means placed little demand on professionals' and patients' time. Thus, it is expected that practical treatments to prevent undue emotional response can be designed that are both effective and efficient.

There are many benefits to be expected when patients' emotional response is low. Patients who can maintain cooperative behavior during a treatment or examination are more apt to receive maximum benefit from the procedure. There is less likelihood of injury from the equipment used. There is reduced need for drugs to assist patients in maintaining emotional control, and this attenuates many potential dangers. Perhaps experiencing low distress during initial health care procedures will increase the number of people who seek care aimed at prevention and early detection of pathology.

Threatening events can be conceptualized in several ways. Leventhal (1970) proposed that there are two types of response during a threat: (a) emotional response and (b) danger control response. These types of response are parallel and may interact with each other. In the Leventhal model, it is postulated that cognitive processes mediate each type of response. In addition, threatening experiences could be thought of as occurring in phases. A broad categorization of those phases would consist of the anticipatory phase, impact phase, and the postimpact phase. The research reported here was concerned with the emotional response during the impact phase. The cognitive processes guiding each of the parallel responses during each phase of the threatening experience and the interactions between situational factors and response are still to be identified, and a theoretical framework formulated.

A theoretical framework that explains response to threatening experiences can have a great impact on health care. Health care workers are aware of the influence of psychological factors on patient behavior. However, there has been little theory to explain response and to guide the selection of interventions. When such theory is available, it may be possible to confidently predict response and to prescribe specific types of psychological interventions to alter the response within the context of known characteristics of both situations and patients. Then, management of psychological aspects of physical health care will become as specific as current management with drugs and other treatment techniques that are derived from the theories of the natural sciences.

REFERENCES

Beecher, H. K. Relationship of significance of wound to pain experienced. *Journal of the American Medical Association*, 1956, 161(17), 1609–1613.

Beecher, H. K. Measurement of subjective responses: Quantitiative effects of drugs. New York: Oxford University Press, 1959.

Casey, K. L., & Melzack, R. Neural mechanisms of pain: A conceptual model. In E. Leong Way (Ed.), *New concepts in pain and its clinical management*. Philadelphia: F. A. Davis, 1967.

Hebb, D. O. On the nature of fear. *Psychological Review*, 1946, 53, 259-276.

Janis, I. L. Effects of fear arousal on attitude change: Recent developments in theory and experimental research. In L. Berkowitz (Ed.), *Advances in experimental social psychology*. Vol. 3. New York: Academic Press, 1967.

Janis, I. L. *Psychological stress*. New York: Wiley, 1958.

Johnson, J. E. The effects of accurate expectations about sensations on the sensory and distress components of pain. *Journal of Personality and Social Psychology*, 1973, 27(2), 261-275.

Johnson, J. E., Kirchhoff, K., & Endress, M. P. Altering children's distress behavior during orthopedic cast removal. *Nursing Research*, in press, 1975.

Johnson, J. E., & Leventhal, H. Effects of accurate expectations and behavioral instructions on reactions during a noxious medical examination. *Journal of Personality and Social Psychology*, 1974, 29(5), 710-718.

Johnson, J. E., Morrissey, J. F., & Leventhal, H. Psychological preparation for an endoscopic examination. *Gastrointestinal Endoscopy*, 1973, 19, 180-182.

Johnson, J. E., & Rice, V. H. Sensory and distress components of pain: Implications for the study of clinical pain. *Nursing Research*, 1974, 23(3), 203-209.

Lazarus, R. S. Emotions and adaptation: Conceptual and empirical relations. *Nebraska Symposium on Motivation*, 1968, 175-269.

Leventhal, H. Findings and theory in the study of fear communication. In L. Berkowitz (Ed.), *Advances in experimental social psychology*. Vol. 5. New York: Academic Press, 1970.

Mandler, G., & Watson, D. L. Anxiety and the interruption of behavior. In C. D. Spielberger (Ed.), *Anxiety and behavior*. New York: Academic Press, 1966.

McClelland, D. C. *Personality*. New York: Sloane, 1951.

Melzack, R., & Wall, P. D. Pain mechanisms: A new theory. *Science*, 1965, 150, 971-978.

Nisbett, R. E. & Schachter, S. Cognitive manipulation of pain. *Journal of Experimental Social Psychology*, 1966, 2, 227-236.

Ross, L., Rodin, J., & Zimbardo, P. G. Toward an attribution therapy: The reduction of fear through induced cognitive-emotional misattribution. *Journal of Personality and Social Psychology*, 1969, 12, 279-288.

Schachter, S., & Singer, J. E. Cognitive, social and physiological determinants of emotional state. *Psychological Review*, 1962, 69, 379-399.

Smith, G. M., Egbert, L. D., Markowitz, R. A., Mosteller, F., & Beecher, H. K. An experimental pain method sensitive to morphine in man: The submaximum effort tourniquet technique. *Journal of Pharmacology and Experimental Therapeutics*, 1966, 154, 324-332.

Zimbardo, P. G., Cohen, A. R., Weisenberg, M., Dworkin, L., & Firestone, I. Control of pain motivation by cognitive dissonance. *Science*, 1966, 151, 217-219.

AUTHOR INDEX

Numbers in italics refer to the pages on which the complete references are cited.

SUBJECT INDEX